THE NEW YORK TIMES
GUIDE TO RESTAURANTS
IN NEW YORK CITY

The New York Times

Guide to Restaurants in New York City

Bryan Miller

Times BOOKS

Library of Congress Cataloging-in-Publication Data
Miller, Bryan.
The New York times guide to restaurants
in New York City.
1. Restaurants, lunch rooms, etc.—New York (N.Y.)—
Directories. I. New York times. II. Title.
TX907.M536 1987   647'.95747'1   86-5896
ISBN 0-8129-1313-2 (pbk.)

Book design by The Sarabande Press

Manufactured in the United States of America

*This book is
dedicated to Pierre Franey,
my generous mentor,
sagacious dining companion,
and most of all,
valued and unwavering
friend.*

Contents

Ethiopian • French Bistro • Gelato • Hamburgers • Ice Cream • Italian • Japanese • Moroccan • Outdoor Cafes • Pizza • Seafood • Soul Food • Tea • Tex-Mex • Vegetable Platters • Wall Street Dining

Acknowledgments

Foremost on my gratitude list are the intrepid and perpetually hungry members of my gastronomic SWAT team, who have stared down enough gray steaks and foam rubber desserts to scare off a band of Visigoths. The silver spoon award goes to my wife, Anne de Ravel, who selflessly made the rounds with me nightly after her own long work day, and lent her invaluable expertise to every column in this book.

My sincere thanks also go out to my editors at *The New York Times*—Annette Grant, Myra Forsberg, and the hawk-eyed professionals of the copy desk—who have saved me from dining on crow au poivre more than once; and to Arthur Gelb, who first persuaded me that eating out more than four hundred times a year would suit me just fine. He was right.

Introduction

One does not need a census survey to see that there has been a restaurant explosion in New York City over the past several years. From the Upper West Side to TriBeCa, from Hell's Kitchen to Turtle Bay, dining establishments of every persuasion are sprouting like zucchini in July. For better or worse, restaurants have become much more than merely places to sate appetites and socialize in a relaxed setting. They are New York City's newest theatrical attraction, rivaling the most glittery Broadway musical.

The reasons are varied. In a city teeming with restless and self-indulgent baby boomers—many of whom occupy apartments the size of Volkswagen vans—restaurants have become the living rooms of the rising middle class. Whereas people in many other cities tend to entertain at home, New Yorkers entertain in restaurants. Moreover, the passion for food and wine in the country in the past decade has also fueled the boom.

According to the latest statistics of the National Restaurant Association, about 40% of all food dollars are spent on meals eaten away from home, compared with 33.6% in 1972. Sales at so-called full-menu, white-tablecloth restaurants grew by 22% during the same period; fast food was up an astonishing 85.7%.

Not only has the number of restaurants in this city reached

a staggering height—there are about 15,000 in the five boroughs —but the cost of whiling away several hours in some of the better known dining rooms has risen as well. I reported in *The New York Times* more than a year ago that the average dinner tab in the upper echelon restaurants had reached the $100 plateau (including tax, tip and a modest bottle of wine). This is all the more reason a guidebook like this is essential. Most people simply can't afford to make mistakes. I have run gastronomic interference for you, discovering the best that local chefs have to offer while at the same time enduring more gray slabs of meat substance and cardboard tarts than I care to remember. This book represents two years and nearly one thousand restaurant meals—not to mention enough antacid tablets to supply the Seventh Fleet—spent trying to sort it all out.

A word about *The New York Times*'s system of restaurant reviewing is in order for those who may not be familiar with the newspaper's method. In the course of my work as food critic for *The Times* I visit restaurants anonymously every day. In the event I am known to the establishment—this is unavoidable in some cases—I reserve a table under a different name and send dining companions ahead of time to claim it. Frequently I send confederates to dinner before writing the review to determine how unknown patrons are treated.

Readers often ask me if it is possible to review a restaurant when the owner happens to know me. While it is always easier to work anonymously, such a circumstance does not obviate an honest assessment. I realized this during a year-long kitchen apprenticeship in a French restaurant seven years ago during which time several local critics came in. When the owners told us what was happening I realized there was little we could do. By this time all our sauce stocks had been prepared, the fish, meat and vegetables purchased, and the desserts made. We could have given the critic extra-large portions, but that might well have backfired and caused a negative reaction. On any given day a kitchen can perform only up to its level of competence (or incompetence, as the case may be); nothing magical can be done for a critic's sake.

Of course the service staff can put on the white-glove treatment, but any professional reviewer can see through that by simply observing how others in the dining room are being treated.

The definition of a good restaurant guidebook, I believe, is one that allows a reader to find precisely what he or she wants within three subway stops (assuming there are no track fires or stuck doors).

- If you're looking for a specific restaurant, see the Restaurant Index, beginning on page 393.
- If you're looking for a particular type of restaurant (Open Sunday, Broadway Theater, etc.) see Special Offerings, page xxxi.
- If you're looking for restaurants in a particular neighborhood, see the Maps, beginning on page 375.
- If you're looking for a particular dish, see Best Dishes, beginning on page 363.

The Diner's Journal selections, which appear every Friday in the weekend section of *The New York Times*, grew out of a desire to fill the needs of younger and budget-minded readers. These are often restaurants that are too small or too narrowly focused to merit a full review but for one reason or another are worth pointing out. It might be a place that makes a terrific couscous, or a storefront Italian spot that has a grandmother in the back turning out hand-rolled cannelloni that could bring tears to a Neapolitan's eyes. And in the Wine Scene section, I provide a comprehensive rundown of wine bars around town. Finally, the Best Dishes section offers a quick way to satisfy any food craving that takes you hostage, be it for french fries or foie gras.

TIPPING

One matter of constant confusion to diners is tipping. In some restaurants, not only is there a waiter to tip but there is also a captain, a maître d'hôtel and perhaps a sommelier. There are guidelines, however.

Since waiters generally earn minimum wage, their income is derived primarily from tips, which average roughly 16 to 20% of the bill. Many New Yorkers find it convenient to double the sales tax of 8.25% to arrive at a 16.5% tip. In effect, the tip is paying the waiter's salary and is not necessarily a gratuity for satisfactory performance. My feeling is that, unless service is exceptionally poor, the standard tip is expected. If service is unacceptable, less can be left to signal displeasure. Extraordinary service could merit 20% or more.

Payment for captains, who usually supervise teams of waiters, varies with the restaurant. In older and traditional restaurants, captains often receive substantial salaries and keep all their tips. In most newer restaurants, captains earn slightly more than waiters but, like them, still depend on tips for much of their income. In these establishments all tips are pooled. In either case, diners should remember that the rule of thumb for restaurants with captains is 16 to 18% of the pretax total for waiters plus 5% for captains.

If, however, you want to single out a particular captain or waiter for extraordinary work, you can hand him or her a supplementary cash gratuity upon leaving and say, "This is for you, thank you," to indicate that it is not intended for the tip pool. The amount should be commensurate with the bill, although the range is generally $5 to $10.

Maîtres d'hôtel seat guests and should keep things running smoothly in the dining room. They do not usually receive tips unless they have performed specific favors, such as finding you a table on a busy night. In that case, a cash gratuity is appropriate. The amount depends on the type of restaurant and the circumstances but could be as little as $5 or as much as $20 or more.

A few restaurants around town are trying a new trick that diners should watch for. These are establishments that accept credit cards yet ask diners to leave cash tips. Use your own judgment in this situation; obviously, there is no obligation to comply—you pay taxes, why shouldn't waiters?

Sommeliers are an increasingly rare breed these days, an unaffordable luxury in this era of six-figure annual rents. If a restaurant has a sommelier and he or she is genuinely helpful, the rule of thumb is 10% of the cost of the wine. If the sommelier does little more than hand you the wine list and pour the first round, no tip is necessary.

WHAT TO EXPECT FROM SERVICE

Here are twelve points of good service that customers should expect in all middle-class and upper-class restaurants:

- *Personal appearance.* All service personnel should be clean and wear fresh clothes.
- *Attitude.* Courtesy and pleasantness are the cornerstones of customer relations. The greeting and good-bye are particularly important. There is nothing more uncomfortable than arriving at a restaurant and standing on the fringe of the dining room unnoticed by the staff. Customers who are not recognized by the staff should be greeted warmly but not effusively.
- *Product knowledge.* Those who serve food should have a basic knowledge of the ingredients and cooking techniques used in each dish on the menu. Once I had a waiter describe a dish as "veal with some sort of brown sauce on top." Appetizing, isn't it?

- *Wine.* Those who serve wine should have at least minimal knowledge about grape varieties and general flavor characteristics.
- *Table setting.* The tableware should be clean and set in the proper fashion before customers are seated.
- *Watchfulness.* Waiters should always be within hailing distance of customers, close enough to respond to eye contact. This way, when guests are ready to order or need something, the waiter can come promptly. (Diners, on the other hand, should never try to get a waiter's eye by snapping fingers or bellowing, "Waiter!")
- *Ashtrays.* Ashtrays should be cleared frequently, especially before food is brought to the table.
- *Table clearing.* The table should be cleared and crumbed between the serving of the entree and the dessert.
- *Serving.* The old rule about serving on the left and removing on the right applies only to classic French-style presentation, in which foods are served from platters. Having food arranged on plates in the kitchen has rendered that rule nearly obsolete. Food should be served on the side that is least disruptive to the diner.
- *"Everything O.K.?"* Waiters should never ask this question while customers are eating. It is annoying and reflects a lack of confidence about the food on their part. They should be nearby to respond to comments or complaints.
- *"Who gets the chicken?"* The service staff should never auction its food at tableside. It doesn't take a photographic memory to jot down on a pad who gets what.
- *The check.* Waiters should not present the check while guests are still drinking coffee unless it is requested. This gives diners the impression of being rushed. When diners ask for the bill, it should be presented promptly to the person who made the request.

RESERVATIONS

In fairness it must be pointed out that many problems in the flow of service can be attributed to inconsiderate diners who arrive late for their reservations without calling ahead and letting management know, or worse, failing to show up altogether. This has forced some restaurants to adopt the airline practice of overbooking to cover their losses. If everyone happens to show up, of course, a crisis ensues. Some top New York restaurants including La Côte Basque and Le Cirque report no-shows approaching 50% on weekends and holidays. Diners who change their plans should always give restaurants as much advance notice as possible.

GRIPES

If you have a complaint about the food, wine or service, bring it up discreetly with the manager or owner. Too often diners vent their wrath on waiters who may not be responsible for the problem—certainly not if the food is substandard. Never make a scene. That only exacerbates the situation and makes everyone defensive. You would be surprised how much more you can accomplish by talking to management in a polite but firm tone. If you still do not get satisfaction, find out if there is a higher-up, perhaps a major investor or absentee owner, and write a cogent, thoughtful letter. Take it from somebody who gets more than his share of irate letters: A smart-alecky tone only lessens your chances of success.

If the problem involves sanitation in the dining room or kitchen, contact the New York City Department of Health, Complaints Office, Room 301, 280 Broadway, New York, NY 10007; 285-9503.

♦ ♦ ♦ ♦ ♦ ♦ ♦ ♦ ♦ ♦ ♦ ♦ ♦ ♦ ♦ ♦ ♦ ♦

Restaurant Categories

To locate the review and neighborhood map for each restaurant in this section, please consult the index beginning on page 393.

◆　◆　◆　◆　◆　◆　◆　◆　◆　◆　◆　◆　◆　◆　◆

Restaurant Ratings

THE STAR SYSTEM

The Times's star system rates restaurants on the following scale:

★　★　★　★	**extraordinary**
★　★　★	**excellent**
★　★	**very good**
★	**good**
no stars	**poor to satisfactory**

Stars are intended as a quick visual clue to the overall quality of a restaurant. I assign the stars based on a formula that breaks down like this: roughly 80% for food quality, 20% for service and atmosphere. These factors are evaluated without regard to price. That means that an "excellent" restaurant costing $40 per person and an equally good one for $60 per person would receive the same three-star rating. This does not mean I am unconcerned about price. If I feel the food or wine is excessively costly, that is always pointed out in the review. Keeping price out of the star formula simply allows me to compare apples to apples without the complication of adding various price levels to the equation. The information box at the top of each review gives an idea of a restaurant's price range. Based on the cost of a three-course dinner with tax (excluding tip and drinks), the price range is as follows:

Inexpensive	less than $20
Moderate	$20 to $30
Moderately Expensive	$30 to $40
Expensive	$40 or more

◆ RATINGS* ◆

★ ★ ★ ★
Le Bernardin
Lutèce
The Quilted Giraffe

★ ★ ★
Aurora
The Four Seasons
Gotham Bar and Grill
Hatsuhana
Huberts
La Côte Basque
La Réserve
La Tulipe
Le Cirque
Le Cygne

Mitsukoshi
Montrachet
River Cafe

★ ★
Akbar
Alo Alo
An American Place
Arcadia
Arizona 206
Au Troquet
Auntie Yuan
Brive
Bud's
Cafe Luxembourg
Cellar in the Sky

*Full restaurant reviews only

Chikubu
The Coach House
Darbar
Devon House Ltd.
Dieci X
The Dolphin
El Internacional
Fu's
Greene Street Restaurant
Il Nido
Indochine
Jams
John Clancy's Restaurant
La Caravelle
La Grenouille
Le Périgord
Le Régence
Marcello
Maxwell's Plum
Meridies
Nanni il Valletto
The Nice Restaurant
Omen
Orso
Oyster Bar and Restaurant in Grand Central Station
Palio
Pig Heaven
The Polo
Positano
Prunelle
Rosa Mexicano
Sabor
Sistina
Sparks Steakhouse

Terrace
Trastevere
Union Square Cafe
Wilkinson's Seafood Cafe

★

Amsterdam's
Andrée's Mediterranean Cuisine
The Ballroom
Barking Fish Cafe
Bukhara
Cafe des Artistes
Cafe du Parc
Cafe 58
Cafe 43 Restaurant and Wine Bar
Cafe Marimba
Carolina
Casual Quilted Giraffe
Cent'Anni
Contrapunto
Cuisine de Saigon
Da Silvano
Felidia
Harlequin
Il Cantinori
Keen's
La Boîte en Bois
La Mirabelle
La Metairie
La Petite Marmite
Lavin's

Lola
Maxim's
Metropolis
Morgans Bar
The Odeon
Ozeki
Palm
Petaluma
Peter Luger
Primavera
The Ritz Cafe
The Russian Tea
  Room
Siam Inn
Sukhothai
Tandoor
20 Mott Street Restaurant

Water Club
Windows on the World

Satisfactory

Ancora
Christ Cella
Harry Cipriani
Kuruma Zushi
Roxanne's
Tavern on the Green
Woods on Madison

Poor

America

Types of Cuisine*

American

America
Amsterdam's
An American Place
Arcadia
Arizona 206
Barking Fish Cafe
Bud's
Cafe 43 Restaurant and Wine
  Bar
Carolina
Casual Quilted Giraffe
Cellar in the Sky
The Coach House
The Four Seasons
Gotham Bar and Grill
Greene Street Restaurant
Huberts
Jams
Lavin's

Maxwell's Plum
Meridies
Metropolis
Morgans Bar
The Odeon
The Ritz Cafe
River Cafe
Roxanne's
Tavern on the Green
Water Club
Windows on the World
Woods on Madison

Chinese

Auntie Yuan
Fu's
The Nice Restaurant
Pig Heaven
20 Mott Street Restaurant

*Full restaurant reviews only

French

Au Troquet
Aurora
Brive
Cafe des Artistes
Cafe du Parc
Cafe 58
Cafe Luxembourg
Devon House Ltd.
La Boîte en Bois
La Caravelle
La Côte Basque
La Grenouille
La Metairie
La Mirabelle
La Petite Marmite
La Réserve
La Tulipe
Le Bernardin
Le Cirque
Le Cygne
Le Périgord
Le Régence
Lutèce
Maxim's
Montrachet
Petrossian
The Polo
Prunelle
The Quilted Giraffe
Terrace

Indian

Akbar
Bukhara

Darbar
Tandoor

Italian

Alo Alo
Ancora
Cent'Anni
Contrapunto
Da Silvano
Dieci X
Felidia
Harry Cipriani
Il Cantinori
Il Nido
Marcello
Nanni Il Valletto
Orso
Palio
Positano
Primavera
Sistina
Trastevere
Union Square Cafe

Japanese

Chikubu
Hatsuhana
Kuruma Zushi
Mitsukoshi
Omen
Ozeki

Mexican

Cafe Marimba
Rosa Mexicano

Middle Eastern

Andrée's Mediterranean
    Cuisine

Russian

The Russian Tea Room

Seafood

The Dolphin
John Clancy's Restaurant
Le Bernardin
Oyster Bar and Restaurant in
    Grand Central Station
Wilkinson's Seafood Cafe

Spanish/Cuban

The Ballroom
El Internacional

Harlequin
Sabor

Steak

Christ Cella
Keen's
Palm
Peter Luger
Sparks Steakhouse

Thai

Siam Inn
Sukhothai

Vietnamese

Cuisine de Saigon
Indochine

West Indian

Lola

Special Offerings

Breakfast

American Festival Cafe
Brasserie
Broadway Diner
Cafe Pierre
Cafe Un Deux Trois
Carnegie Deli
Empire Diner
Exterminator Chili
Friend of a Farmer
Good Enough to Eat
Le Régence
Les Délices Guy Pascal
The Polo
Restaurant Florent
Southern Funk Cafe
Sylvia's Restaurant
Windows on the World
(All major hotel dining
    rooms)

Broadway Theater

American Festival Cafe
Barking Fish Cafe
Broadway Diner
Cabana Carioca
Cabana Carioca II
Cafe Des Sports
Cafe 43 Restaurant and Wine
    Bar
Cafe Un Deux Trois
Carnegie Deli
Carolina
Chez Napoleon
Darbar
Hamburger Harry's
Joe Allen
La Bonne Soupe
La Caravelle
Lavin's
Le Bernardin

Le Madeleine
Mike's American Bar and
   Grill
Orso
The Russian Tea Room
Siam Inn
Southern Funk Cafe
Square Meals
Tastings
Victor's Cafe 52
The Wine Bistro

Business Entertaining

American Harvest
Aurora
Cafe Pierre
The Four Seasons
Huberts
La Caravelle
La Côte Basque
La Réserve
La Tour d'Or
Lavin's
Le Bernardin
Le Cygne
Le Périgord
Le Régence
Palio
The Polo
Prunelle
Union Square Cafe

Fun for Children

America
Boathouse Cafe

Caribe
Chicken Kitchen
Chirping Chicken
Contrapunto
Cafe Marimba
Exterminator Chili
Fountain at Macy's
Great Shanghai
Hamburger Harry's
Hayato
Les Poulets
Oyster Bar and Restaurant in
   Grand Central Station
Pig Heaven
Sidewalkers'
Southern Funk Cafe
Tavern on the Green
20 Mott Street Restaurant
Yellow Rose Cafe

Good Deals

Amsterdam's
Cabana Carioca
Cali Viejo
Caribe
Checkers
Chicken Kitchen
Chirping Chicken
Contrapunto
Crisci
Cuisine de Saigon
Exterminator Chili
La Bonne Soupe
Les Poulets
Manhattan Chili Co.

Moroccan Star
The Nice Restaurant
Pete's Place
Provence
Siam Inn
Southern Funk Cafe
Sukhothai
Sylvia's Restaurant

Lincoln Center Area

Cafe Des Artistes
Cafe Destinn
Cafe Luxembourg
La Boîte en Bois
Sidewalkers'

Notable Wine Lists

Aurora
Bud's
Cellar in the Sky
The Four Seasons
Il Nido
Jams
Keen's
La Côte Basque
Lavin's
Le Cirque
Lutèce
Oyster Bar and Restaurant in
    Grand Central Station
Quilted Giraffe
River Cafe

SoHo Kitchen and Bar
Sparks Steakhouse
Tastings
Tastings on 2
Windows on the World

Open After Midnight

America
Brasserie
Cafe Luxembourg
Carnegie Deli
Exterminator Chili
Frank's Restaurant
Joe Allen
Le Zinc
Marvin Gardens
Maxwell's Plum
Mezzaluna
The Odeon
Pig Heaven
P. J. Clarke's
The Russian Tea
    Room

Open Sunday

Alo Alo
America
Amerigo's
American Festival Cafe
Au Grenier Cafe
Auntie Yuan
Bridge Cafe

Broadway Diner
Bud's
Cabana Carioca
Cadillac Bar
Cafe Des Artistes
Cafe Destinn
Cafe 58
Cafe Luxembourg
Cafe Marimba
Cafe Pierre
Carnegie Deli
Carolina
Cent'Anni
The Coach House
Contrapunto
Cuisine de Saigon
Da Silvano
Darbar
Docks Oyster Bar and Seafood
  Grill
The Dolphin
El Internacional
El Rio Grande
Friend of a Farmer
Fu's
Gotham Bar and Grill
Grapes
Great Shanghai
Greene Street Restaurant
Hamburger Harry's
Harlequin
Harry Cipriani
Il Cantone
Jams
John Clancy's Restaurant
La Boheme

La Bonne Soupe
La Metairie
La Tulipe
Le Madeleine
Le Régence
Lion's Rock
Lola
Manhattan Chili Co.
Maxwell's Plum
Meridies
Metropolis
Mezzaluna
Montrachet
The Nice Restaurant
The Odeon
Omen
Ozeki
Palm
Peter Luger
Pete's Tavern
Pig Heaven
Pizzico
The Polo
Primavera
Quatorze
Restaurant Florent
Rosa Mexicano
Roxanne's
River Cafe
The Russian Tea
  Room
Sabor
Siam Inn
Sistina
65 Irving Place
Sukhothai

Tap Room, Manhattan
    Brewery
Tavern on the Green
20 Mott Street Restaurant
Water Club
Ye Waverly Inn
Windows on the
    World
The Wine Bar

Outdoor Cafes

American Festival
    Cafe
Boathouse Cafe
Caffe Vivaldi
Da Silvano
Friend of a Farmer
Le Madeleine
Liberty Cafe
Lion's Rock
Meridies
Pete's Tavern
Provence
River Cafe
Roxanne's
65 Irving Place
Tavern on the Green
The Terrace, American
    Stanhope Hotel
Tout Va Bien
Victor's Cafe 52
Water Club
The Wine Bistro
Ye Waverly Inn

Romantic

Aurora
Au Troquet
Brive
Cafe Des Artistes
Cafe Pierre
Cellar in the Sky
Devon House Ltd.
The Four Seasons
Huberts
La Metairie
Le Refuge
Le Régence
Maxim's
Petrossian
Prunelle
River Cafe
Terrace

A Taste of New York City for Out-of-Town Visitors

Alo Alo
American Festival Cafe
Boathouse Cafe
Cafe Des Artistes
Carnegie Deli
Cellar in the Sky
The Coach House
The Four Seasons
Keen's
La Côte Basque
Le Bernardin
Le Cirque

Liberty Cafe
Lutèce
Oyster Bar and Restaurant in
  Grand Central Station
Palm
Peter Luger
P. J. Clarke's
River Cafe
The Russian Tea Room
Sylvia's Restaurant
Tavern on the Green
Terrace
Terrace Five
Water Club
Windows on the World
The Wine Bistro

Weekend Brunch

Alo Alo
America
American Festival Cafe
Bridge Cafe
Broadway Diner
Cadillac Bar
Cafe Des Artistes
Cafe Luxembourg
Cafe Marimba
Cafe Pierre
Darbar

El Rio Grande
Friend of a Farmer
Fu's
Greene Street
Harlequin
Harry Cipriani
La Metairie
Le Madeleine
Le Régence
Lion's Rock
Lola
Maxwell's Plum
Metropolis
The Nice Restaurant
Omen
Palm
Pig Heaven
Pizzico
Restaurant Florent
River Cafe
Roxanne's
The Russian Tea Room
Tap Room, Manhattan
  Brewery
Tavern on the Green
20 Mott Street Restaurant
Water Club
Ye Waverly Inn
Windows on the World
The Wine Bar

Restaurant
Reviews

✦ AKBAR ✦

★ ★

475 Park Avenue, between 57th and 58th streets, 838-1717.

Atmosphere: Dimly lit, comfortable, spacious.

Service: Somewhat slow and indifferent.

Price range: Moderate. Inexpensive prix fixe lunch and dinners available.

Credit cards: All major cards.

Hours: Lunch, Monday through Saturday, 11:30 A.M. to 2:45 P.M.; dinner, daily, 5:30 to 10:45 P.M.

Reservations: Recommended.

Akbar, an aristocratic-looking Indian restaurant on Park Avenue that is frequented largely by urban Moguls from the northeastern steppes of Manhattan, has surprising appeal for commoners as well—namely some beguiling food at reasonable prices. While the cooks here may not dazzle with inventive twists and impressive presentations, their straightforward, almost textbooklike approach to refined Indian cuisine usually pleases. Vindaloos are appropriately hot, condiments are cool, curries are complex, and tandoor-roasted foods are succulent. One cannot ask for much more.

The long rectangular dining room is soothing and comfortable with its deep red rugs, white walls, beveled columns, backlit stained glass and cozy alcoves. The phlegmatic service staff

3

sometimes must be flagged down for water or other requests, and don't expect much help when it comes to explaining the menu.

A good way to start is with the assortment of vegetable appetizers that features two types of cleanly fried fritters, one stuffed with mild white goat cheese, the other with sweet wilted onions, peas and cubed potatoes. A second mixed-appetizer platter, this one including meat, combines tasty lamb samosas redolent of cumin; dried-out nubbins of baked, yogurt-marinated chicken (tikka); battered cauliflower, and spicy ground lamb called seekh kebabs, which is molded on roasting skewers.

The wondrous breads of India are well turned out here; best among them is the airy onion-filled nan known as kulcha. Earthy whole-wheat chapatis and parathas go well with all the sauces, and dirigible-light puffed poori bread comes to the table all golden and pulsing as if ready for flight.

Fans of tandoor roasting will not be disappointed here, for the various chicken dishes are paragons of the art, mildly hot outside from a coating of mixed spices and succulent within. Only tandoori lobster seems ill suited to this treatment; the meat tends to tighten and lose its characteristic flavor in the super-hot oven.

One quizzical preparation is called chicken jalfrezi, described on the menu as a chicken casserole with homemade cheese, assorted vegetables and spices. Upon failing to detect any cheese in it, I asked the waiter what had happened. "Oh, we didn't put any cheese in tonight," he replied matter-of-factly, then walked away.

Lamb vindaloo, a smoldering dish from southwestern India, excels here because it has much more than mere BTU's going for it—the pulpy sauce is stratified with sensations of cumin, garlic, ginger and cinnamon. Dal, a side dish of buttery lentils, is soothing but underseasoned. Another winning lamb dish is saag gosht, cubed lamb simmered slowly with creamed spinach and spices. One superb rice dish not to be missed is called chicken biryani, which melds nuggets of chicken, saffron rice, cashews and almonds.

One weak spot on the menu is seafood. Prawns cooked in a subtle ginger- and cumin-perfumed sauce were dry from overcooking, and fish begum bahar combined pieces of scrod in a bland cream sauce. Beer is the best beverage with this dynamic food, and it's just as well, because the small, narrow wine card offers little of interest.

Standard Indian desserts are generally well made, such as the fried milk rounds in a pool of honey called gulab jamun, and rasmalai, crumbly cheese flecked with pistachios and doused with rose water. Mango ice cream is creamy and ripe tasting; rosewater ice cream tastes like perfume to me, but several diners at my table enjoyed it.

Don't be intimidated by Akbar's pricey location—it offers good mileage for the dollar, and in a colorful and alluring setting.

✦ ALO ALO ✦

★ ★

1030 Third Avenue, at 61st Street, 838-4343.

Atmosphere: Grand cafe setting; colorful, convivial and international.

Service: Young professionally trained waiters and waitresses who sometimes get overwhelmed at busy times.

Price range: Moderate.

Credit cards: All major cards.

Hours: Open daily. Lunch, 11:30 A.M. to 3 P.M.; light dishes served from 3 to 6 P.M.; dinner, 6 to 11 P.M.; supper, 11 P.M. to 2 A.M.

Reservations: Suggested.

Alo Alo is the kind of high-spirited and sophisticated Italian restaurant I would go to if I ever had a night off from professional dining. It is the creation of Ricardo Amaral, a Brazilian-born entrepreneur who started Club A, the East Side discotheque, and Dino De Laurentiis, the moviemaker.

The whimsically chic dining room is in the grand-cafe style. It has a towering ceiling supporting futuristic disk-shaped chandeliers, cartoon-like papier-mâché characters perched on ledges above the room, a wraparound glass exterior and inside walls sporting dreamy pastel murals of forest scenes. The glass fishbowl effect creates a bright and breezy ambiance during the day, and at night it becomes a glittery urban setting in which the boundaries between outside and inside blur.

The clientele is decidedly upscale and polyglot; the after-work bar scene is colorful and bonhomous. It's fun to stop here for a glass of wine or a caipirinha, which is the Brazilian national cocktail, made with fresh lime and sugarcane liquor. Diners should be warned that this is not a place to have an intimate conversation, because the music and mirthmaking can reach Shea Stadium pitch.

As for the food, it is as uplifting as the setting. Francesco Antonucci, a talented young chef from Italy, has a spirited style that is modern yet not affected. What he offers is invigorating fare at affordable prices, something this city sorely needs. The wines suit the brassy style of food well; and while there is no pastry chef, the owners buy desserts from one of the best commercial sources.

All Mr. Antonucci's sauces are intense and boldly seasoned, employing the freshest of ingredients. For starters, there are several outstanding salads—arugula in a good vinaigrette; fresh endive with anchovies, and radicchio with Parmesan cheese slices.

The most interesting appetizer, though, is the swordfish salad. It is really a carpaccio of raw, fresh marinated swordfish sliced into translucent sheets and garnished with tiny juliennes of carrots, parsley, oregano and lemon basil. The swordfish has a delicate oceanic flavor and a texture similar to very lean salmon.

The grilled vegetable platter is as pretty as it is delicious. The large serving combines thin, barely charred slices of smoky eggplant, endive, zucchini and red and yellow peppers. The flavors are so pure they need only a drizzle of olive oil. Of the two soups sampled—pasta e fagioli and a veal soup with vegetables—the former was the hands-down winner at my table. It was thick and rustic, heavy on the beans, with a pleasing balance of seasonings. The veal soup by comparison was pale and salty with strips of dry meat and leeks.

The unrivaled stars of this menu's cast are the pastas. A good example is pennette with duck sauce, which features resilient little tubes of al dente pasta tossed with small cubes of fresh duck meat in an earthy duck-stock-and-tomato sauce redolent of fresh rosemary. Another pasta that received raves was the spaghetti with arugula, anchovies and butter. The tart arugula played off the saline anchovy flavor beautifully.

A special one evening, penne with Bolognese sauce, was a paragon of that lusty regional dish, rich with the flavors of meat and fresh tomatoes. On another evening, the special was fusilli with pancetta—the Italian smoked bacon—tossed with fresh tomatoes and shreds of radicchio. The mélange of smoky, sweet and tart sensations was superb. Only two dishes were lacking: the undersauced penne with zucchini and tomatoes and the bland lasagna oozing with a surfeit of béchamel sauce.

If you crave a good risotto, try the one here, which is offered as a special in various guises. I had it mixed with radicchio. The rice, cooked in a good beef broth, had just the proper semifirm texture; the shreds of radicchio throughout imparted a pleasing sharp edge.

Pastas are not the only crowd pleasers. Two standout fish dishes are the expertly steamed salmon fillet presented on a fan of summer squash and accompanied by stewed tomatoes, and sautéed snapper alongside a basil-perfumed mixture of sweet onions, carrots and celery. All the veal preparations are worth trying. Don't miss the succulent veal chop roasted with whole garlic cloves.

For dessert, all fruit tarts—apricot, kiwi and strawberry, grape and raspberry—are recommended. The young waiters and waitresses are competent and nimble, although they sometimes could use reserve troops on busy nights.

Alo Alo is a grand cafe in the best European sense—the kind of place you can enter tired, hungry and carrying the weight of the world on your shoulders, and leave with a spring in your step and a smile.

✦ AMERICA ✦

Poor

9 East 18th Street, between Fifth Avenue and Broadway, 505-2110.

Atmosphere: One enormous room seating 350 with an oversize elevated bar, American scenes painted on the wall and neon tubes overhead. Noise level akin to Shea Stadium's in the bottom of the ninth, tie game.

Service: Young untrained staff tends to get lost in the shuffle.

Price range: Moderate.

Credit cards: All major cards.

Hours: Daily, 11:30 A.M. to 4 A.M.

Reservations: Suggested.

If noise and grandiose space are your idea of high dining, then America is a restaurant of Himalayan appeal. However if good food is your quest, don't risk the trip.

8

Ordinarily I would not review such a place. An exception was made in this case because, despite its substantial shortcomings, this massive feeding institution is more than a restaurant. It is a cultural phenomenon, a totem to the new urban generation. Spending an evening at America, where you can watch the fervid goings-on at the three-deep bar and sit among scores of mirthful diners devouring their freezer-burned Tex-Mex dinners followed by S'Mores, reveals as much about the recreational habits of so-called yuppies as any Gallup poll. The curiosity seekers have largely passed on to other hot spots in town, so America is not quite as frenzied as it was when it opened in 1985.

This 10,000-square-foot, 350-seat patriotic barn represents the apotheosis of the new style bar and grill—the biggest, brashest and most bibulous of them all. Cheap eats, $2 drafts and an exciting environment full of promise—that is the appeal of America.

You enter from relatively tranquil 18th Street and slam into a wall of sound that nearly bounces you back out the door. America is awesome to behold. The enormous room has soft murals of all-American scenes on the walls and neon tubes skirting along the towering ceiling. Two sprawling seating areas are separated by a wide central corridor leading to an enormous elevated bar.

Upon opening America's menu I knew I had entered hazardous territory. More than 160 items are listed covering breakfast through dinner, give or take a dozen or so specials. Not only is the volume of food unrealistic for any restaurant, but the range is astonishing. There is something inherently suspicious about a menu that offers sushi, Cajun chicken lips and three-color fusilli primavera.

Don't expect much help from the green young waiters and waitresses in their open flowered shirts. As for the food, which comes in ranch-hand portions, it is ineffably bad at dinner, slightly better at lunch. Prices are remarkably low, which could partly account for the lines at the door.

Many of the appetizers taste as if they had been made in advance and frozen, then thawed in a microwave oven. That would explain freezer burn on the tasteless New Mexican black bean cakes, the stale leftover-tasting barbecued lamb ribs and the dried-out shrimp cooked in banana leaves with an overly sweet tomato dressing.

My fellow diners couldn't decide which was worse, the so-called hot and spicy homemade alligator sausages, which had all the flavor of a pocketbook, or the "dry-cured Virginia ham scrapple," an oversalted mound of mush that would bring tears to a Philadelphian's eyes. The only edible appetizers encountered were the Buffalo chicken wings, which were little more than fried chicken with blue cheese dressing and hot sauce, and the char-grilled wild mushrooms.

Only two of the more than a dozen dinner entrees sampled can be recommended: grilled chicken with herbs and garlic and an herby soup called New Mexican sopa de fideo, which combines vermicelli with shrimp, red onions, snow peas, carrots, scallions, mushrooms and coriander.

The list of calamities includes gummy, unseasoned crab cakes, rewarmed barbecued pork with gloppy commercial-tasting dressing, leathery chicken-fried steak in an unctuous batter that slid off onto the plate, and a greasy duck stew with sloppy mixed vegetables, nearly raw wild rice and bland pine nut pilaf.

Two of the pizzas sampled at lunch—eggplant, leek and pepper; and tomato, Cheddar and chilies on cornmeal crust—at least had been freshly made and had flavor.

The best desserts are the brownies with ice cream and rice pudding with raspberry sauce.

I doubt that America was conceived as a temple of fine regional dining, but even so it is perplexing why it tries to salute the cuisine of every ethnic group from sea to shining sea. It is an effort doomed from the start, and instead of a salute it is a slap.

✦ AMSTERDAM'S ✦

★

454 Broadway, at Grand, 925-6166.

Atmosphere: High-ceilinged, two-tier restaurant done in black and white. Open rotisserie kitchen and long, comfortable bar. Informal.

Service: Pleasant young staff, generally efficient. Service tends to be better in rear dining room.

Price range: Moderate.

Hours: Lunch and dinner, Monday through Saturday, noon to 1 A.M. (kitchen closes around midnight).

Credit cards: All major cards.

Reservations: Suggested.

The winning formula that made the original Amsterdam's on the Upper West Side enormously popular has been cloned on lower Broadway by its youthful team of owners. It is such a sensible approach one wonders why so few have followed suit: a limited menu of simple appetizers, inexpensive rotisserie entrees, good desserts and affordable wines, served in a smart and functional setting.

The long, rectangular two-tier restaurant is done in sharp-edged shades of black and white, with a long bar along one side and an open rotisserie grill on the other. No fussy table settings here, and if you want to pick up the fire-blistered and moist roast chicken with your hand and gnaw on the bones, there is no

11

maître d'hôtel around to roll his eyes toward the ceiling. Crisp, golden french fries are better than average—and you can eat these with your hands, too.

One evening, a special of warm roast chicken stuffed with curried apples, chutney, rice and raisins won a split decision at my table because it was served room temperature. The yeas were universal when it came to the well-burnished and lean roast duck in a zinfandel and cranberry sauce.

One of the appealing aspects of Amsterdam's is that you can drop in for a glass of wine and eat just an appetizer or an entree, and leave with cab fare from your $20 bill. If it's a salad you crave, the formidable mound of mixed greens mingled with assorted meats and vegetables is fresh and sprightly. Ingredients vary slightly from day to day, but foraging usually turns up roasted red and yellow peppers, Black Forest ham, rotisserie-grilled chicken, sirloin strips, sun-dried tomatoes, zucchini, smoked Gouda, duck and anything else within arm's reach of the chef.

Like the food, the wine list is straightforward and priced for the average financially overextended New Yorker.

You can expect more attentive service in the back dining room than in the front one near the bar. In general the waiters and waitresses are earnest and helpful.

The short roster of lighter dishes (there is no distinct appetizer list) includes a meatloaf-thick slab of smooth-textured duck liver mousse that could use a bolstering of seasonings; pretty red-tinted Swedish shrimp—they were pleasantly saline though not as fresh-tasting as those at the uptown restaurant—and delicious, glossy gravlax with a dill-mustard sauce. Pastas have been added to the menu, and most are al dente and well seasoned.

Desserts are intended not to dazzle but to delight, and they succeed, particularly the sharp gooseberry tart and lustrous chocolate velvet mousse cake.

✦ AN AMERICAN PLACE ✦

★ ★

969 Lexington Avenue, between 70th and 71st streets, 517-7660.

Atmosphere: Small, slightly cramped dining room in muted colors.

Service: Generally efficient, although on weekend evenings it can be slow.

Price range: Expensive.

Credit cards: All major cards.

Hours: Dinner, Monday through Saturday, 5:45 to 10:45 P.M. Closed Sunday.

Reservations: Required.

There is no better textbook on the evolution of so-called new American cuisine than the menu at An American Place, created by Larry Forgione, the Thomas Paine of America's culinary revolution. On his menu, you find such Early American artifacts as planked salmon, buffalo steak and apple pandowdy next to such voguish 1980s preparations as barbecued squab, grilled free-range chicken and domestic fresh foie gras. Mr. Forgione was among the first to hop on the now crowded haywagon of all-American cooking when he was chef at the River Cafe; his new restaurant, which he owns, shows how exciting American cuisine can be, although it is not a uniformly smooth trail.

An American Place is a tiny place, and a rather frumpy-looking one at that. Except for a handsome little wooden bar near the entrance, where traffic jams up between seatings on busy nights, the rest of the premises is relatively colorless.

The ever changing seasonal menu is small yet well rounded.

One of the foremost appetizers is Mr. Forgione's signature dish, a terrine of three smoked fish—salmon, whitefish and sturgeon —garnished with their respective caviars. The fresh and smooth terrine, stratified with layers of each fish, is nicely seasoned, and the diadem of colorful caviars is as stunning as it is delicious. Less lofty but equally rousing starters are the generous deviled-crab and oyster fritters, animated with black pepper, and a lusty assortment of country hams and sausages.

Southern-fried rabbit with vegetable pasta sounds intriguing, and while the boneless rabbit is moist and well fried, the pasta in creamy garlic sauce needs more zip.

The Stars and Stripes gets a good showing among the entrees, especially in game preparations such as the succulent roast partridge in an apple-cider-and-vinegar sauce with chestnut puree, and rare-roasted slices of tender mallard duck breast. Mr. Forgione likes to surprise diners with unlikely juxtapositions of ingredients, and those surrounding the duck—a slab of ruddy country ham and sweet-edged red-eye gravy—work better than one might think. The most memorable element of the dish is the country samp, nuggets of hominy that have a pasta-like texture, enlivened with minced red onions, bell peppers and coriander.

Grilled free-range chicken, moist, meaty and flavorful, which comes with wonderful fettuccine loaded down with wild mushrooms, is superb. Barbecued squab with wild rice and apple griddle cakes would have been high on the applause meter as well, had it not been for uneven roasting that left certain sections of the squab too pink inside. If you are in the mood for red meat, go with the lustrous loin of lamb in a bracing dark stock sauce rather than with a light asparagus custard over a bland buffalo steak.

Among seafood entrees, the broiled lobster arrangement looks like something out of a Georgia O'Keeffe painting. The perfectly cooked meat is removed from the shell and reassembled graphically on the plate over a nouvelle version of Newburg sauce, heady with sherry. I was nonplussed by the planked Alaskan king salmon, which had a slightly fishy smell, in a hard-boiled-egg sauce.

Desserts are an adolescent's American dream: velvety and intense chocolate pudding, picture perfect banana Betty, cinnamon-perfumed apple pandowdy with a buttery crust, and mile-high strawberry shortcake. Also-rans are the lemon and raspberry layer cake in a pool of sour raspberry coulis made with underripe berries, and dry devil's food cake.

The service staff at An American Place has always seemed well honed; however the pace can be thrown off on busy weekend nights. An all-American wine list is exceptionally well chosen, and prices are more than fair.

Even with its inconsistencies, An American Place can be as wholesome and uplifting as a Fourth of July parade—and what's wrong with a little flag-waving once in a while?

◆ ANCORA ◆

Satisfactory

2330 Broadway, at 85th Street, 496-9240.

Atmosphere: Expansive postmodern brasserie style, with open pizza kitchen and well-spaced tables. Lively crowd, but noise level is moderate.

Service: Knowledgeable and good natured, but the kitchen can be slow.

Price range: Moderate.

Credit cards: All major cards.

Hours: Lunch, daily, noon to 3:30 P.M.; dinner, daily, 5 P.M. to midnight; bar, daily, noon to 2 A.M.

Reservations: Recommended for lunch; necessary for dinner.

One of the most conspicuous—and ambitious—of the upper Broadway establishments is Ancora, at 85th Street, a cavernous, two-tier Italian restaurant specializing in grilled foods, salads and pastas. Like so many of its flashy counterparts, Ancora expends as much, if not more, effort on its impressive ambiance as it does on the food. There are several first-rate dishes scattered among the densely populated menu, but you may need the doggedness of an archaeologist to find them.

Upon entering, you encounter an expansive room done in pale yellow with a long wooden bar on one side and a dining room on the other. The thirty-foot-high atrium that soars to the second level imparts a feeling of grandeur. The cynosure of the main level is a handsome wood-burning pizza station.

The more comfortable and spacious upstairs is reached via a wide, rust-colored stairway rising from the middle of the ground-floor room. Tables upstairs are well spaced, and the noise level is considerably lower. The food at Ancora, which is served on quaint Italian ceramic plates, is most puzzling. It is somewhat like buying a new Mercedes-Benz that left the assembly line without polish—The internal parts are top quality, but lack of final touches leaves the product dull.

This is most evident in the wide assortment of grilled and broiled meats and fish. While one can't quibble about the quality of the veal chop, lamb steak, chicken or squab, the minimalist style of presentation, with no detectable seasonings or sauces on the meats, leaves them lacking. Indeed, as one of my companions noted, some dishes are reminiscent of the food at a high-class weight-loss camp.

For example, the grilled lamb steak—the menu says it is marinated, but there is no evidence of it—is cooked to order perfectly one evening, seriously overdone on another occasion. It is served with some cotton-dry deep-fried potato rounds. The same applies to the thick veal chop and the baby chicken. The mixed grill (well-charred pieces of lamb, veal, steak and chicken) does have more flavor than the others, but a light sauce or even herb butter would help.

Grilled seafood fares better. Whole rainbow trout, grilled with fresh mint, can be as fresh as a spring morning. Giant whole shrimp from Italian waters, a special—they are about seven inches long—are superb simply grilled and sprinkled with lemon. If Ancora can pull off feats like this, one must ask, why does it consistently overcook swordfish and salmon steaks?

Pizzas—tomatoes, mozzarella and basil; Gorgonzola, goat cheese and mozzarella; and black olives, capers, anchovies, tomato and garlic—are fresh and flavorful. Calzone pumped up with ricotta, goat cheese and spicy lamb sausage is also satisfying, if a bit doughy and skimpy on the fillings.

Of the eight pastas sampled, all made with the finest ingredients, every one suffers from the blahs.

For dessert, the fruit and cheese plate is colorful and fresh; sorbets are a gamble. Tarts range from dry and flat (lemon) to fresh and moist (kiwi).

While dishes at Ancora are wildly inconsistent, commitment to quality is evident, and the service staff is friendly and well informed (if occasionally disorganized). The kitchen is only a saltshaker away from one or more stars.

✦ ANDRÉE'S MEDITERRANEAN ✦
CUISINE

★

354 East 74th Street, 249-6619.

Atmosphere: Comfortable small dining room with colorful tapestries and brick walls.

Service: Young and green, yet they manage to get the job done.

Price range: Moderately expensive.

Credit cards: None. Will accept checks with proper identification.

Hours: Dinner, Tuesday through Thursday, 6 to 9:30 P.M., Friday and Saturday, 6 to 10 P.M. Closed Sunday and Monday.

Reservations: Required.

The earthy brick walls set off by exquisite tapestries in this tiny dining room provide a delightful setting for Andrée Abramoff's couscous, tabbouleh and other specialties from North Africa and the Middle East. Based on my experiences, though, the food can be good at times but is rarely as magical as the ambiance. Couscous is one of the better options, and the ethnic appetizers are unsurpassed, but a host of other dishes fails to excite.

The road to satisfaction at Andrée's begins with the assorted Middle Eastern appetizers. The baba ghannoush is one of the best I've had: a marvelously smoky eggplant puree blended with olive oil, garlic and lemon. It is a special treat when slathered over pita bread. The hummus, a chick-pea puree accented with lemon and cumin, is equally addicting. Tabbouleh, which in lesser establishments can taste like lawn clippings with bark chips, is a bright and balanced combination of parsley, bulgur, scallions, mint, lemon juice and olive oil. Stuffed grape leaves are fresh and citric, while the Greek dip taramasalata, which melds pink carp roe, milk, bread, scallions and lemon, has a refreshing briny flavor. Only the fava bean-and-parsley croquettes called falafel are ho-hum; they are spongy and over-fried.

Frying is better executed with the light triangles of phyllo dough stuffed with spinach and cheese. When I last tried the

18

duck liver salad, a special, it was over the hill and acrid tasting; salmon mousse was grainy and had a suspicious off-flavor, and shrimp ravigote, with capers, onions and parsley, was ordinary. As for the entrees, my advice is to play it safe and go straight for the couscous. One rendition is based on meaty beef shanks combined with chicken, zucchini, chick-peas and the farina-like grain after which the dish is named. The couscous comes with a small crock of harissa, the Moroccan hot-pepper paste, which is mixed into the broth. The seafood version, to which almonds give an extra dimension, also has a rich stock with a variety of fish.

Simple grilled fish with basil butter or other seasonings is a good bet. I have been disappointed with some of the more involved specials, such as Cornish hen stuffed with raisins, pine nuts, giblets and bulgur, which was dry. If you call at least twenty-four hours in advance, Andrée will prepare a special meal for parties of four or more, such as bouillabaisse or paella. Service is inexperienced and halting, but the room is so small you can usually make your requests known. The restaurant serves wine and beer.

The most intriguing dessert is a moist semolina cake flavored with honey and almonds called basboussa. Khochaf, a Middle Eastern fruit salad combining prunes, dried apricots, almonds, pine nuts, pistachios and raisins in a cool soup of rose water, is as refreshing as it is unexpected. Coffee parfait is light and with the dry edge coffee fans will enjoy, and the flourless chocolate-walnut torte will cause palpitations among the chocolate brigade. By confining your trip to Mediterranean standards at Andrée's, it is possible to have a gratifying experience in a cheerful ethnic environment.

✦ ARCADIA ✦

★ ★

21 East 62nd Street, 223-2900.

Atmosphere: Small, cozy and colorful—and cramped.

Service: Competent but occasionally confused.

Price range: Expensive.

Credit cards: American Express, MasterCard, Visa.

Hours: Lunch, Monday through Saturday, noon to 3 P.M.; dinner, Monday through Saturday, 6 to 11 P.M. Closed Sunday.

Reservations: Necessary.

Arcadia is one of the preeminent American restaurants to arrive in New York City in recent years. Co-owned by Ken Aretsky and Anne Rosenzweig, the gifted young chef, it has forged a distinctive menu melding the best of American regional cuisine without lapsing into the cutsies.

Arcadia is a cozy and colorful spot, with an inviting little mahogany bar up front and a larger rectangular dining room in the back ringed by mauve banquettes; on the walls is an enchanting wraparound mural by Paul Davis depicting the four seasons. Overcrowding has become a serious problem since it became so popular, so it might be wise to go at off hours if you want relative peace and quiet.

Almost everything on the lunch and dinner menus, which change every six weeks or so, sounds tempting. The food is not inexpensive: $38.50 prix fixe at dinner, à la carte at lunch with entrees in the $15 range. One might start dinner with a succulent roulade of rabbit and a rosemary-tomato mousseline or lean and spicy grilled duck sausages accompanied by sweet sautéed apple slices and roast chestnuts. One of the prettiest, and tastiest, appetizers is the golden corn cakes crowned with a dollop of crème fraîche and two kinds of caviar, golden whitefish and osetra.

The lunch menu carries one of the best starters of all, grilled leeks in puff pastry. The perfectly cooked leeks, glossed with butter, are crowned with a square of brittle puff pastry. They rest on a swath of onion puree surrounded by a pool of sweet beurre blanc with chives.

Dinner entrees are as warm and soothing as a favorite old sweater, starting with the partly boned roast quails with assertive kasha and cabbage. Venison fillet with an orange-tinged poivrade and kale is another warming winter meal. So is the lovingly prepared loin of veal stuffed with minced carrots, celery and herbs accompanied by scalloped potatoes and stewed tomatoes and onions.

A dish of char-grilled salmon fillets sprinkled with fresh dill sprigs was lustrous and fresh over sautéed onions and slivers of Jerusalem artichokes. This is far better than the mundane grilled swordfish. One of the house specialties is called chimney-smoked lobster. The lobster is smoked and grilled at the same time over a wood-fired grate and served with aromatic tarragon butter. The meat, which has the slightest hint of smoke, is precut and served in the shell, accompanied by deliciously crunchy deep-fried celery-root cakes.

Miss Rosenzweig, who began her career as a pastry chef, makes the desserts, and they are sublime. Chocolate bread pudding with brandy custard sauce has me seriously considering a move to East 62nd Street. The rectangle of spongy dark chocolate is rich but not excessive, and the brandy custard is good enough to drink. On the lighter side is vibrant mango mousse garnished with fresh raspberries served in a parchment-crisp tuile cone lying in a lake of multicolored strawberry puree and crème anglaise.

Another stunning dessert is fresh pear in puff pastry with a warm chocolate sauce, its flaky carapace a marvel to behold and the chocolate sauce adding a dose of decadence. And then there are the crunchy macadamia nut tart and the exquisite lemon curd tart. Overall, the wine list is limited but varied, and the wines are priced fairly. Both house wines are superior.

Some of the waiters are wobbly, and service can break down under the pressure of nightly mob scenes. Nonetheless, I highly recommend Arcadia for those who want to see what new American cooking is all about at its highest level of refinement.

✦ ARIZONA 206 ✦

★ ★

206 East 60th Street, 838-0440.

Atmosphere: Rough plaster walls and glowing hearth suggest a southwestern cave. The decor's theme is carried out without resorting to hokey props.

Service: Enthusiastic and friendly, although occasionally forgetful.

Price range: Moderate.

Credit cards: All major cards.

Hours: Lunch, Monday through Saturday, noon to 3 P.M.; dinner, Monday through Saturday, 6 to 11 P.M. Closed Sunday.

Reservations: None.

The name Arizona 206 sounds more like a highway than a restaurant. In a way, though, it is aptly named, because this exuberant new spot offers a direct route to some of the best California- and southwestern-style food around. At a time when voguish grill restaurants are turning up like Christmas lights in December, Arizona 206 stands out above the crowded display with a sparkling array of dishes.

The kitchen is run by Brendan Walsh, a young dynamo who has created an exciting and diverse menu that is sure to run your taste buds through Olympic-like trials. He does not, however, assemble unusual dishes merely for shock value. Virtually all his recipes are intelligently conceived and demonstrate just how appealing this style of cooking can be in skilled hands.

As you enter the long, narrow restaurant, the first sensation is the soothing aroma of a crackling fire in the small lounge. The whimsical decor includes undulating molded plaster walls that suggest the Southwest, natural-wood floors and tables, and lovely arrangements of desert flowers—"haute cave," they call it. The banquettes have desert-toned cushions that are more comfortable than the bare straight-backed chairs. Conversation and music ricochet off the hard-edged surfaces, so on busy nights it can be clamorous.

The menu is mercifully limited, so you can get right down to business without having to plow through a hand-scrawled encyclopedia of western botanical oddities. The bouncy young waiters and waitresses take pride in the food and are happy to answer questions. Service is casual—"Who gets the chicken?"—and occasionally forgetful.

Two of the appetizer salads are highly recommended: grilled lamb salad with fennel, artichoke, green-leaf lettuce and chopped tomatoes; and a warm mélange of dark, fibrous mustard greens, hickory-smoked bacon and exquisite morsels of sautéed sweetbreads coated with corn flour. In the former, thin slices of lamb are grilled to rare pink, and the sweet-edged honey-cumin vinaigrette helps the diverse flavors come together. The sweetbreads, which are fresh and firm, take on rustic extra dimension in their carapace of crunchy corn flour.

One of the better soups is a velvety, sweet puree of assorted squash. It is garnished with a lovely cirrus pattern of red pepper cream sauce.

The wine list is limited but adequate, and well matched with the food. Iron Horse Brut, which is sold by the glass, is a nice way to start. Mr. Walsh has a golden touch with game. Don't miss the rare-grilled barbecued quail nestled in a bed of creamy polenta, or the squab in a cactus-pear sauce accompanied by peppery spinach and wild rice (a special). One highlight of fall and winter is a superb venison chili in which tender morsels of well-marinated meat are combined with firm-cooked black beans, corn, red peppers, coriander, garlic cloves and tomato. This serendipitous combination is served with a slab of roast red pepper brioche.

Desserts do not fly at the same altitude. Chocolate walnut cake with espresso ice cream is satisfying, although sweet potato pie is run-of-the-mill. A slightly tart cactus-pear sauce enlivens the passion fruit sorbet.

◆ AU TROQUET ◆

★ ★

328 West 12th Street, 924-3413.

Atmosphere: Simple, cheerful French ambiance.

Service: Helpful and pleasant but unpolished and at times slow.

Price range: Moderate.

Credit cards: American Express, MasterCard, Visa.

Hours: Dinner, Monday through Saturday, 6 to 11 P.M. Closed Sunday.

Reservations: Suggested.

Everything about this compact restaurant in the West Village evokes France—the lettered awning shielding white-framed windows with gauzy curtains, the small bar where handsome young waiters flirt with a pair of neighborhood girls who have stopped in for a drink, the simple and lovingly arranged dining room highlighted with paintings by the owner, and the sincere feeling of hospitality—not a well-rehearsed "Good evening, I'm Reginald your waiter and we will be dining together tonight" type of welcome, but the kind conveyed by a warm smile and a bottle of cool white wine.

François le Morzellec, former maître d'hôtel at Le Relais, runs Au Troquet (the name means "little cafe") with his young son, Marc. The small menu, which changes every few months, is contemporary but not flashy, colorful but not contrived. And prices are quite reasonable for what you get; a couple can have a three-course dinner, including a $10 bottle of wine, for about $60.

Intensely flavorful homemade stocks, the mortar with which all French cooking is built, contribute to some first-rate sauces. One example is the mignonnettes de veau à l'estragon. This dish consists of thin medallions of buttery veal cloaked in a meaty veal-stock sauce flavored with aromatic leaves of fresh tarragon. A wedge of crusty potatoes dauphinoises (a casserole of potato slices, cream, nutmeg, salt and pepper) and a grilled tomato half are typical vegetables. Among the roughly ten daily entrées, others worth singling out are the grilled baby pheasant with raspberry brandy, sautéed shrimp stuffed with celery and bacon, duck with Pommard wine sauce and chicken breast served with a mustard-cream sauce. The mild-flavored pheasant, charred on the outside, moist and tender within, came with a lustrous semi-sweet raspberry brandy sauce. In the shrimp dish, the medium-size shrimp are slit down the middle and stuffed with lightly cooked bacon and celery, then sautéed briefly. It's a simple and tasty combination.

The young waiters can be charming and helpful, but for some reason they are often laggard getting food out, even on slow weeknights. Of course, the kitchen may be equally at fault. In any case, it is wise to plan an evening at Au Troquet, not around it. The wine list is short, but the prices are fair.

The two best appetizers on the menu are the crab in puff pastry set in a pool of mustard sauce, and raw salmon marinated with basil. Other good choices are a salad of endive with Roquefort, avocado and cucumber; escargots with garlic butter and anise-flavored Ricard, and an assortment of woodsy wild mushrooms tossed in light cream and crowned with a slab of puff pastry. Only the grainy duck liver mousse is disappointing.

Au Troquet is the sort of homey place where one tends to linger well into the evening sipping espresso or a snifter of cognac. Try either with a pretty fan of apples marinated in red wine and rum, served with fresh cassis sauce and garnished with almond slivers.

Overall, Au Troquet is a restaurant I would return to frequently. It offers value for the dining dollar and provides—for Francophiles like myself—the closest experience there is to following one's nose along the Left Bank.

✦ AUNTIE YUAN ✦

★ ★

1191A First Avenue, near 65th Street, 744-4040.

Atmosphere: Dramatic all-black dining room with pinpoint overhead lighting.

Service: Knowledgeable and efficient.

Price range: Moderately expensive.

Credit cards: American Express, Diners Club.

Hours: Lunch, noon to 4 P.M.; dinner, Monday through Saturday, 4 P.M. to midnight, Sunday, 4 to 11 P.M.

Reservations: Suggested.

Many purists insist that the best Chinese food is found only in restaurants that are (a) cramped and deafening, (b) as brightly lit as a supermarket and (c) filled with tables of Chinese families fiercely poking at wondrous creations that never seem to be on the menu. An exception is Auntie Yuan, the stylish Upper East Side establishment owned by David Keh that turns out a host of compelling dishes rivaling some of Chinatown's finest—albeit at steep uptown prices.

What the higher tab gets you is a coal-black, sleekly cool dining room with overhead pinpoint lighting illuminating solitary flowers on each table, elegant tableware, an extensive wine list and captains in black tie. Tables are well separated and conversations are muted. The captains, virtually all non-Oriental, have a good grasp of the food and assure that no dish remains a mystery.

Two giveaway munchies are so good I would return for them alone: One bowl holds shredded Chinese cabbage and ground shrimp in a coriander–sesame oil vinaigrette, the other has strips of carrots and daikon in a smoldering chili-pepper dressing. Among the appetizers, cold noodles in a peppery sesame sauce flecked with scallion are bright and fresh, while a cold salad mingling shredded duck meat with strips of crackly skin, scallions, Chinese cabbage and coriander offers a lovely contrast of flavors.

One arresting hot starter is succulent barbecued quail glazed with a zippy garlic paste. Of the four types of dumplings served, only the shrimp-filled Shanghai-style ones were memorable, seared golden-brown on the outside and so juicy that upon biting into one I nailed a waiter at six paces.

Seafood entrees are fairly reliable. Salmon is prepared in an engaging way—steamed to just pink in the center and garnished with salty fermented black beans and strips of fresh ginger. Steamed flounder is exceptional, set under a snowfall of garlic, fermented black beans and flecks of hot peppers.

Orange beef is one of those benchmark dishes that can give quick clues about a kitchen. The version here is one of the better ones in town—crisp outside, fibrous and tender within and not overly sweet.

Peking-duck fanciers should note that Auntie Yuan turns out one of the best—layers of brittle skin with a thin sheen of fat underneath to add flavor, wrapped in a rice pancake, followed by the lustrous meat, which is so rich it needs no sauce.

Desserts are few and forgettable.

As diverting as an evening in Chinatown can be, it is nice to know there is a more tranquil alternative when the mood strikes.

✦ AURORA ✦

★ ★ ★

60 East 49th Street, 692-9292.

Atmosphere: Luxurious and quiet with well-spaced tables and super-comfortable chairs and banquettes.

Service: Generally professional. Can be imperious.

Price range: Expensive.

Credit cards: All major cards.

Hours: Lunch, Monday through Friday, noon to 2:30 P.M.; dinner, Monday through Saturday, 5:30 to 11 P.M. Closed Sunday. Bar menu available between lunch and dinner.

Reservations: Suggested.

Joseph Baum might be called New York's gastronomic Vivaldi, orchestrator of the world's second most famous "Four Seasons," and the man who brought respectability to rooftop dining (Windows on the World). Aurora, his most personal creation, is as expected, provocative and controversial.

You are compelled to take an aesthetic stand immediately upon passing the uniformed doormen and entering the winsomely plush dining room. The interior design, by the graphic artist Milton Glaser and the architect Philip George, precludes neutrality. The room combines a very establishment, corporate ambiance (burnished-wood wainscotting, muted colors, plush leather chairs) with a playful bubble theme more appropriate to a trendy yuppie bar—a blend of martinis and margaritas. Bubbles are everywhere: on the plates, the windows, the rug, the waiters' jackets. Even the fanciful overhead lights support the theme. I haven't seen so many bubbles since "The Lawrence Welk Show."

Tables are broad and generously spaced, tableware is weighty and expensive, and best of all, the noise level is muted. The vaguely horseshoe-shaped bar in the middle is a good spot to order lunch from a special grill menu.

As for the food, under the direction of Gérard Pangaud, a well-known Parisian chef, it can soar as high as Mr. Glaser's bubbles on a windy day. Mr. Pangaud brings with him the newfound Gallic affection for unpretentious "real food": that is, dishes that stress flavor over flair. A good example is the appetizer of crisp-skinned duck confit in a nest of fresh greens, enhanced with strips of cured duck and nuggets of gizzard confit, all in a lively hazelnut dressing. Or the firm, golden-sautéed sweetbreads paired with sliced potatoes, truffles and a caper-parsley vinaigrette. Other first-rate starters are the luxurious pheasant terrine layered with buttery foie gras, a glistening mosaic of salmon and leeks, and florid fresh tartare of tuna (a lunch appetizer), jazzed up with lots of pepper and lemon. Globules of golden caviar throughout burst in the mouth, adding a rousing saline accent.

Many of Mr. Pangaud's more refined portraits jump off the canvas as well. A dome of helium-light red pepper mousse is flanked by shrimps in a zesty basil vinaigrette, while a palette of baby vegetables in puff pastry with a sherry vinegar sauce also succeeds admirably. Sautéed fresh foie gras is as stunning as it is seductive on a layer of mâche and garnished with sheer slices of black radish. A tangy vinaigrette sauce makes a fine foil.

A few spectacular-sounding dishes fail to live up to their billing. One example is overcooked pasta with scallops and sea urchin roe in a soupy curry sauce. And doughy Roquefort-filled ravioli are not rescued by a good walnut sauce.

The service staff, donning spiffy cream-colored jackets, gets high marks in general for efficiency. But some customers have complained about imperious attitudes among waiters. Ray Wellington, former wine wizard at Windows on the World, is a great asset to the dining room. He approaches his métier with an unpretentious consumerist attitude. Aurora's reasonably priced wine card, updated daily, is intelligently assembled to harmonize with the ever-changing menu.

Entrées are not uniformly flawless, but the odds are well in your favor. Game fanciers will swoon over Mr. Pangaud's sublime roast pigeon with aromatic garlic sauce and sautéed potatoes, his toothsome venison in a poivrade sauce with pearl onions, and the stuffed pheasant breast roasted in a jacket of caul fat until it is golden and succulent. An incredibly tender veal chop, as thick as a Russian novel, comes with cabbage pockets filled with rice and wild mushrooms.

On the seafood side of the menu, salmon steak baked in a mild horseradish crust is always pleasing. So is red snapper Antiboise, a perfectly cooked fillet on three croutons, slathered respectively with a rustic black olive tapenade and purees of parsley and garlic. A potentially stunning dish of lobster meat in a lime and Sauternes sauce has been vitiated by slight over-cooking on several occasions, while bland tuna steak mounted on a raw-tasting tomato coulis disappointed twice.

What rarely disappoints, though, are desserts. Whoever dreamed up saffron ice cream should be canonized. And the fragile-crusted apple tart with cinnamon ice cream is no slouch either. The cast is large and ever changing: lemon-hazelnut torte, chocolate raspberry cake, warm chocolate mousse cake, an intriguing "nirvana of five oranges" featuring various citric delicacies. I wasn't thrilled, however, with the pallid terrine of fruit in tasteless gelatin.

Presiding over everything is the ever vigilant Joseph Baum, looking as edgy as a long-tailed cat in a room full of rocking chairs. He set out to make a statement about the return of gracious dining in New York. With Aurora, he has succeeded.

✦ THE BALLROOM ✦

★

253 West 28th Street, 244-3005.

Atmosphere: Countrified and inviting dining rooms in a low-key Spanish motif. A giant mural depicting well-known American painters and art dealers sitting in the cafe dominates one room. The long, wide bar filled with tapas offers an alternative to sitting at tables.

Service: Slow and indifferent.

Price range: Moderately expensive.

Credit cards: All major cards.

Hours: Lunch, Tuesday through Friday, noon to 3 P.M.; dinner, Tuesday through Saturday, 4 P.M. to midnight. Closed Sunday and Monday except for private parties.

Reservations: Suggested.

The long wooden bar displays a stunning array of strange and wonderful foods: baby octopus in a sea of red sauce, giant marinated mushrooms, bulbs of baked fennel, stuffed squid, snails with red beans, roasted eggplant, seafood casserole and more. Dangling overhead like an edible raised curtain are braids of blood-red hot peppers, rosy hams, sheets of powdery dried cod and plump black sausages. "This is it!" I said to myself upon entering, awash in nostalgia for my former home in Castile. "Just like a tapas bar in Madrid."

Well, not exactly, I discovered in the course of four visits to The Ballroom, the Iberian-style restaurant-cum-cabaret. A good number of the tapas—meaning finger foods served at bars in Spanish restaurants—are too timidly seasoned or inconsistently cooked. And some of the entrees are uneven in these rustic dining rooms, where a classical guitarist sets a soothing mood. Nonetheless, ample good offerings are available in a setting that is comfortable and sociable without the forced conviviality found in so many of the newer hot spots in town.

You will have no trouble identifying the chef-owner, Felipe Rojas-Lombardi; his grinning, bearded visage is plastered all over the place. Mr. Rojas-Lombardi is a conscientious chef who strives for authenticity. He does things the right way, with no short cuts. I suspect, though, that the minions who execute his recipes don't always exhibit the same commitment.

How else does one account for a time-consuming pied de veau (calf's foot gelatin) made with a reduction of calf's feet and morels that has no perceptible seasonings? Or resilient baby octopus in paprika sauce that is sharp and invigorating one day, insipid the next?

Tapas can be a meal in themselves or appetizers. If you plan to have a full-course meal in the dining room, it is advisable to reconnoiter at the tapas bar beforehand. Although waiters bring a large tray of these tidbits to your table, often the best ones are missing. Among the most pleasing are the grilled eggplant brushed with a peppery coriander sauce; whole squid stuffed with a herbaceous combination of ground pork, pine nuts and raisins; spicy cold chicken in tomato sauce; baked fennel; lemony and fresh ceviche of scallops with scallions; orejas (thin slices of pig's ears) in balsamic vinegar sauce, and a tasty caponata (eggplant salad). Spanish tortilla, which is akin to a potato omelet, is well seasoned and expertly cooked.

Waiters are generally slow and sloppy, always seeming to disappear just when you need them.

The tapas that fail to excite are the bland mixed vegetables with tarragon (but no salt), grilled calamari marred by sand, and chicken in a lackluster curry sauce. Entrees are limited and change slightly from day to day. Roast pheasant in a peppery brown sauce with homey braised cabbage is a first-rate autumn dish that is served in cooler months; get a side order of the sweet fried plantains or yucca, a potato-like tropical root sliced to resemble steak fries. The scallops with their coral are perfectly cooked and set in a lemon-butter sauce.

The Ballroom has an adequate wine list of French and Spanish selections, though you could do well with the pleasing house wines, Viña Sol red and white. The cabaret theater in a separate room, where pop singers and other entertainers perform, serves tapas during the show. The restaurant also offers a colorful buffet lunch composed of tapas and special entrees.

Desserts are not included in the price of the buffet, which is no great loss. The German chocolate cake is gummy, coffee pecan pie has a granitic crust, and tarts are undistinguished. If the rye cake, made with rye flour, raspberry puree and cinnamon cream, is available, go for that. The leaden version of Spanish bread pudding, filled with pineapple chunks, is appealing in a macho sort of way. A fittingly Spanish ending to the meal is a glass of sherry and assorted cheeses.

✦ BARKING FISH CAFE ✦

★

705 Eighth Avenue, between 44th and 45th streets, 757-0186.

Atmosphere: Informal, bustling.

Service: Friendly but can be very slow at busy times.

Price range: Moderate.

Credit cards: All major cards.

Hours: Lunch, Monday through Friday, 11:30 A.M. to 4 P.M.; dinner, Monday through Friday, 5:30 to 11 P.M., Saturday, 4:30 to 11 P.M. Closed Sunday.

Reservations: Requested.

Barking Fish Cafe took root on Eighth Avenue near 44th Street during the height of the Cajun craze in New York several years ago, when everybody's tongue seemed to be stained red and corn bread was considered the height of gastronomic chic. The mania has subsided, although a good number of Cajun restaurants remain in its wake trying to keep the embers alive.

The cafe's front dining room and bar are decorated in a riverboat theme, sporting white deck railings and lots of brass. The pale-yellow back room has a trompe l'oeil staircase on one wall, presumably heading to the upper deck. Fried seafood is available in sandwiches, with tartar sauce, at lunch; po'boys, traditional Southern fish sandwiches served at lunch and dinner, are small French baguettes garnished with shredded cabbage, tomato, pickle and dressing. Another good bet is the chicken-and-ribs combination platter. The meaty pork ribs are glazed with a woody barbecue sauce and are not too fatty; the chicken can be moist and crackly if barbecued to order. At busy times, however, it is cooked in advance and becomes shriveled and greasy while waiting. Good ole Southern boys and girls who were nurtured on rough and crumbly corn bread will be disappointed by the cakelike version here, which is more suitable to a ladies' tea than to sopping up gumbo broth.

Speaking of gumbo, the one served here is dense and spicy, fortified with filé powder that leaves an afterglow at the back of the palate. It has a crab floating on top, as well as sausage, rice and assorted vegetables. In contrast, the oyster stew with a milky broth is subtly seasoned, as it should be, and the oysters are not overcooked. Crab bisque, a special, was redolent of shellfish, but too viscous and bland.

Underseasoning is a recurring flaw, as if the chef fears Yankees can't take the heat. The blackened catfish, for example, which traditionally is coated with spicy Cajun seasonings and seared in a red-hot skillet, is prepared here with little or no spices, resulting in a pallid imitation of the real thing. The same flaw mars the hot barbecued shrimp appetizer—the shrimp are firm and tasty, but the sauce is oily and dull. Try instead the smoldering Cajun jambalaya, a mélange of smoked ham cubes, two kinds of sausage (hot and moderately spiced), chicken and tiny Gulf shrimp in a pepper-laced tomato and vegetable sauce.

A pleasant way to end this sojourn in Dixie is with the heady bread pudding drenched in bourbon and a cup of sharp chicory-laced coffee.

✦ BRIVE ✦

★ ★

405 East 58th Street, 838-9393.

Atmosphere: Soft and cushioned town house restaurant that is romantic, relatively quiet and comfortable.

Service: Gracious and welcoming.

Price range: Expensive.

Credit cards: All major cards.

Hours: Dinner, Monday through Saturday, 6 to 10 P.M. Closed Sunday.

Reservations: Necessary.

Brive is the sort of eccentric restaurant that evokes pro and con reactions popping with exclamation marks, like abstract art. This softly upholstered town house on East 58th Street is the domain of Robert Pritsker, who operated the nouvelle-cuisine Doudin-Bouffant in the same spot between 1979 and 1982. While Mr. Pritsker has moved from the kitchen to the dining room, the food turned out by his crew still reflects his devotion to quality ingredients leavened with a puckish attitude about haute cuisine. If you can get over Brive's relentless case of the cutes on the menu, some arresting food is to be had.

The long, narrow dining area begins in the flower-strewn front room with rust-orange walls and burnished antiques, then tumbles into a slightly more confined back room and finally into a dark and romantic alcove overlooking a small garden. The welcome at Brive is warm and genuine, and the service, while at times overly mannered, could not be more helpful. And you will need help when it comes to this menu, which is cluttered with silly descriptions usually associated with family restaurants designed to resemble pirates' galleons.

If you can muster the courage to order an appetizer described as "calves' brains wrapped and sent from Spain," what you get are delicate poached brains enveloped in almond crepes ringed by a vibrant gazpacho. Wild? Yes, but the combination works. Salmon terrine flecked with its golden roe that gives off a burst of salinity is delightful. A two-course appetizer consists of a warm flan of chicken livers that is silky and mild, followed by a creamy, cold chicken-liver mousse flanked by a good home-made aspic and French bread.

Less serendipitous starters are an overorchestrated dish of mussels that are poached, removed from the shells, swathed in an olive-oil mixture and huddled in the center of a large plate under bread crumbs. All the manhandling saps the mussels of flavor.

Some of the entrees are stellar. Roasted veal chop with a bright basil sauce is superb. Perfectly grilled squab fanned over orso in a savory stock sauce could not be improved upon, nor could the special of roast tuna steak in a garlic-flecked parsley sauce. Perhaps the most distinctive dish is calf's liver. Dusted with bread crumbs and mustard seeds and black peppercorns, the liver is sautéed and presented next to a clump of tart mustard greens and sweet pears.

"Sweet, sweet, sweet sweetbreads" describes you-know-what poached in sweet vermouth and set inside a circle of fettuccine tossed in a light cream sauce studded with sweet red and green peppers, sweet corn and bacon—a beguiling combination. One entree that fails is a clashing combination of beef carpaccio with ginger mayonnaise and dry strips of sauerbraten larded with ginger.

Brive has a limited but engaging wine list and splendid desserts. The ultra-rich and smooth chocolate-pistachio praline torte is not to be missed. Another winning combination is poached peaches, canteloupe and nectarines surrounding an igloo of lustrous mint ice cream. Blueberry sorbet and marjolaine cake oozing with hazelnut cream also leave nothing to the imagination.

Brive's idiosyncratic flirtations may be off-putting to some at first, but give the restaurant a chance and you may be surprised.

✦ BUD'S ✦

★ ★

359 Columbus Avenue, at 77th Street, 724-2100.

Atmosphere: Palms, bamboo and rattan set a California theme. Bustling scene nightly with conversation sometimes reaching a thunderous level. Can be crowded and cramped.

Service: Generally pleasant and knowledgeable. Sometimes long waits between courses.

Price range: Moderately expensive.

Credit cards: All major cards.

Hours: Dinner, Sunday through Thursday, 6 P.M. to midnight, Friday and Saturday, 6 P.M. to 1 A.M.; supper (appetizers and selected entrees), Sunday through Thursday, 11 P.M. to midnight, Friday and Saturday until 1 A.M.; lunch, Saturday and Sunday, noon to 4 P.M.

Reservations: Necessary.

Jonathan Waxman, the chef and co-owner of Jams, and his partner, Melvyn Master, have planted their California flag on the Upper West Side in hopes that the hungry masses foraging along Columbus Avenue will be disposed to pay more than $20 for roast chicken—that is, if the free-ranging bird in question has the well-toned body of an aerobics instructor, is grilled to a turn and arrives with a heavenly batch of golden-fried onion rings.

Judging from the swarms of customers who descend nightly upon Bud's, they are. This rakish addition to the avenue sports a leafy two-tier dining room with rattan chairs, soft lighting and hip background music.

Mr. Waxman has been generally recognized as one of the first major exponents of California cooking in New York since the opening of Jams in 1984. The popularity of Bud's emphasizes that the essence of California cuisine—a light touch and uncompromising freshness combined with a dash of Mexican zest and a pinch of American ingenuity—has universal appeal when executed with intelligence. Haute cuisine? No. Diverting and provocative? Yes.

Take, for example, the stimulating appetizer salad, which mingles lime-accented laces of jìcama—a texture similar to water chestnuts—with fried strips of blue corn tortillas, ripe avocado, red and yellow peppers, hot chilis and grilled scallions. It makes your taste buds jump to attention, as a good appetizer should.

Another winning salad is made with an egg poached in red wine and seated in a nest of glistening wild greens accented with shiitake mushrooms and pancetta bacon in a smooth vinaigrette. Among the warm dishes, earthy and robust black bean soup will warm you to your fingertips throughout the winter. Succulent grilled chicken on skewers with a mound of crunchy white daikon is delicious too, although the jarring papaya-tomatillo sauce could be dispensed with at no great loss.

Another good bet is the blue corn tortillas rolled around cubes of tender pork and sliced avocado in a zippy tomato salsa charged with fresh coriander. Fluffy deep-fried squid in tempura batter presented on a banana leaf is habit forming. Be sure to spoon over it some of the hot corn-and-pepper relish. Fish dishes are cooked to a turn and deftly seasoned, whether it is sea bass baked in rock salt with a light lemon-and-tomato butter or red snapper cooked in parchment paper and tinged with orange zest, lime juice and julienne vegetables.

The bouncy and well-trained young staff is rather self-consciously attired in West Coast getups—captains wear dark suits and white sneakers, waiters don flowered shirts and green khakis. Their enthusiasm is palpable, although occasionally there are long lags between appetizer and entree.

39

The more than ample wine list wisely complements the food, including good choices in the $15 to $25 range.

Mr. Waxman's spirited approach soars right through to dessert, with such engaging combinations as fresh figs poached in Beaujolais with vanilla ice cream, mango-rice tart, chocolate–pine nut tart and Himalayan-size profiteroles supporting glaciers of chocolate sauce.

Simplicity and freshness have been strangers to the Upper West Side quiche belt, so it's no wonder the locals are rushing to Bud's like surfers to ten-foot swells.

✦ BUKHARA ✦

★

148 East 48th Street, in the Helmsley Middletowne Hotel, 838-1811.

Atmosphere: Handsome and low-key with sandstone-colored walls and soft lighting.

Service: A bit confused but improving.

Price range: Moderate.

Credit cards: All major cards.

Hours: Lunch, Monday through Friday, noon to 3 P.M.; dinner, daily, 6 to 11 P.M.

Reservations: Suggested.

Bukhara is not your typical Indian restaurant. For one, this midtown establishment, modeled after the original in New Delhi, is the most handsome and comfortable of its type to come along in years. Moreover, the food, described as "frontier cuisine" from the northwest, is a bright and brassy change of pace from more familiar Indian fare around town. Every entree is grilled over charcoal or roasted in the ancient clay oven, the tandoor; diners wear big checkered bibs and eat with their hands. While Bukhara may not be everyone's cup of Darjeeling, I found it overall to be a diverting experience with some spirited food.

The dining room has rough sandstone-tone walls holding gleaming hammered-brass-and-copper trays and colorful embroidered rugs, soft indirect lighting and stout teakwood tables set with copper water tumblers and pretty flower-painted plates. Behind a glass partition is a spiffy slate-walled kitchen where chefs tend the tandoor ovens.

The menu is limited to about a dozen main courses, with no appetizers and only three desserts; some of the entrees, however, make good starters if split among two or four. When you are seated, a waiter brings hot hand towels and the menus.

The tandoor ovens turn out a host of terrific breads: nan, a fluffy white-flour disk; roti, a flat, earthy whole-wheat round, and khasta roti, which is a toasted whole-wheat bread sprinkled with cumin seeds. The best is mint paratha, the slightly puffed and charred whole-wheat bread that is dusted with dried mint. Bharvan kulcha, an inflated nan stuffed with onions, potatoes and fresh cheese, is delicious when dipped in a mint-ginger chutney set out on the table.

Bukhara had some service shortcomings in the first few months after opening, but by now one hopes they have been ironed out.

This "frontier" style of cooking, said to originate with the Pathan tribes of Peshawar, now part of Pakistan, revolves around marinating primary ingredients in yogurt (or another moistening agent), herbs and spices, then cooking in the super-hot tandoor. This technique reaches a sublime level with chicken Bukhara, in which the whole sectioned bird is infused with yogurt, chili powder, ginger and garlic, then roasted to falling-off-the-bone succulence. Veal chops, marinated in dark rum and yogurt that is accented with cinnamon, then grilled, also share best-of-show honors. A hint of sweetness from the rum melds with the sharp-edged cinnamon and lingers on the palate. All portions are large enough to share around a table of four.

Another recommended chicken dish, called mellow cream chicken, features bite-size pieces of meat marinated in cream, lime juice, green peppers and mild cheese, then skewered and nicely charred over the grill.

It is ironic that lamb, for which Indian cooking is justly renowned, is the least appealing of the entrees—it tends to be overcooked and underseasoned. The most expensive item on the menu, duck Bukhara ($38), is to be avoided. It is bland and tastes more like beef than duck.

Two good side dishes are the delicious grilled cubes of fresh cottage cheese flavored with cumin seed and ginger paste, and the exceptionally creamy and rich lentil dish called dal. The dal is best scooped up with one of the flat breads.

The menu writer got fancy when it came to dessert, switching to French to describe l'orange crème, which is a sprightly orange-perfumed frozen cream served in a carved-out orange peel (spoons are allowed with dessert). The other desserts are humdrum.

Bukhara is a good option for large groups since the serving style lends itself to sharing.

✦ CAFE DES ARTISTES ✦

★

1 West 67th Street, 877-3500.

Atmosphere: Gracious cafe with dark wood walls and splendid murals.

Service: Well schooled in the food but at times forgetful and slow.

Price range: Moderately expensive.

Credit cards: All major cards.

Hours: Lunch, Monday through Friday, noon to 3 P.M.; brunch, Saturday, noon to 3 P.M., Sunday, 10 A.M. to 4 P.M.; dinner, Monday through Saturday, 5:30 P.M. to 12:30 A.M., Sunday, 5 to 11 P.M.

Reservations: Necessary.

Cafe des Artistes, in a historic turn-of-the-century building off Central Park West, is one of the most gracious and romantic spots in town. Its dark, burnished-wood walls, lead-paned windows, sparkling tableware and famous bucolic murals by Howard Chandler Christy contribute to an ambiance of gentility and anticipation—in such a setting the world suddenly feels full of promise.

When it comes to food, however, that promise is not entirely fulfilled. The menu can be likened to the saucy yet innocent Christy nudes on the walls—both revel in the flirtation more than the follow-up. The cafe's menu is big, perhaps too big, and it takes several run-throughs to locate the potholes. Once you know your way around, though, it is possible to have a splendid experience.

The restaurant is perpetually packed, and it is difficult to get a reservation before 10:30 P.M. on short notice. Even with a booking, chances are you will have to cool your heels at the bar, which is hardly penitential, for it is one of the most fashionable perches in town—and great for celebrity watching. In the downstairs room, tables are jammed together along purple banquettes; the bar level is slightly more private. The service staff is well informed and tirelessly enthusiastic, if sometimes slow and forgetful.

While the menu wanders all over the map, its strength lies in certain ingenuous French-bistro dishes. The confit of duck is one of the better renditions around, crisp-skinned, falling-off-the-bone tender and authoritatively seasoned. It comes with

43

tasty white beans. Another high point is the classic combination of rare-roasted slices of lamb in a zesty pan gravy surrounded by tasty flageolets, the small pale-green French beans. Rack of lamb encrusted with basil and bread crumbs can be recommended. The slide comes among seafood entrees, many of which tend to be overcooked.

The wine list has some good selections but at prices that begin at $24. Dom Pérignon (1980) is a real bargain at $65. Every night a special "wine basket" offers preselected labels at $14 each.

Appetizers fare better than entrees. Opt for the creamy and herbaceous squash soup over the pallid seafood gazpacho. Four preparations of salmon presented on a wooden serving board—gravlax, smoked salmon, poached salmon steak and dill-flavored tartare—are fresh and lively. The cold foie gras terrine rolled in black pepper crust is silky and delectable along with its duck cracklings and toasted brioche.

Parties of four or more should try the "great dessert plate," a battalion of heavy-duty cakes and pies. Among the best are the tart and airy Key lime pie, moist and nutty sour cream apple walnut pie, zesty orange savarin cake and velvety chocolate mousse cake. The frozen praline mocha is excellent, far better than the burned-tasting chocolate-truffle ice cream. Those of an intrepid spirit might want to attack the "Great Bonaparte," a Himalayan-size napoleon made with puff pastry under an avalanche of whipped cream, lemon curd and strawberries.

✦ CAFE DU PARC ✦

★

106 East 19th Street, 777-7840.

Atmosphere: Handsome, understated, exposed brick and high ceiling.

Service: Eager but erratic.

Price range: Moderate.

Credit cards: All major cards.

Hours: Lunch, Monday through Friday, noon to 2:30 P.M.; dinner, Monday through Friday, 6 to 10:30 P.M., Saturday, 6 to 11 P.M. Closed Sunday.

Reservations: Necessary.

The cooking at this low-key establishment that caters to the publishing crowd at lunch could be classified as "new French" as opposed to nouvelle; that is, the chef uses imaginative color and texture combinations without lapsing into excessive daintiness. The main dining room, with its high ceiling and track lighting, exposed brick wall and etched-glass room dividers, is well suited to both a relaxed business lunch by day and a less serious rendezvous by night.

Among the better appetizers in summer is salade d'été, a visually stunning combination of fresh fennel and anchovies resting on a star pattern of julienne strips of red and yellow peppers with basil leaves. It is sprinkled with an aromatic basil-and garlic-tinged olive oil. Another winner is a crisply grilled veal and duck sausage, lean and tasty, resting in a nest of radicchio and mâche lettuce and garnished with crunchy nuggets of deep-fried duck skin.

A slice of fresh salmon purportedly marinated in dill and aquavit is devoid of either flavor; steamed mussels in saffron sauce suffered from grit, and leeks and shrimp in puff pastry would have been good had the baby shrimp not been desiccated and frozen tasting. The assortment of homemade terrines are bland.

Inconsistency mars the soup and pasta appetizers. Fusilli with basil and pine nuts was soupy and mundane one time, as was ravioli filled with lobster and spinach; on a second visit, both were much better. Lobster bisque was tepid and underseasoned

45

once, more flavorful the next, especially with a shot of sherry in it.

Some of the waiters can be as fervent as television evangelists when it comes to describing the food; inexplicably, though, once the sermon is over, they tend to disappear just when you need them. If you have limited time for a business lunch, make that clear at the outset.

Most of the fish dishes sampled were exceptionally well prepared, starting with the fillet of salmon served on a bed of spinach with a vernal tomato-sorrel sauce. The salmon was moist and had a delightful smoky flavor. Fillet of sole steamed in parchment with julienne slices of ginger, carrots and leeks was equally alluring. When a waiter sliced open the puffed bag, a blast of ginger swirled around the table.

A lunch special one day, navarin of lobster with tomato and basil over pasta, was lackluster—its only flavor was butter. Two better choices were monkfish in red-wine sauce with pearl onions and mushrooms, and steamed striped bass with julienne of red, yellow and green peppers, tomatoes and basil. Calf's liver with roasted garlic, pearl onions and sherry vinegar was cooked as requested and glazed with a delicious veal-stock sauce. Grilled veal paillard, on the other hand, was tasty but chewy.

For dessert, try the chocolate-cappuccino cake, alternating layers of dense chocolate, frothy cappuccino cream and chocolate layer cake, garnished with fresh walnuts; the uplifting mango mousse with raspberry sauce, or, when they have it, the equally good cassis cake. All the superior tarts are freshly made, and the selection of homemade sorbets—cassis, raspberry, lemon, passion fruit and more—is among the best in town.

✦ CAFE 58 ✦

★

232 East 58th Street, 758-5665.

Atmosphere: Subdued, comfortable, informal.

Service: Amiable but slow at times.

Price range: Moderate.

Credit cards: All major cards.

Hours: Lunch, Monday through Saturday, noon through 4 P.M.; dinner, Monday through Saturday, 4 P.M. to midnight, Sunday, 5 to 11 P.M.

Reservations: Suggested.

When I think of Cafe 58, visions of one of my favorite dishes flash before me: pied de cochon. This peasant dish—succulent breaded and roasted pig's feet, crisp outside and gelatinous within—is superb here, as good as in any Paris bistro. This homey and old-fashioned restaurant has consistency problems, however, which leaves some of the other food tired and bland. Yet prices are more than reasonable, the ambiance is relaxing, and sufficient good selections exist to merit keeping it in mind when you are in the neighborhood.

The walls are covered with a dark plaid fabric—the kind one finds on children's bunk beds—and the ceiling is made of eerie crenulate cement, which is sprayed to resemble a cave. Wall sconces above the banquettes are mounted on gnarled vine roots.

The appetizers are not nearly as esoteric as the setting. All the familiar tunes are played, and among the better ones are the earthy and lean country pâté, beefy onion soup, scallops in a white sauce with mushrooms, and smoked salmon. Mussels ravigote can be gritty, and the escargots are run-of-the-mill. Most appetizers carry supplementary charges, so the prix fixe is not really valid.

Cafe 58 usually offers several daily specials in addition to the regular menu. On weekends, there is bouillabaisse, a dish that proves you don't have to fly in French fish and charge $30 a bowl to create a credible version. This one ($19.50 at lunch, $20.50 at dinner) contains pieces of pompano, red snapper and cod as well as half a lobster, clams and mussels in a well-seasoned red broth. It is enhanced by a garlic mayonnaise and a peppery rouille (hot mayonnaise with paprika).

Another special is cassoulet, which also is good and garlicky with lots of sausage and duck ($11.95 at lunch, $14.95 at dinner). Another peasant dish is a winner: tête de veau, or calf's head. You get slices of tongue, meaty cheeks and brain accompanied by a mild creamy vinaigrette. The onion-flavored boudin, or blood sausage, is simply grilled and served with apple sauce and first-rate french fries. We peasants never had it so good. Seafood does not fare as well. Both fish specials sampled—monkfish in a green peppercorn-cream sauce and broiled scrod—were bland. Grilled Dover sole meunière is better.

The limited wine list matches the food well—a few good crus Beaujolais, some Macons, a Muscadet and a Sancerre, many in the $15-to-$22 range.

Desserts, like the entrees, are meant to satisfy, not dazzle. The fruit tarts are pleasing, as is the festive coupe aux marrons (glazed chestnuts buried in vanilla ice cream with whipped cream). Oeufs à la neige, crème caramel and pears poached in red wine received passing grades. All in all, if you're looking for honest food at an honest price, Cafe 58 is worth noting.

✦ CAFE 43 RESTAURANT ✦
AND WINE BAR

★

147 West 43rd Street, 869-4200.

Atmosphere: Comfortable, bright and bustling cafe ambiance.

Service: Can be forgetful and slow at lunch; better at dinner.

Price range: Moderate.

Credit cards: All major cards.

Hours: Lunch, Monday through Friday, 11:30 A.M. to 3 P.M.; dinner, Monday through Saturday, 5 to 11 P.M.; supper, Monday through Wednesday, 11:30 P.M. to 12:30 A.M., Thursday through Saturday, 11:30 P.M. to 1 A.M. Closed Sunday, Christmas Day and New Year's Day.

Reservations: Recommended.

Convenient to Broadway theaters, Cafe 43 is a place to keep in mind for a drink and snacks before the show or something more substantial afterward. Its food seems to have slipped considerably since it was originally reviewed in late 1984, so order conservatively—leave the razzle-dazzle to Broadway casts.

The restaurant is a cavernous space with high ceilings, blush walls, arched mirrors and wide banquettes in a color that refrigerator salesmen refer to as harvest gold. The dining room is comfortable and bright, and the high ceilings absorb conversation so even at peak hours you don't have to bellow.

The lunch and dinner menus change often, so the following are typical dishes. Cafe 43 has one of the more extensive wine-by-the-glass menus in town—twenty-four kinds in all, including eight champagnes and sparkling wines. The regular wine list is well represented among California and European selections, all priced fairly.

Several appetizers are near misses at lunch. A salad of buttery sea scallops served with avocado chunks, broccoli florets and corn, all swathed in sesame dressing, was marred by an underripe avocado; mozzarella with marinated eggplant was drowned in oil, and acorn squash–leek soup was woefully underseasoned. A better choice at dinner was the shrimp in a light cream sauce dusted with parchment-like flakes of fried celery.

Some of the simplest dishes are the best bets: medallions of beef under a semisweet caramelized onion puree were delicious. The grilled swordfish steak with a pat of tarragon butter can be satisfying, too, if it is not overcooked. A plump hamburger, cooked rare to order and served with sautéed onions and first-rate french fries, was prepared with obvious care.

Desserts sampled were uniformly good: creamy mango and macadamia nut parfait, fluffy chocolate mousse with candied ginger, an airy egg white mousseline resting in a pond of English cream and cranberry sauce (unfortunately the almond slivers on top were stale), moist and chunky chestnut cake and fruit sorbets.

Service, like the food, rises and falls with the tide of customers. If possible, try the cafe before or after the lunch crunch, or in the evening.

✦ CAFE LUXEMBOURG ✦

★ ★

200 West 70th Street, 873-7411.

Atmosphere: Stylish and lively West Side crowd that gets younger and more colorful as the evening wears on. Can be noisy.

Service: Friendly and casual.

Price range: Moderately expensive.

Credit cards: American Express, MasterCard and Visa.

Hours: Dinner, Monday through Thursday, 5:30 P.M. to 12:30 A.M., Friday until 1:30 A.M., Saturday, 6 P.M. to 1:30 A.M., Sunday, 6 P.M. to 12:30 A.M.; brunch, Saturday, noon to 3 P.M., Sunday, 11 A.M. to 3 P.M.

Reservations: Necessary.

When Cafe Luxembourg opened in 1982, it became an overnight hit, a stylish and serious restaurant in the gastronomic tundra surrounding Lincoln Center. It has slightly more competition today, but not much.

Every evening a polymorphic parade of Upper West Siders passes the gleaming zinc bar up front and into the sleek tile dining room with its period sconces, Parisian cafe chairs and red banquettes. The dark-suited local gentry and business types hold forth from about 8 to 10 P.M., academia and literati settle in next, and after 11, restless young fast-trackers, meticulously disheveled and in buoyant spirits, linger until closing. Service is casual in a brasserie manner yet overall professional. At peak hours the room can be loud.

The straightforward, essentially American menu is intelligently balanced to serve such diverse demands, allowing one to partake of a substantial three-course meal or a simple late-night light repast. Two tantalizing starters are the grilled shrimp with a bright and tasty herb butter and the golden-sautéed crab cakes that are bolstered with minced green peppers and set in a sparkling tomato sauce tinged with salty capers and parsley. The eggplant and red pepper terrine is exceptionally pure and bright. All the salads are good, especially the combination of tart chicory and other green lettuces with Roquefort and garlic croutons.

The entrees represent American bistro food as it should be: nothing too elaborate or quizzical, just down-to-earth good food. Rare roasted leg of lamb in natural juices with an eggplant-and-red-pepper flan, macadamia-coated sautéed calf's liver, chicken paillard and steak pommes frites are all right on the mark. One of the best entrees is the brittle-skinned roast duck in a rousing honey-lemon sauce. The sweet and sour play off each other beautifully. Another unqualified winner is the grilled split lobster, remarkably moist, perfumed with smoke and brushed with basil butter. One of the few disappointments is pasta, which is not up to the standards of the other entrees.

Seafood selections change daily. One day it might be steamed halibut set over strands of fresh ginger in light cream sauce bolstered with white pepper or sautéed salmon smothered in wilted onions.

Except for grainy and pallid sorbets, all desserts sampled make for happy endings. Don't miss the soothing square of creamy bread pudding with caramel sauce or the crunchy maple pecan pie.

✦ CAFE MARIMBA ✦

★

1115 Third Avenue, entrance on 65th Street between Second and Third avenues, lower level, 935-1161.

Atmosphere: Enchanting use of shadows and lighting make for a dramatic setting. Noise level can be quite high when busy.

Service: Extremely earnest staff that is sometimes a bit too chatty, but overall does a conscientious job.

Price range: Moderate.

Credit Cards: American Express and Diners Club.

Hours: Dinner, Monday through Thursday, 5 P.M. to 1 A.M., Friday and Saturday, 5 P.M. to 2 A.M., Sunday, 5 P.M. to midnight.

Reservations: Recommended.

Until recently, most of my forays to Mexican restaurants in New York resulted in one gastronomic Alamo after another: a series of assaults on the digestive system that could put me out of commission for days. The whimsical names changed and the margaritas came in different colors, yet the food was, for the most part, greasy and leaden—fast food served slowly. Only in the last several years have a handful of serious establishments appeared that offer something other than deep-fried tortillas heaped with iceberg lettuce and gloppy overcooked fillings. One of the more engaging new spots is Cafe Marimba, an enchantingly designed restaurant on the East Side.

Part of the David Keh empire (Auntie Yuan, Pig Heaven, Safari Grill), it is run by the Mexican-born Zarela Martinez. When Cafe Marimba opened in early 1985 amid much fanfare and anticipation, I was wowed by the innovative decor. The food, however, was something else. Miss Martinez appeared to be spending too much time with customers in the dining room while cooking was left to a young, inexperienced crew.

Eventually, though, reports filtered back that Cafe Marimba had improved, so I returned. In short, the kitchen indeed tightened up its act. The menu carries some uncommon and buoyantly seasoned preparations.

First a word about the design, by Sam Lopata. Mr. Lopata tossed aside all the sombrero and bullfight-poster clichés to create a room that evokes Mexico without being corny. The two main dining areas, flanking a square tile bar, are done in muted earth tones and enhanced by dramatic use of light and shadows to create a feeling of sunset in the desert. Stout wooden chairs, tile banquettes and hardwood floors carry through the theme. They also amplify noise, which seems to swell in direct proportion to margarita consumption during the night. Mexican food is made for sharing, so it is advisable to get an assortment of appetizers. One of the best was a special—red snapper hash, a mound of fresh and firm shredded fillet that tinged the palate with a blend of cumin, cloves and Mexican cinnamon.

Traditional Mexican fajitas were better than most you will find in town—tender marinated strips of fibrous skirt steak served with flour tortillas, guacamole sauce and refried beans.

There is hardly a restaurant in New York, it seems, that does not serve grilled salmon in some guise, yet the version here is exceptionally satisfying. The florid crosshatched fillet carries a hint of oregano and comes with a zippy mayonnaise laced with chipotle peppers. I don't really know if goat cheese has become chichi in certain circles south of the border; regardless, it makes for a rousing starter as part of a sizzling preparation called chilaquiles. The dish combines shredded chicken, flour tortillas, bright tomatillo sauce and tart goat cheese. The kitchen turns out a terrific corn-and-crab chowder that smolders with diced hot chilies and has a haunting charcoal undercurrent.

Two of the least enticing appetizers are the flautas—rolled fried tacos stuffed with dried chicken and served with guacamole —and a bizarre ensalada de chicharron—deep-fried pork crack-lings in a cloying mayonnaise and avocado mixture. If you want something lighter, try the invigorating salad of watercress and jìcama dusted with sesame seeds and tossed in a good vinai-grette.

Some of the entrees require a little explanation. The relent-lessly earnest waiters and waitresses here overdo it a bit, giving dramatic re-creations of each dish, complete with footnotes on their personal favorites. All in all, though, they mean well and manage to keep the pace going. One occasional problem at Cafe Marimba is that food comes out tepid or cold, which could be as much the fault of the kitchen as the service staff.

Entrees are imaginative and distinctive, if not uniformly suc-cessful. Duck fanciers should go straight for the pato en-cacahuetado. It is a beautifully grilled breast of duck, with a lean layer of crusty skin, accompanied by two vivid sauces, one a peppery blend of peanuts and powdered chili, the other a pulpy puree made with mashed pumpkin seeds and roast tomatoes. Ground orange rind and the earthy red spice achiote combine to enliven a spit-roasted baby chicken. This is far better than the "drunken chicken," which is dry and overwhelmed by olives. If you are among those who feel no Mexican dinner is complete if it doesn't ignite a brushfire on the tongue, try the camarones con coco, shrimp cooked in the shell with grated coconut and jalapeño peppers. On the tamer side, another worthy dish featured a smoky grilled slab of veal served with a buttery pumpkin-seed puree. The grilled loin of pork marinated in sherry, vinegar and peppers, another special, was garnished with earthy marinated chili strips and sweet onions. Unfortunately, the dish was flawed on two occasions: Once the meat was overcooked, a second time the entire dish was served nearly cold.

If you do not overdose on floured tortillas during the meal, dessert is worth considering, especially the zesty cinnamon ice cream (it can be had with a crusty and moist cinnamon-flavored brownie). Buttery almond layer cake soaked in Frangelico liqueur is a winner too. A wacky dessert you might want to share around the table features cinnamon-flecked tortilla chips inserted in balls of vanilla ice cream with sliced apples.

Cafe Marimba eschews Mexican stereotypes in both food and decor, and for an evening of fun with some spirited food, it is worth a visit.

◆ CAROLINA ◆

★

355 West 46th Street, 245-0058.

Atmosphere: Pretty main dining room with skylight and mirrors. Low noise level.

Service: Pleasant and informative.

Price range: Moderately expensive.

Credit cards: MasterCard and Visa.

Hours: Lunch, Monday through Friday, noon to 3 P.M.; dinner, Monday through Saturday, 5 P.M. to midnight, Sunday, 12:30 to 8:30 P.M.

Reservations: Suggested.

The smart little restaurant Carolina took root along the West 46th Street Restaurant Row in 1983 just as the campfires of regional American cuisine were beginning to ignite. It was an engaging spot offering a refreshing change of pace from the old French bistros that had dominated the block for decades. It may be hard to believe in this mesquite-crazed age, but only a few years ago the concept of wood-grilled meats and fish was a novelty, at least in these environs, and Carolina did a creditable job.

It's likely that we have become fussier about this kind of cooking through increased exposure, or even more likely that Carolina has become less fussy about its cooking. Whatever, the food has slipped over the years and now lacks the sharp edge that makes wood-fired barbecue so appealing.

The main dining room is still one of the more accommodating on the block, with its arching skylight, gray banquettes and the wraparound glass walls that multiply the sole palm tree in the middle of the room into an urban grove. The effect is even more enchanting at night. A front room near the bar is lively at lunch, too dark at dinner; an upstairs addition is the least appealing of the three. All three are relatively quiet.

The young waiters at Carolina are sincere and well informed. Don't feel obliged, however, to comply with management's written request that they be tipped with cash.

While nibbling on the corn bread—it doesn't seem to taste as good as it used to—consider starting with a bowl of chili. Fresh-tasting, beefy and stoked with lots of hot peppers, it is one of the few boldly seasoned dishes left. Sweet-tinged corn chowder isn't bad either, made with a milk base and firm kernels of corn. Both of these are recommended over the dry and sinewy barbecued beef on lettuce or the smoked salmon with "home-baked" dill bread. At lunch the bread arrived chilled and soggy-bottomed, as if recently thawed.

The wine list is unyieldingly patriotic, offering an adequate and fairly priced selection of American labels.

On the entree card, one of my favorites from the early days, crab cakes, is as good as ever—two hefty disks generous with crab, slightly peppery and skillfully deep fried. I wish other seafood entrees were as distinctive. Grilled swordfish steak and grilled salmon are well cooked but lack woody nuances; skewered shrimp tend to be overcooked and unseasoned.

The restaurant specializes in hot-smoking meats, a technique that involves low-heat cooking with aromatic wood. The meat that profits most from this is the brisket of beef, which is moist and exceptionally flavorful.

Light and puffy corn pudding and homemade coleslaw are worthwhile side dishes. Another special entree that satisfies is called Texas tenderloin, marinated strips of grilled steak swathed with sweet onions and served with mashed potatoes.

Most desserts at Carolina are heavy-hitting winners, from the citric lime pie to dense chocolate mud cake and crunchy pecan rolls dipped in chocolate. While the restaurant has slipped a notch from its earlier two-star level, it still has a certain appeal as a theater-district dining option. I just wish Carolina would return to its roots and get back to basics.

✦ CASUAL QUILTED ✦
GIRAFFE

★

15 East 55th Street, in the AT&T Arcade, 593-1221.

Atmosphere: Distinct, futuristic miniamphitheater with stainless-steel walls and gray leather banquettes.

Service: Young, well-trained and attentive staff.

Price range: Expensive.

Credit cards: American Express.

Hours: Monday through Saturday, 11:30 A.M. to 11:30 P.M.

Reservations: Suggested.

The tongue-in-cheek diner motif of this highly personalized project of Susan and Barry Wine, proprietors of the sumptuous Quilted Giraffe, is bold and exciting, or sterile and cold, depending on your aesthetic predilections (I belong to the former camp). The dining room is a two-tier, miniamphitheater arrangement with gray leather banquettes around the perimeter, black granite tables, Buck Rogers–style steel lighting columns, perforated stainless-steel walls and handsome tableware. To describe this place as a diner is like calling the Metropolitan Opera a vaudeville house.

As for the food, which is listed on an oversize plastic-covered menu carrying an outline of Philip Johnson's Chippendale-topped skyscraper, it is equally paradoxical. How does one characterize a bill of fare that has everything from veal cutlet and sweet-potato fries ($22), creamed corn ($5 as a side dish) and root beer floats ($6) to beluga caviar in crepe pockets ($10 each) and pasta with foie gras ($22)?

Those who plan to breeze in for a snack or light meal should be forewarned that a $15 minimum plus an 18% service charge applies. A simple lunch for two with one bottle of the most modest wine easily breaks the $80 barrier; more substantial dinners can easily run up tabs of $75 a person. As one dining companion quipped upon perusing the menu, "This has got to be the most expensive food ever laminated."

Price notwithstanding, a handful of dishes is very good; the rest range from merely good to humdrum. The menu is divided into appetizers ($12 except caviar, which is $10), soups ($7.50), side dishes ($5), main courses ($22, except salmon brochettes and lamb chops, which are $10 apiece), deluxe main courses ($30) and desserts ($6). Cutely named prix fixe meals range from "coffee break" (brioche with cashew butter, coffee and jelly beans, $15) to "six-pack extravaganza" (six caviar pockets and a bottle of Dom Pérignon, $150).

Hot appetizers are more interesting than cold. Snails nestled among earthy, garlic-scented black beans are exceptionally savory; small pizzas combining ricotta cheese and Japanese wasabi mustard are irresistible—the crust is yeasty and puffed, and the snowy ricotta carries a faintly hot undercurrent from the mustard. Creamy polenta topped with onions and two fried eggs would make a terrific breakfast—unfortunately the restaurant does not open until 11:30 A.M., when my desire for such fare has waned.

Fried chicken nuggets and potato salad are both well made, even if they are nothing more than fast food served slowly. The nostalgia prize goes to spicy duck meatballs clinging to a crater of mashed potatoes. Served on rain-slicker-yellow diner-style plates, they look like something Ozzie and Harriet would have contributed to a pot-luck supper. The meatballs are indeed tasty, and the potatoes are buttery and smooth. The best cold appetizers are charred lamb cubes over mixed greens and Japanese radishes, the vibrant summer salad, and a selection of New York State goat cheeses.

The changing wine selection is divided into four tiers with three to five wines in each: good ($20), fine ($30), great ($50) and superb ($125). I would prefer to make my own judgments on quality and would like to see more inexpensive selections befitting a "casual" restaurant.

The earnest young waiters and waitresses decked out in spiffy white shirts with navy blue "Quilted Giraffe" suspenders try hard to please, and they are succeeding.

Entrees offer more variety than appetizers. The salmon brochettes garnished with bacon, tomato and onions are cooked to a turn and presented over freshly prepared creamed corn. Tuna steak, while fresh and also deftly grilled, curiously had no flavor, and the accompanying strips of fennel and carrots didn't help. Grouper, also cooked to a turn, came with bursting ripe grilled tomatoes.

All the deluxe main courses sampled were on the mark: steamed lobster, double-cut veal chop with sweet-potato fries, and well-aged sirloin with potato crumbs.

Desserts are the most consistent course on the menu. Chocolate cake is moist and shamelessly rich, and cinnamon bread pudding with caramel and whiskey is worth every calorie. A caramelized pear comes with luxurious pistachio ice cream and a cluster of sweet champagne grapes. The one dessert I passed up was "jelly beans and gummy bears."

The problem with the Casual Quilted Giraffe is not so much the food—on the whole it is on a one-star level and likely to improve—but rather the fuzzy concept of the place. For all its multimillion-dollar glitz, it lacks identity. Part high-tech, part low-brow, part Barry Wine, part Betty Crocker, it is neither informal bistro nor elegant restaurant. It would be nice to see the Casual Quilted Giraffe loosen its tie and become truly casual.

◆ CELLAR IN THE SKY ◆

★ ★

1 World Trade Center, 107th floor, 938-1111.

Atmosphere: Tranquil cellar-like ambiance with classical guitarist.

Service: Attentive and efficient.

Price range: Expensive.

Credit cards: All major cards.

Hours: Dinner, Monday through Saturday, one seating at 7:30 P.M.

Reservations: Required.

Compared with the stadium-like scene at Windows on the World, the more exclusive Cellar in the Sky seems downright monastic. This slightly more ambitious restaurant-within-a-restaurant, seating only thirty-six, offers a leisurely pre-set five-course meal built around an aperitif and four wines. If you don't mind surrendering personal choice to fate, Cellar in the Sky can be one of the more enchanting and delectable experiences in town.

The dimly lit, romantic dining room has a cavelike motif sporting wine racks along glass walls. It does not offer the celestial views of the main restaurant, although what you gain in the trade-off is more varied and refined food that is artfully presented and paired with intelligently selected quality wines—not 1966 Château Latour quality, but always substantial and interesting. A classical guitarist plays nightly. The $70 prix fixe might sound stiff, but considering that no supplements are levied and wines are included, it is really no more expensive than many other first-class establishments in New York City.

The menu changes about twice a month. Recent dinners

began with finger foods such as silken foie gras mousse on toast, bite-size vegetable tartlets, caviar on buttered brown bread, and buttery smoked sea scallops set over a tangle of julienne leeks. The wines for starters: a zesty 1982 Trimbach Riesling on one occasion, a bright and dry 1984 Wente Chardonnay another time.

Subsequent courses are gracefully orchestrated to embrace a range of flavors and textures. It might be a terrine of fresh foie gras (not as flavorful as it could be) served with brioche and assorted greens, or a superb dish of fresh and mild calf's liver set over wilted sweet onions with veal stock. The summertime soups are always light and delicate—I prefer the sweet oyster bisque redolent of oyster brine to the cream of sole with chives.

The service staff is attentive and accommodating. Waiters make certain your wine well never goes dry.

Both fish courses excelled: a perfectly cooked, meaty fresh turbot brightened with the lightest of cream sauces, one colored with parsley, the other with carrots. Lobster out of the shell in a truffle beurre blanc was as prettily arranged as it was delicious, surrounded by spokes of asparagus and flecked with black truffles. A luscious 1982 Pommard from one of the region's premier vineyards, Rugiens, set the stage for tender squab in a Pinot Noir–based sauce flanked by red and white cabbage; rare-roasted strips of duck breast were surrounded by lively fettuccine flecked with fresh sage and nubbins of crisped duck skin.

A small but well-chosen cheese course follows with an appropriate wine. Desserts are satisfying though not memorable—lime tartlet paired with lemon mousse and lime sherbet one day, and somewhat dense profiteroles encasing coconut ice cream surrounded by fresh berries another time. Best of all was the dessert wine, a 1983 late harvest Gewürztraminer from Jean Geiler.

Cellar in the Sky is a celebratory sort of place, where decisions are few and the wine flows freely from a regal fountain. For any lofty occasion, it is well worth the ascent.

✦ CENT'ANNI ✦

★

50 Carmine Street, between Avenue of the Americas and Seventh Avenue South, 989-9494.

Atmosphere: Small, minimally adorned dining room with a friendly Greenwich Village ambiance.

Service: Veteran waiters are informed and genial, but not terribly attentive.

Price range: Moderate.

Credit cards: American Express.

Hours: Lunch, Monday through Friday, noon to 2:45 P.M.; dinner, Monday through Saturday, 5:30 to 11:15 P.M., Sunday, 5 to 10:45 P.M.

Reservations: Recommended.

"Where are the sun-dried tomatoes?" a diner at my table asked our waiter after tasting a sauce supposedly made with this distinctive and expensive delicacy, but detecting none.

"They're in the sauce," the waiter replied with an expression of bemused astonishment. "Do you know what they taste like?" "Yes, that's why I ordered them," the diner responded. "But this is just plain tomato sauce."

Seeing no point in extended debate on the matter, the waiter dashed into the kitchen and reappeared proffering two strips of sun-dried tomato on a saucer. "You see? There they are," he said triumphantly.

Dining out can sometimes be a frustrating experience, especially at a homey and well-intentioned place like Cent'Anni, the diminutive restaurant with the oversize banner hanging above Carmine Street. I am drawn to these lively ethnic establishments and want them to succeed—imagine a city with only mesquite grills and three-figure French restaurants. But try as I do, it is difficult to warm up to Cent'Anni, which bills itself as a Florentine country restaurant. The case of the invisible tomatoes is merely one illustration. While the kitchen is clearly capable of pleasing when the team is on a roll, it suffers recurring slumps—a two-star performance one day, barely fair the next.

The ambiance is diverting in a threadbare Greenwich Village sort of way—crowded, bustling and friendly. White-frocked waiters are enthusiastic and well informed, but not much when it comes to the fine points of service, such as pouring wine and tidying up tables. Even the most diligent of them get lost reciting the unnecessarily long list of specials.

The best starter by far is the cold seafood salad, a sparkling assortment of shrimp, lobster, scallops and squid bathed in a mild olive oil dressing. There are four pastas on the printed menu and several daily specials, all of which can be split as appetizers. Shells all'amatriciana were on the mark in their fresh tomato sauce bolstered with onions, prosciutto and olive oil. So was the capellini con aragosta, thread pasta in tomato sauce with chunks of well-cooked lobster and fresh clams. Two disappointments were the rigatoni alla Medici—tube pasta in a buttery but characterless sauce combining chicken, onions, carrots and cream—and the pappardelle in rabbit sauce, which could have been pork for all the flavor it had.

One problem with the number of specials is that the kitchen appears overtaxed. Some dishes do not get the attention they deserve. For example, the shellfish special that includes fresh lobster, scallops and squid can be ruined by sandy and off-tasting mussels and clams. Overcooked roast loin of pork has the texture of a softball, and tripe alla Fiorentina is rubbery from undercooking. On a good night, though, we enjoyed a lovely osso buco—the veal shanks were fork-tender and infused with vegetable and herb flavors from long braising. The double-thick veal chop, which is first broiled to impart a nice crust, then sautéed with wine and fresh sage, was as delightful as it was copious.

Among the notable seafood dishes are the exceptionally fresh broiled whole red snapper basted with garlic and olive oil, and two specials, sea bass fillet in a briny and well-seasoned fish stock, and grilled jumbo Mediterranean shrimp in a sweet-tinged, cognac-spiked red sauce.

Fruit and cheese are the most suitable desserts. If you're in the mood for something sweet, both the pear tart and the tartufo, chocolate ice cream in a dense chocolate skin, are preferable to the grainy zabaglione. The lavish-looking chocolate mousse cake crowned with chocolate curls is a cruel coquette, an empty tease.

Cent'Anni is one of those restaurants that are difficult to rate with all-encompassing symbols, whether they are stars, forks or "Have a nice day" buttons. I am siding with the optimists and going with one star, hoping to find a smaller banner with brighter colors on a future visit.

✦ CHIKUBU ✦

★ ★

12 East 44th Street, 818-0715.

Atmosphere: Soft gray and natural wood dining rooms; low noise level.

Service: Long on politeness, short on performance.

Price range: Moderate.

Credit cards: American Express and Diners Club.

Hours: Lunch, Monday to Friday, noon to 2:30 P.M.; dinner, Monday through Saturday, 5:30 to 10:30 P.M. Closed Sunday.

Reservations: Requested.

Chikubu is one of those inconspicuous midtown Japanese restaurants that I have passed dozens of times without paying much notice. Only when some Western friends who have kept it to themselves for years decided to break their code of silence did I venture inside. First impressions were promising—at a long table in one of the two dining rooms were six tipsy Japanese businessmen, their silk ties askew and normally rigid expressions softened by sake. Judging by the gusto with which they were eating and drinking, I had high hopes.

Chikubu is indeed a find in this part of town, offering some first-rate vegetable dishes, broiled entrees and casseroles. It specializes in the cuisine of Kyoto, which is known for its cooked dishes. However, exceptionally fresh sashimi is available, while sushi is served only at lunch.

The narrow restaurant is trim and neat, in shades of light gray and blond wood. The noise level is generally low. The service staff is good natured and exceedingly polite if not always terribly efficient.

It might be a good idea to bring along a Japanese dictionary. Otherwise, since much of the menu is not translated, you'll have to rely on the staff for explanations. One of the best appetizers is dengaku eggplant, which resembles the earthen monolith that haunted Richard Dreyfuss in *Close Encounters of the Third Kind*. This mound of tasty eggplant is coated in a sweet soybean paste sprinkled with tiny sesame seeds. Another light primer is called takiawase vegetable, which often changes ingredients. It might feature little squares of acorn squash, turnips, eggplant and potato, resting in a slightly sweet broth tinged with mirin wine.

Broiled dishes are far superior to fried ones. Shioyaki flounder is best of all—a perfectly cooked whole fish is presented on a stunning blue-and-white ceramic plate in a clear broth under a snowfall of minced Japanese radish. The fried whole flounder is stiff and dry, while both the shrimp tempura and the tatsuta age chicken are greasy.

Try instead the crusty salt-grilled shioyaki salmon or the broiled kabayaki eel. Such familiar standards as chicken teriyaki (glazed skewered chicken) and negimaki (grilled beef rolls with scallions) also make pleasant light lunch entrees. Also notable is yosenabe, an earthenware crock holding a similar broth that is set over a burner at your table. A waiter fills it with pieces of flounder, scallions, chicken, cabbage, enoki mushrooms, shrimp, clams, noodles and more. The broth acquires an intriguing complexity along the way.

Japanese persimmons, engagingly sweet with an acidic edge, are a suitable finale at this unassuming little spot in the heart of the business district.

✦ CHRIST CELLA ✦

Satisfactory

160 East 46th Street, 697-2479.

Atmosphere: Drab and colorless dining rooms with a masculine feeling.

Service: Perfunctory, informal.

Price range: Moderately expensive.

Credit cards: All major cards.

Hours: Lunch and dinner, Monday through Thursday, noon to 10:30 P.M.; dinner, Friday and Saturday, 5 to 10:45 P.M. Closed Sunday.

Reservations: Required.

Christ Cella is another pillar in the pantheon of New York steakhouses, and like the Roman original, it is deteriorating with age. Everything about Christ Cella has a faded, almost sad, patina. Groups of two-fisted ex-linemen still frequent the wood-paneled bar before hunkering down to a meal that likely rekindles memories of the pregame steak dinner. The remaining patrons appear to be older New Yorkers who made a habit of going there in its heyday and continue.

The dowdy downstairs dining rooms could probably be described as homey if the food were better. The upstairs front room, the largest of all, at least benefits from sunlight and a street view.

Menus are superfluous. Steaks, chops and several fish entrees were rattled off so quickly in a rote manner by our waiter that we had to ask him to repeat them twice. The veteran service team—our waiter had been there nearly thirty years—has its routine down pat, but don't expect any fine touches.

On the first visit our group ordered veal chops, lamb chops, steak and broiled snapper. Lamb chops were the best entree, char-blackened outside and buttery within. Veal chops were cooked to order and relatively tender but had little flavor. New York strip steak was rich and beefy but overcooked and lacked texture. Broiled snapper dusted with paprika had all the flavor of typing paper. It came with a cereal bowl full of tartar sauce, but even that failed to rescue it.

The anachronistic wine list offers no specific names for Bordeaux châteaux but rather describes them as merely St. Emilion, St. Julien, Médoc and so on. When I asked our waiter what the St. Emilion of the house was, he put his nose to the list, squinted, and declared, "It's French!"

On a second visit, swordfish, a dinner special, was desiccated beyond rescue. A better selection was the cold poached salmon, a special at lunch, which lay in a garden of lettuce, cucumbers, tomatoes, onions, pickles, carrots and eggs. The giant portion of salmon was fresh and moist, enhanced by its accompanying mustard mayonnaise.

The biggest disappointment was the famous Christ Cella lobster, which for years has been renowned for its size. Ours was indeed a hefty critter—about three pounds—but its mushy texture hinted that it had passed on to lobster heaven some time before the chef made its acquaintance.

Considering the limited number of side dishes served, one would think the kitchen could do a better job. Not so with the leathery hash brown potatoes, soggy premade Caesar salad and assorted salad greens with gloppy blue cheese dressing. The crabmeat salad, which is the best of the lot, comes with the same cliché ketchup cocktail sauce that you find at Peter Luger.

After the meal, a waiter comes to your table lugging a tray holding a giant napoleon the weight of a barbell. Actually, it is pretty good, in a gooey sort of way. Rum cake with chocolate filling is vastly enhanced by a dousing of rum. The fainthearted are allowed to have fresh fruit, but only if they promise to finish all the whipped cream.

◆ THE COACH HOUSE ◆

★ ★

110 Waverly Place, west of Washington Square, 777-0303.

Atmosphere: Early American charm. Red leather banquettes, colorful artwork, brick-and-paneled walls, formally attired staff.

Service: Captains are polite and strive to please. Generally efficient.

Price range: Moderately expensive.

Credit cards: All major cards.

Reservations: Suggested.

The venerable Coach House relishes its reputation as the Model T of American cuisine. While all the zealous young whipper-snappers chase their free-ranging chickens and slather goat cheese on everything but the candlesticks, this Greenwich Village landmark put-puts along with its rack of lamb, chicken potpie and other reliquiae from the original *James Beard Cookbook*.

That in itself is no reason for criticism; these dishes are the roots upon which our new American cooking style have been grafted, and it's important to keep them alive. But the problem at The Coach House several years ago was complacency. Quality slipped as it tried to roll along on reputation alone. Happily, though, Leon Lianides, the resident archivist and owner, realized this folly before it was too late. He has tuned up the Model T's engine and given the buggy a fresh coat of polish. I was pleased to discover that it is worth taking out for a spin again.

Any discussion of The Coach House menu must begin with its signature dish, black bean soup, which is back to the level that made it famous. The thick, inky puree was rich with the essence of ham and bolstered with sweet Madeira, giving it an earthy aftertaste. Now the restaurant should work on the lackluster gazpacho. Another house special, warm buttery corn sticks, arrive soon after you are seated. They can be a bit dry but the flavor is good.

Appetizers worth trying are the bright and herbaceous eggplant Provençale, which combines cubes of eggplant, capers, raisins, onions and tomatoes; sautéed shrimp in a mild mustard sauce, and first-rate crab cakes, which are replete with sweet meat and contain no bread filler. The crab cakes are subtly seasoned and golden-fried in clean oil (they are available as both an appetizer and entree).

Service at The Coach House has improved considerably. It is one of the few restaurants in which captains still refer to women in the third person—"Would the lady care for more sauce?" Such deference seems fitting in this patrician setting. The captains are disarmingly pleasant and efficient. The main dining room is one of the most enchanting in the city. The brick-and-paneled walls adorned with early American and French art, red leather banquettes, spindly brass chandeliers, lavish flower arrangements and formally attired staff exude a sense of style and period that is rare today. The upstairs area, used for overflow and parties, has an appeal of its own with a similar color scheme and wine racks lining the walls.

Without question, the best black pepper steak in town comes out of this kitchen—a well-aged slab of tender beef embedded with black peppercorns and blanketed in a dark, intensely flavorful veal-stock sauce. As a good pepper steak should, this one takes you right to the threshold of pain, then backs off. Get it with the crusty sautéed potatoes. The all-American chicken pie, which several years ago slipped to the level of the "two for 99 cents" frozen variety, is now chock-full of moist white meat, fresh peas, carrots and other vegetables in a light cream sauce.

Prime ribs of beef, a real he-man portion, and rack of lamb are good quality and competently prepared. So are the simple but good sautéed lobster tails atop a heavily reduced and buttery shellfish sauce. Among the disappointments is a dry grilled squab with a sweet-edged sherry sauce, and one preparation that sounded far more tempting than it was: mignonettes of veal with glazed chestnuts. The veal can be slightly dry and the dark brown sauce with mushrooms and chestnuts characterless.

One area in which the old American cooking seems as contemporary as ever is desserts, and The Coach House knows how to show them off. The deep-dish apple pie layered with almonds and encased in a thick cinnamon-flavored crust stands alone as an icon of our cooking heritage; the deep-dish peach and plum pie is equally beguiling. Blueberry tart on a brittle sugar crust is ethereal with a crown of unsweetened whipped cream, and the chef's eggy and remarkably light custard set in raspberry sauce would give that cliché of the with-it set, crème brûlée, a run for its money.

A restaurant like The Coach House reminds us of our culinary roots. Who knows, when all the "new American" fun and games are over, we may need a safe place like this to call home.

✦ CONTRAPUNTO ✦

★

200 East 60th Street, 751-8616.

Atmosphere: Informal; all white; open kitchen.

Service: Confused and haphazard when busy; not very professional.

Price range: Moderate.

Credit cards: All major cards.

Hours: Lunch, Monday through Saturday, noon to 5 P.M.; dinner, Monday through Saturday, 5 to 11:30 P.M., Sunday, 4 to 10 P.M. Closed Christmas Day.

Reservations: None.

When a restaurant menu starts off with a declaration of its cooking philosophy or the admonition "Good food takes time to prepare, so please be patient," that is usually a signal for wise diners to flee. Contrapunto, a chic, informal pasta restaurant at 60th Street and Third Avenue, above a sister establishment called Yellowfingers, is a serendipitous exception. This restaurant, while limited in scope, puts considerable energy and imagination into making its pastas tasty and distinctive.

The menu begins with four appetizers, all good: a mixed green salad with a walnut oil dressing; grilled mushrooms with garlic; air-dried beef with Parmesan cheese, and a salad of Italian cheeses and roast peppers. Following are twenty pastas, both fresh and imported, and a handful of specials. There isn't a real clunker among them.

Almost anything with seafood is a safe bet. Try the cappelli marina piccola, strands of al dente angel hair pasta flecked with dried tomatoes, shallots, leeks and basil, all crowned with a diadem of littleneck clams in the shell; or the fettuccine with chunks of sweet fresh lobster in a mild sage-and-butter sauce.

One of the best dishes is brodetto, a souplike mélange of red snapper, half a lobster, sea scallops, squid, clams, garlic and fresh herbs. The seafood is served atop flaxen strands of angel hair pasta swathed in a strong fish stock.

The only seafood dish that doesn't make the grade is malfatti aragosta, large pasta squares filled with paltry bits of lobster in a lackluster sauce. Most of the artistically presented vegetable and cheese pastas are bright and flavorful. Among the more intriguing offerings was the fusilli tossed with dandelion leaves, arugula, watercress, fennel, tomato, garlic and a generous dusting of hot pepper. The heat of the peppers playing off the cool sensation of the fennel is a delight. There are many vegetable variations—some with mushrooms, or leeks, or varied herbs—and most work well.

Another good choice is the giant ravioli stuffed with mascarpone cheese, spinach, watercress, sage and Parmesan glistening under a sauce of white wine, butter and olive oil. The fresh pasta is resilient to the bite and the stuffing wonderfully herbaceous.

The wide-open, slightly cramped dining room, all white with spotlit tables, can be deafening at peak hours. Service sometimes resembles a Keystone Kops routine. One white-aproned waiter dashes over breathlessly to take your order, another delivers it ("Who gets the capelli?"), and yet a third tends to wine and other matters. Keep this in mind if you plan to go to a movie or catch a sale at nearby Bloomingdale's.

Most of the cakes and tarts for dessert taste like decent commercial quality—a bit heavy-handed with sugar. The homemade gelati also were too sweet. A better choice is the homemade sorbet, particularly strawberry or orange.

◆ CUISINE DE SAIGON ◆

★

154 West 13th Street, 255-6003.

Atmosphere: Faded Oriental ambiance; low-key, harsh lighting.

Service: Halting and slow; occasional language problems.

Price range: Moderate.

Credit cards: All major cards.

Hours: Dinner, Sunday through Thursday, 5 to 11 P.M., Friday and Saturday until 11:30 P.M.

Reservations: Requested for weekends.

If New York City has a conspicuous gap in its crowded parade of ethnic restaurants, it is in the Vietnamese contingent. This is a shame, for the cooking of what was once called Indochina is among the most delicate and refined in Asia.

Cuisine de Saigon in Greenwich Village is among the most prominent in this tiny fraternity. Those familiar with some of the better Vietnamese restaurants in other American cities will not be wowed by the straightforward fare here; nonetheless, enough pleasing dishes can be found to etch a reasonable picture of what Vietnamese cooking is all about.

Situated on the ground floor of an old brownstone, the restaurant has been minimally disguised in Southeast Asian attire. As you enter, you pass through a dark bar–waiting room into the dining area with its arched ceiling painted dark red, faded blue-gray walls reminiscent of an old classroom, Oriental paintings, harsh overhead lighting and simply appointed tables. Waiters are slow and may pretend they understand English better than they do.

The four-page menu is tempting to read, but don't be deceived by its size—in many cases you face a Hobson's choice. Two or three of the chef's basic sauces go by several aliases and show up unexpectedly.

For example, the crispy bass features a nicely fried and meaty whole fish sprinkled with shredded ginger and scallions. It is set in a sweet-and-salty sauce based on nuoc mam, a saline fish condiment, soy sauce and seasonings. We experienced a flash of déjà vu, however, when the shrimp Saigon-style (shrimp blended with bits of pork and scallion) arrived in the same sauce. Chicken Saigon-style plays nearly the same tune; so does a dish called crispy chicken, which is well seasoned but not crispy.

The two barbecued selections—beef and pork—are tasty variations on the same theme, served with lettuce for making little rolls, julienne of vegetables for garnish and hoisin sauce.

The kitchen's strong suit is broiling; its weakest is frying. Try the shrimp with sugarcane, an engaging combination of shrimp paste molded to a stalk of sugarcane before broiling and served with translucent rice paper, lettuce, coriander sprigs, fresh mint and pickled onions. The idea is to make cigar-shaped rolls with the ingredients and swab them with sweet hoisin sauce. Lemon grass, a long, thin herb that resembles scallions, is a staple in Vietnamese cooking. I have a passion for it, so it was disappointing to find barely any in the lemon-grass chicken, which was overpowered by a sharp, peanut-laced curry sauce.

Another standard in Vietnamese cooking is the spring roll, which at its best is extraordinarily light, crisp and exploding with the flavors of fresh mint and vegetables. On a scale of one to ten, these are about seven—the pork and shrimp filling is well seasoned and the roll is skillfully fried, but it lacks zip. The shrimp rolls and vegetarian rolls are lighter and tastier. Both the fried Vietnamese toast with minced pork and shrimp and the fried dumplings, holding the same fillings, are tasty if a bit greasy. Steamed dumplings stuffed with pork and shrimp are glossy and light, resting on a bed of steamed bean sprouts.

Desserts are forgettable with the exception of the steamed banana cake, a resilient and quivering specimen, really more of a pudding, garnished with coconut milk and peanuts.

Cuisine de Saigon has modest ambitions and manages to achieve a fair percentage of them. If you go there with modest expectations and choose correctly, you should come away satisfied and yearning for a wider sampling of this exciting cuisine.

◆ DA SILVANO ◆

★

260 Avenue of the Americas, between Bleecker and Houston streets, 982-0090.

Atmosphere: Rustic Tuscan ambiance but cramped. Outdoor cafe.

Service: Sloppy and slow.

Price range: Moderately expensive.

Credit cards: American Express.

Hours: Lunch, Monday through Friday, noon to 3 P.M.; dinner, Monday through Thursday, 6 to 11:30 P.M., Friday and Saturday, 6 P.M. to midnight, Sunday, 5 to 11 P.M.

Reservations: Suggested.

Da Silvano is a victim of its own success. What was once a leisurely rustic setting in which to enjoy engaging Tuscan specialties has become a chaotic and unpredictable place, about as relaxing as the rush-hour IRT. Too many customers, too many dishes, too few waiters—it's a familiar story. I tried to be understanding on the first of several revisits when more than half an hour passed before we managed to secure some wine as aperitifs. When that turned out to be the pace of the evening—we arrived at 8:15 and finished dessert at 11:30—my patience meter was quivering in the red. Subsequent lunch and dinner service was equally slow and haphazard. More important, the cooking has slipped noticeably.

I suggest you take a tape recorder for the mile-long list of specials recited by waiters. Among the better special appetizers are a salad of fresh and resilient baby octopus in a lemony vinaigrette, and a heaping bowl of meaty steamed mussels in a fresh, oceanic broth. Another seafood salad on the menu, combining calamari rings and mussels in a garlic-and-lemon vinaigrette, was sparkling and invigorating one evening, overcooked and underseasoned another time. Crostini—Italian bread slathered with seasoned chicken liver—is always a good starter. Some tasty cold appetizers were enjoyed at lunch in the restaurant's charming outdoor cafe, including bread salad with red onions, eggplant parmigiana and braised baby artichokes.

Most of the pastas, though, were disappointing: watered-down spaghettini puttanesca, an oily and bland tagliarini with duck liver—both specials—and gummy cannelloni. A nicely seasoned pasta roll filled with spinach, prosciutto and ricotta suffered from being served tepid. One intriguing combination was tagliarini crowned with sea urchin roe and slices of avocado— you mash them into the pasta to form a deliciously saline sauce.

The best dish overall was succulent lamb shanks braised with white wine, carrots and celery. Of the grilled entrees, salmon with rosemary was done to a turn and breaded jumbo shrimp were simple and tasty. Failures seem to arise from an overworked kitchen. One example is the roast squab, which, while crisp and succulent, lacked the promised cayenne pepper. Fennel-perfumed Italian sausages were partially burned, and lobster stuffed with crabmeat was spoiled.

Flan and good zabaglione with strawberries are recommended over the diner-quality chocolate mousse and the grainy raspberry sorbet. The neglectful service continued to the end—I nearly needed a subpoena to get the check one evening.

Da Silvano's decline in food and service clearly invalidates its former two-star rating; until it controls the crowds and gives both its kitchen and service staffs a break, one is more appropriate.

◆ DARBAR ◆

★ ★

44 West 56th Street, 432-7227

Atmosphere: Elegant multilevel restaurant with handsome brass wall hangings and vivid color scheme.

Service: Adequate and low-key.

Price range: Moderate.

Credit cards: All major cards.

Hours: Lunch, Monday through Friday, noon to 3 P.M.; dinner, Sunday through Thursday, 5:30 to 11 P.M., Friday and Saturday, 5:30 to 11:30 P.M.; buffet, Saturday and Sunday, noon to 3 P.M.

Reservations: Recommended.

An often overlooked option for distinctive and moderately priced dining in midtown is Darbar, a consistently rewarding Indian restaurant on West 56th Street. Offering primarily the refined Mogul cuisine of northern India, Darbar performs with self-assurance and elan, rarely compromising for supposedly timid Western palates.

The restaurant is a multilevel affair with a bar downstairs and magnificent hammered copper hangings on fabric-covered walls. Upstairs the tables often seem too small for the quantities of food that arrive, but aside from that the setting is essentially comfortable and soothingly illuminated.

When a dish calls for hotness, such as gosht vindaloo, the smoldering condiments come at you like an arching curve ball, first making a wide and deceptive approach, then suddenly changing course and zapping into the target. The vindaloo, while delightfully complex and pleasingly hot, is tame compared to murgh madras, a south Indian specialty in which chicken pieces are simmered in a rust-colored pepper sauce camouflaged with cinnamon and a touch of lemon. When that detonates on the palate, there is not enough water in Lake Champlain to douse the flames. This, of course, is authenticity in excessive doses.

A more reasonable chicken dish is reshmi kebab, buttery pieces of dark meat rubbed with a mix of Indian spices and roasted on skewers in the tandoor oven. Marinated morsels of lamb aromatic of cardamom and cumin from the tandoor are exceptionally tender, too.

Frying is one of the kitchen's many strengths. This is most graphically seen in the crinkly hot-air balloons of poori, golden puffs of fried bread. Tandoori roti, a round whole-wheat bread baked in the tandoor, has an earthy and charred flavor. Perhaps the standout, though, is onion kulcha, which is a baked pocket of bread stuffed with sweet onions and fresh coriander. All the breads are wonderful accompaniments to the creamy lentil dish, dal, and the restorative potato-yogurt mixture called raita.

Vegetarians have a good range of fresh and boldly seasoned dishes from which to choose. My favorites are the grilled eggplant mixture called bayngan bhurta, blended with onions, tomatoes and spices.

The service staff performs adequately in a low-key fashion, although some waiters can be a bit aggressive trying to sell extra bottles of wine.

Appetizers embrace all the little fritters familiar to fans of Indian cuisine: crisp and fresh vegetable-filled samosas, meltingly tender chicken pakoras, and sour-cream-marinated shrimp in light batter. All come with a sweet-and-sour tamarind sauce and a cooling mint sauce. The one unusual starter, crab Bombay, should stay in the subcontinent; the sinewy strips of crab come in a watery coconut-and-tomato sauce. Palak shorba, a spinach soup fragrant of clove, was inedibly salty.

Among the standard Indian desserts, a cardamom-flavored rice pudding called kheer is a refreshing semisweet punctuation mark, as is nutty kulfi ice cream perfumed with rose water.

Overall, Darbar is noteworthy not for any unusual fancy footwork, but rather for its steady and reliable performance.

◆ DEVON HOUSE LTD. ◆

★ ★

1316 Madison Avenue, at 93rd Street, 860-8294.

Atmosphere: Formal and understated with two cozy and romantic dining rooms.

Service: Well informed if slightly mannered; generally efficient.

Price range: Expensive.

Credit cards: All major cards.

Hours: Dinner, daily, 6 to 11 P.M.

Reservations: Suggested.

You approach the unmarked entrance and press a small buzzer. The door opens slowly and you are greeted by a young man in a navy blue blazer and bow tie who looks like a recent graduate of an English school for butlers. He asks your name, nods knowingly and beckons you to enter. The foyer is formal and tastefully understated, with a little mahogany bar and, on either side, cozy, compact dining rooms that sparkle like crystal goblets.

Welcome to Devon House Ltd., New York's most proper and patrician restaurant. The hushed ambiance here is as far removed from those cacophonous new California-style grilleries as Tower Records is to the Pierpont Morgan Library's manuscript room. The food is essentially Continental, with a dash of West Indian salsa sprinkled in by the Jamaican-born owner and chef, Yvonne Scherrer. Those looking for a romantic, serene setting and food that usually satisfies, and occasionally excites, would do well to visit Devon House.

Daily specials are numerous, and among the best are the coarse-textured and deftly seasoned rabbit pâté glazed with flambéed port, and a bowl of huge and meaty fresh mussels steamed in an exquisite broth containing fennel, saffron, tomato and scallions. Escargots are prepared in an unusual way that is exceptionally tasty. The escargots, without shells, are served in a satiny garlic-tinged cream sauce colored with little bits of tomatoes and scallions.

Some of the soups sampled were standouts. One evening it was a thick, stewlike blend of pureed leeks, lettuce and spinach in a flavorful chicken stock.

The earnest if slightly mannered service staff is well versed in the food—occasional lags seem to originate in the kitchen. The well-heeled and soft-speaking patrons don't seem to mind, as Devon House's courtly pace casts a pleasing sedative spell on all who enter.

Some of the classic French and Italian dishes fall short of the mark: veal chop with a lackluster imitation of osso buco sauce, and tough medallions of veal with foie gras and a morel cream sauce. The more engaging entrees are those with Jamaican accents. Fresh salmon takes on an entirely new personality when prepared in the Caribbean style. The fillet is lightly marinated in oil and seasonings, then briefly braised in salmon stock, white wine and Jamaican peppers. As a finishing touch, it is popped under a broiler just to sear the top, leaving the bottom nearly raw. Game fanciers might enjoy the nicely roasted half pheasant, crisp skinned and moist, presented with a red-wine sauce aromatic of fresh sage. Equally pleasing is the roast Cornish hen with an exotic-tasting sauce combining pineapple, green peppercorns and lime. Rack of lamb comes in a tasty green peppercorn sauce, but when I had it, the meat tasted halfway to muttonhood. A better choice would be the well-aged, tender fillet of beef cooked to order in a zippy Pickapeppe sauce (a condiment bottled in Jamaica) with capers.

For those who enjoy cheese before dessert, or in lieu of it, there is a cart with a limited but good selection; cheeses are served with a glass of port.

Desserts can be heavenly. Try the airy and intensely fruity raspberry mousse cake or the invigorating lemon custard tart.

The sedate scene at Devon House may not be everyone's idea of an exciting night on the town, but for those seeking a tranquil refuge on this frenzied island, there are few places like it.

✦ DIECI X ✦

★ ★

1568 First Avenue, between 81st and 82nd streets, 628-6565.

Atmosphere: Cozy, low-key and relatively tranquil.

Service: Prompt and earnest if occasionally careless.

Price range: Moderately expensive.

Credit cards: American Express and Visa.

Hours: Dinner, daily, 5:30 to 11:30 P.M. Closed Sunday in July and August.

Reservations: Required.

While I cringe at the thought of a $17 bowl of pasta—even one spiked with vodka and sprinkled with caviar—I must admit this specialty at Dieci X is delightful, in a decadent sort of way. As one might guess, Dieci X is one of those swanky East Side Italian restaurants that cater to a polished, meticulously groomed clientele that rarely cringes at dinner tabs. What makes it stand out among this gilded circuit of restaurants is some zesty and intelligently conceived food.

In fairness it should be added that, aside from this extravagant pasta, prices at Dieci X are comparable to those at similar establishments in the area. Al dente penne with its rich, assertive tomato sauce, faintly briny with the caviar, is indeed the best in a strong lineup of pastas. Don't expect to detect nuances of an extra-dry vodka martini in this dish—the alcohol all but evaporates in the cooking and what remains is a hint of hot peppers that are marinated in it to impart flavor. Another superior option is the angel hair pasta with mussels and scallops in a sprightly red sauce. One of the more original dishes is called pizzoccheri ortolana, robust buckwheat fettuccine tossed with mushrooms, assorted vegetables and thin slices of tender veal.

Dieci X offers all the creature comforts associated with this genre of restaurant—a cozy, low-decibel dining room with softly illuminated tables and urbane Italian ambiance. The waiters in black tie can be careless at times, especially when it comes to getting orders straight and explaining dishes. The pace of the meal, though, is leisurely but not laggard.

Seafood is fresh and prepared with care, whether it is an

appetizer of sautéed jumbo shrimp with mushrooms, garlic, white wine and cherry tomatoes or the entree of fresh, meaty red snapper baked in a balloon of parchment paper along with summer vegetables julienne and a dabble of fresh tomato sauce. The single soup offered, called summertime minestrone, was a surprise. It turned out to be full-bodied and dark, replete with mushrooms, assorted vegetables, black truffles and tomatoes—ideal for après-ski parties, perhaps, but not steamy city nights. Mushroom fanciers may want to try an occasional special if they have it, giant cultivated mushrooms from Italy that are nearly the size of Frisbees. They are sautéed in olive oil and garlic until crisp. Their firm meaty texture and surprisingly mild flavor are not unlike veal.

Speaking of veal, that comes in several forms. A good summer version is called veal giardino, in which a veal chop is dipped in eggs and bread crumbs then sautéed and presented under a mound of arugula, endive, radicchio, onions and tomato. A veal chop special one evening, purportedly sautéed with cognac, was nondescript with little detectable seasoning. Calf's liver, by contrast, was exceptional: pink, delicate and paired with wilted sweet onions and a heady wine sauce cut with vinegar, which added a vibrant edge.

Dieci X is one of the few places in town where roast baby goat is on the regular menu. The tender and mild-flavored meat is cut into bite-size chunks and marinated with rosemary and sage.

Desserts are a fifty-fifty proposition. It would be difficult to find a better tirami sù—this one is an espresso-soaked vanilla cake that is pumped up with satiny custard and mascarpone cheese, all dusted with bittersweet chocolate. Fresh apricot tart and tartufo, the Italian chocolate-covered ice cream ball, are pleasing as well. Skip the gelatinous raspberry mousse, gummy crusted apple tart and flossy and pallid zabaglione bloated with egg whites.

Judged solely on the basis of food and service, Dieci X merits two stars. A bargain it is not, but for a splurge it is worth keeping in mind.

✦ THE DOLPHIN ✦

★ ★

227 Lexington Avenue, between 33rd and 34th streets, 689-3010.

Atmosphere: Pleasant, simple brick and blond wood; insufficient lighting at lunch.

Service: Earnest and enthusiastic, but sometimes slow.

Price range: Moderately expensive.

Credit cards: All major cards.

Hours: Lunch, Monday through Friday, noon to 3 P.M.; dinner, Monday through Friday, 5 to 10:30 P.M., Saturday, 5 to 11 P.M., Sunday, 4 to 10 P.M.

Reservations: Recommended.

For a major seaport city, New York offers lean pickings when it comes to good no-nonsense fishhouses. Devoted seafood eaters enjoy their fish the way connoisseurs of bourbon take their drink: straight, unembellished and often. A simple broiled or poached red snapper, for example—served whole, please, so it resembles the dignified swimmer it recently was—is all that is desired. And unassailable freshness goes without saying.

The Dolphin, a relative newcomer to Murray Hill, offers this formula. The owner and chef, Elio Rugova, used to run the kitchen at The Captain's Table on Second Avenue and 46th Street, where his skillful handling of the daily catch attracted an enthusiastic following.

The Dolphin dining room is trim and neat, with a long brick

wall on one side, blond wood paneling on the other, bent-cane chairs, simply appointed tables and a large mural of a frolicking dolphin. At lunchtime, the lights are so dim it takes five minutes to accustom yourself; afterward, when you head into the bright sunlight, the optic blast can bring you to your knees.

An impressive variety of domestic and imported fish is served, either broiled with a coating of oil and mixed herbs or poached with hollandaise sauce. Shellfish is prepared in several ways. The fish of the day are presented on a large platter, wide eyed and glistening fresh. The platter might hold red snapper, sea bass, Dover sole, flounder, trout, striped bass and a seafood brochette, as well as filleted fish that are too large to serve whole, such as salmon and turbot.

Virtually every broiled and poached fish is first-rate. Broiled sea bass, for example, has a crackling skin and moist, glossy white meat. The light coating of oil and a dusting of mixed herbs impart an aromatic Provençale accent. The fish comes on a large oval plate with a supporting cast of boiled potatoes and garlicky sautéed spinach.

The chef has a delicate touch with soft-shell crabs when they are in season. They are sprinkled with seasoned bread crumbs and quickly sautéed, which is all they call for. The only loser is the seafood brochette, a mixture of lobster tail, shrimp, onions and green pepper, which can be quite dry.

One of the few more elaborate dishes is red snapper baked in parchment paper, garnished with mussels, bay scallops, tomatoes and herbs. I have had it twice—once it was heady with herbs and delicious, but another time it was overcooked. The menu carries some token meat dishes; however, going to the Dolphin for steak is like going to Queens to ski.

Several appetizers are worth mentioning. Oysters on the half shell—usually bluepoints or Belons—are sparkling and delicious, served with a tart mignonette sauce; cherrystone clams, nearly the size of quahogs, are remarkably tender. Calamari salad here is usually excellent.

Service is adequate, although busy evenings can be a bit hectic.

Dessert is not a priority here. Your sweet tooth may be sated with a goblet of strawberries under an avalanche of heady zabaglione; if not, walk down to Second Avenue, where there are ice cream parlors galore.

✦ EL INTERNACIONAL ✦

★ ★

219 West Broadway, between White and Franklin streets, 226-8131.

Atmosphere: Informal, convivial, noisy late at night.

Service: Enthusiastic but at times harried and slow.

Price range: Moderate.

Credit cards: American Express.

Hours: Lunch, Monday through Saturday, noon to 4 P.M.; dinner, Monday through Saturday, 4 P.M. to 1 A.M., Sunday, 5 P.M. to 1 A.M.

Reservations: Necessary.

El Internacional, a wacky, kitsch-laden TriBeCa establishment, was one of the first restaurants to introduce New Yorkers to the Spanish tradition of tapas, or finger foods served at a long, colorful bar. The original owners, an artsy couple from Barcelona, departed last year, and with them went some of the eccentric charm they brought to it. The new owners are struggling to keep the kitchen's integrity.

Along a handsome 1920s gold-trimmed tile wall behind the

bar dangle long garlic braids, whole dried codfish, ruddy preserved hams and all sorts of hot peppers. The tapas are in earthenware casserole dishes along the counter. One can order a tapa, which is a bite-size portion, or a ración, an appetizer-size dish, by the plate. The selections change often, so some of those described may not always be available.

Among the best are baby mushrooms in sherry sauce ($2 a tapa; $4 a ración), grilled squid ($3, $6) and codfish with eggplant and peppers ($3.50, $6). The squid, milky white and sparkling fresh, is seared in a hot iron pan until it is golden. Try it with a slab of earthy Spanish bread. The fresh and briny cod salad is marinated in a spicy dressing with tomatoes, scallions and black olives.

The sine qua non of a tapas bar is the tortilla, or Spanish omelet, which is made with lots of potatoes and onions and just enough egg to bind it. Here it is lovingly executed, moist and flavorful ($1.50, $3.25). It is fun to begin the evening by spending half an hour at the bar sampling tapas with a glass of a rough house wine before going in for dinner. In contrast to the bar, the dining rooms are decidedly un-Spanish. The larger room is done in surreal clashing colors, red-flocked flowered wallpaper, green tablecloths, a rose-colored ceiling.

One can make a meal of raciónes in the dining rooms or order from the daily menu. Service is congenial and enthusiastic but tends to get harried and slow when the place fills up after 9 P.M.

A Spanish delicacy worth trying is angulas, or baby eels, in hot sauce ($10, $15). Normally these mild-flavored shoestring-thin white eels, which come from freshwater rivers in Spain, are served in a small earthenware crock, swathed in sizzling olive oil and seasoned with whole cloves of garlic. The best entree on the prix fixe dinner was braised shoulder of lamb with sweet potatoes. The sinewy meat was fork tender and suffused with the earthy spices of the braising liquid. Stewed lamb chunks also were homey and soothing.

If there is a quintessential Catalan dish, it is duck with pears, and here it is well prepared. The huge braised duck leg was served in a semisweet sauce of pureed pears with tomato, onions and carrots. It was garnished with a poached pear half. The other nightly special was a deftly poached red snapper in a bright lime-butter sauce with shallots.

Spanish cuisine does not evoke images of exceptional desserts, but El Internacional intends to do something about that. The crema Catalana is a paragon of a perfectly made French crème brûlée. It is silky and rich inside, with a seared brittle sugar crust. Guava pudding, which has a soft bready texture, could have used more guava. Those seeking a light dessert might try something called lemon fantasy, an airy fresh-lemon pudding. For a typical Spanish dessert, try the goat's cheese with honey and pine nuts. The cheese is tart enough to make your hair bristle, but the honey cuts it down to size, creating a tantalizing finish to an unusual dining experience.

◆ FELIDIA ◆

★

243 East 58th Street, 758-1479.

Atmosphere: Upscale rustic setting; cramped and overcrowded in the evening, more pleasant at lunch.

Service: Professional but overtaxed at dinner, therefore slow and rushed.

Price range: Expensive.

Credit cards: All major cards.

Hours: Lunch, Monday through Friday, noon to 3 P.M.; dinner, Monday through Saturday, 5 to midnight. Closed Sunday.

Reservations: Required.

Felidia, the most handsome and talked-about restaurant on East 58th Street, the uptown Little Italy, is so popular that dinner reservations are often required up to five days in advance. The handsome bar is a bibulous holding pen of impatience and famine, where patrons wait sometimes an hour past their reservation time. Many knowledgeable diners rave about Felidia, declaring it the best Italian restaurant in New York. All this strikes me as most curious. Although Felidia is capable of turning out some exceptional dishes, I have found its overall performance to be uneven at best.

The two-level restaurant with its brick walls, lush foliage and barreled skylight would be more enjoyable if several tables were removed from each level. As it is, customers are literally back to back and waiters have to suck in their stomachs to get through the mob.

The vast menu—four pages and as many as three dozen daily specials—focuses on northern Italian cooking, especially the cuisine of Trieste. But freshness problems plague the kitchen, no doubt because of the overly ambitious offerings. Highly touted specials such as Adriatic scampi can be over the hill and mushy.

At the same time, though, if you hit it right, some fish specials can be fresh and nicely prepared: sautéed snapper in a white wine and thyme sauce; branzino (a delicately textured Italian sea bass) prepared similarly; deep-fried calamari, which was resilient to the bite and fried to a crispy golden color; grilled Dover sole meunière; seppia (cuttlefish) cooked in the oven with olive oil, and a perfectly cooked striped bass served with a lusty sauce of green and black olives, onions, mushrooms, capers and tomatoes. But black risotto with squid—the color and flavor come from the squid's ink—tends to be pale gray and lackluster.

Say hello to the $18 bowl of pasta. And nondescript pasta at that. The trenette primavera is a clumsy combination of large zucchini chunks, broccoli florets, green beans and peas in an underseasoned cream sauce. Fusilli puttanesca comes with a sauce featuring black and green olives, capers, tomatoes, peppers and garlic. It flops because the competing ingredients are not integrated into a sauce but rather taste as if they have been thrown together at the last minute.

Many meat and poultry dishes are disappointing. While lamb chops in a brown sauce with chives cannot be faulted, the last time I was there overcooking ruined the roasted baby lamb, a special. Roast suckling pig, another special, was succulent and moist inside, but the skin, which our waiter had described enthusiastically as "crisp and dry," was flaccid and greasy.

The service staff is well meaning and generally knowledgeable, but overextended. Be prepared for exasperating delays.

The wine list is exceptionally rich in Italian labels. If you are in the mood to splurge, there are plenty of opportunities to sample some rare old Barolos.

Appetizers offer some of the tastier choices: mussels in wine and garlic, asparagus au gratin, tangy broccoli di rape sautéed in olive oil and garlic, and a soothing soup from Trieste called yota, combining sauerkraut, white beans and pork. A buffet table near the bar also offers a colorful assortment of cold appetizers, ranging from assorted cheeses to smoked fish and roast peppers.

Felidia is much more enjoyable at lunchtime, when, because of less stressful conditions, the service and food are better. If you choose one of the first-rate salads and simple grilled or sautéed fish, chances are you will have a satisfying meal. Desserts are rich and spirited. Among the best: vanilla semifreddo filled with almonds and garnished with raspberry sauce, and zuccotto Fiorentino, a dome-shaped genoise lined with crushed hazelnuts and holding a mass of dense whipped cream.

✦ THE FOUR SEASONS ✦

★ ★ ★

99 East 52nd Street, 754-9494.

Atmosphere: Palatial scale that affords the luxury of privacy at well-spaced tables. The rosewood-paneled Grill Room is masculine and trim, while the glittering Pool Room is romantic and plush.

Service: The huge platoon of captains, waiters and busboys works as a crack team.

Price range: Expensive.

Credit cards: All major cards.

Hours: Lunch in Pool Room, Monday through Friday, noon to 2:30 P.M.; dinner, Monday through Saturday, 5 to 11:30 P.M. Lunch in Grill Room, Monday through Saturday, noon to 1:45 P.M.; dinner, Monday through Friday, 7:30 to 11:30 P.M. Closed Sunday.

Reservations: Required; two weeks in advance for weekend evenings.

The Four Seasons, the venerable New York institution, marked its quarter of a century of pampering the power elite in 1986. Such longevity alone in this volatile business merits at least a silver spoon award; even more impressive, though, is how this grand vessel of luxury has managed to stay right on course during its long voyage, maintaining standards of food quality and service that are paragons of the industry.

As with any restaurant of this size and scope, lapses occur. I have received complaints from customers who have been unhappy with the food or service; however, disappointments seem rare based on my six visits.

Food, of course, is of paramount importance, and the Swiss-born chef, Seppi Renggli, has over the years proved to be one of the most intelligent and independent-minded in the business.

His eclectic style melds Oriental accents with regional American and modern French cooking to forge a cuisine of his own. And long before American chefs began clucking about "new American cooking," Mr. Renggli was turning out stunning dishes using native provender.

Dining at The Four Seasons differs dramatically according to when you go and where you sit. The legendary Grill Room, with its Astrodome ceiling, rippling copper-chain curtains and dark, masculine rosewood walls, is the ultimate power-lunch spot, an unrivaled arena of high-rolling executives.

The menu in the Grill Room is lean and spirited. Typical of the chef's approach is a grilled tuna steak that is glossed with sweetish hoisin sauce and cooked until blush pink in the center. Accompanied by wok-fried green beans, carrots and zucchini, it makes a beguiling lunch that won't have you dozing at your desk by 4 P.M. Another invigorating entree is lime-marinated chicken breast broiled to a turn and topped with a tart lime sauce. A peppery lemon compote served on the side imparts a rousing extra dimension. Two lightly breaded and golden crab cakes burst with snowy shards of meat (they should at $12.50 apiece). The accompanying curried mustard sauce flecked with crunchy deep-fried capers is terrific.

In contrast to the Grill Room, where almost no one eats dessert, the lavish Pool Room with its graciously appointed tables, lofty foliage and gurgling illuminated marble pool is for romance and extravagance. A laundry list of all the dishes tasted could run on forever, so the following is a representative sampling.

Terrines are consistently superior, especially the one combining pheasant, quail and mallard duck served with cranberry relish. Cold breast of pigeon with tart red currants is another winner.

The hot appetizers are unqualified successes. The mildly spicy and generous crab gumbo is loaded with shards of sweet white meat, okra, celery and green and red peppers; another good choice is the oversize ravioli stuffed with minced lobster spiked with jalapeño peppers and root vegetables mired in a bracing lobster-cream sauce. It is ringed by speckled pieces of lobster meat sautéed in black butter. Game fanciers will not be disappointed with the pappardelle swathed in a winy venison ragout sauce.

If I had to pick a favorite entree from Mr. Renggli's repertory, it would be his duck au poivre. He serves two perfectly cooked legs and a breast. Atop the breast is a potato-chip-crisp layer of skin. The brassy cracked pepper sauce is piquant enough to warm the soul without searing the lips. Wild rice dotted with pine nuts complements it beautifully. It is ironic that the chef can make such a peppery duck yet turn out an anemic imitation of Paul Prudhomme's blackened redfish. The fish's skin tasted acrid, and the sauce of sweet peppers and onions didn't rescue it.

Those pitfalls aside, the roster of superior dishes is extensive: from snapper baked in a crust of sea salt and pepper with two sauces—a rich tarragon or a lighter blend of lemon, olive oil and parsley—to scallops of veal with ginger, and breast of pheasant with golden Gorgonzola polenta. Desserts are justly renowned. The Gibraltar-like "fancy cake" soaked with curaçao is a must. Hazelnut layer cake is outstanding too, as are all the homemade sorbets and soufflés.

Overall, the Four Seasons is a tightly run ship that is a marvel to behold. As its voyage toward the half-century mark begins, it certainly deserves to fly three stars on its mast.

◆ FU'S ◆

★ ★

1395 Second Avenue, between 72nd and 73rd streets, 517-9670.

Atmosphere: Modern, comfortable, semiformal.

Service: Friendly and helpful, although the kitchen can be slow.

Price range: Moderate.

Credit cards: All major cards.

Hours: Lunch, daily, noon to 3 P.M.; dinner, daily, 3 P.M. to midnight; dim sum brunch, Saturday and Sunday, noon to 4 P.M.

Reservations: Recommended.

Fu's, a sleek and handsome establishment on Second Avenue near 73rd Street, is one of the better Chinese restaurants to come along in some time. It wears no regional badge; selections include dishes from Peking, Sichuan, Hunan, Shanghai and Canton. The food is seasoned with authority, and sauces are light and pure—the chef doesn't believe in heavy cornstarch thickeners. Moreover, many preparations are as pretty to look at as they are delicious.

Fu's has a sporty little black-lacquer bar near the entrance facing Second Avenue. The two-tier dining area is covered by the obligatory gray felt wallpaper of upscale Chinese restaurants, with comfortable cranberry banquettes around the perimeter, inset lighting, fresh flowers and crisp linen (set with knives and forks, which you can exchange for chopsticks).

Everything in the restaurant is orchestrated by Gloria Chu, an ebullient, welcoming host who overflows with more energy than the Hoover Dam. She is a walking encyclopedia of Chinese food and customs, and will happily walk you through (sprint is more like it) the menu, recommending dishes to match individual tastes. The service staff also is cordial and helpful, if occasionally hampered by a slow kitchen.

Ask Mrs. Chu about the daily specials, particularly the exquisite blanched and seared calamari. The fresh, resilient rings are swathed in a black bean sauce bolstered with hot red peppers, scallions, green peppers and onions. The seasonings create a sensation on the palate that is just this side of burning and slightly salty.

Appetizers represent mostly familiar fare. Start with the various dumplings, such as the combination of two pork and two shrimp steamed dumplings that are gracefully seasoned with fresh coriander and ginger and enveloped in delicate fluted skins; and the crescent-shaped fried dumpling featuring the same fillings and a slightly crunchy scored exterior.

Spareribs can be the most prosaic appetizers in a Chinese restaurant, but the two versions at Fu's are irresistible. The regular barbecued pork ribs are meaty, well trimmed of fat and perfectly charred so that they are still moist and succulent. The honey baby spareribs consist of pork ribs hacked into bite-size nuggets that have been glazed with honey before grilling. It is the kind of dish children go wild over, that is if adults don't beat them to it.

One of the few disappointments among the appetizers is the doughy and greasy spring roll.

There is a baker's dozen of special entrees on the menu, among them first-rate Peking duck (it is available every day so there is no need to call ahead). A female chef with a little girl's smile and a big man's cleaver performs the surgery at tableside. Rice pancakes are filled with crackly golden skin moistened with a thin layer of fat, rosy duck meat, scallions, hoisin sauce and translucent slices of cucumbers.

Orange beef garnished with hot and sweet preserved strips of orange rind is as good as you will encounter anywhere; another superior selection is pan-fried whole flounder under a shower of ginger, scallions and parsley. Delicious duck meat comes with an earthy black bean sauce, and eggplant family-style is made from sweet purple eggplants that are mashed and laced with red pepper strips.

Fu's offers some special steamed dishes for customers on low-cholesterol, -sodium or -carbohydrate diets. Those sampled were fresh and satisfying, if at times a bit underseasoned to the nondieting palate. Among them were steamed shrimp with ginger and scallion sauce, steamed flounder with the same sauce, steamed chicken with black mushrooms, and steamed shrimp dumplings.

You may want to end the meal with a glass of the surprisingly pleasant house cocktail, plum wine cut with brandy—it is undietetic, uncompromisingly Oriental and utterly bone-warming on a frigid winter evening.

✦ GOTHAM BAR AND GRILL ✦

★ ★ ★

12 East 12th Street, 620-4020.

Atmosphere: Spacious and comfortable multitier dining room with postmodern decor including a pink-marble bar, tall columns, high ceiling and parachute shades.

Service: Attentive and professional.

Price range: Moderately expensive.

Credit cards: All major cards.

Hours: Lunch, Monday through Friday, noon to 3 P.M.; dinner, Monday through Saturday, 5:30 to 11:30 P.M., Sunday 6 to 11:30 P.M.

Reservations: Suggested.

Gotham has made a comeback that is every bit as remarkable as the 1986 New York Mets. After opening to great fanfare in early 1984, this stunning postmodern restaurant slowly sank under the weight of its fussy and bland food. In 1985 an intelligent, French-trained young chef, Alfred Portale, came aboard. In a short time, Mr. Portale transformed Gotham into one of the most exciting and talked-about restaurants in town. His cooking approach is contemporary and personal, but not free-wheeling; his dishes are visually dazzling but rarely incongruent.

The roster of appetizers is so alluring you will be hard pressed to choose. You would do well to begin with the freshly made chicken terrine, which is bursting with the flavor of earthy morels. It is accompanied by slices of mild French garlic sausage and well-seasoned lentils—a meal in itself. A succulent roast quail, crisp-skinned and pink inside, comes with celery root, sliced potatoes and a nest of marinated shiitake mushrooms and curly endive swathed in a walnut-oil vinaigrette. Gotham's seafood salad is the best I have had in town. Arranged around a pretty fanned avocado is a sparkling assembly of mixed greens laden with exquisitely fresh squid rings, lobster, scallops, octopus slices and mussels. Tiny red beads of flying-fish roe add a lovely saline edge. The entire combination is tossed in a lively olive-oil-and-lemon vinaigrette.

Among the dozen regular entrees, remarkably, there is not a clunker. Every one of Mr. Portale's seafood dishes is uncompromisingly fresh and exceptionally well presented. Typical of his style is a meaty loup de mer draped in a reduction of port wine and aged vinegar with an accent of garlic and shallots. It comes with shiitake mushrooms, sautéed leeks, baby squash and turnips; equally alluring are the fillets of sautéed Norwegian salmon set atop a mound of spinach and accompanied by grilled fennel and a superb shallot-and-saffron custard.

On the meat side of the menu, one of the best selections is

a dish of rosy slices of roast squab with pan juices over a bed of wild mushrooms and Swiss chard. It comes with delicious spaetzle in mustard butter. Rolled veal tenderloin stuffed with spinach and pine nuts in a port-wine sauce makes a harmonious marriage. Grilled loin of lamb with sweet roast shallots and thin golden slices of potatoes surrounding an artichoke heart could not have been improved.

The wine list is full of good choices at fair prices.

The kitchen's impressive pace does not flag near the finish line. Desserts are sublime, from the lustrous warm raspberry gratin with Grand Marnier butter and the heady bourbon soufflé to the old-fashioned apple-and-apricot charlotte made with slices of French bread. It is served with a ball of seductive honey-vanilla ice cream atop a brittle tuile cookie and garnished with tiny lavender flowers.

✦ GREENE STREET ✦
RESTAURANT

★ ★

101 Greene Street, between Prince and Spring streets, 925-2415.

Atmosphere: Dramatic multitier SoHo loft with a bandstand.

Service: Confused and laggard.

Price range: Moderately expensive.

Credit cards: All major cards.

Hours: Dinner, Monday through Thursday, 6 P.M. to midnight, Friday and Saturday, 6 P.M. to 1 A.M., Sunday, noon to 8:30 P.M.

Reservations: Suggested.

Considerable evidence exists to buttress the theory that good food and good music are rarely found under the same roof. One serendipitous exception is Greene Street, the vast, dramatic nightclub and restaurant in SoHo.

Only last year did the kitchen begin to harmonize on a par with the jazz and pop musicians who entertain nightly, making it one of the best bets for downtown dining and entertainment.

The dining arena is in a cavernous breakthrough loft with a sky-high ceiling, sixty-foot-high mural depicting vintage New York scenes and a bandstand against a spotlighted brick wall. Waiters in black tie scurry around the shadowy environs—they seem to run in circles, though, because service can be confused and slow.

The well-balanced menu offers something for all tastes. Among the best opening acts are the hefty homemade scallop ravioli in a lustrous butter sauce with leeks and fennel sprigs, and the vibrant salmon sausage studded with shards of salmon. An herb-flecked mayonnaise and a cucumber-dill salad make up the supporting cast.

Chef Stefan Kopf's knack with fresh seasonings also makes a winner of the sautéed shrimp in a glistening herb-butter sauce with cubed tomatoes and spinach; and even oyster purists who prefer theirs straight and on the rocks should try the minimally poached bluepoints under a glossy lemon-butter sauce with fresh chervil. All the special salads are lovely.

The only flat note among the appetizers is smoked stuffed quail, which had an unpleasant acidic bite as if the forcemeat was over the hill.

The wine list is deep and amply stocked with reasonably priced selections; the ten or so wines by the glass, which change regularly, offer a good opportunity to experiment with unknown labels.

When it comes to entrees, among the biggest hits are pink-roasted loin of lamb in a light yet richly flavored stock sauce, and an equally engaging veal steak that is sautéed golden outside and tender within, under a fistful of pleurote mushrooms and accompanied by squiggly spaetzle.

Simple Dover sole à la meunière could not be faulted, and the roasted baby pheasant with onions, mushrooms and potatoes was cooked to pink perfection—the sauce, though, could have used more seasoning. Mr. Kopf may have stumbled on several occasions, but he never really had a face-first fall. Al dente fettuccine tossed with chunks of chicken and lobster in an asparagus-and-butter sauce just missed the mark because of underseasoning; two other entrees that needed more rehearsal before show time were the tough sirloin steak in a green peppercorn sauce and grilled tuna in a lifeless citrus sauce.

I can recommend almost all the desserts: silky black velvet cake, excellent crème brûlée, light and refreshing lemon soufflé and an assortment of superb fresh fruit sorbets (they come from Pierrot in the Bay Ridge section of Brooklyn). Only the gelatinous raspberry bavarian disappointed.

The spirited new tempo in the kitchen combined with a classy nightclub ambiance places Greene Street on the top of my hit parade when the mood strikes for musical dining.

◆ HARLEQUIN ◆

★

569 Hudson Street, corner West 11th Street, 255-4950.

Atmosphere: Sophisticated and distinctive all-gray decor.

Service: Professional and efficient.

Price range: Moderate.

Credit cards: American Express (others will be accepted soon).

Hours: Dinner, daily, 5:30 to midnight. Brunch, Saturday and Sunday, noon to 4 P.M.

Reservations: Suggested.

José Barcena, the chef at Harlequin, is capable of turning out some first-rate Spanish specialties—his knockout paella, for example—that are so delicious they could keep a matador home on Sunday afternoon. But for some reason he feels compelled to offer a menu half filled with French fare, much of it undistinguished. The first look at Harlequin is a surprise. It doesn't have the usual blood-red walls, black banquettes, bullfight posters or pitchers of sangria on the bar. And where are the flamenco hats, the silly waiters' costumes, the map of old Iberia?

What you encounter instead is a Castilian version of La Caravelle—cool and dove-gray, soft and soothing, with matching napery and exquisite custom-made dishware carrying the frolicking harlequin logo. On one side of the dining room is a sparkling little bar and on the other a glass display case filled with Lladro porcelain statuettes. In a way, Harlequin appears more preciously French than cliché Spanish, and therein lies a hint of the problem.

The paella for two at Harlequin is the best I've had in New York, reason in itself to head for West 11th Street. In Spain there are as many recipes of this national dish as there are provinces—some with meat, some with shellfish, some with neither. Mr. Barcena does not take sides. He throws in everything—chunks of fresh lobster, shrimp, crayfish, sausage, clams, mussels, pork and chicken, all fresh and well cooked. The yellow rice is moist and complex with a blend of saffron, garlic, crushed tomatoes and chicken stock.

Several appetizers are displayed on a buffet table near the restaurant's entrance, including such cold dishes as fresh asparagus, rosy tuna fillets in a lively hot-pepper-flecked marinade, sweet sea scallops in a similar marinade, carrot salad and beets with onions.

One of the best choices on the regular menu is shrimp in cream of garlic, a half-dozen grilled shrimp arranged atop two sauces: one an aggressive blend of garlic, cayenne, white wine, lemon and brown stock; the other a thick and heady combination of garlic, white wine, fish stock and cream. Another good bet is the light and custardy vegetable terrine filled with fresh peas, carrots, asparagus, mushrooms and green beans. This typically Spanish preparation was enlivened by a similar garlic-cream sauce covering one-half of the plate and a fiery pepper-stoked red sauce on the other. The terrine is preferable to a bizarre concoction dubbed escargot feuilleté in which undercooked snails are embedded in a little volcano of puff pastry sitting in a pond of spicy tomato sauce. The flavors clash like a pair of cymbals.

Hard-core Spanish-food aficionados will be delighted to find angulas, the bean-sprout-size white eels, prepared in the traditional manner: placed in a little earthenware crock and cooked in sizzling olive oil flavored with shards of fresh garlic. Angulas are not on the menu, so if the waiter fails to mention them, ask. Mixed seafood salad with herbs and hot peppers was returned because it had an off odor; instead, we tried dense and livery duck pâté accompanied by a pleasantly sweet sauce combining currant jelly, raspberries, mustard and duck. Skip the bland sausages in white-wine sauce and the overly vinegared white gazpacho. The genial and well-disciplined service staff is helpful. The wine list is reasonably priced and split between relatively inexpensive French and California labels and a host of wines from Rioja and Penedès in Spain. Bouillabaisse Catalonian is a briny, anise-flavored red broth filled with firm, fresh monkfish, mussels, clams, calico scallops and lobster tail. The first time I tried it, the combination was delicious, especially with a hunk of bread to soak up the broth; the second time, it was marred by an overdose of anise.

The Spanish sweet tooth is reflected in the desserts. A house special, called crêpes Harlequin, includes two thin crepes swathed with chestnut puree and blanketed in chocolate-brandy sauce and crème anglaise. This one-two combination is so sweet that it makes your teeth throb. A better choice is the firm, rich flan garnished with tiny melon balls. If Mr. Barcena would toss his French beret into the sea and don a matador's cape in the kitchen, Harlequin might be one of the standout Spanish restaurants in town.

✦ HARRY CIPRIANI ✦

Satisfactory

783 Fifth Avenue, at 59th Street, in the Sherry-Netherland Hotel, 759-9020, 759-9021, 759-9047.

Atmosphere: Streamlined, classy cafe with great people-watching. Can be noisy.

Service: Overall professional and polite bistro-style service. Lunch service slow.

Price range: Expensive.

Credit cards: All major cards.

Hours: Lunch, daily, noon to 3 P.M.; dinner, Monday through Saturday, 6 to 10:45 P.M., Sunday until 9:30 P.M.

Reservations: Suggested.

Ernest Hemingway might feel ill at ease if he were to wander into the New York clone of his beloved Harry's Bar in Venice and find (a) a stratospherically chic restaurant with an undersized marble-topped bar serving $8 champagne cocktails, (b) a rakish clientele of impeccably preened women paired with more men in pinstripes than at a Yankee doubleheader and (c) not a canal in sight. No, this is not the Harry's Bar of literary fame.

This is Harry Cipriani, a Manhattan version under the same Cipriani family management in the Sherry-Netherland Hotel on Fifth Avenue. Following its opening in early 1985, this polyglot gathering spot became the biggest hit among the gilded set since Trump Tower.

Even if you've never been to the famous original, Harry Cipriani is worth a visit, primarily for its superb people-watching—rivaled only by Le Cirque in this category—and only secondarily for the dearly priced food, which on the whole is unexciting cafe fare.

The Cipriani family, with the help of the international hotel empire Trusthouse Forte, has done a faithful job re-creating the understated glamour of the Venice restaurant. The new rendition is a bright and animated place of modest dimensions, with grass-paper-covered walls holding black-and-white photographs of Venice, simple brass light sconces and a platoon of urbane Italian waiters. The high-spirited crowd creates a din at peak hours that makes casual conversation difficult. I don't know if it has something to do with the decor or the legend of Harry's Bar, but for some reason nearly everybody in the place looks vaguely famous.

Harry Cipriani benefits from the hot-dogs-taste-better-at-the-ballpark syndrome; in a less electrified setting, I suspect, some of the mundane dishes here might not elicit such smiles from patrons. The ever-changing menu is relatively small, which is a blessing in this age of overreaching kitchens. A good way to begin is with the house fish soup, based on a good fish stock filled with vegetables and a rotating cast of seafood—fresh salmon one night, buttery scallops another. Bean noodle soup is a fine winter warmer, while lightweight minestrone is a distant runner-up.

Pastas and risottos round out the appetizers. The vegetable

risotto, called printanier, ranges from insipid to acceptable; the shrimp risotto is well textured but lackluster. They are stiffly priced at $21 and $19 respectively. Overcooked baked green noodles in a béchamel sauce flecked with shards of prosciutto is flat and gummy. A better option is homemade meat-filled ravioli in a silky tomato sauce garnished with chopped asparagus.

Considering the crowds at Harry Cipriani, the service staff has held up rather well. Waiters generally are patient and polite, however at lunch the pace is exceedingly slow. A couple ordering a full dinner à la carte can expect to leave at least $100 leaner (with one $20 bottle of wine, but before tax and gratuities).

Of the half-dozen desserts, only two are worth mentioning. Chocolate layer cake is unstintingly rich, and fruit sorbets are pure and refreshing. Other pies and cakes are cloyingly sweet.

If you order carefully, Harry Cipriani can provide some satisfying food and a chance to rub shoulders with the insouciant international set. And even if the meal disappoints, as one of my dining companions rationalized it, "At least I can say I've been to Harry's."

✦ HATSUHANA ✦

★ ★ ★

17 East 48th Street, 355-3345.

Atmosphere: Bright, clean and trim dining rooms on two levels, each with long sushi bars.

Service: Better at sushi bars than tables; can be slow at busy times. Staff is congenial and earnest.

Price range: Moderately expensive.

Credit cards: All major cards.

Hours: Lunch, Monday through Friday, 11:45 A.M. to 2:30 P.M.; dinner, Monday through Friday, 5:30 to 9:30 P.M., Saturday and Sunday, 5 to 9:30 P.M.

Reservations: Required for dinner.

Aficionados of Japanese food rate their favorite restaurants on a three-part scale: freshness, variety and presentation. The original Hatsuhana continues to rank highly on all three counts, although a few rough spots encountered recently indicate that relentless crowds can take a toll on the kitchen.

The cheerful dining rooms on two levels, each with elongated sushi bars flanked by rows of simple wooden tables, provide a suitable stage for the colorful production put on by the personable sushi chefs. I have found that the best place to enjoy the show is front row center at the sushi bar, where a dialogue can be established with one of the masters. If you leave your fate in their hands, some strange and wonderful surprises may be in store.

The extensive menu is not without its charms, either, especially among the unusual appetizers. With fish as fresh as this, some of the least elaborate presentations are the most appealing: negihamachi, consisting of chopped, mild-flavored yellowtail flecked with scallions; negitoro, chopped belly of tuna, which is more assertive and rich, prepared the same way; and sabagari-maki, slices of silver-skinned mackerel blended with pickled ginger and wrapped in Japanese white radish. Two soy-based sauces are set out for dipping. Another delicious if unfelicitously translated dish is broiled squid feet (geso-yaki). The resilient little tentacles, broiled to a turn, are available in a butter sauce, miso or just plain salt.

A few of the cooked appetizers, however, are forgettable. Hatsuhana dumplings, bite-size packets enclosed in gossamer sheets made of pressed vegetables, are filled with dry, tasteless

107

ground beef. The familiar dish of scallions wrapped in beef strips, called negimayaki, can be superb when made with first-rate meat. At Hatsuhana the beef is thick and tough.

If you want a cooked appetizer, try chawanmushi, an ethereal steamed egg custard enhanced with bits of shrimp, white fish and minced vegetables; the broiled strips of duck breast with scallions, or the fantastic meat-stuffed broiled eggplant with soybean paste. A personal favorite is torame, or "tiger's eye," which is rings of squid stuffed with salmon, then broiled. The saline and faintly smoky salmon marries beautifully with the tender charred squid.

Should you be in an experimental mood, sample the tiny fried Japanese crabs. These red creatures, no wider than a quarter, resemble those whimsical little refrigerator-door magnets. You pop them in your mouth like candies, shells and all. The crunchy texture and saline flavor are surprisingly good. They are usually available Tuesday and Friday nights.

The highlights of Hatsuhana's menu, though, are sushi and sashimi, which come in many varieties. A good way to get acquainted with the chefs' style is with the Hatsuhana special, which includes both of the raw fish specialties as well as tempura and grilled skewered fish. The sashimi features sparkling strips of roseate tuna, white fluke and mackerel, each over a mound of white radish and two kinds of seaweed. The sushi arrangement, served with hot wasabi mustard, soy sauce and pickled ginger, is equally colorful and fresh—tuna, yellowtail, avocado and briny giant clam over hand-packed rice. On two occasions, though, the sushi rice had none of the traditional vinegar flavor, which left it flat.

Included as well in the Hatsuhana special is the expertly fried tempura of shrimp, fish, broccoli and sliced sweet potato; it can also be ordered as an entree by itself. The grilled skewered tuna with shrimp and vegetables is succulent. In fact, all grilled teriyaki-style fish are highly recommended.

When the dining room is full, which is almost always, service can get bogged down. The sushi bar is a better bet if you are on a tight schedule. It is advisable to make dinner reservations no later than 8 P.M. since the kitchen closes down at 9:30.

✦ HUBERTS ✦

★ ★ ★

102 East 22nd Street, 673-3711.

Atmosphere: Understated, warm, comfortably formal.

Service: Earnest and well-versed staff who hold their own except occasionally when the room is full.

Price range: Expensive.

Credit cards: American Express, MasterCard and Visa.

Hours: Lunch, Monday through Friday, 12 to 1:30 P.M.; dinner, Monday through Saturday, 6 to 10:30 P.M. Closed Sunday.

Reservations: Recommended.

The handsome little step-down dining room, with its pale yellow walls, parquet floors and soft lighting, is soothing and romantic. Guests are greeted by Karen Hubert, the petite, courteous owner, whose partner, Len Allison, toils in the back of the house as part of a five-man team. The waiters, with their button-down shirts and muted ties, look like moonlighting English teachers down from Choate. They are well versed in the eclectic menu, though, and fairly professional, if not always available when the room gets full.

The food at Huberts might be defined as untraditional American; that is, some familiar native recipes are borrowed and held up to the light, then turned upside down, inside out, disassembled and reinterpreted with a surprise twist. Almost always the surprise is delightful; very occasionally, however, it's like receiving a hand-crocheted dickey from Aunt Flo for Christmas—one appreciates the effort, but . . .

A pleasing twist on what could be a run-of-the-mill appetizer is blush-pink shrimp arranged over a bed of "smashed" cucumbers with a vibrant Oriental sauce of sesame oil, mustard and honey. The owners are Japanese aficionados, and it shows in many of the Oriental accents throughout their repertoire. Another engaging appetizer is grilled fresh tuna basted with a sweet mixture that includes sherry, sherry vinegar, sesame oil, tahini and plum paste. It is served at room temperature over stalks of endive with a mustardy dressing.

The standout among the starters, however, is the lean and herb-flecked grilled rabbit sausages with mole sauce. Slightly charred and with crackly skin, the sausages blend beautifully with the pungent Mexican sauce.

Entrees follow the same cross-cultural highway. Grilled baby lamb—two rosy chops and three succulent medallions in a savory brown sauce—is nearly overshadowed by its sidekick, a luxuriously creamy goat-cheese lasagna. Gamy and succulent, the roast squab is stuffed with wild rice and pecans and is accompanied by a colorful cast of baby green zucchini, baby yellow squash, caramelized onions, sugar-snap peas and sweet-potato puree.

Seafood dishes are equally inventive. Among the best is steamed fluke in a rousing ginger broth served with winter radish. Crunchy buckwheat noodles rolled in a seaweed sheet are a lovely counterpoint. Sautéed pompano with a zippy lime-mole sauce, crisp apple fritters, eggplant caviar and sautéed cucumbers is an unusual but winning liaison; more equivocal is the aggressively seasoned pan-blackened salmon. I felt that this faddish preparation of the aristocratic salmon, which can work well with mild whitefish, was a bit like making a foie gras sandwich with Ritz crackers, but several companions disagreed and applauded it.

The wine list is engaging, with a good range of California labels, and fairly priced. A recently added lunch, which features a host of appetizer-size dishes, features some terrific creations at bargain prices.

Nearly all the desserts are winners, from the luscious tangelo Riesling sorbet to the cornet (a cone-shaped tuile) filled with prune-Armagnac cream to the apple charlotte with apricot puree.

✦ IL CANTINORI ✦

★

32 East 10th Street, 673-6044.

Atmosphere: Charming Tuscan ambiance with stucco walls, dark woodwork and appetizer-filled sideboards. Front room can be loud.

Service: Professional and considerate. Well informed about the food and wine.

Price range: Moderately expensive.

Credit cards: American Express, Carte Blanche and Diners Club.

Hours: Lunch, Monday through Friday, noon to 3 P.M.; dinner, Monday through Thursday, 6 to 11:30 P.M., Friday and Saturday, 6 to midnight, Sunday, 5 to 11 P.M.

Reservations: Required.

Il Cantinori is one of the more imaginative and ambitious Italian restaurants in town. If it has a fault it is overambitiousness—the menu and specials are too copious for the kitchen to handle. If the cards are dealt in your favor, it is possible to leave Il Cantinori with a passion for this hearty northern Italian cuisine. Then again it is just as easy to be sorely let down.

The dining rooms blend rusticity with sophistication—stucco walls, handsome sideboards filled with regional appetizers, and soft lighting. One of the charms of Tuscan restaurants in Italy is the colorful array of cold antipasti always on display that one can nibble for starters. The selection here is visually alluring and tasty—zucchini with capers, sliced eggplant, marinated artichokes, slabs of snowy mozzarella, marinated mushrooms, silvery sardines and more. One evening a waiter suggested we try some deep-fried baby artichokes that had just come out of the kitchen, and they were a delight: seductive fresh florets with crisp golden petals.

One of the best appetizers, though, is a special assortment of grilled vegetables—endive, white chicory and asparagus—teamed with wild mushrooms, fresh mozzarella and basil, all under a dousing of balsamic vinegar and olive oil. Dry veal carpaccio, on the other hand, tasted as if it had been sliced in advance.

The service staff is exceedingly professional and considerate. The regular menu carries a half-dozen pastas that are usually supplemented by three or four specials. Odds for success are fifty-fifty in either camp. The best among the standards are a classic spaghettini alla puttanesca (a zesty mélange of olives, tomatoes, capers and anchovies) and the al dente tagliolini swathed in a buttery tomato-accented sauce bolstered with ground hot and sweet sausage and fresh peas. One superior special includes spaghetti and a garlic-tomato sauce studded with delicious fingernail-size squid.

Other pastas I would pass up are the gummy penne in a ground veal sauce and a special, fettuccine in game sauce that tasted oddly like strong chicken livers. We had the same seesaw experience with risotto: the so-called seafood version was dry and appeared to contain nothing but squid; the one flavored with fresh spinach and mint was sprightly and well textured.

The kitchen seems more confident with entrees, whether it is a succulent homespun osso buco with carrots and mashed potatoes, or juicy roast quails with polenta cubes in a tomato-herb sauce (both specials).

Two game-dish specials got thumbs down from my table: papery dry pheasant, and venison overpowered with grappa.

The traditional sweet wine called vin santo, into which Italians dunk hard almond biscuits, is a fitting dessert. If you are in a more expansive mood, the tirami sù is one of the better renditions around, espresso-drenched ladyfingers with mascarpone cheese. Zabaglione with strawberries and zuppa inglese are over-sugared and commercial tasting, while profiteroles are old and dry.

✦ IL NIDO ✦

★ ★

251 East 53rd Street, 753-8450.

Atmosphere: Tuscan ambiance, comfortable and elegant.

Service: Professional and congenial.

Price range: Moderately expensive.

Credit cards: All major cards.

Hours: Lunch, Monday through Saturday, noon to 2:15 P.M.; dinner, Monday through Saturday, 5:30 to 10:15 P.M. Closed Sunday.

Reservations: Necessary.

Il Nido blasted onto the scene in the late '70s and within a short time garnered a three-star rating for its combination of graceful setting, first-rate food, superior service and excellent wines. It has had a hard time keeping up that pace based on recent visits.

The handsome Tuscan decor with its rough plaster walls criss-crossed by timber beams, the cordovan banquettes and gentle lighting are still inviting, the service staff is as nimble and professional as ever, and the wine list, a passion of the owner Adi Giovannetti, gets more exciting by the year.

It is just that many of the dishes, which rarely change, sometimes seem tired and perfunctory. It is akin to a college professor giving the same lecture for five years—the substance is all there, but it is delivered with less spice and élan. To be sure, only the best ingredients are used. But some dishes have lost their luster. For example, most of the preparations that call for red sauce taste as if only the main ingredients have been switched while the tomato sauce remains the same.

Take, for instance, two of the restaurant's seafood specials: crostacei marinara, a $30 bowl of lobster, shrimp, clams and mussels in a light tomato broth; and scampi fra diavolo with pasta. The seafood in both dishes is top quality, but the red sauce, which tasted identical in both, lacks zip.

Superior choices among the seafood dishes are red snapper with clams and zuppa di pesce, a heaping bowl of shrimp, mussels, clams, squid and red snapper fillet in a well-seasoned tomato broth. Pastas are uneven. Two better selections are linguine matriciana, sporting a sauce of tomatoes, prosciutto and onions deftly balanced between salty ham and sweet onions; and tortellini with four cheeses—taleggio, fontina, Gorgonzola and Bel Paese—is surprisingly subtle and complex.

One of the best dishes under the pasta category actually has no pasta at all: ravioli malfatti. The name means "badly made ravioli" because it is essentially the filling for ravioli—spinach, eggs and cheese—without the pasta envelope. One gets three tasty green igloos of filling seasoned with nutmeg on top of a tomato sauce with Parmesan sprinkled over them. A special one evening, agnolotti filled with pumpkin puree, was superb, served in a creamy tomato sauce.

Appetizers are the highlights of the meal. Both the bresaola, air-dried beef, and the carpaccio, gossamer slices of raw beef, are as delicious as they are attractively presented. The former has just enough moisture so it is not leathery to the bite, while the latter is lustrous and fresh, drizzled with olive oil, minced onions and herbs. Spiedino alla Romana, deep-fried skewered layers of bread, ham and cheese, is golden-crisp and enhanced with a pleasantly salty anchovy sauce.

Meat entrees offer little excitement. Probably the most interesting dish is boneless chicken with chicken livers and eggplant smothered in melted cheese—a homey if heavy combination. Chicken with prosciutto and cheese, and chicken with garlic cannot really be faulted, but they are nothing one couldn't find at a neighborhood pasta house. The same goes for breaded veal chops and breaded lamb chops.

For dessert, there are always plenty of ripe fruits and berries, which are sublime when mired in the excellent zabaglione—ask for the version made with Cointreau and champagne. If you are up to it, try the button-popping zuppa inglese, which looks like a giant napoleon that has tumbled off the back of a bicycle. This asymmetrical concoction has multiple layers of rum-soaked puff pastry sandwiching whipped cream and fresh raspberries, all crowned with a dollop of zabaglione. Afterward, the staff is very accommodating about carrying you off the banquette.

✦ INDOCHINE ✦

★ ★

430 Lafayette Street, between Astor Place and E. 4th Street, 505-5111.

Atmosphere: Large and airy dining room; can be clamorous when busy.

Service: Enthusiastic, but uneven and occasionally slow.

Price range: Moderate.

Credit cards: None.

Hours: Dinner, daily, 6 P.M. to 12:30 A.M. Closed Christmas Day.

Reservations: Necessary.

The name Indochine reflects the menu's mix of Vietnamese and Cambodian food. Since opening in late 1984, the restaurant, which has an ownership tie with the Odeon on West Broadway, has attracted a late-night polyglot crowd—men with asymmetrically chopped hair and funky thrift-shop jackets, and women with either too much makeup or not enough wearing everything from leather miniskirts to silver-fox stoles.

The dining room is hollow and airy with a neo-colonial feeling. Large green palm leaves decorate the walls, complementing green banquettes and yellow tablecloths. Despite the departure of the original Asiatic chef last year, Indochine's food quality has remained fairly consistent. One of the biggest hits on the menu is sweet-and-sour shrimp soup. The orange broth, generous with perfectly cooked shrimp, gets its sweetness from slices of pineapple and its tartness from chunks of tomato and a generous amount of tamarind seasoning. This combination attacks the tip of the tongue first with sweetness, then with a slightly sour sensation, and finishes with the smooth, lingering aftertaste of a good fish stock.

Another exceptional soup is the sliced beef with rice noodles, onions, Chinese cabbage and bean sprouts, all cooked to a turn. The sweetened beef broth, cut with aromatic fresh coriander, adds an extra dimension.

The young and eager service staff at Indochine sometimes gets overwhelmed when the place fills up.

Appetizers shine more brightly than entrees. Steamed shrimp

with a supporting cast of fresh mint, basil, red peppers, shallots and lemon juice in a slightly sweetened vinaigrette is a sparkling success. The same steaming treatment is given to mottled strips of fresh squid, with equally tantalizing results. Rouleau de printemps, a staple of Vietnamese cuisine, is a bright and fresh mixture of chopped chicken and shrimp, mint, scallions, vermicelli and lettuce wrapped in a large rice pancake. It is dipped in a sweetened sauce based on nuoc cham, a condiment made with salted anchovies and spices. Pâté impériaux, golden deep-fried tubes of rice pancakes stuffed with seasoned pork, carrots and Oriental vegetables, is a crunchy delight—it also is good with the dipping sauce.

Steamed Vietnamese ravioli, served in a bamboo box, can be bland; better choices are the puffy scampi beignets and the salad of thin, carpaccio-like beef in a stimulating hot sauce with shallots, Chinese cabbage, red peppers and mint.

The best entree is boneless, deep-fried chicken wings stuffed with vermicelli, bean sprouts, lemon grass, galanga (in the ginger family) and diced chicken. This labor-intensive enterprise, when bolstered with the dipping sauce, is a real palate teaser. Fish is prepared in interesting ways, such as a fillet of sole wrapped in a banana leaf and infused with the haunting tropical flavors of banana and coconut.

Brochettes of beef fillet garnished with lemon grass, red pepper and resting on angel hair noodles were underseasoned. So were roast chicken chunks with lemon grass.

Indochine is always a good place to take out-of-town visitors who want to brush shoulders with the downtown artsy scene, yet eat good food too.

✦ JAMS ✦

★ ★

154 East 79th Street, 772-6800.

Atmosphere: Upbeat and trim setting with colorful abstract art and open kitchen; gregarious but not too loud.

Service: Enthusiastic and efficient.

Price range: Expensive.

Credit cards: American Express, Diners Club, MasterCard, Visa.

Hours: Lunch, Tuesday through Friday, noon to 2:30 P.M.; dinner, Sunday through Thursday, 6 to 11 P.M., Friday and Saturday until 11:30.

Reservations: Necessary.

Of all the culinary trends that have sprouted in New York City in recent years, however fleeting, one that has thrown strong roots and become part of the landscape is so-called California cuisine. This winsome approach to cooking involves minimalist techniques of grilling and sautéing fish and meat, and mating them with light, vegetable-based sauces and enough fresh greenery to make a nutritionist swoon.

Whatever one thinks of this Garden of Eden style of cooking, it must be acknowledged that Jams, the first major California restaurant to open in New York, remains the preeminent practitioner in the city. This upbeat, two-level establishment on East 79th Street, with its rakish and well-heeled clientele, has maintained a high level of food and service. Though some customers grumble about paying $23 for grilled chicken with french fries, they continue to pay up—you won't find a meatier, tastier grilled chicken anywhere, and the haystack of thin, brittle french fries is the best in town.

Jams is the creation of Jonathan Waxman, a young, expatriate

California chef, and Melvyn Master, the dapper co-owner. They also have interest in two other restaurants: Bud's, at Columbus Avenue and 77th Street, and Hulot's, on Lexington Avenue between 72nd and 73rd streets.

The atmosphere at Jams is breezy and casual, yet, because of its prices and East Side location, decidedly urbane—dark suits far outnumber Hawaiian shirts. The lively downstairs dining room, with its terrazzo floor and buoyant artwork on white walls, meets an open kitchen in the back; the upstairs is equally diverting if somewhat less crowded. The racket level, which was occasionally distracting when the restaurant opened, seems to have diminished—or maybe I'm inured to it by now.

The menu is beguiling and manageable in size. It is one of those documents that leave nothing to the imagination, spelling out every herb and vegetable in every dish except salt and pepper. At times it reads like a seed catalogue. One of the most invigorating starters is "ceviche of salmon and red snapper, accompanied by a salad of romaine, papaya, mango, red pepper and onion." I had reservations about tropical fruits in a ceviche, but they were added with restraint, lending a touch of sweetness that complemented the superbly fresh seafood combination. A similarly arresting presentation was the carpaccio of fresh and smoked salmon set over a lush bed of greens: arugula, mâche, basil, thin green beans and plum tomatoes in a lemon-and-lime vinaigrette.

One of Mr. Waxman's signature dishes is his red pepper pancakes crowned with yellow whitefish caviar and golden salmon caviar. They are served over a sheen of crème fraîche flecked with chives and strips of lean smoked salmon. The combination of saline and tart sensations makes a spirited light palate teaser.

If you are a crab cake fan, don't miss the meaty, crisply sautéed ones here. They are terrific with their corn and tomato salsa. Another standout is incredibly moist strips of brittle fried chicken encased in a peppery batter nestled among a virtual greenhouse of plant life. The one letdown among appetizers is the two-colored pastas—one white egg pasta, the other colored with beet roots—tossed in a light, herby tomato sauce with shrimp. Over-the-hill shrimp drags down an otherwise good combination.

The young bright service staff has not flagged in enthusiasm. Waiters are amiable without being overly familiar, and they perform their tasks well. The wine list is intelligently chosen, with a good range of prices and styles, especially among California wines.

Entrees are equally alluring. Tops among them are the plump and succulent grilled quail marinated in soy sauce, ginger and garlic, and rare sautéed tuna steak swathed with a tapenade (a black-olive puree). All three grilled seafood dishes can be recommended: lobster out of the shell surrounded by al dente baby vegetables (turnips, carrots, beans and potatoes); swordfish with grilled shiitake mushrooms and sage butter; and wolffish (a firm, white-fleshed species also known by its French name, loup de mer) in a glossy basil and garlic-butter sauce. All come with the al dente assorted baby vegetables.

With the exception of an excessively sour lemon pie, desserts are uniformly excellent. Among my favorites are the dry-edged chocolate-coffee mousse, the ripe raspberry tart and a luscious mixed-berry sorbet.

Woody Allen once said of Los Angeles that its major cultural contribution was turning right on a red light. I would add California cuisine to that and credit Jams with introducing it to us.

⋄ JOHN CLANCY'S ⋄
RESTAURANT

★ ★

181 West 10th Street, 242-7350.

Atmosphere: Cheerful restaurant in white and gray with colorful garden prints. Moderate noise level. Upstairs room more intimate.

Service: Punctual and workman-like.

Price range: Moderately expensive.

Credit cards: All major cards.

Hours: Dinner, Monday through Saturday, 6 to 11 P.M., Sunday, 5 to 10 P.M.

Reservations: Advised for weekends; suggested for weekdays.

I have always suspected that mesquite-wood grilling is 75 percent menu hype in restaurants because the flavor is only rarely palpable. One exception is at John Clancy's Restaurant in Greenwich Village, where expertly grilled seafood is suffused with the beguiling flavor of light, woody smoke. Many other entrees are available in this cheerful fishhouse, but when I return it is for the grilled swordfish, Dover sole, snapper, tuna or whatever specials are offered on that day.

The walk-down dining room is graceful and welcoming, with whitewashed brick walls on one side, pearl-gray panels on the other and framed pastel garden prints all around. White bentwood chairs surround well-spaced tables. Despite the low ceiling, noise level is moderate. An upstairs room, equally attractive, is more intimate.

Cold appetizers include excellent littleneck clams and a variety of oysters on the half shell. Cold mussels are clean and plump, served with a piquant sauce combining diced green peppers, onions, coriander and hot red pepper flakes. Also recommended are the firm and mild smoked trout with a billowy cloud of whipped cream and horseradish, and the silky gravlax under a sweet mustard-dill dressing.

Hot appetizers come in a distant second. Skip the mushroom caps filled with a bland crab-and-cream combination, the under-seasoned clam-and-corn chowder (a special), and the floury lobster bisque.

All this stands as prelude to the chef's exemplary skills on the mesquite grill. Grilled tuna steak in a soy-based teriyaki sauce is moist and meaty with hints of mesquite. A fillet of fresh and firm red snapper is remarkable for its size and delicate taste. The grilled flesh soaks up the essence of mesquite, adding a wonderful extra dimension. Other winners include the thick and meaty Dover sole, swordfish on skewers and rosy salmon steaks. Many entrees come with either pureed broccoli or sliced potatoes. Lobster Américaine, the most expensive item on the menu, is not worth it.

John Clancy's wine list is well in tune with the menu and priced fairly.

The service captains are an earnest and well-informed team; waiters are less polished but manage to keep things going at a steady pace.

After a healthful meal of grilled fish and vegetables, you can throw self-restraint to the wind and order one of the most monumentally rich desserts in town. John Clancy's dome-shaped mousse cake is a Vesuvius of chocolate mousse enveloped in vanilla cake and covered with ripples of whipped cream. The chocolate core is fudgelike and bittersweet. Also notable are the slightly less rich chocolate roulade topped with almonds, and the multilayered English trifle moistened with sherry.

✦ KEEN'S ✦

★

72 West 36th Street, 947-3636.

Atmosphere: Clubby and masculine, replete with mementos from the turn of the century.

Service: Amateurish and slow.

Price range: Moderately expensive.

Credit cards: All major cards.

Hours: Lunch, Monday through Friday, 11:45 A.M. to 3 P.M.; dinner, Monday through Friday, 5:30 to 11 P.M., Saturday, 5 to 11 P.M. Closed Sunday. Pub menu of lighter fare, including oysters, mussels and chowder, in the barroom from lunchtime to 9:30 P.M. Monday through Friday.

Reservations: Recommended.

The century-old Keen's, a celebrated chophouse at the turn of the century, closed its doors in 1976, a victim of old age and changing tastes. The landmark building lay dormant until late 1981, when it was renovated and reopened by new owners. The new Keen's suffered from an identity crisis for several years until arriving at today's blend of the traditional—grilled chops and steaks—leavened with some contemporary preparations of seafood and game.

The four main dining rooms and the gleaming old bar still have the look and aroma of a creaky old men's haunt (in 1905, the actress Lillie Langtry broke the sex barrier by successfully suing Keen's for discrimination). Thousands of numbered clay pipes hang from the ceiling. One could spend a day perusing the vintage photographs, newspaper clippings and posters covering the walls. While the food has improved significantly under the current chef, service remains amateurish and slow.

Appetizers include many old standards—shrimp cocktail, smoked salmon and escargots—as well as some more alluring selections. Oysters—plump and tasty Chincoteagues while they're in season—are prepared differently every night. Sometimes they are dredged in flour and briefly sautéed, then napped with a subtle red-wine-and-butter reduction laced with julienne of leeks and tiny cubes of baby yellow beets. A similar preparation pairs oysters with a light Riesling sauce studded with scallops.

Ragout of wild mushrooms with cabbage and parsley in a buttery red-wine sauce is a good starter, as is scallop-carrot-and-potato chowder. Grilled rabbit sausages, though, are skinny and dry, and cold poached salmon with horseradish sauce (an appetizer for two or an entree) is served too cold and on the dry side.

The star of the menu is still mutton chop, a massive section of double-cut loin that is deliciously charred outside and succulently pink in the center. The flavor is surprisingly tame for mutton.

Broiled filet mignon, rack of lamb and a thick, crusty veal chop smothered in wild mushrooms are all skillfully grilled.

Ordinarily, I steer away from seafood in a chophouse, but the chef here makes a concerted effort. Whole spicy sizzling fish is prepared by rolling a black bass in chestnut flour and spices, then sautéing it. While I could not detect any spices, the fish was moist and flavorful nonetheless. It was presented over wild rice with a bizarre blend of apple sauce and wasabi, which tasted as strange as it sounded.

On Saturday evening, which is the slowest night of the week in this part of town, diners are invited to have coffee and dessert in front of a crackling fire in the Bull Moose Room. Warm gingerbread with whipped cream and an unrepentently rich hazelnut meringue cake with layers of chocolate ganache and butter cream are the recommended choices. Sitting in snug leather chairs under the watchful eye of a massive bull moose mounted above the hearth, one feels like old J.P. himself, wheeling and dealing with his cronies. All that's missing is the pipe, so bring your own.

◆ KURUMA ZUSHI ◆

Satisfactory

18 West 56th Street, 541-9030 or 541-9039.

Ambiance: Simply appointed sushi bar and dining room with a private tatami room.

Service: Perfunctory.

Hours: Lunch, Monday through Friday, noon to 2:30 P.M.; brunch, Saturday, noon to 2:30 P.M.; dinner, Monday through Saturday, 5:30 to 10 P.M. Closed Sunday.

Credit cards: American Express, Diners Club, MasterCard, Visa.

Reservations: Recommended.

What can you say about a Japanese restaurant that serves commercial-tasting beef Wellington and something misidentified as "poulet a la Kive"? For one, it can be surmised that Kuruma Zushi, which garnered three stars in its old Madison Avenue location under different ownership, lost more than a few fragile dishes in the move to West 56th Street in 1983. For while many of the raw fish preparations are still laudable, the kitchen seems to have developed an identity crisis, weaving in and out of Continental cuisine for no apparent reason.

The restaurant has a simple Oriental decor with a sushi bar up front, a small dining room in the back and a large private tatami room.

Don't tempt logic by ordering the beef Wellington, which is sodden, as if it has been defrosted poorly, and comes with bland, canned foie gras. A creation called hamachi hollandaise, described as grilled yellowtail flounder, is surely not that delicate white fish. The fillet has the consistency of swordfish; the hollandaise sauce, if it existed, is expertly disguised. One hot Oriental entree, described as chicken teriyaki with peach, is even more bizarre—the meat is soaked in shallots and soy sauce and garnished with wilted watercress and iceberg lettuce (and, when I had it, crowned with a wizened pear, not a peach).

The irony of all this is that much of the sushi and sashimi is quite good. One of the better appetizers is usuzukuri, composed of pearly sheets of mild-tasting yellowtail flounder arranged in a fan pattern around a dollop of seaweed. Also enjoyable is the bright and wonderfully briny sea urchin nested on seaweed.

One of the more exotic dishes is grated fresh Japanese yam potato with fresh tuna. This Oriental oddity takes some time to appreciate, sort of like sumo wrestling. The neutral-tasting white potato has a slimy texture, similar to okra, but somehow it works well with the rich tuna and some dipping sauce. Broiled squid legs are a misnomer—they are actually dry and rubbery slices of squid body—while a preparation called nuta turned out to be morsels of lovely fresh tuna steak over boiled scallions. The achingly sweet sauce, though, spoiled it for me.

Several options are available for complete Japanese-style dinners that combine sushi and starters and a special entree. The one we chose featured sort of an Oriental surf-and-turf for the main course: a tasty fried fillet of yellowtail flounder paired with slices of bland steak. We always seemed to do better à la carte, beginning with some of the first-rate sushi—either tuna, yellowtail flounder, squid, crab roe or fluke—followed by some seaweed rolls called tekka maki. The seaweed rolls at Kuruma Zushi are some of the best I've had in a long time. The seaweed sheets are lightly toasted so they are crisp, the rice is well seasoned with vinegar and sugar, and the ingredients, whether fish or vegetables, are always fresh and vibrant.

Lunch is a better option than dinner since the sushi bar is going full tilt and the options seem more varied and fresh. If Kuruma Zushi would drop its silly European affectations on the menu—if I want chicken à la Kiev, I'll go to the Russian Tea Room—and focus on what it does best, it could soon restore the cachet enjoyed in its old location.

◆ LA BOÎTE EN BOIS ◆

★

75 West 68th Street, 874-2705.

Atmosphere: Attractive country French setting in tiny, slightly cramped room.

Service: Competent but not overly helpful in describing the menu.

Price range: Moderate.

Hours: Lunch, Monday through Saturday, 11:45 A.M. to 2:30 P.M.; dinner, Monday through Saturday, 6 to 11 P.M., Sunday, 5:30 to 10 P.M.

Credit cards: None; will accept personal checks with proper identification.

Reservations: Necessary.

The question I am asked most frequently is where to dine in the Lincoln Center area. For all the brouhaha about a restaurant explosion along Columbus and Amsterdam avenues, there are precious few places where a concertgoer can eat nearby without risking exposure to dreary bar fare or ersatz ethnic in a clamor that puts construction sites in a favorable light.

La Boîte en Bois (The Wooden Box), a French country-style restaurant on West 68th Street just off Columbus Avenue, is a happy exception. It is the creation of Alain Brossard and Jean-Claude Coutable, who toiled side by side in the kitchens of

Régine's, Vienna Park and Chez Pascal before setting out on their own. Mr. Coutable tends the fires in the back while Mr. Brossard works the dining room. They offer straightforward and for the most part well-prepared bistro-type food at reasonable prices.

When the owners chose the name Wooden Box, they must have had a matchbox in mind, for the tiny step-down dining room, while cheerful and tastefully done, is exceedingly cramped on busy nights. The French-speaking waiters, who are competent in a laconic sort of way, have mastered the task of shuffling sideways across the room with their elbows high, resembling old vaudeville teams.

Mr. Coutable is not trying to make any statements with his cooking, thank heavens—we get plenty of that elsewhere. If anything, he is just saying, "Eat, it's good for you." His strength seems to be seafood, including such winning preparations as salmon baked in parchment paper with a mustard-cream sauce, and monkfish in saffron sauce. The pink and moist salmon fillet arrives in an inflated parchment balloon accompanied by boiled potatoes and julienne of well-seasoned carrots and zucchini. The thick and firm fillets of lotte, or monkfish, rest in a pool of heady saffron sauce. The other fish on the regular menu, fillet of snapper in a lustrous herb-butter sauce lightened with champagne, was marred by slight overcooking on my last visit.

Among the better meat dishes are succulent lamb chops garnished with fresh rosemary, veal cutlet with three types of wild mushrooms (chanterelle, shiitake and white) in an earthy veal-stock sauce, and the firm, fresh veal kidneys in a flavorful Bordelaise sauce. Chicken fricassee, in which a cut-up chicken was braised with mushrooms and thick country bacon, can be timidly seasoned; filet mignon under a sward of shallots is all pomp and little substance.

The best appetizer is Marseilles-style fish soup, an intensely flavored homemade fish stock perfumed with saffron and thickened with flecks of fish. The only improvement needed is more zip in the garlic mayonnaise that comes with it.

The kitchen turns out some nice fruit tarts, a good oeufs à la neige with hazelnuts, and a delightful orange sorbet with confit of orange rind floating on top. Frozen bitter-chocolate mousse is a big letdown because of the inferior chocolate used.

La Boîte en Bois tends to fill up early before show time at Lincoln Center so it is wise to reserve well in advance.

✦ LA CARAVELLE ✦

★ ★

33 West 55th Street, 586-4252.

Atmosphere: Old-world charm with good noise control.

Service: Highly skilled and amiable but slow.

Price range: Expensive.

Credit cards: All major cards.

Hours: Lunch, Monday through Friday, noon to 2:30 P.M.; dinner, Monday through Saturday, 6 to 10:30 P.M. Closed Sunday and from August 1 through September 8.

Reservations: Recommended.

The winds of change that propelled French restaurants toward sunny new climes in the 1970s passed right over La Caravelle without effect. This once celebrated luxury liner remained anchored to its secure home port, convinced that the foolhardy adventurers would disappear over the horizon, never to be heard from again.

Of course, that didn't happen. It was La Caravelle that risked being forgotten. Fortunately, the current owners, Roger Fessaguet, the former chef, and his partner, André Jammet, decided to revamp the uncompromisingly French institution before it was too late, which included hiring a gifted young chef, Michael Romano, a disciple of Michel Guérard. Only in his early thirties, Mr. Romano is one of the youngest chefs at an old-line New York French restaurant, and the first American. The turnaround for the better has been a pleasure to behold.

Recent visits to La Caravelle leave the impression that while Mr. Romano has nominal control of the kitchen, the influence of Mr. Fessaguet, a respected champion of classic French cuisine, can still be seen. Consequently, La Caravelle's campaign to modernize has been somewhat limited—a three-foot leap across a five-foot ditch.

The dining room has been brightened through little touches here and there but otherwise unaltered. One enters a long corridor flanked by bright red banquettes that are populated by privileged old-time customers. The main room, wrapped in murals of vernal Parisian street scenes, has a soft genteel glow. Well-distanced tables and acoustical tiles allow for discreet conversation.

Mr. Romano has many strengths, and among the first you encounter are his ethereal terrines. The best is a helium-light hot mousse of sole, snow white on the bottom, basil green on top, set in a lovely tomato-cream sauce. At lunch a cold buffet cart holds a silky scallop terrine studded with tender sea scallops, a florid salmon terrine embellished with a coil of spinach in the center, and an earthy-textured terrine of trout layered with carrots and zucchini. Of the meat terrines, one made with duck liver was good and peppery while the quail terrine blended with foie gras and truffles was oddly characterless.

Fresh foie gras is now available in a score of New York restaurants, but rarely have I had it prepared as well as at La Caravelle. One evening the delicate liver was flash-sautéed to leave it seared outside yet pink within and paired with a mild vinegar-edged stock sauce and fresh chervil.

One vestige from the old La Caravelle is French style of service in which captains prepare plates at table side. The service team is highly skilled and engagingly fussy.

Entrees at dinner seem to hold up better than those at lunch. Perfectly cooked sea scallops nested atop braised lettuce in a vibrant chervil-cream sauce served in the evening are far better than the lunch offering of overcooked scallops mired in a bland cream sauce with endive. Grilled red snapper at lunch was dried out, while at dinner sautéed Dover sole was delicious amid cubes of potatoes, artichoke hearts and tomatoes. The only fish that disappointed at dinner was blandly poached turbot that came with a mustard-cream sauce.

One aspect of La Caravelle that needs rethinking is the extensive but overpriced wine list.

Desserts trundle by on a three-tier cart, and there are plenty of winning options. A towering chocolate charlotte is terrific, intense, moist and set in a pool of crème anglaise. Sugar-dusted lemon custard cake is tart and refreshing, as is a luscious plum tart loaded with ripe fruit that bursts in the mouth. Crème brûlée is more like a flan than a rich custard. Chocolate mint soufflé is not to be missed—the aroma of fresh mint bursts from the crust like a geyser.

The updated La Caravelle is seaworthy again, reflected in its rise from one- to two-star status. While it may not be a culinary Columbus, its voyages can be enchanting nonetheless.

◆ LA CÔTE BASQUE ◆

★ ★ ★

5 East 55th Street, 688-6525.

Atmosphere: Old-world charm and glamour in a glowing and comfortable dining room.

Service: Proper and attentive, although not always congenial with new-comers.

Price range: Expensive.

Credit cards: All major cards.

Hours: Lunch, Monday through Saturday, noon to 2:30 P.M.; dinner, 6 to 10:30 P.M., Saturday until 11 P.M. Closed Sunday.

Reservations: Necessary.

Twice a day, six days a week, a procession of gleaming limousines lumbers up to La Côte Basque on East 55th Street, discharging prosperous citizens into its soft and familiar environs. They come seeking the old verities, to be reassured that the once genteel Manhattan dining scene has not gone completely mini-malist and hard edged with its nouveau warehouses, T-shirted waiters, oversize plates and hamster-size portions.

Habitués of this twenty-eight-year-old fortress of classic French cuisine look for comfort, cosseting and food they can really get their teeth into. And that, for sure, is what they get from the chef-proprietor, Jean-Jacques Rachou. La Côte Basque is to the pastel tableaux of new American cuisine as Rubens is to Georgia O'Keeffe. The wraparound dining room, which was much expanded several years ago, still exudes a timeless glamour with its murals of coastal France, red leather banquettes, splen-did flower clusters and a well-turned-out crowd.

Some longtime customers grouse that service has lost its per-sonal touch after the expansion. Still, familiar customers get a gushing welcome, although hoi polloi are lucky to get a second glance. Because I was known to the management, I sent two dining companions in advance one evening to claim our table under their name. They were coolly dispatched to a bench in the foyer until my arrival, at which point we were whooshed into the dining room. The service staff in general, though, is attentive and professional.

Mr. Rachou's cooking style is as deeply rooted as a Bordeaux vine. It is characterized by intensely reduced sauces, lavish presentation and prodigious portions. Certain appetizers, such as the couronne de fruits de mer, a spectacular-looking seafood salad, are larger than entrees in some other restaurants. The salad features sweet, fresh cold lobster, crab and shrimp encircled by summer vegetables with a tarragon mayonnaise. A lobster terrine, more modestly proportioned, is built upon a foundation of lobster mousse alternating with layers of green beans, tomato and carrots—all bright and lively.

Another hefty, though superb, starter is le vol au vent de St. Jacques, a beehive of puff pastry holding buttery bay scallops in a rich fish-stock-and-cream sauce brightened with Sauternes. The addition of chives and a touch of vinegar gives it a sprightly edge. The seafood casserole changes daily, and it is worth trying. Served in a silver terrine, my version combined a rich, creamy fish stock replete with perfectly cooked morsels of lobster and scallops. This is a better option than the salty fish soup.

Fresh foie gras is treated with dignity. Quickly seared and pink in the middle, it is nestled among shiitake mushrooms and a first-rate veal-stock sauce. Lighter appetizers are available—sparkling cold salads, rosy cold poached salmon, vegetable combinations and the like—and the attentive staff is reasonable about preparing various combinations.

La Côte Basque has one of the most impressive wine cellars in town; unfortunately, it is aimed at the limousine crowd. The overpriced list is top-heavy with $30 and up bottles and is heavily biased toward reds.

Entrees religiously follow the bible of classic French cooking, and most dishes are paragons of the genre. It might be as rudimentary as homey roast chicken with pan juices and tarragon sauce, lusty steak au poivre or a more intricate creation such as succulent stuffed quail in pastry crust with truffle sauce. All reflect the Rachou style—brassy, indulgent and comforting.

Roast duck is similarly memorable, with puffed crisp skin, savory meat and a well-balanced pepper sauce. Pasta with shiitake mushrooms makes a good earthy sidekick.

If elephants had edible sweetbreads, they would probably be about the same size as those served here. Once you get over their staggering size, you will find them to be fresh, firm and delicious, in an engaging veal-stock sauce tinged with Madeira and garnished with pearl onions. Simple grilled seafood—sole, salmon and red snapper—is always good. What is described as salmon with sorrel, though, turned out to be rather heavily battered fillets in a thick red-wine sauce that suffocated the delicate fish.

Polite protestations will not keep the pastry cart from your door. Assuming your will is broken, let me suggest the airy vanilla bavarois with raspberry sauce, the excellent hazelnut dacquoise, a ripe white-peach tart and the silky, concentrated chocolate mousse. Frozen raspberry soufflé is as stunning to behold as it is delicious, luxurious with vanilla and fresh fruit.

La Côte Basque's traditional style, like a button-down oxford shirt, may not suit everyone in this lean and restless era. But for those who yearn for unabashed luxury and uncompromising classic fare, it is still the place to go.

✦ LA GRENOUILLE ✦

★ ★

3 East 52nd Street, 752-1495.

Atmosphere: Plush and glowing dining room with opulent flower arrangements and comfortable banquettes.

Service: Efficient but sometimes lacking personality.

Price range: Expensive.

Credit cards: American Express, Diners Club.

Hours: Lunch, Monday through Friday, noon to 2:30 P.M.; dinner, Monday through Friday, 6 to 10:30 P.M.; supper, Monday through Friday, 10:30 to 11:30 P.M. Closed Saturday, Sunday and during August.

Reservations: Necessary.

La Grenouille, which was once among the heavy hitters on New York's A-team of French restaurants, has dropped to minor leagues. In the past several years the chef and many top staff members have left as rumors circulated about morale problems and squabbles among management.

To a patron who knew the restaurant in its heyday, the main difference can be seen in the food, much of which has lost its glitter. Presentation also leaves much to be desired. Take, for example, a lunch special of poached, skinless chicken. We were served part of the breast and the leg under a white cream sauce accompanied by white rice. Presented on a white plate without even a sprig of parsley, it both looked and tasted institutional.

Dover sole with sage was obscured under the kind of viscous butter sauce that went out of style twenty years ago—a recurring theme here. A less stodgy preparation was salmon aux blettes, a lunch entree. It consisted of poached escalopes of fresh pink salmon with a verdant chive-butter sauce. Langoustines in a lustrous sauce of shellfish bolstered with what tasted like vermouth were overcooked. Breaded lobster sections in a richly seductive butter-and-shellfish stock at lunch are preferable to a lamb casserole with potatoes and onion called champvalon. The last time I had it, the lamb was seasoned well, but was insufficiently braised, leaving it chewy.

Simple dishes fare better. Beef fanciers should enjoy the rosy strips of sirloin cloaked with a luxurious black truffle sauce; roast chicken with pan juices and girolle mushrooms also is uncomplicated and tasty—a fine light dinner or supper.

Two game dishes offered in season as specials display some

135

imagination and enthusiasm. Partly boned quail stuffed with foie gras, truffles and wild rice under a sauce combining green grapes and truffles is a regal and savory combination; duck meat in a citric lemon sauce accompanied by crispy straw potatoes also is a winner.

One could do quite well at La Grenouille composing a meal entirely from appetizers. Start with the sprightly mixed appetizer plate, which changes slightly from day to day. It may have a wedge of good pork terrine, well-seasoned ratatouille, cold poached salmon with mustard mayonnaise, crunchy celery root in a light dressing, and shrimp with homemade mayonnaise. The house salad is also a treat: a pair of coral-pink shrimp flanked by dabs of whitefish caviar, crescents of ripe avocado and julienne of carrots in a good olive oil vinaigrette. Skip the dry duck terrine in favor of the buttery pheasant terrine stuffed with pistachios and truffles with a core of silky foie gras.

Desserts have lost some of their former luster. Among the best are the chocolate concoctions: cocoa-flavored soufflé served with Grand Marnier whipped cream, and heady chocolate mousse.

Those who remember La Grenouille at its four-star peak can only hope that it will recapture its youth and blossom anew, like the stunning flowers that made the room famous.

✦ LA METAIRIE ✦

★

189 West 10th Street, 989-0343.

Atmosphere: Small, dark, romantic dining room.

Service: Informal but efficient and friendly.

Price range: Moderate.

Credit cards: MasterCard and Visa.

Hours: Lunch, Monday through Friday, noon to 3 P.M.; dinner, Monday through Saturday, 6 to 11:30 P.M., Sunday, 5 to 11 P.M. Closed Christmas Day and New Year's Day.

Reservations: Required.

La Metairie, a warm and welcoming French bistro in the West Village, is such a pint-size place it gives the resident of a Manhattan studio apartment the impression of returning home to Gracie Mansion after dinner. Some might call it intimate, others romantic. Whatever, it is a charming neighborhood spot that favors solid bistro food that is as honest as a country prior.

The dining room, which can squeeze in about two dozen with a crowbar, has a dark, lodgelike feeling with several tables in the center and banquettes around the walls. Two doves in a cage hanging from the ceiling oversee the proceedings. The owner, Sylvain Fareri, a Tunisia-born Frenchman who spent most of his professional life in Nice, is a casual and accommodating host.

Many patrons are drawn to the restaurant because of its superior couscous. Replete with sausage, lamb, chicken, chickpeas and zucchini over the semolina-like grain with a heady meat broth, it is a perfect toe-warming dish on frigid nights. Treat the accompanying inflammable harissa sauce with respect.

For starters, there is a pleasantly gamy and well-seasoned duck pâté. It comes with a small terrine of airy duck liver mousse tinted with port wine. Puff pastry filled with lobster is well made but marred by a stodgy brown sauce. Roseate gravlax is sparkling, firm and redolent of dill, while the lamb's lettuce salad with a warm bacon dressing tends to be too much of a good thing— the dainty greens are sometimes inundated in dressing.

Mr. Fareri often brings in special products from France, such as delicious oversize fresh Mediterranean sardines that he chargrills and drizzles with lemon. Other grilled fish are prepared

137

with care too, whether Dover sole with mustard butter or salmon-dill sauce.

The last time I had the sautéed boneless lamb with mint sauce it was on the tough side and lacked mint flavor. Better was the deboned duck in a Calvados-accented sauce with raisins and apples. The duck was tasty, relatively lean and greaseless.

The chef turns out some fine French desserts, such as tarte Tatin, a multilayered upside-down apple tart with a caramelized glaze, and a good bombe glacée with praline ice cream. My favorite, however, is the richly smooth and tropical papaya ice cream served in a frozen papaya shell.

✦ LA MIRABELLE ✦

★

333 West 86th Street, 496-0458.

Atmosphere: Quaint and simple little dining room off the lobby of a residential hotel. Moderate noise level.

Service: Amiable and efficient.

Price range: Moderate.

Credit cards: American Express, MasterCard and Visa.

Hours: Dinner, Monday through Thursday, 6 to 10 P.M., Friday and Saturday until 10:30. Closed Sunday.

Reservations: Suggested.

La Mirabelle, a little pearl of a French restaurant ensconced in a thread-worn aristocratic hotel residence on West 86th Street, is a far cry from the splashy pastel grilleries that are becoming ubiquitous on the Upper West Side. La Mirabelle is about as chic as a pair of brown brogues, and any inquiry about mesquite would probably yield the response "Eat lots of garlic and they won't sting you."

The restaurant belongs to Annick Le Douaron and Denise Vienot, two welcoming and delightful entrepreneurs who worked together at La Bonne Bouffe in midtown. They handle everything up front, while the chef, Joel Gaidon, and his nephew, Frank Rozet, run the kitchen. The tiny dining room—fewer than twenty tables—is a charming, tranquil spot in its own anachronistic way: pink and white wall panels with ornate moldings, icicle chandeliers, a little service bar on one side and simply appointed tables. You are greeted warmly by the owners and offered a cocktail or a selection from the limited wine list while perusing the short, classically oriented menu.

This is nostalgia food, the kind of straightforward, flavorful repasts that the owners no doubt served to their families back home. There are no surprises here, but plenty of delights—and at affordable prices. Start with the vernal soupe au pistou, a restorative mélange of fresh spring vegetables in a flavor-packed broth, or creamy coquilles St. Jacques with its thin lid of molten cheese. Glossy sautéed chicken livers with bacon and raspberry vinegar is another invigorating starter. So is the subtly exceptional vichyssoise. The only disappointments are the house pâté and three-fish mousse, both of which are oversalted.

Eight regular entrees are supplemented by two or three daily specials. Almost all are French standards performed to the letter of the old book. Some of the sauces may be a bit thick for modern tastes, but they do not lack flavor, as is so common in today's lighter style of cooking. Dover sole with lemon and butter, sautéed soft-shell crabs with chopped fresh tomatoes (a special), monkfish in a sauce of tomatoes, white wine and tarragon—all are nicely cooked and served with al dente buttered carrots and creamed green beans. No cuisine minceur disciple, this chef.

The signature dish of the house, canard aux mirabelles (duckling with plums), was one of the better roast ducks I've had recently. It seemed to have been cooked in a low oven to allow much of the fat to drip away, leaving a layer of burnished, but not crisp, skin. The semisweet plum sauce was soothing and tasty. Nicely roasted chicken with a light truffle-speckled cream sauce, a special, made the rounds at my table of earnest tasters more than once. Entrecôte with green peppercorn sauce was beefy and mildly piquant; however, the meat was a bit chewy. Savory rack of lamb moistened with garlic-tinged pan juices was cooked precisely to order. It came with buttered flageolets. One case in which the sauce was a bit stodgy was veal medallions with a mustard-cream combination filled with what tasted like canned mushrooms.

All desserts are homemade. Among the best are the fragile-crusted and delicious tarte Tatin, a rich strawberry-and-whipped-cream cake and an embarrassingly intense chocolate mousse cake made with good-quality chocolate. Ideally, that is how it should be—every neighborhood should have a modest restaurant serving wholesome, lovingly prepared food for a fair price. Unfortunately, though, that is the ideal. La Mirabelle is a special little place, and its neighborhood is lucky to have it.

✦ LA PETITE MARMITE ✦

★

5 Mitchell Place, at 49th Street and First Avenue in the Beekman Towers Hotel, 826-1084.

Atmosphere: Bright, modern, upbeat.

Service: Polite and professional, if sometimes laggard.

Price range: Moderately expensive.

Credit cards: All major cards.

Hours: Lunch, Monday through Friday, noon to 2:30 P.M.; dinner, Monday through Friday, 6 to 10:30 P.M., Saturday, 5:30 to 11 P.M. Closed Sunday.

Reservations: Recommended.

For nearly two decades La Petite Marmite has been quietly servicing the United Nations community and the solid citizens of the Beekman Place neighborhood. This is no small achievement in a city where the average restaurant's life span is about as long as that of a first-run movie. One reason La Petite Marmite has endured could be that it represents a mirror image of its clientele: worldly but conservative, amiable yet reserved, inventive but cautious.

The restaurant had cosmetic surgery a few years ago to give it a trendy Art Deco look. Thin stainless-steel-link chains cover the windows, illuminated green glass panels that resemble video screens are set into the center support column, and futuristic metal light sconces in the walls could double as chin-up bars.

The style of cooking, which could be described as modern French built on classical roots, has remained more or less the same over the years. Simple seafood preparations and some daily specials such as stews and roasts are the best bets. Two felicitous starters are the asparagus under puff pastry with a thyme-accented butter sauce, and the broiled bluepoint oysters (a special). Oysters come on the half shell as part of the plâteau du pêcheur, or fisherman's platter, along with sparkling cherrystone clams, sweet marinated bay scallops and a salad of bland baby shrimp in mustard sauce.

The house terrine is a lusty creation—vigorously seasoned, roughly textured and livery. Smoked duck breast over a sward of mâche is a happy liaison, as is the salad of pearly bay scallops with radicchio, endive, mâche and green lettuce tossed in an herby tomato sauce. Not as successful is a similar salad to which rather dry frogs' legs are added.

The entree list is varied but manageable in size. Seafood is treated with respect, so it is a wise choice. Skate, which is a flat, fan-shaped fish in the ray family, is filleted and browned in butter with capers. The slightly sinewy flesh has a pleasant mild flavor. Salmon poached with seaweed is another winner. It is enhanced with a white-wine sauce garnished with grapes. Lightly battered pompano under a chunky sauce of diced red and green peppers, garlic and bacon is as colorful as it is delicious. However broiled salmon with dill sauce is a bit dry.

The waiters, who are correct and proficient if sometimes laggard when the dining room is more than half-full, are effective salesmen of the daily specials.

Desserts are hard to ignore. If your willpower crumbles, consider going all the way with either the bulbous pear soufflé laden with chunks of fresh pear and mint, garnished with fresh raspberry sauce, or the almond frangipane under a mound of vanilla ice cream. Paris-Brest, the cream-filled puff pastry, is aptly rich, as is a mocha ice cream cake with a layer of hazelnut in the center, all drizzled with chocolate sauce.

La Petite Marmite, while not the most exciting restaurant in Manhattan, is the kind of place that gives the city its culinary ballast in these trendy and turbulent times.

✦ LA RÉSERVE ✦

★ ★ ★

4 West 49th Street, 247-2993.

Atmosphere: Elegant cafe-like dining rooms with comfortable fabric banquettes, oversize paintings and soft lighting.

Service: Snappy; mostly European veterans, thoroughly professional and congenial.

Price range: Expensive.

Credit cards: All major cards.

Hours: Lunch, Monday through Saturday, noon to 3 P.M.; dinner, Monday through Saturday, 7 to 11 P.M.; pretheater dinner, Monday through Saturday, 5:30 to 7 P.M. Closed Sunday.

Reservations: Suggested.

When La Réserve opened in 1983, the Rockefeller Center area was overshadowed by its celebrated midtown neighbors Le Cirque, Le Cygne, La Côte Basque and The Four Seasons. Jean-Louis Missud, the owner, decided to do something about that reputation and sent out a posse to capture a talented chef. It found its man toiling behind a stove at La Côte Basque and took him back—not only alive, but full of enthusiasm and ideas for the challenge ahead.

André Gaillard, a young Burgundian, managed in just a few months to revitalize the menu at La Réserve with his refined and serendipitous style of cooking. Like an eighth-place baseball club that acquires a powerhouse cleanup batter in midseason, team players at La Réserve show a new pride.

While Mr. Gaillard's cooking orientation is strongly classical, his touch is light. This is evident in some of his appetizers, such as the warm lobster and asparagus flan, which is an ethereal delight infused with shellfish flavor and garnished with a diadem of lobster morsels. It is presented in a pool of tangy watercress sauce with asparagus spears. Watercress was well chosen, for its slight sharpness cut through the rich lobster flavor like a razor, yielding a vivid taste sensation.

One of his most dazzling creations, a special, is the seafood charlotte. It consists of a silky sole mousse cooked in a charlotte mold and filled with pieces of scallops, shrimp, tomato and mushroom, seasoned with flecks of fresh tarragon. Clinging to the surface are strips of carrots and turnips. The sauce, a beurre blanc garnished with laces of pousse-pied, a seaweed from Brittany, forms a tableau that is as arresting as it was delicious.

Less elaborate starters include slices of fresh salmon and calico scallops marinated with dill, and a delectable slab of fresh foie gras sautéed with hydromel (a fermented honey mixture), garnished with baby vegetables and served with a crunchy potato basket filled brim-high with woodsy wild mushrooms. In the near miss department are a chewy lobster salad and a pâté of duck liver that leaves an acrid aftertaste.

One of the soups sampled—jellied lobster tail flavored with chili peppers—is outstanding, ideal for a warm summer day. The cold aspic soup, intensely flavored with lobster essence, is as briny and refreshing as an ocean spray, and the pinch of chili adds a rousing extra dimension.

A crew of mostly veteran European waiters provides sharp and attentive service. The captains are familiar with the wine list, which is a bit pricey on the lower end of the scale but offers a good range.

Mr. Gaillard happily does not belong to what might be called the "kitchen sink" school of cooking—a little of this and a little of that and a little more of this until the dish is so cluttered one's palate goes tilt like a pinball machine. His fish preparations, for example, are well focused and straightforward. A crisp-skinned grilled fillet of red mullet is memorable, with the judicious addition of clove giving a subtle zip to the sauce. A sprinkling of fresh coriander does the same with a beurre blanc–coated poached salmon. But turbot with lemon grass and caviar fell flat because the fish was overcooked and the lemon grass imperceptible.

If you try only one fish, though, get the regal poached Dover sole: two firm and fresh fillets sandwiched around a well-seasoned layer of creamy artichoke mousse. The fillets, embellished with threads of various root vegetables and slivers of truffles, are served in a glossy pool of beurre blanc dotted with tiny lobster-filled ravioli.

In the meat category, you can enjoy a good roast duck with a gingered cranberry sauce, tender fillets of lamb in an aromatic saffron-and-mint sauce, equally good veal in a sherry-vinegar sauce, and a wonderfully earthy fricassee of veal kidneys and sweetbreads with red cabbage in a mild curry sauce.

Mr. Gaillard is not beyond a little showmanship on occasion. One special is quail cooked in clay. Beaming like a new father, he brings to the table an ornate platter holding two entombed little birds. The quail are exceptionally moist and slightly gamy, stuffed with a tasty combination of sweetbreads, foie gras and mushrooms. Their lustrous sauce combines Madeira, foie gras and capers.

Desserts are copious and ever changing. Tops among them is a mango mousse cake oozing with the flavor of that tropical fruit under an unsweetened soft meringue lid. Equally good is the warm, ripe pear enclosed in phyllo sheets that folded open at the top like a budding flower, surrounded by a semisweet chocolate sauce. Other winners include the plum tart with fresh raspberry sauce, an intensely fruity bavarois of raspberries, and moist carrot and pistachio layer cake veined with whipped cream. Exceptions were a dark and textureless version of crème brûlée, a sodden-crusted apple tart and a run-of-the-mill chocolate cake topped with a dry cream puff.

La Réserve's two dining rooms are as enchanting as ever, with their beige- and peach-colored banquettes, high ceiling, giant paintings of birds in marshlands and soft lighting. With the marked improvement in food, La Réserve has moved out of the shadows and can stand tall among its towering French confreres.

⋆ LA TULIPE ⋆

★ ★ ★

104 West 13th Street, 691-8860.

Atmosphere: Intimate and formal.

Service: Cool and perfunctory; extremely long wait for entrees.

Price range: Expensive.

Credit cards: All major cards.

Hours: Dinner, Tuesday through Sunday, 6:30 to 10 P.M. Closed Monday.

Reservations: Necessary.

La Tulipe is a charming and intimate little restaurant with a Parisian-style bar up front, chocolate-colored walls, corduroy banquettes and graceful tulip sconces. It has maintained a high altitude over the years largely because Sally Darr, the chef-owner, has never left the cockpit for long to chat with passengers. She stays at the controls and personally prepares every dish to order. While this dedication assures a certain consistency of quality, it has its drawbacks. Service can be maddeningly slow. Those willing to grant the cook this self-indulgence will enjoy some of the best food in the village.

The seasonal regular menu carries five appetizers. Shrimp is prepared with a delightful Oriental touch in a salad with ginger, scallions and a warm Oriental sesame- and peanut-oil sauce. Fresh foie gras, an appetizer that is becoming as commonplace as breadsticks, reflects the Darr touch. It is sautéed lightly and placed over a slice of garlic toast with raisins, pearl onions and a sweet duck-stock sauce.

Even tomato soup can be memorable. You receive an empty

bowl with leaves of fresh mint and basil on the bottom as well as julienne strips of tomato and a dab of crème fraîche. The steaming soup, thick and unseasonally flavorful, is poured over the condiments, then stirred.

During the long wait between the first and main courses, one can become quite familiar with the staff, some of whom can be brusque and rather cold.

Mrs. Darr's entrees are nearly always well conceived; she stresses flavor over flashiness. A magnificent game dish is blush-red slices of grilled squab laid over a hillock of sautéed spinach, onions and pine nuts, all surrounded by a parapet of couscous. Another inspired country preparation is confit of duck legs with lentils.

That old workhorse of classic French cuisine, tournedos Rossini, is well prepared here with a slab of fresh foie gras atop the fillet and a savory truffle sauce. The menu describes sweetbreads as being prepared with white wine and shallots, but what I sampled was an overworked dish with pasta in a swampy cream-and-vegetable sauce.

Seafood dishes excel: Typical of the preparations are red snapper cooked in parchment paper with herbs and vegetables; remarkably sweet sautéed bay scallops presented over sautéed spinach and doused with sizzling brown butter; and an oceanic ragout of seafood—scallops, whitefish, lobster, mussels, shrimp —in an excellent red shellfish stock.

La Tulipe is dessert heaven, able to break the will of the most resolute. You can see the dieter begin to crumble as a fellow diner's spoon pierces the apricot soufflé, its golden nectar slipping down the sides. He begins to tremble as the thin glazed apple tart, warm from the oven, is swathed with kirsch-perfumed whipped cream. The forehead breaks out in a cold sweat as a fork cuts through a two-layer ganache-and-bittersweet-chocolate cake.

The dieter surrenders, calling out "Waiter! Waiter!" as an intensely flavorful tangerine sherbet served with iced kirsch is devoured next to him. The other choices are crumbly tulip-shaped tuiles filled with vanilla ice cream, toasted almonds and hot chocolate sauce, and a cloudlike disk of l'île flottante with praline sauce. He eats both.

✦ LAVIN'S ✦

★

23 West 39th Street, 921-1288.

Atmosphere: Classy cafe ambiance with excellent wine bar.

Service: Competent and congenial.

Price range: Moderately expensive.

Credit cards: All major cards.

Hours: Lunch, Monday through Friday, noon to 3 P.M.; dinner, Monday through Friday, 6 to 10 P.M. Closed Saturday and Sunday.

Reservations: Necessary.

Lavin's, a comely American-style restaurant in midtown, is a victim of the mysterious black-hole phenomenon that afflicts certain neighborhoods in Manhattan. Situated in the heart of the busy garment district on West 39th Street, midday finds Lavin's as mobbed as the fitting room at Bloomingdale's, yet in evening it is a cool and lonely place.

Richard Lavin, the owner, seems to have directed his energies toward lunch at the expense of dinner, for the differences between the two are, quite clearly, like night and day. The large rectangular dining room has a classy cafe feeling with carved oak-paneled walls and symmetrical rows of neighborly tables. In the front of the house is Mr. Lavin's pride and joy, a comfortable wine bar offering an ever-changing selection of by-the-glass offerings. Mr. Lavin, an oenophile with a particular fondness for California, always has delightful surprises on his wide and fairly priced list.

The lunch menu is not only bigger but also better than that at dinner. The cooking here is particularly well suited to working people because of its light and salubrious approach, minimizing cream, butter and salt. Sometimes the kitchen goes a bit too far, especially in omitting salt, which can result in healthful but flat-tasting food.

Winning appetizers at lunch and dinner include lustrous mesquite-perfumed carpaccio of beef, wonderfully smoky and moist, and a vivid carpaccio of tuna with capers. Oysters on the half shell are unassailably fresh and flavorful—all the more reason not to gussy them up with a confetti of vegetables that only muddles their flavor and texture. The only soup sampled, a rough-textured gazpacho, was refreshing and delicious with a zippy hot undercurrent.

Pastas, which can be split as appetizers, have their ups and downs. The best sampled were spaghetti Provençale-style colored with green beans, carrots, broccoli and red peppers, all glossed with a light butter and chicken-stock sauce; a more hearty rendition blended mild and lean veal sausage, asparagus and tomato. One pasta appetizer to sidestep is ravioli filled with sinewy scallops and shrimp in a jarring lemon sauce.

The service team at Lavin's, mostly well-scrubbed collegiate types, manages to keep a fairly steady pace at lunch, which is no minor feat.

As for entrees, simple grilled items fare best, such as the terrific swordfish steak, cooked to just pink in the center and jazzed up with a spirited tomatillo sauce spiked with coriander. Grilled veal chop is done with equal skill, and paired with deliciously crunchy straw potatoes. One flop among the grilled items was calf's liver, which was overcooked and had to be returned; the reprise was better but sorely needed salt.

All notions of health food are tossed overboard when it comes to the uniformly excellent desserts: chunky bread pudding moistened with a heady bourbon sauce, profiteroles with luxurious mint ice cream and chocolate sauce, silky crème brûlée and a flourless chocolate cake that is so rich it should be subject to a windfall-profits tax.

While it is likely you will have a two-star lunch at Lavin's, the less favorable odds at dinner preclude a two-star overall rating. One is more appropriate.

◆ LE BERNARDIN ◆

★ ★ ★ ★

155 West 51st Street, 489-1515.

Atmosphere: Luxurious and clubby room with well-spaced tables.

Service: Knowledgeable and efficient.

Price range: Expensive.

Credit cards: All major cards.

Hours: Lunch, Monday through Saturday, noon to 2 P.M.; dinner, Monday through Saturday, 6 to 11 P.M. Closed Sunday.

Reservations: Required.

Le Bernardin is a stunning restaurant serving an all-seafood menu in the new Equitable Assurance Tower on Seventh Avenue at 51st Street. The fish is so fresh and lovingly prepared as to be an epiphany of sorts.

The restaurant is the creation of Gilbert and Maguy Le Coze, the dynamic siblings who own the acclaimed Parisian restaurant by the same name. The first impression that strikes you upon entering this perpetually booked Manhattan establishment is of what is missing: clatter. The dining room, designed by Miss Le Coze with the architect Philip George (and bankrolled by Equitable, with which the owners have a lease arrangement), exudes a lavishly clubby and corporate feeling: a soaring teak ceiling, gray-blue walls, generously spaced tables and larger-than-life paintings of fishermen and their catch.

Mr. Le Coze, who grew up on the Brittany coast, where his family has a hotel and restaurant, is a fanatic about freshness. Such dedication can be seen in a glistening array of oysters (Belons, Cotuits, bluepoints) and addictive littlenecks on the half shell, and in the lagniappe of periwinkles that you pick out of their shells with pins. The flavor is akin to being gently washed by an ocean wave.

Under the category of raw appetizers, don't miss the pearly sheets of black bass flecked with coriander and basil and lacquered with extra virgin olive oil, a sensational combination, or the sparkling salad of marinated fish. The pristine quality of a tuna carpaccio, though, was obscured by an oversalted ginger sauce.

The rest of the starters are terrific and, like all dishes here, are minimally cooked to allow the freshness of the sea to shine through. Among my favorites are sea scallops in various guises. In one preparation, attributed to the French chef Georges Blanc, three giant scallops on the half shell are served in an exquisite sauce combining the scallops' brine, some butter and a dash of saffron. They are garnished with asparagus, thin strips of fresh tomato and fennel sprigs—a heavenly combination. Equally memorable are the same scallops in a salad with a gossamer cream sauce perfumed with truffle juice.

If you have never tried a sea urchin, those saline little porcupines of the sea, let Mr. Le Coze make the introduction. He scoops out the orange roe and blends it with butter, then returns it to the shell, where it is mixed with the urchin's warm briny nectar.

The tone of the crack service team is set by the beguiling hostess, Maguy Le Coze, a wisp and a smile that twirl around the room like a benign cyclone. She is extremely knowledgeable about the first-rate wine list—consider the little-known French whites in the $20 to $25 range.

As for entrees, thin strips of blush-pink salmon are presented on a red-hot platter in a bubbling sorrel-and-white-wine sauce. Mr. Le Coze times the presentation so perfectly that the fish actually finishes cooking at the table on the hot plate. A thick slab of salmon, just this side of sushi in the center, comes in a small casserole atop an ethereal tomato-cream sauce, and garnished with fresh mint. There was some quibbling at my table about whether the poached halibut in a warm herb vinaigrette was a tad too acidic, but all agreed they had never tasted halibut so moist and fresh. The only disappointing entree was pasta in a stodgy lobster-cream sauce. The list of superlatives goes on, changing slightly with the season and availability.

When it's time for dessert, you can either remain afloat with a palette of intense, fresh fruit sorbets or sink to the ocean floor with the meltingly rich chocolate cake, a buttery thin apple tart or a dazzling sampler of caramel sweets: caramel ice cream, flan, oeufs à la neige and caramel mousse. My favorite is the trio of pears, which combines a cinnamon-tinged poached pear along with a warm tiny pear tart and pear sorbet.

The only question that remains is whether the Le Coze can maintain such a world-class pace on two continents simultaneously. As a purely selfish motive, I would like to see their passports confiscated and their movement restricted to this fish-starved island.

✦ LE CIRQUE ✦

★ ★ ★

58 East 65th Street, 794-9292.

Atmosphere: Classically elegant room with cramped banquettes and closely spaced tables.

Service: Extremely professional veteran staff.

Price range: Expensive.

Credit cards: American Express, Diners Club and Carte Blanche.

Hours: Lunch, Monday through Saturday, noon to 2:45 P.M.; dinner 5:45 to 10:30 P.M. Closed Sunday.

Reservations: Necessary well in advance.

Nowhere in the United States, nor anywhere else as far as I have seen, is there a dining room that crackles with the high-voltage energy of Le Cirque. There is indeed something magical about the fetes thrown twice a day by the suave Italian-born owner, Sirio Maccioni, that have the rich and famous from around the world clambering to squeeze into one of his elbow-to-elbow banquettes. While so many other chic restaurants blaze for a short time in the night and then fade like a shooting star, Le Cirque has remained white-hot for most of its twelve years.

Why? The food, to be sure, is of the highest quality, classically rooted and generally conservative. The enormous menu is cleverly attuned to the insouciant aristocrats who make this their home away from home—it is like a tasteful painting, adding luster to the room but never distracting.

Another attraction is the discreet service team, nimble Europeans all, who exhibit more fancy moves than the Harlem Globetrotters. Undeniably, though, the star attraction is Mr. Maccioni himself, a hawk-eyed perfectionist who one minute is aligning salt and pepper shakers as if the success of his establishment rests on table symmetry, while the next he is kissing the hand of a parting customer, making her feel like the Princess of Wales as she floats out the door.

Le Cirque, like most other restaurants in its class, is not always a democratic institution. Preferred tables—those with the best views of the comings and goings—are unofficially reserved for the legion of regulars. However, the bleacher seats in this timelessly elegant room are few and not entirely isolated from the playing field. As for the overly neighborly tables, Mr. Maccioni contends that whenever he tries to create breathing space, some customers complain. Would you rather sit six inches or six feet from Woody Allen?

The menu is so extensive—and annoyingly all in French— that the help of waiters may be necessary. There are any number of spirited light starters. Ceviche of meaty red snapper fillet is vibrant in an aromatic vinaigrette under ribbons of red and yellow peppers; a similar sauce, this one warm, glosses sweet bay scallops set over a fan of endive and mixed greens. One of the prettiest presentations is a plate of saline-poached mussels on the half shell arranged in a circle and showered with a confetti of different colored sweet peppers and red onions. The mussels are impeccable and the mild vinegar-laced cream sauce lets them take center stage.

Top quality fresh foie gras is deftly handled, simply sautéed and framed by multicolored salad greens under a light vinegar sauce that cuts the fattiness; less successful is the terrine of foie gras studded with pistachios, which had a bitter off flavor. Pastas change daily, and those I sampled were unqualified successes. One combined whole-wheat thin spaghetti with shrimp and bay scallops in a rich fish-stock-based cream sauce seasoned with chervil; another had smoky charred langoustines perched on a tangle of tagliarini in a nearly identical sauce.

The wine list is deep, broad and fairly priced for this kind of establishment. Pay attention to some of the unusual Italian whites, which tend to be the better bargains, some in the $20 neighborhood.

Entrees are straightforward, invariably very good, occasionally extraordinary. You can't go wrong with meticulously prepared grilled and sautéed selections, especially at lunch, where a more abstemious crowd holds forth—thick fillets of perfectly grilled Dover sole with mustard sauce (or, as an occasional special, with a lively Provençale sauce of olives, capers and tomatoes), grilled turbot in a soothing beurre blanc sauce, paillard of beef or veal, succulent lamb chops redolent of fresh herbs, and so on. Game birds are one of the restaurant's specialties. The best I had was a succulent roast pigeon, golden-skinned and tender, surrounded by shreds of cabbage flavored with bacon cubes and a brittle potato basket holding well-seasoned steamed spinach—a delightful and earthy combination. Duck with ginger and cassis did not reach such heights. The duck was humdrum and the ginger was barely perceptible.

Le Cirque's desserts are legendary, and rightly so. The renowned crème brûlée is as seductive as ever, a golden egg custard under a burnished lid of thin caramelized sugar. An ineffably light four-layer napoleon is constructed with a fluffy mortar of faintly sweetened whipped cream and brittle puff pastry and embellished with fresh raspberries. Other irresistible temptations include the tart lemon mousse, gratin of poached pears, hazelnut mocha cake and assorted soufflés, particularly the mango with chocolate sauce.

Le Cirque is something much grander than the sum of its parts. When the world is gray and somber outside, it is still bright and filled with possibilities inside Le Cirque. The party can be expected to roll on for years.

◆ LE CYGNE ◆

★ ★ ★

55 East 54th Street, 759-5941.

Atmosphere: Elegant and colorful two-level town house. Moderate noise level.

Service: Excellent.

Price range: Expensive.

Credit cards: All major cards.

Hours: Lunch, Monday through Friday, noon to 2 P.M.; dinner, Monday through Friday, 6 to 10 P.M., Saturday, 6 to 11 P.M. Closed Sunday.

Reservations: Required.

Le Cygne is one of those dependable and discreet institutions that hum along from year to year at a steady pace while rarely making a splash or attracting much public attention. Its comely clientele, refined and low-key, likes it that way, preferring reliability over rakishness—a Mercedes rather than a Lamborghini.

Opened in 1969 by the partners Gérard Gillian and Michel Crouzillat, the restaurant moved next door to a two-story town house four years ago. The two small dining rooms on both levels sport distinctive charms. Muted lighting and cool peach-and-gray tones lend a bright and cheerful mood; misty murals of wildflowers brighten the gloomiest Manhattan day, as do vibrant fresh bouquets on the tables, which appear to have been snipped from the painted countryside. The upper level, reached by dual winding staircases, has an airy and contemporary feeling with its arched ceiling and backlighted opaque glass panels.

A new chef, Pierre Baran, former second in command at Le Cirque, came on in January 1986. His style follows the restaurant's tradition of straddling the middle of the French highway. Mr. Baran has a fine touch with seasonings and a graceful, but not faddish, eye for presentation. All in all, though, plenty of first-rate options exist to compose a superb meal in one of the most civilized and soothing settings in town.

Appetizers are uniformly wonderful. Try the succulent little scallops from Maine in a bright lime-accented fish stock with julienne of endive, or the sparkling salmon terrine in a cool and flavorful aspic. The salmon terrine is presented on crinkly leaves of purple kale with a zesty tarragon dressing and cucumber salad. Both meat terrines are paragons of the art: a rough-textured and mildly livery country pork terrine and, my favorite, a luxurious duck rendition, speckled with nutty black truffles, and molded around a pink core of silky foie gras.

Oyster fanciers will not be disappointed by the icy Belons when they are in season, or, even a rare treat when in season, the oceanic thumbnail-size Olympias from Washington State. A more substantial starter would be the firm, thin medallions of sweetbreads, simply sautéed and set over a glossy vinegar-edged veal-stock sauce. The only loser was fricassee of baby shrimp. The Provençale-style broth was fresh and herbaceous, but the shrimp were tasteless.

A subcategory among the entrees offers house specialties, and all those sampled are worth seeking out. Beautifully sautéed fresh foie gras, silken and delicate, rested in a pool of port wine and cognac sauce ringed by tiny tart gooseberries; lemony seafood salad—lobster, scallops and shrimp—was right on the mark (although crab remoulade on the side had telltale signs of age). Often prosaic escargots came to life in a fragrant tomato-based broth with wild mushrooms. If they have the smoked maigret, don't miss it: a florid slice of moist duck breast with haunting woody nuances, served with a buttery foie gras mousse.

From the moment you enter the cool gray portals of Le Cygne, the staff keeps a distanced eye on you to fill every need or whim, but never in an ingratiating or overfamiliar way. First-time customers seem to get the same cosseting as regulars.

The wine list is stiffly priced with paltry selections in the $20 to $25 range.

Among the entrees, one of the more unusual offerings is highly recommended: a deftly sautéed fillet of baby silver salmon prepared like a pepper steak. The salmon is coated with crushed black pepper, sautéed, and served with a sauce combining fish stock, tomato and cognac—the interplay of hot and sweet is a delight. Lobster ragout comes in a heady shellfish and tomato broth, although the lobster meat is a bit overcooked; the same flaw marred grilled Dover sole on two occasions. If you like frogs' legs, the version here, simply prepared in garlic and butter, is the best I have had in New York.

Other highlights include the rosy roast squab—just gamy enough to let you know what you are eating—in an earthy mélange of cloves, cèpes and artichokes; another engaging preparation is the duck breast in a yin-yang sort of sauce balancing tart vinegar and sweet honey.

When the pastry cart rounds the bend, it is worth taking a ride. Crème brûlée is excellent, glassy crusted and embarrassingly rich, as is an orange-and–Grand Marnier mousse and a chocolate layer cake with bittersweet chocolate curls on the roof and intense chocolate mousse on alternating levels. Most tarts sampled—apricot and raspberry in particular—were stellar. Only a white-and-dark-chocolate charlotte disappoints because of dryness.

Le Cygne's appeal is multifarious. While its gastronomic gifts can be delightful, the sophisticated packaging adds to their luster. Le Cygne is indeed humming along the high road— comfortably, contentedly and with a backseat full of happily pampered passengers.

◆ LE PÉRIGORD ◆

★ ★

405 East 52nd Street, 755-6244.

Atmosphere: Soothing old-world charm with well-spaced tables, low noise level and low-key colors.

Service: Proper and knowledgeable but slow at times.

Price range: Expensive.

Credit cards: All major cards.

Hours: Lunch, Monday through Friday, noon to 3 P.M.; dinner, Monday through Saturday, 5:30 to 10:30 P.M. Closed Sunday.

Reservations: Necessary.

Le Périgord is a survivor among an endangered species in New York: a solid French restaurant in a civilized setting that is conducive to both tranquil socializing and discreet business entertaining. This cozy spot with an old-world ambiance on the eastern reaches of 52nd Street is far from the business executives' midtown lunch circuit, so if you are trying to steal a client from the competition, it is a relatively safe place to do it.

Le Périgord caters to a regular and well-heeled clientele, mostly older, mostly conservative, who enjoy being cosseted by the seasoned team of captains. The dining room is attractive in a genteel way—no jarring murals or theatrical lighting here. The swirled peach and pale blue fabric-covered walls are soothing and warm; extravagant flower arrangements and well-spaced tables add to a sense of luxury.

The food harmonizes with the atmosphere. The French-trained chef, Antoine Bouterin, is skilled at mixing up his pitches to offer something for everyone. His menu pays obeisance to classic cuisine yet at the same time keeps in step with the latest trends. You will find dishes as homespun as Cornish hen Périgourdine and braised beef with carrots or as au courant as sliced duck breast with essence of passion fruit or gratin of shrimp coated with sesame seeds in lobster and shrimp sauce.

Overcooking is a nagging flaw with certain dishes, but if you become familiar with the chef's many strengths a two-star experience is virtually assured. The appetizer list is somewhat daunting at first—nearly two dozen choices including soups. One can minimize guesswork by picking from a cold buffet table that holds cold poached bass with green sauce, shimmering Scottish smoked salmon and fresh vegetables. One of the best items, which is not on display, is the cold vegetable pâté filled with little cubes of firm-cooked carrots and zucchini bound in a cooling, full-flavored aspic. It is served with a sour cream–based herb sauce.

A standout appetizer, sometimes offered as a special, is salmon tartare blended with Worcestershire sauce, capers and a touch of curry, which gives it a piquant edge.

Among the hot starters, try the vegetable tart with truffles. It is really more like an airy quiche made with pureed leeks, celery, carrots, zucchini and tomato; the subtle lemon-butter sauce around it is laced with truffle slices. This one is beautifully displayed on the plate, as are most of Mr. Bouterin's preparations.

Another sure bet is the foie gras, either sautéed with apples and capers ($10 supplement over the prix-fixe dinner) or cold in a rim of sweet Sauternes aspic ($15 supplement). One disappointment is mushy sweetbreads inside a crepe with vinegar butter.

Service is professional in the best French tradition, yet there are often inexplicably long lags between courses. The captains are exceptionally well informed about the entrees and wines, which is a blessing since there are wide selections of both.

The chef has an innovative touch with seafood. One stellar

dish is rolled fillets of sole, crowned with truffle slices and set in a mild garlic puree garnished with caramelized garlic cloves and baby carrots; another typical of his style is deftly roasted turbot fillets resting in a nest of homemade noodles swathed in a light curry sauce.

If you are in the mood for more familiar fare, such as rack of lamb or sliced veal au jus with tarragon (a special), you can't do better than here. Kidneys Bordelaise also are paradigmatic—the firm, dark kidneys are served with a burnished stock sauce studded with sweet roast shallots. Get them with a side order of sarladaise potatoes, a thick disk of sautéed sliced potatoes layered with truffles ($6 supplement at dinner).

The overloaded dessert cart carries something for everyone, from ripe and luscious fresh fruit sorbets and seasonal berries with sabayon sauce to towering chocolate layer cakes with bitter-sweet-chocolate shavings clinging precariously to the sides, to first-rate fruit tarts and citric lemon meringue pie.

If your potential client doesn't defect to you after all this, he is probably not worth your company.

✦ LE RÉGENCE ✦

★ ★

Hotel Plaza-Athenee, 37 East 64th Street, 606-4647, 606-4648.

Atmosphere: Plush, hushed and ultra-French.

Service: Professional and congenial.

Price range: Expensive.

Credit cards: All major cards.

Hours: Lunch, daily, noon to 2:30 P.M.; dinner, daily, 6 to 10 P.M.

Reservations: Suggested.

You sweep past a beaming doorman into the marmoreal opulence of the Plaza Athenee hotel, then down a few steps to a clubby paneled anteroom where a comely maître d'hôtel greets you with diplomatic aplomb. The dining room, all crisp turquoise with white trim, is plush, formal and as unmistakably French as the Champs-Elysées: velvet banquettes, leather armchairs, ornate mirrors, well-separated tables. The overall effect is old-world but not old-fashioned, and as comfortable as a cashmere sweater.

The menu at Le Régence follows the same script—it is classically rooted yet bright and contemporary. Daniel Boulud, the young chef, wears the school tie of his mentor, Roger Vergé, whose cooking style evokes the sunny Mediterranean coast.

Typical of Mr. Boulud's repertory is a smashing appetizer combining lightly sautéed jumbo shrimp and a vivid shellfish stock seasoned with rosemary and a touch of fresh orange to impart a hint of citric sweetness. Another rousing starter is a cold aspic terrine of shredded beef shanks and sweet leeks, redolent of fresh herbs, accompanied by a mild horseradish sauce. A cold lobster salad flanked by crescents of ripe asparagus and shoelace-thin green beans and garnished with chervil also is first-rate, although the kitchen is too stingy with the truffle vinaigrette.

Le Régence turns out some lustrous pasta appetizers as daily specials. Of the two best I sampled, one was glistening raviolis filled with morsels of delicate lobster and spinach and glazed with a buttery shellfish stock sauce; the other paired homemade fettuccine tossed with julienne of carrots, shards of lobster and chives in a similarly silky stock sauce.

The predominantly French waiters cosset the well-groomed cosmopolitan clientele—yuppies are as scarce in this rarefied world as blue margaritas. The wine list is more than adequate across the board, and prices are within reason.

Le Régence originally billed itself as a seafood restaurant. Ironically, it earns the lowest grades in that category. One letdown is the scallop soup, which is served with all the pomp of a state visit. A waiter presents a shallow bowl holding a huddle of bay scallops and herbs; right behind him comes a cohort who ceremoniously ladles a sublime creamy broth over them—a nice show, but the scallops are dry and rubbery. Salmon steak with an insipid sauce made with ginger and overcooked crayfish, a special, also disappoints.

The kitchen makes partial amends with a meaty white fillet of braised brill (known as barbue in French) set over a puree of well-seasoned mushrooms and blanketed with watercress and chopped ripe tomatoes. Another winner is flaky red snapper braised with artichoke hearts and a light sauce melding rosemary, chives and Italian parsley. It comes with a buttery disk of crisped potatoes.

All meat dishes are on target. Roast free-range chicken is palpably superior to the run-of-the-mill variety. The veal chop is extraordinarily tender and rich in its burnished stock-based sauce brightened with asparagus, endive and artichoke hearts. And duck fanciers will not be let down by the savory version here combining a succulent leg and florid strips of rare breast surrounding a cinnamon-flecked pear.

Le Régence offers a lovingly presented cheese course—we tried first-rate Reblochon, goat cheese, St. Nectaire, St. André —that comes with a glass of good port. For dessert, the winner by a mile is the croquant aux fraises et menthe, paper-thin disks of mille-feuille pastry sandwiching chopped strawberries and mint-flavored whipped cream with a dollop of strawberry sherbet on the side. Crème brûlée jazzed up with fresh cherries and kirsch liqueur is delicious; so is the lemony warm gratin of red plums and apricots. Only a chestnut mousse cake, served at lunch, was gelatinous and bland.

The low-key atmosphere and professional service make the

setting ideal for tranquil business entertaining. Le Régence exemplifies the best of the revived hotel dining scene in New York. You don't have to be a Francophile to love it, but it helps.

✦ LOLA ✦

★

30 West 22nd Street, 675-6700.

Atmosphere: Elegant cafe ambiance with pastel-colored walls adorned with attractive prints and drawings and soft lighting. Annoyingly loud when full.

Service: The comely young staff is outgoing and helpful but occasionally awkward.

Price range: Moderately expensive.

Credit cards: American Express.

Hours: Lunch, Monday through Friday, noon to 3 P.M.; dinner, Monday through Thursday, 6 P.M. to midnight, Friday and Saturday until 1 A.M., Sunday until 10 P.M.; Sunday brunch, noon to 5:30 P.M.

Reservations: Suggested.

It is always refreshing to see a relatively unfamiliar cuisine appear in New York, such as the spicy and spirited fare of the West Indies at Lola, a stylish restaurant in the blossoming Madison Square neighborhood. This rakish, pastel-washed establishment is the creation of Eugene Fracchia, former owner of Pesca, and the Jamaican-born Yvonne (Lola) Bell. The menu is only about half Jamaican; Mr. Fracchia asserts his own ethnicity via a handful of Italian dishes.

On paper, at least, the lineup is beguiling. In reality, though, the cooking and service are as unpredictable as island weather. During the course of four visits, my experiences varied so greatly that I sometimes thought I had wandered into a different restaurant. Moreover, the noise level can be numbing. There is barely a soft surface in the house, so when conviviality peaks, usually about 10 P.M., the dining room becomes a huge echo chamber.

While perusing the menu, you can be priming your palate with sharp little cayenne-spiked shortbread cookies made with cheese and pecans. And when choosing, keep in mind that on the whole, the appetizers are better than the entrees. Bermuda seafood chowder is consistently pleasing, a rich sweetish broth chock-full of fresh tuna and vegetables; sweet-potato vichyssoise, which is served hot, is another winner. West Indian potato-and-shrimp fritters sound intriguing, but upon first sampling they were a letdown, undercooked and 90 percent potato; several nights later, they were a pleasant surprise—crisp, well seasoned and amply filled with shrimp. Even the accompanying chopped-tomato-and-basil garnish came to life.

The outstanding appetizer is grilled calf sweetbreads, which are firm, fresh and infused with a faint smoky flavor. They come with a tart salsa of parsley, garlic, capers and olive oil. Skip the watery and tasteless grilled polenta, and try instead the mountain of ultra-thin cayenne-laced onion rings.

The service team, led by the ebullient Miss Bell, is long on personality though occasionally short on finesse. No useful help is offered regarding the wine list, which is fairly priced but includes several clunkers. Play it safe with well-known producers and you'll do fine.

If you'd like to try something with a West Indian accent, you might choose the sharp shrimp-and-chicken curry served with rough-textured wild-rice waffles. As for the so-called hundred-spice Caribbean fried chicken, it sounds more ominous than it is. What you get is perfectly acceptable fried chicken coated with mildly hot dried spices and a Chinese-inspired three-cabbage salad.

Even the most humble West Indian restaurant should be able

to turn out a creditable shellfish gumbo; the rendition here, though—with shrimp, clams, mussels, ham and rice—is lackluster. So are the ersatz osso buco, the dried-out veal paillard and the colorless tenderloin of pork roasted in milk and garlic. Simple grilled dishes fare better, such as the lovely lamb chops with golden-fried shoestring potatoes, and the swordfish steak enhanced with a caper-dill crème fraîche sauce.

The ricotta-flavored gelato, while not exactly a staple of Jamaican cuisine, is still worth trying. So, too, is the light and creamy Frangelico pumpkin cheesecake.

✦ LUTÈCE ✦

★ ★ ★ ★

249 East 50th Street, 752-2225.

Atmosphere: A town house with an airy and cheerful garden dining room, an intimate anteroom and formal, old-fashioned pair of upstairs rooms.

Service: Cordial and extremely professional.

Price range: Expensive.

Credit cards: American Express, Carte Blanche and Diners Club.

Hours: Lunch, Tuesday through Friday, noon to 2 P.M.; dinner, Monday through Saturday, 6 to 10 P.M. except from Memorial Day to Labor Day, when the restaurant is closed Saturday. The restaurant also closes for summer vacation in August.

Reservations: Necessary well in advance.

In its 25 years of exemplary service, Lutèce has become bigger than life—indeed, the name itself is a metaphor for superior dining. Carrying such a burden is a mixed blessing. As with a great painting or sculpture, a legendary restaurant must continually satisfy inflated expectations of the public, many of whom come with magnifying glasses, searching for imperfections.

André Soltner, the amiable chef-owner who has been associated with the restaurant virtually from its beginning, would be the first to acknowledge that perfection is merely the elusive goal that keeps good chefs on their toes. On a day-to-day basis, however, his restaurant offers some of the most consistently engaging, inventive and intelligent cuisine in the city.

Before visiting Lutèce I had heard grumblings about difficulty in getting reservations and cool, if not rude, treatment to first-time customers. My experiences as an anonymous diner over five visits did not bear that out. Indeed, reservations need to be made at least two weeks in advance, lunch at least a week (reservations are accepted up to a month ahead of time). As for the reception to first-timers, we were always treated with professionalism and warmth.

In keeping with the personality of Mr. Soltner, the decor of his town-house restaurant is unpretentious and comfortable. My favorite room is the cheerful enclosed garden downstairs with its high Quonset-hut-like ceiling. At lunch, the filtered sun casts a soft, soothing glow across the flower-dappled garden with its white trellised walls. My next favorite spot is a cozy anteroom at the garden entrance.

The menu at Lutèce is manageable in size and always carries special preparations worth considering. Among the appetizers, the choices could be as simple as plump, firm sweetbreads pan-fried to golden crispness and served in a sparkling white-wine-and-caper sauce or strips of fresh salmon swabbed with a mustard mousse mixture and glazed under the broiler. A more lofty starter might be sea scallops sliced into equal-size disks and coated with minced truffles and Italian parsley. The scallops are quickly sautéed and served in a sauce made with butter and some white wine in which the truffles have been preserved. The aroma of the earthy and nutty truffles swirls to the ceiling, but the delicate flavor of the scallops is not lost. Two other exceptional starters are the coarse, well-seasoned suckling pig terrine and the silky, complex gazpacho.

Portions are adequate, but not overwhelming. If you order from the $70 menu degustation, eight or more courses are marched out of the kitchen. Such feasts may begin with rosy fresh foie gras sautéed with apples followed by the aforementioned scallops coated with truffles. Then comes lobster meat in a fresh tomato coulis; fillet of St. Pierre, a firm-textured white fish, in an airy beurre blanc accented with fresh tarragon leaves and a hint of orange zest; fresh plum sorbet (it was too sugary); gamy morsels of squab in a savory wine sauce; a towering puff pastry square filled with custard and stewed strawberries, and finally, a tart and sweet frozen lemon mousse enveloped in a thin layer of almond cake.

Other standout dishes included braised baby spring lamb with carrots, turnips, tomatoes and fresh noodles, and a wonderful navarin of lobster and scallops in a Pernod-tinted lobster bisque. Lutèce has a strong wine list that includes some delightful Alsace selections at moderate prices.

Desserts are equally arresting: glistening tarte Tatin; white chocolate mousse filled with shards of white chocolate and draped in a fresh kumquat sauce; tiny, succulent, wild strawberries from France with whipped cream; and velvety chocolate mousse under lacy strips of preserved orange. The list could go on and on; however, the reason Lutèce deserves its four-star rating goes beyond a clinical listing of its superior dishes. It has to do with the total experience of Lutèce. From the risible, good-natured barman at the tiny cafe waiting area to the capable captains, waiters, and finally the chef, this is a class act.

✦ MARCELLO ✦

★ ★

1354 First Avenue, near 73rd Street, 744-4400.

Atmosphere: Contemporary, understated setting in shades of beige and rose. Large photo mural of Florence on back wall. Can be very loud when busy.

Service: Professional and well informed about the food.

Price range: Moderately expensive.

Credit cards: All major cards.

Hours: Dinner, daily, 5 P.M. to midnight.

Reservations: Necessary.

Marcello Sili is a big, compactly built man with an earnest demeanor and a smile as wide as the Verrazano-Narrows Bridge. He is no stranger to habitués of Italian restaurants in New York, having logged twenty years in the business. His latest venture, Marcello, is in many ways his crowning achievement.

Situated on the Upper East Side, where high-priced pasta houses are commonplace, Marcello is noteworthy on two accounts. While not exactly cheap, it is a notch below much of the competition in price; more important, though, is the spirited cooking of the chef and co-owner, Gianvito Fanizza, formerly of Nanni il Valletto and Sign of the Dove. A third partner in the venture is John Roland, an anchorman on Channel 5.

The contemporary dining room is done in shades of beige and rose, with plants here and there to soften the hard edges. However, the greenery is insufficient to muffle the distracting clatter on crowded evenings. The rear wall, near the kitchen, is covered with a striking floor-to-ceiling black-and-white photograph of Florence. As waiters scurry back and forth with orders, it seems as though they are making fleet-footed tours of the Uffizi museum. Overall, the professional and well-informed service staff is holding up well.

Pastas, which can be ordered in half portions for appetizers, are more compelling than most of the starters. One of the best is al dente fresh fedelini (thin spaghetti) with firm-cooked shrimp and tart radicchio with a touch of tomato for color. Equally memorable is the fusilli in a luxurious blend of creamy mascarpone cheese with a dash of brandy. A mixed seafood pasta, offered as a special one evening, was outstanding: flossy egg noodles glossed with an herby white wine replete with mussels, clams, shrimp and bay scallops, each perfectly cooked. A diverting dish to share among several diners is the trio of fresh pastas on one plate—shells in a vibrant pesto sauce, tortellini stuffed with porcini mushrooms and ricotta in a light tomato sauce, and thin pasta with a smoky blend of pancetta, porcini and fresh peas.

Gnocchi fans no doubt will be pleased with the firm, fresh version here swathed in fontina cheese and butter. Spaghetti with clam sauce is a paragon as well.

If you want to begin with a lighter antipasto, try the salad of orange sections, shrimp and black olives. A special of sautéed porcini with garlic curiously lacked flavor.

When Mr. Sili describes the entrees, gesticulating effusively, one is hard pressed to decide. Seafood blue-ribbon winners include the sparkling fresh red snapper sautéed in wine, tomatoes and herbs, and the meaty Dover sole paired with a faintly sharp blend of mustard, green peppercorns and brandy. A mound of brittle fried zucchini is a side dish not to be missed. Zuppa di pesce, a ubiquitous dish that is a swampy bore in many restaurants, is exceptional in the hands of Mr. Fanizza. A shallow pool of thyme-scented shellfish stock overflows with shrimp, salmon, monkfish, mussels and clams. Only the baby squid with olives and artichokes is disappointing. The dark sauce is viscous and cloying.

The chef respects good-quality veal, allowing the meat to shine through when prepared Milanese-style with a sprightly garnish of marinated tomatoes, onions and peppers. Other winners are scallops of veal prepared with a sauce of wild mushrooms or with an earthy combination of chestnuts and wine.

Don't miss the ethereal dessert called tirami sù, a fortress of espresso-soaked ladyfingers, mascarpone and whipped cream. This dish has become somewhat of a cliché in Italian restaurants around town, but none surpasses Marcello's. The combination of fresh raspberries with balsamic vinegar is rousing too. The gelati, though, are icy.

If this capable crew manages to hold a steady course, Marcello's 1,000-watt smile can be expected to illuminate the neighborhood for a long time.

◆ MAXIM'S ◆

★

680 Madison Avenue, at 61st Street, 751-5111.

Atmosphere: Lavish belle époque dining rooms with bucolic murals, stained glass and ornate woodwork.

Service: From formal and well informed to callow and forgetful.

Price range: Expensive.

Credit cards: American Express, Diners Club.

Hours: Lunch, Monday through Friday, noon to 3 P.M.; dinner, Monday through Thursday, 6 P.M. to 1 A.M., Friday and Saturday until 2 A.M. Closed Sunday.

Reservations: Required (formal wear Friday and Saturday evenings).

It is like entering a time warp, circa 1893, an era when women carried parasols and gentlemen wore hats. The expansive, multilevel dining rooms are agleam with burnished rosewood supporting vines of hammered brass, intricate wall moldings, sylvan murals, stained glass galore, oversize sconces, plush banquettes and tables holding pink roses and matching lampshades. While I didn't sport a top hat, I was decked out in black tie, which is de rigueur on weekends at Maxim's.

Modeled after the original establishment on the Rue Royale in Paris, this belle époque icon of excess, in the Carlton House on Madison Avenue, is the ninth link in a worldwide chain owned by the designer Pierre Cardin. It opened in November 1985.

No detail has been spared, from the monogrammed crystal wineglasses to the strolling violinists. The food, which occasionally lives up to the surroundings, is somewhat of a throwback too. Patrick Pinon, who put the Garden City Hotel on Long Island on the gastronomic map, is saddled with a vast and overreaching menu of classic French cuisine that makes consistency difficult.

Maxim's was frighteningly expensive when it opened, but it recently eliminated its $65 prix fixe with many supplements and went to à la carte—a three-course dinner costs $50 to $60, including tax and tip but not drinks. An informal bistro downstairs, called L'Omnibus, under the same ownership, done in mirrored high-tech, serves salads, sandwiches and the like at more modest prices.

In Maxim's you might begin dinner with the chiffonnade of seafood, a nest of shredded salad greens cushioning morsels of lobster, langoustines, shrimp and scallops in a bland mayonnaise dressing. More appealing are the little langoustine tails poached inside cabbage leaves with a julienne of carrots, celery and truffles. The dainty and delicious packets are enhanced with a light vermouth-accented shellfish-stock sauce. Scallop terrine, an old Maxim's standard, is forgettable—grainy, underseasoned and accompanied by a commercial-tasting green mayonnaise.

Entrees follow the same hilly road. The standout is perfectly aged venison steak, tender and mild, in a highly reduced red-wine sauce that has a sweet edge from marinated grapes. Firm and fresh sweetbreads in mild mustard sauce also received nods of approval from all at the table. No matter what entree you choose, get a side order of the renowned Maxim's potatoes, ultra-thin disks pressed into a hot buttered pan, then baked until marvelously crisp.

Maxim's employs enough waiters to field a respectable college marching band. The more experienced ones—most of them French—know how to pamper the well-heeled types who come here; some, though, are bush leaguers in big-league uniforms. Take, for example, the young man who held an uncarved rack of lamb behind two diners at my table and barked, "Hey, look at this!"

The wine list, which is reasonably priced for a luxury restaurant, has something for every taste and most budgets.

The dishes are too numerous to describe in detail, so I will highlight some recommended preparations and point out the land mines. Gratinéed oysters, plump and saline, have a layer of creamy watercress lining the shell and a glaze of champagne-leavened hollandaise sauce—a delicate and pleasing combination. Scallops and langoustines in a tarragon-garnished aspic are as fresh as they are pretty. Too bad the aspic lacks flavor.

A dried-out plank of duck terrine should be passed over for crêpes océane, two thin crepe pockets concealing minced shellfish in a lustrous Américaine sauce.

As for the entrees, game and meat offer the best odds. Aside from venison, roast pheasant for two is lovely. The deboned meat is superbly juicy and tender, resting on a fan of sautéed apples napped with a Calvados cream sauce. Rolled saddle of lamb for two stuffed with a well-seasoned mixture of basil, cream, wild mushrooms and sweetbreads is another winner. Two expensive seafood dishes, however, are duds. A combination of lobster, langoustines and scallops comes in a milky, underseasoned cream sauce with truffles. Lobster meat served in the shell under a glazed frothy hollandaise sauce is curiously mushy and tough at the same time.

Desserts, like the restaurant itself, are big and glittery. Of ten sampled, those worth the calories are the unusual but good tarte Tatin—it's the shape of deep-dish apple pie—as well as minimally sweet yogurt and ricotta pie, profiteroles with excellent hot fudge sauce and fruit sorbets. Skip the leathery pear tart, a frozen raspberry mousse that tastes like chilled whipped cream, and dreadfully sweet crepes suzette.

The lights dim about 10 P.M.—the cue for violinists on a little stage to begin playing "La Vie en Rose." A mist of nostalgia envelops the room, drawing couples to the dance floor. They twist and twirl and laugh and flirt well past midnight.

◆ MAXWELL'S PLUM ◆

★ ★

1181 First Avenue, at 64th Street, 628-2100.

Atmosphere: Art Nouveau gone psychedelic—stained glass galore, carved beams, gas lanterns, stuffed animals, balloons and more. Front cafe less formal but more neighborly and loud; main dining room is a Technicolor high-style cafe.

Service: Earnest and cheerful; generally efficient.

Price range: Moderately expensive.

Credit cards: All major cards.

Hours: Lunch, Monday through Friday, noon to 5 P.M.; Saturday brunch, noon to 5 P.M., Sunday brunch, 11 A.M. to 5 P.M.; dinner, Sunday through Thursday 5 P.M. to midnight; Friday and Saturday until 1 A.M.

Reservations: Suggested.

In 1985 Maxwell's Plum, the rococo all-American restaurant on First Avenue at 64th Street, jettisoned its dated steak, burgers and eggs Benedict menu and leaped into the forefront of California cuisine by hiring two rising culinary stars from Spago in Los Angeles. The revolutionary menu—for Maxwell's, at least —caused quite a stir among longtime customers and lured a cadre of new ones. However nine months after the California duo arrived, they suddenly packed their surfboards and left, saying the restaurant was too large to suit their style of cooking.

Happily their capable replacement, Philippe Selaya-Mendez, has salvaged the best of his predecessors' creations while offering a number of more traditional dishes from the past—in short, a little for everyone. Spirited appetizers include meaty steamed mussels mariniére with a lovely saffron mayonnaise, and thin sheets of grilled tuna glistening under a soy-based vinaigrette. Nouvelle pizzas have remained, and they are buoyantly good, especially the one scattered with peppery pieces of chicken, artichoke and cilantro.

Other rousing dishes are the black pepper fettuccine tossed with smoked bacon and al dente asparagus tips (it can be had as an appetizer or entree) and pepper-speckled fettuccine tangled with bits of salty pancetta bacon, firm asparagus tips and crisp arugula in a light and flavorful veal stock and red wine sauce.

Among entrees seafood is one of the kitchen's strengths. Try the sautéed salmon steak, encrusted in cracked white pepper and set over a rousing coulis of roasted sweet red peppers. The white pepper imparts a sharp edge to the fish without masking its flavor. Grilled whole red snapper with a crackling skin in lime-butter sauce is another spirited offering.

For more traditional tastes, there are plenty of roasted and grilled steaks, chops and fish. When it is available, loin of venison in a glistening, heady stock with caramelized chestnuts is a standout—you would be hard-pressed to find such tender and succulent venison anywhere. Snow peas, broccoli and carrots round out the cast.

Desserts are a winning team as well. Try the lush raspberry tart garnished with crème anglaise, the first-rate chocolate hazelnut dacquoise or the extravagantly rich chocolate-raspberry terrine with two sauces.

Maxwell's Plum is a celebratory, good-time place. The youngish service staff, which does a commendable job, even seems to be having a good time in this unabashedly corny setting. If your spirits need a lift, Maxwell's just might be the prescription—and a tasty one at that.

✦ MERIDIES ✦

★ ★

87 Seventh Avenue South, between Bleecker and Christopher streets, 243-8000.

Atmosphere: Bright and clean glass-enclosed dining room and bar, with an outdoor cafe.

Service: Functional if unprofessional.

Price range: Moderate.

Credit cards: American Express.

Hours: Lunch, Monday through Friday, noon to 4:30 P.M., Saturday and Sunday, 11 A.M. to 4:30 P.M.; dinner, Monday through Friday, 6 P.M. to midnight; late-night supper, Friday and Saturday, midnight to 2 A.M.

Reservations: Recommended.

It is easy to miss the glass-enclosed restaurant with a shady little outdoor terrace along kaleidoscopic Seventh Avenue South in Greenwich Village, as I did for months until a friend raved about the spirited food there. Meridies, a reincarnation of the old Buffalo Roadhouse under the same ownership, is indeed one of the more engaging places to open downtown in recent years. It offers a bright and cross-cultural menu, part Italian grilled items, part contemporary American cooking and even a couscous tossed in for good measure. The driving force behind the kitchen is Susan Sugarman, who made her mark at Sabor, one of the best Cuban restaurants in town, then later moved on to Wise Maria and La Colonna before joining Meridies last August.

The new design is clean and spare, with a raised-platform dining area done in blond wood and glass on one side, a bar and scattered tables on the other, and a leafy outdoor cafe that is far enough from the avenue to preclude the need for a gas mask. Meridies tends to be a late spot, as customers stream into the dining room after 9 P.M. Young waiters and waitresses lack the fine points of service, such as replacing tableware and pouring wine, and the pace can be slow at peak hours.

Appetizers range from satisfying to excellent. At the top of the scale is a terrific puree of roast eggplant, smoky and fresh, flanked by strips of roast sweet red peppers; bresaola, the air-cured sheets of deep red beef glossed with olive oil, rosemary and juniper berries, is also invigorating. Gravlax was buttery but lacked dill flavor, and beef carpaccio set over tart field lettuce was first rate.

Little pizzas are as commonplace now as Villeroy & Boch china, and the thin-crusted versions served here can be delicious. The white pizza combines assertive Parmigiano-Reggiano, fontina Val d'Aosta and asiago; the red is crowned with overlapping thin slices of tomato dusted with oregano and rosemary. (Occasionally the red pizza is overpowered by a surfeit of herbs.) Finally there is a succulent and crisp-skinned confit of duck. In the pasta category, all dishes can be split as appetizers. I recommend the lustrous little gnocchi bathed in a vernal tomato-and-sage sauce. Cannelloni with two fillings—a lovely beet puree and a blend of basil and cheese—were tasty but served nearly cold.

There is hardly a loser among the entrees. Simple grilled dishes are executed with care, such as the pepper-flecked Cornish hen, large sweet shrimp served in the shell, and the florid slices of duck breast perfumed with clove and accompanied by sautéed apples and sweet potatoes. A baked fillet of salmon is perfectly done and delivered in an airy saffron-and-ginger sauce. Lobster pan roast is a particularly serendipitous creation, featuring a hacked-up 1½-pounder in the shell and set in a superb creamy bisquelike broth. A note of caution: It's nearly impossible to eat the lobster without splashing Rorschach-like patterns all over your shirt.

I did not find the nouvelle-style couscous here up to the level of other dishes—the vegetables were added at the end to keep them firm but at the expense of flavor. Two excellent meat dishes are the delectable baby lamb chops encased in a Parmesan cheese breading, and tender veal slices under a lovely and light tuna-and-caper sauce. Deep-fried soft-shell crabs were superb when I stole a bite from a friend's plate; when I ordered my own portion the next evening, however, the combination of fried crabs and deep-fried parsley turned out to be excessively oily.

Dessert highlights are a brittle, buttery, tulip-shaped cookie filled with blueberries, strawberries and mango; colorful fruit tarts, and an extra-thick and rich baked chocolate cream. A lime cream puff had good flavor but a day-old texture, and unripe strawberries were not rescued by a dousing of moscato wine.

✦ METROPOLIS ✦

★

444 Columbus Avenue, between 81st and 82nd streets, 769-4444.

Atmosphere: Grand interior with towering arched skylights, trees, main dining area in central courtyard and banquettes behind peripheral brick arches. Noise level tolerable.

Service: Inexperienced and awkward for the most part, with occasional long delays.

Price range: Moderate.

Credit cards: All major cards.

Hours: Dinner, Sunday through Thursday, 6 to 11:30 P.M.; Friday and Saturday until midnight; brunch, Saturday and Sunday, noon to 3 P.M.

Reservations: Suggested.

Metropolis has had its share of tribulations since opening in 1985 in the luxurious former quarters of the ill-fated DDL Foodshow on Columbus Avenue. Despite an impressive roster in the kitchen and out front, it never really got its act together. One thing is without doubt: the setting is a knockout—a towering ceiling with arched skylights, lofty trees, lots of brick and polished wood, and a handsome raw bar.

The menu follows the culinary curriculum that we are seeing all over town—a little pasta, a few modern pizzas, grilled meats and fish with herb sauces, and whimsical desserts. Appetizers, which change slightly from day to day along with the entrees, are the most memorable selections. Spicy potato fritters, redolent of coriander and turmeric, are lively starters with their two sauces: a blazing dip of yogurt, mint and jalapeño peppers, and a blend of avocado, cumin, yogurt and lime juice. Barbecued pork tostada, composed of shredded meat that is simmered with two kinds of chilies and served atop a toasted tortilla, is another good choice—especially with its pair of sauces, sour cream–cilantro and roast tomato, on the side. The most unusual appetizer, and probably the best, is called snails and dumplings. In this rendition, the snails are poached, then immersed in chicken stock along with some brandy, Pernod, fennel and scallions. The thick, bready dumplings are added to the broth, which is then glossed with some escargot butter.

Several of the pastas are overreaching disappointments. One exception is the shells with tapenade, a brassy blend of black olives and olive oil, garlic, anchovies, capers and lemon. Saffron-and-black-pepper fettuccine with a cream-and-oyster sauce has none of the attributes of the first two ingredients, so the result is bland.

The kitchen rolls out a mean pizza dough, puffed, light and nicely burnished around the edges. One of the more enlivening toppings is piquant chorizo and sun-dried tomatoes; others are tomato sauce, roast garlic, mozzarella and basil, and the clam and calamari with tomato sauce.

Choosing a wine to go with the potpourri of flavors on this menu is a challenge, but the wine list reflects intelligence and forethought, with interesting selections across the board and a few gems.

The restaurant had some serious problems trying to coordinate its green young service staff, who are long on smiles and short on basic skills.

Grilled and rotisserie foods are generally safe bets. Roast chicken with a zippy sauce combining tomatoes, chicken stock, roast sesame seeds, chili ancho and yogurt can be first-rate if they don't overcook it. Roast tenderloin of beef with béarnaise sauce, and roast leg of lamb with tarragon mayonnaise are blissful couples. Grilled fish, such as the salmon with lime and coriander, is reliable too.

Metropolis is a card-carrying member of the nostalgia dessert club, which promotes such fond memories as hot fudge sundaes, banana cream pies and butterscotch sundaes with sautéed apples —all are as soothing as a Norman Rockwell painting. Crème brûlée, however, is merely loose flan with some caramelized sugar on top, and old-fashioned devil's food cake with Italian meringue icing is humdrum. If they have it, go with the puckering lemon tart or the smooth and intense strawberry sorbetto.

✦ MITSUKOSHI ✦

★ ★ ★

461 Park Avenue, at 57th Street, 935-6444.

Atmosphere: Comfortable, though overly lit; clean and colorful sushi bar; tatami rooms Westernized for comfort.

Service: Charming and well meaning if occasionally hampered by overburdened kitchen.

Price range: Moderately expensive.

Credit cards: All major cards.

Hours: Lunch, Monday through Saturday, noon to 2 P.M.; dinner, Monday through Saturday, 6 to 10 P.M. Closed Sunday.

Reservations: Recommended.

Mitsukoshi, the polished restaurant below a porcelain and pottery shop of the same name at Park Avenue and 57th Street, attracts a standing-room-only lunch business on weekdays and a respectable evening trade. The seafood, both raw and cooked, is of the highest quality, and you pay dearly for it.

There are three seating areas: the rather garish, over-illuminated main dining room with faded yellow-gold wallpaper, the sushi bar and the private tatami rooms. Don't worry, these tatami rooms are Westernized with a sunken well under the table so you can dangle your feet below. In the main dining room, traditionally garbed waitresses with permanently etched smiles do their best to please, although understaffing seems to be a problem that causes delays. I left an unusually generous tip at lunch when our waitress saved me from embarrassment in front of friends. In a foolhardy show of bravado, I ordered something called natto sengyo ae, having no idea what it was. "Maybe you not like fish guts so much?" she warned discreetly.

There are plenty of other dishes that I do like, starting with the long list of appetizers. Salmon caviar wrapped in a seaweed sheet with rice and grated white Oriental radish (ikura oroshi) is particularly good; the large golden eggs are bright and firm so that they pop when chewed. Slices of resilient fish cake with marinated cucumbers (itawasa) are delightfully evocative of the sea. They are complemented nicely by a wasabi-stoked soy sauce.

For those who seek a really fresh oceanic sensation, the squid or whitefish sashimi swathed with sea-green urchin roe is worth trying. One of my dining companions remarked, "It's like lying in the surf facedown."

Several appetizers fall short of the mark. Deep-fried tofu cubes with a scallion-and-ginger soy sauce (agedashi tofu) are soggy and bland. Yamakake, a crock holding grated Japanese potato over cubes of tuna sashimi, is a peculiar preparation. The potato tastes like warm egg whites, and all it does is blunt the flavor of the tuna.

Many of the entrees are expanded versions of appetizers. Among the better ones are a light and brittle tempura featuring vegetables, shrimp, whitefish and a tangy ginger dipping sauce (there also is a succulent if expensive lobster-tail tempura for $17). Grilled fish of the day—usually red snapper or salmon—is perfectly charred and moist. Grilled filet mignon (filet kuwayaki) is top quality and cooked to order. Shabu shabu, a caldron of simmering broth heated at the table in which diners cook their own food, is as diverting as it is delicious. The colorful selection includes lustrous thin slices of lean beef, Chinese cabbage, mushrooms, tofu, scallions, carrots and rice pasta.

Excellent sushi and sashimi are available in the dining room and tatami rooms, but it is more fun to have them at the sushi bar. Places should be reserved in advance. The cozy, aseptic bar has ten seats facing three chefs. The basic sushi platter is a vivid palette of contrasting tastes and textures. The plate holds about six tuna rolls wrapped in dried seaweed sheets and rice, two tuna sashimi, one salmon, one salmon caviar roll, a fluke, a large shrimp and two triangles of sweet Japanese omelet, which should be eaten last as dessert.

The other selections are dictated by market availability. Lightly smoked eel, which is almost always available, is a real delicacy, as is the luxurious quail egg and sea urchin combination. The watery octopus is disappointing. One of the most extraordinary sashimis is baby Gulf shrimp that are about two inches long and wondrously sweet.

During our last visit to the sushi bar we ate nearly all we could and, under the firmament of several sakes, challenged the chef to create something special for the road. His eyes lit impishly as he popped something into the oven. Minutes later, he handed us a seaweed sheet rolled like an ice cream cone filled with rice, scallion flowers, cucumber and a strip of tasty firm-textured fish. When we failed to identify the fish, the chef held up his arms in muscleman fashion and declared with a grin, "Fluke muscle! Thank you for coming."

✦ MONTRACHET ✦

★ ★ ★

239 West Broadway, 219-2777.

Atmosphere: Casually spare dining room with soft lighting and rust-pink banquettes.

Service: Friendly and efficient.

Price range: Expensive.

Credit cards: American Express.

Hours: Dinner, Monday through Saturday, 6 to 11 P.M.

Reservations: Suggested.

Montrachet is a minimalist, low-key establishment housed in one of those high-ceilinged downtown industrial spaces. It has been tastefully done with a polished mahogany-and-onyx bar, pale green walls, pinkish-rust banquettes and soothing lighting. It blasted off the starting block in early 1985, fueled largely on the talents of David Bouley, a young French-trained American who has since left to open his own establishment.

The current kitchen crew, headed by Brian Whitmer, has managed to uphold the early high standards while at the same time sticking to the light Provençale-style established by Mr. Bouley. The only significant difference is prices, which have risen significantly since Montrachet received its three-star rating. The $16 prix fixe special dinner is now $27. It begins with a deliciously smoky eggplant and roasted red pepper terrine, followed by savory roast duck with ginger and a first-rate crème brûlée. The more expensive prix fixe, for $45, begins with either bass fillet in an herbaceous olive oil–based sauce or a superb salad of roast pigeon and baby corn, followed by loin of veal and a luxurious warm soufflé (flavors change daily).

Another superior à la carte starter is a small circular tart topped with warm fresh oysters and bits of salty pancetta. Fresh New York State foie gras is deftly prepared, sautéed till buttery pink in the center and flanked by sweet glazed shallots.

At most of the restaurants I visit, the bread is not worth writing about; most of it comes from the same three or four commercial sources. Montrachet's rolls, which also come from the outside, are exceptional—thick-crusted, earthy and with a little crunchy "lid" giving them the appearance of tiny soup terrines.

The intelligent and generally moderately priced wine list has something for everyone and complements the food nicely.

Drew Nieporent, the owner, a former captain at La Grenouille, Le Périgord and several other French restaurants in town, sets a rather frenetic pace at this often packed establishment. His waiters scurry around the room in black shirts, pants and ties looking like a team of cat burglars. They usually keep on top of things, although a good number of diners have complained about abrupt treatment or having to cool their heels for half an hour or more waiting for a table when they arrive on time for a reservation.

The entree list is limited but amply diverse, carrying about ten items, including daily specials. A standout on the permanent roster is the fillet of red snapper, in which the fish is broiled until the skin is parchment crisp, while the meat remains moist and flaky. It is presented with sweet roasted peppers and lemon. Another recommended seafood selection is sea bass in a zesty tomato vinaigrette. On the meat side, roasted kidneys in a fresh and faintly fruity Beaujolais sauce is an ingenious combination, and rare-roasted baby pheasant with orzo and olives is a lovely match.

Desserts maintain the kitchen's high standards. The most extravagant is the duo of hot soufflés in various flavors—raspberry and pear with chocolate, or maybe apple and strawberry —inflated disks bursting with fruit essence, dusted with sugar and draped in multicolored fresh fruit purees. Crème brûlée is the real thing, with a glassy caramelized crust enclosing a dense, eggy custard.

A slice of layered hazelnut ice cream topped with Grand Marnier truffles and a coffee sauce is beyond resistance, while tarte tatin of pear and apple, with a thin, buttery crust and molten caramel sauce, melts in the mouth. If you are too impatient to let it cool, Calvados sorbet comes to the rescue.

✦ MORGANS BAR ✦

★

237 Madison Avenue, between 37th and 38th streets, 689-7401.

Atmosphere: High-tech, all-gray basement restaurant with cozy banquettes and low lighting.

Service: Casual and at times laggard.

Price range: Moderate.

Credit cards: American Express and Diners Club.

Hours: Lunch, Monday through Friday, 11:45 A.M. to 3 P.M.; dinner, Monday through Friday, 4 P.M. to 12:30 A.M. Closed Saturday and Sunday.

Reservations: Accepted.

Larry Forgione, the celebrated chef-owner of An American Place, has taken on this eclectic little grillery in the celebrity-studded Morgans Hotel on Madison Avenue called Morgans Bar

186

but never really managed to make much of a mark there, partly because of extended difficulties getting a liquor license from the city. Moreover, while some of the food is inventive and colorful, the overall effect is sort of underwhelming.

The fifty-seat dining room is in a windowless, gray-toned, high-tech, low-lit basement. The minimalist decor includes overhead pinpoint lights and cozy little banquettes set along the walls in a jagged pattern. This may be fine for romantic couples, but a quartet of bankers discussing interest rates might feel a bit cramped. A few larger banquettes are up for grabs near the entrance.

The all-day menu, which reflects Mr. Forgione's commitment to American provender, gets an A for concept. One part contains what are described as "finger foods," intriguing little appetizers that can be picked up and eaten with the hands. The other section features fancy salads, oven-baked sandwiches, grilled and fried entrees and desserts.

Sharing several tidbits with fellow diners before the entrees is an appealing way to start. The finger foods, in fact, are the highlight of the menu. Among the best are Buffalo-style chicken wings, a heaping portion of wings rubbed with a fiery blend of ground spices and served with a first-rate blue cheese dip. Bite-size nuggets of buffalo-meat sausage, lean and mildly spicy, are tasty when dipped in a mild mustard-cream sauce. One of the more unusual preparations features corn pancakes filled with strands of shredded pork and toasted corn kernels, garnished with sour cream and a tame salsa. The smoky corn and the moist pork make for a deliciously earthy combination.

Among the special salads, choose the grilled duck and red peppers resting in a pretty nest of mixed greens. The spicy fried chicken and country ham salad is a letdown: spiceless chicken, ham and greens in a listless vinaigrette.

Oven-baked sandwiches are a good idea for this type of restaurant. Lamentably, those at Morgans look like something a teenager would slap together from leftovers during commercials for the late show. Roast lamb with garlic mayonnaise and sweet peppers was a sorry sight—the meat was leathery and the mayonnaise had turned sour from sitting unrefrigerated. A salty glazed brisket sandwich with slaw and tired french fries was no better. Try instead the old-fashioned New England lobster roll, which is a ballpark hot-dog bun chock-full of fresh lobster swathed in a creamy tartar sauce.

Desserts, which make one nostalgic for the Eisenhower administration, are unqualified winners. Three cheers for a chef who jettisons chocolate mousse for an old-fashioned chocolate pudding with whipped cream. And the strawberry shortcake is a paradigm of the art—real baking-powder biscuits, gobs of unsweetened whipped cream and luscious ripe berries. Then there are fudge brownies, banana Betty and apple pandowdy, all uncompromisingly outdated and fun.

◆ NANNI IL VALLETTO ◆

★ ★

133 East 61st Street, 838-3939.

Atmosphere: Plush quarters that fairly glow with money and power; cavernous main dining room with high ceiling, oversize mirrors and comfortable banquettes.

Service: Generally excellent and intelligent, although some first-time visitors report receiving perfunctory treatment.

Price range: Expensive.

Credit cards: American Express, Carte Blanche, and Diners Club.

Hours: Lunch, Monday through Friday, noon to 3 P.M.; dinner, Monday through Saturday, 5:30 P.M. to midnight. Closed Sunday.

Reservations: Necessary.

188

Nanni il Valetto, the glamorous younger sibling of the home-spun Nanni on East 46th Street, is one of the more splendiferous —and expensive—Italian restaurants in town. Every evening a soigné parade of perennially tanned gentlemen in dark European-cut suits escorted by polished and bejeweled ladies glide past the little horseshoe-shaped bar in front, where they are greeted warmly by the staff. Luigi Nanni himself, a gruff yet endearing host, may come to the table, dismiss the menu with a wave of the hand, and suggest an assortment of the daily specials.

If you happen to be one of these lucky and pampered few, you could be in for a truly serendipitous evening of food and wine fit for a Venetian prince. If you are an unknown, however, it's possible to feel like a commoner at the royal banquet.

One privilege of entering the regal circle is being seated at the cozy dining area between the bar and the grandiose main salon. The larger dining room isn't exactly second-rate, though; it is an imposing space, with a soaring ceiling, gold-striped wallpaper, towering mirrors, opulent flowers and comfortable banquettes. Service ranges from the superb to the so-so, depending on one's status.

The daily specials at Nanni il Valletto are so numerous and intriguing that it is often wise to go with the captain's suggestions. You might begin with giant and meaty New Zealand mussels floating in a high tide of oceanic broth, rilled shards of fresh and barely chewy cuttlefish glossed with olive oil, or delicious lightly fried ovals of eggplant rolled around spinach and ricotta cheese, then baked under a molten layer of mozzarella and tomato sauce.

Another must special—they always have it but you have to ask—is the irresistible bruschetta, a garlicky slab of Italian bread slathered with a vibrant spread of tomatoes, basil and herbs.

The cold appetizer assortment of marinated and stuffed vegetables is preferable to the hot version. The latter carried rubbery little scallops and slightly dry shrimp bathed in white wine, fish stock and shallots; next to them were baked clams on the half shell under a raw and acidic blanket of chopped peppers and pimientos.

The kitchen at Nanni il Valletto is capable of turning out some spectacular pastas. Mr. Nanni's creations, many of which are assembled à la minute at tableside, are light, herbaceous and exquisitely fresh. A superb example is his al dente bow-tie pasta tossed with a simple but explosively flavorful mélange of diced tomatoes, fresh basil, zucchini and eggplant (a special). Other memorable selections were pappardelle in a rich and mellow oxtail sauce and thin spaghetti with minced shrimp, clams and fresh herbs. Seafood risotto, another special, generous with morsels of shrimp and cuttlefish, was perfectly textured and delightfully peppery. Only a trenette in pesto sauce came up short on the flavor meter.

The regular entrees list combined with the copious specials has more twists and turns than a Venetian canal. Branzino, that brawny fish from the North Atlantic that is similar to bass in texture, was prepared in the best Italian fashion on two occasions—simply roasted with a light perfume of garlic and olive oil or with a sheen of butter sauce.

Some of the other entrees do not glow as brightly. Chicken scarpariello, sautéed nuggets of chicken breast in a salt-edged garlic and wine sauce, can be dry; moreover, the $26 tab for such a modest preparation is a shocker. When I sampled the entrecote alla pizzaiola, it was cooked beyond medium despite a request for medium rare, and the sauce lacked zip. The best veal dish sampled was prepared Milanese-style, featuring a pounded and tender cutlet that was breaded and golden fried. Osso buco, long simmered and richly flavored, also excels.

Desserts are appropriately majestic looking in their multitiered chariot, and most are good. My preference is the brassy warm zabaglione with fresh fruit, and the exceptional Marsala-soaked tirami sù.

✦ THE NICE RESTAURANT ✦

★ ★

35 East Broadway, 406-9776, 406-9510.

Atmosphere: Expansive, bright and festive. Large circular tables and comfortable bent-cane chairs. Noise level moderate.

Service: Good-natured and generally efficient waiters. Some have difficulty speaking English.

Price range: Moderate.

Credit cards: American Express.

Hours: Lunch and dinner, daily, 8 A.M. to 11 P.M.

Reservations: Suggested.

The Nice Restaurant is one of those airy, animated and overly adorned places that specialize in Hong Kong–style Cantonese cuisine. That is where all generalizations end, however, for some of the food is superb. The expansive upstairs dining room exudes a festive air with its shiny gold columns, bright lighting and tables full of voracious families. The downstairs is used for overflow and parties.

The waiters, a small army of them, are a good-natured and efficient lot, though some have real difficulty with English. The Nice Restaurant serves only beer and soft drinks, but patrons are allowed to bring their own wine. Through trial and error I have arrived at a list of recommendations that would constitute a memorable feast.

191

A good way to start is with the shrimp-paste rolls. They are not on the printed menu but in a little photo album that comes with it. The dishes are not identified, so you have to go on faith. On the bottom of page four is a picture of white eggroll-size cylinders of shrimp paste that have been wrapped in translucent rice paper and lightly deep-fried. The crackling wrapper and mild-flavored shrimp are wonderful when dipped in one of the several sauces provided—sweet, hot, and hotter. A soup pictured on the first page filled with shredded crab and dried scallops is rich with shellfish flavor but far too gelatinous for my taste.

Another shellfish recommendation from the photos is deep-fried prawns. Like all fried dishes sampled, these tasty little balls are skillfully prepared in clean oil, leaving them puffed and light. Both the shrimp-paste rolls and the prawns are engagingly presented with carved turnip flowers and cucumber fans.

The roast suckling pig is one of the best in town. Its lacquered skin is lined with a thin layer of fat and rests upon slices of succulent and moist pork. The sweet and salty meat lies upon a base of sweet-cooked soybeans that are so good you can eat them like candy. Roast duck prepared in a similar manner is equally delicious. Bypass the insipid steamed fish and another humdrum dish called filet mignon on skewers.

I have saved the best three exhibits for last. First is the traditional Cantonese dish of minced squab in lettuce. This rendition is more complex in flavor than most, combining moist cubes of squab, diced salty Chinese bacon and sour preserved vegetables. Diners wrap the ingredients in lettuce, choose from several sauces, and eat it like a taco. One of the most intriguing preparations is called soyed squab in pot, in which a whole squab, head and all, is cut up and placed in a small ceramic crock and baked in a blend of soy sauce, wine, vinegar, sugar and spices. When the lid is removed at the table, puffs of perfumed steam rise to reveal the exquisite meat, which is imbued with the heady marinade.

Finally, there is salt-baked chicken, an incredibly moist and velvety preparation that will disappear instantly at your table because of its universal appeal.

Don't miss the dessert of coconut-tapioca-melon soup (last photo in the album), a cool and refreshing finale to such a varied meal. If you want the soup served in an elaborately carved melon as presented in the photograph, it is necessary to make a request a day in advance. It is a fitting punctuation mark to a meal that strays from the familiar path followed in New York.

◆ THE ODEON ◆

★

145 West Broadway, at Thomas Street, 233-0507.

Atmosphere: Art Deco cafeteria with close tables, and rattling noise level in the evening.

Service: Young and congenial staff tries hard to keep up with the fervid pace at night; lunch service better.

Price range: Moderately expensive.

Credit cards: American Express and Visa.

Hours: Lunch, Monday through Friday, noon to 3 P.M.; dinner, daily, 7 P.M. to 12:30 A.M.; light supper, Sunday through Thursday, 1 to 2:30 A.M., Friday and Saturday, 1 to 3 A.M.; Sunday brunch, noon to 3:30 P.M.

Reservations: Recommended.

This Art Deco former cafeteria, one of the pioneer restaurants in TriBeCa in the early 1980s, has a long bar against one wall, a tile floor and bistro tables crammed in tighter than cars in a midtown parking lot. On busy evenings, which is to say all the time, the din is loud enough to wilt your salad. One soon notices, though, that some of the crackling artistic energy that once made this scene so diverting is fading as the clientele metamorphoses from brash bohemian cool to corporate gray.

That is beyond the restaurant's control; the neighborhood has been discovered. What is within its control, however, is the food, which, like the crowd, has lost some of its vibrancy.

Overcooking and underseasoning drag down a number of potentially appealing dishes, which may indicate an overworked kitchen. Consider the pan-roasted loin of lamb in a walnut-butter sauce, with spinach and golden sautéed potatoes. At a recent dinner, everything was tasty except the medallions of lamb, which were tough and dry. The same fault marred the chicken breast with fresh ginger and summer vegetables. And at lunch a gray paillard of veal resembled the steam-table meat substance served at my college cafeteria.

Such strikeouts aside, The Odeon still turns out a host of appealing preparations that make it worth recommending. Two of the best entrees are homemade fettuccine with Gulf shrimp and a baked red snapper in saffron broth with artichoke hearts. The pasta sauce is assertive with shellfish flavor and laced with sweet red, green and yellow peppers; the moist, meaty snapper is delicious in its bright herby broth. Of the remaining fish dishes sampled, rare-grilled tuna bolstered with a zippy red pepper–and–jalapeño vinaigrette is vivid and fresh; poached salmon in a green pepper sauce garnished with salmon caviar is a winner also—the combination of hot and salty play off each other nicely. Poached sole under a pretty blanket of fanned cucumbers was mealy and old the last time I had it.

New York strip steak, well seared and flavorful, is the best meat entree, but the french fries, which were once first-rate, are now limp.

The affable young waiters and waitresses wearing floor-length bistro aprons do as well as they can under the clamorous circumstances. (Service at lunch is better.) The Odeon has a limited but intelligently chosen wine list that complements the food.

Appetizers have a higher percentage of winners than entrees. Crab cakes are excellent—brittle outside, meaty and faintly peppery inside. Another good choice is chilled Gulf shrimp framed in salsa mayonnaise exploding with fresh coriander.

The meal can end on a high note if you opt for the terrific chocolate terrine with a hint of orange, the poached white peach in Sauternes sabayon or the puckering lemon tart.

✦ OMEN ✦

★ ★

113 Thompson Street, between Prince and Spring streets, 925-8923.

Atmosphere: Comfortable brick and wood multilevel dining rooms suggesting a Japanese country inn.

Service: Gracious and sincere, if occasionally slow on busy evenings.

Price range: Moderate.

Credit cards: American Express and Diners Club.

Hours: Dinner, Tuesday through Sunday, 5:30 to 11:30 P.M.; Saturday and Sunday brunch, 11:30 A.M. to 4:30 P.M. Closed Monday.

Reservations: Suggested.

The casual charm of a restaurant in rural Japan is evoked by the brick-and-wood interior of Omen, a local favorite in SoHo that continues to turn out high-quality, distinctive fare at reasonable prices. In contrast to the sleek and minimalist uptown sushi bars, which are designed for speed, Omen is a place for winding down with a sake and a steaming bowl of fish soup. Oriental lanterns hang from a timbered ceiling, spacey electronic music pulses from above, and striking calligraphy adorns the walls.

The restaurant's signature dish, called Omen, is a beguiling soup made by steeping seaweed in chicken stock and spiking it with soy sauce, sake and mirin, a sweet and syrupy rice wine. It is accompanied by a pretty ceramic plate holding a colorful array of partially cooked vegetables including white radish (also known as daikon), lotus root, broccoli, carrots and burdock root, as well as raw spinach and scallions. All of the vegetables are plunged into the broth followed by the long, white wheat-flour noodles called udon. The crowning touch is a sprinkling of crunchy sesame seeds.

You can order from among five-course prix fixe menus or choose à la carte. Although the obliging young waiters and waitresses are a little shaky in the English department, they make a valiant effort to explain unusual dishes. It is always prudent to ask questions in Japanese restaurants, for they are known to offer innocent-sounding dishes that turn out to resemble the sort of creatures that wash up at the seashore and cause children to squeal. The staff is generally efficient; however on crowded evenings the pace slows down considerably.

Surprisingly, sushi is not served at Omen, yet a wide range of uncompromisingly fresh sashimi is available. A good sampling is the assorted sashimi plate, which holds pieces of florid and smooth tuna and cool thin slices of octopus, as well as squid, giant clam and fluke. One of the more intriguing preparations is raw tuna with Japanese yam. Deep-red tuna cubes rest in a pool of soy sauce and are covered with matchstick strips of Japanese yam and crowned with a quail egg. The neutral-tasting yam has a texture that suggests egg whites. The combination is a singular sensation that took me two samplings to begin to appreciate.

Two other uncommon preparations worth trying are the avocado and shrimp with miso sauce, and the spinach and scallops with peanut cream. The former consists of a ripe avocado half stuffed with marinated cucumber slices and topped with whole shrimp. The savory sauce combines egg yolks, rice vinegar, salt and sugar. The second dish, one of my favorites, features scallops and blanched spinach swathed in a peanut-cream sauce tinged with mirin, sake and soy sauce.

Other winning choices are the blanched spinach with meaty shiitake mushrooms and sesame seeds (goma-ae), which has a delightful contrast of textures; spinach salad sprinkled with briny flaked bonito (oshitashi); crunchy Chinese bok choy cooked in a strong fish broth flavored with sake (nappa-ni), and scallops tossed in a blend of lemon juice, sake, soy sauce and sugar, garnished with snow peas. The tempura dishes—shrimp and vegetable, vegetable only, and tofu—are unremarkable.

The three chicken dishes on the menu are superior—all are variations of boned roast meat marinated in a sweetish soy sauce cut with sake and mirin. The sansho chicken is extraordinarily buttery and moist, with what tastes like hints of orange (I was told later that is the effect of sake). It comes with hair-thin strands of carrot and white radish. The others are chicken with grated radish (tori-mizore) and cold chicken with cucumber (tori-tosazu).

Japanese beer is the best accompaniment to these salty flavors. A nice way to clear the palate at the end is with some ice cream: the dry-edged green tea or the creamy red bean.

While Omen's unconventional dishes contribute to its appeal, so too does the staff's easygoing, unreverential approach to Japanese dining. It's worth the trip.

✦ ORSO ✦

★ ★

322 West 46th Street, 489-7212.

Atmosphere: Bright, sunny and casual setting with open kitchen and skylight.

Service: Good natured and generally efficient.

Price range: Moderately expensive.

Credit cards: MasterCard, Visa.

Hours: Lunch, dinner and late supper, Monday, Tuesday, Thursday and Friday, noon to 11:30 P.M.; Wednesday and Saturday, 11:30 A.M. to 11:30 P.M. Closed Sunday in July and August.

Reservations: Necessary.

The Broadway theater district is not exactly a shining chorus line of quality restaurants. Theatergoers face depressing odds when trying to choose a dining spot at random—it's sort of like trying to pick a play solely by looking at marquees. One place that I often recommend with confidence is Orso, the sunny and casual Italian restaurant on West 46th Street specializing in moderately priced pastas, individual pizzas and grilled entrees.

Orso is owned by Joe Allen, whose namesake restaurant is next door, and is managed by family members. The front room has a small bar flanked by several tables and followed by a step-down main dining room under an arching skylight that makes for a cheerful setting at lunch. The restaurant is done in clean tans and oak, sporting celebrity photos on the walls and an open tile-and-steel kitchen in the rear. In recent years Orso has become somewhat of a youthful Sardi's as theater people mingle with agents and journalists over salads and thin-crusted pizzas. Even the comely and generally efficient young service staff exudes a certain dramatic flair, although not in an overbearing way.

Orso's menu is wisely limited in size and emphasizes freshness over elaborate preparation. Consider, for example, the individual-size pizzas. They have thin, yeasty crusts and vibrant toppings: fennel-perfumed sausage, mozzarella, garlic and tomato; red peppers, onion, garlic and tomato; and basil, Parmesan, mozzarella and tomato. My favorite is the pizza bread, shards of thin, brittle pizza dough infused with garlic and olive oil. It is absolutely addictive.

One of the better appetizers is delicious salt-crusted grilled shrimp served in the shell—the sweet meat is heady with smoky nuances. Other good options are bresaola, the air-dried beef, paired with radicchio salad and asiago cheese, and a tender slab of cold veal with a caper-speckled puree of tuna sauce. On the debit side are undercooked grilled eggplant and overmarinated raw salmon with green peppercorn sauce.

A well-chosen all-Italian wine list has some good bottles in the $13-to-$18 range that marry well with this style of food.

The chef makes sprightly à la minute sauces for pastas, and virtually all are satisfying. Among the best are spaghetti with mussels and clams; fusilli with broccoli di rape, chopped tomatoes and pecorino cheese, and tagliarini alla puttanesca that is lusty with anchovies and black olives.

Meat entrees fare better than seafood. Succulent little grilled quail with a brandy-laced stock sauce were stellar; so, too, was a lovely rolled veal tenderloin stuffed with spinach and mildly tart goat cheese. The only real flop among meat dishes is the desiccated and tasteless roast pork chop with leeks and currants.

Desserts range from a first-rate tortoni to a ripe blueberry tart and the traditional almond biscuits with sweet dessert wine. A pear ice was pallid; far superior was an unusual dessert combining sweetened cream of ricotta with fresh whole cherries.

If Orso continues to maintain this admirable pace, it can be assured a long and enthusiastic run.

✦ OYSTER BAR AND RESTAURANT ✦
IN GRAND CENTRAL STATION

★ ★

Grand Central Station, lower level, 42nd Street and Vanderbilt Avenue, 490-6650.

Atmosphere: The sprawling main dining room with its vaulted ceiling has a grandeur reminiscent of the heyday of rail travel. The wood-paneled tavern room is more sedate. Dress is informal.

Service: Variable. Efficient overall if not terribly professional. Off-peak dining times are better and more relaxed.

Price range: Moderate.

Credit cards: All major cards.

Hours: Lunch and dinner, Monday through Friday, 11:30 A.M. to 9:30 P.M. Closed Saturday and Sunday.

Reservations: Recommended.

The grand vaulted ceiling with its rim of twinkling lights is as impressive today as it was back when trains were clean and rail schedules were more than ballpark estimates. And unlike the commuter trains that thunder beneath the dining room, the Oyster Bar has upheld its quality over the years, so that it is still one of the best spots in town for uncompromisingly fresh seafood.

The main dining room, which has both counter service and tables, is a dish-clattering, cacophonous and fast-paced dining arena that exudes a sense of urgency. If you seek a more soothing setting, try the handsome tavern with its wood-paneled walls, old ship prints, softer lighting and diminished noise level.

Trying to describe the enormous menu in a short review is like reducing a whale to a fish stick. As a rule, stay with simple preparations and savor the seafood's freshness; sauces are not the kitchen's métier.

Oyster fans invariably begin with a sampling from the dozen exquisitely fresh varieties posted. All those listed are not always on hand, although I have sampled as many as nine types on one plate. Every one is as fresh as an ocean mist and distinctly flavorful. When the kitchen tries to gussy up oysters with cream sauces and the like, the results can be dispiriting.

Of the two clam chowders, the milky and chunky New England version has more shellfish character than the timidly seasoned red-broth Manhattan. Smoked salmon, which is flavored over fruit wood on the premises, is too intense for my taste.

One of the famous old preparations at the Oyster Bar is pan-roasted shellfish: either oysters, sea scallops, shrimp, lobster, clams, mussels or the works. Every one is terrific. If you sit at the counter near the white-frocked cooks, you can watch these remarkable stewlike dishes being prepared.

The Oyster Bar wine list is renowned for its selection of California whites, more than one hundred, at reasonable prices. Fewer than half a dozen token reds are available. The service staff is enormous, and your treatment varies greatly, depending on the luck of the draw.

Of the house specialties, bouillabaisse is a standout. Its herby tomato-based broth, generous with saffron, is filled above tide level with mussels, shrimp, lobster, clams and whitefish. Also recommended are the meaty golden-fried crab cakes accompanied by good thin french fries. The long list of mostly broiled fish fillets changes daily according to availability, and they are consistently pleasing.

Desserts are surprisingly good. The hefty deep-dish apple pie with an earthy whole-wheat crust is homey and satisfying. Strawberry galette features a layer of brittle puff pastry garnished with almonds, fresh whipped cream and ripe strawberries. The only losers are a gelatinous blueberry pie and commercial-tasting raspberry cheesecake.

I hope the Oyster Bar continues chugging along the tracks for another seventy years. For those who seek the finest fish, it is still one of the straightest routes to the sea.

✦ OZEKI ✦

★

158 West 23rd Street, 620-9131.

Atmosphere: Low-key Japanese ambiance with a medium-size sushi bar, small yakitori bar and two small dining rooms with colorful Japanese prints on the walls. The ventilation needs improvement.

Service: Language can be a problem at times, especially at the sushi bar. Service is occasionally slow.

Price range: Moderate.

Credit cards: All major cards.

Hours: Lunch, Monday through Friday, noon to 2:30 P.M.; dinner, Monday through Thursday, 6 to 11 P.M., Friday, 6 to 11:30 P.M., Sunday, 5 to 10:30 P.M. Closed Saturday.

Reservations: Usually not necessary.

If there is a Japanese equivalent to the new American grilleries that have become ubiquitous around town, it is the yakitori bar, in which portions of seafood and meat are brushed with special sauces and seared over charcoal. At Ozeki, a handsome little restaurant on West 23rd Street, this technique is performed with considerable skill.

Near the entrance to the restaurant is a sushi bar refulgent with glistening fresh fish ranging from blood-red tuna to silvery mackerel. Next to it is a smaller yakitori bar, where a chef tends little hibachi grills. A wooden partition holding potted plants separates the larger back area into two dining rooms. Colorful Oriental prints add to the pleasing, understated environment. One area in which improvement could be made is ventilation; cooking fumes sometimes fill the restaurant.

Ozeki is a good spot for a light lunch—that is, if you are not on a tight schedule. Service in the back room runs hot and cold. It is much better in the evening; at lunch the sushi bar, with sometimes only one chef on duty, can be exasperatingly slow.

Try several tidbits from the yakitori menu for starters: ikanosugatayaki, which is an eight-syllable way to say grilled squid, and chicken yakitori, bite-size pieces of chicken coated with teriyaki sauce and grilled on skewers with onions. The chalk-white fresh squid, about four inches long, is perfectly cooked, sliced into a half-dozen rings, and reassembled on the plate with the blackened tentacles set on the side as garnish. The delicious, resilient rings come with a zesty soy-ginger sauce. The less exotic chicken nuggets, glazed in a reddish orange sauce, are tender, moist and sweet.

Two other noteworthy selections from the yakitori grill are the smoky peeled eggplant, set in a light broth perfumed with fresh ginger, and the "surprise" grilled item, described on the menu as "For Your Stamina." This, of course, could not be passed up, even at the risk of being served some bizarre-looking creature from the murky waters under docks. It turns out to be grilled chicken gizzards, chicken livers, chicken hearts, mushrooms and green peppers, all coated in a light, semisweet glaze. The hearts and livers are the most tender and enjoyable; the gizzards I find bland and cartilaginous.

Among the more conventional fare, beef negimaki—thin slices of grilled beef rolled around scallions—is recommended over the mushy pork loin in ginger sauce. Many of the soups are richly flavored and complex. Only the tempura soba, a vegetable broth filled with tempura shrimp and vegetables, is ill conceived —the crackling tempura crust inevitably gets soggy and slides off. We moved on to sample the shrimp tempura, a generous lineup that is billowy, golden and well drained.

The dinner menu is a slightly expanded version of the lunch card. A good way to begin is with the succulent little pan-fried pork dumplings that are so moist they pop when you bite into them. Airy, golden-fried tofu squares with a soy-based tempura sauce also are good starters, preferable to the soggy cold tofu cubes on ice. One of the better raw-fish appetizers is sunomono, which includes shrimp and strips of assorted fish in a shallow pool of vinegar-and-sesame-oil sauce garnished with lettuce and crunchy sesame seeds. The assorted sashimi and sushi plates are fresh and oceanic if prosaically presented.

Language barriers prevent a give-and-take between customer and chef, which is so important at sushi bars.

No one goes to Japanese restaurants expecting a fantasyland of desserts. Ginger ice cream is as whimsical as they get. Skip the green-tea and red-bean ice cream, which were crystallized on three occasions.

The yakitori bar offers a light and tasty cooking style especially appropriate for summer. Let's hope that more Japanese restaurants stoke up their grills and follow suit.

◆ PALIO ◆

★　★

151 West 51st Street, 245-4850.

Atmosphere: Awe-inspiring decor, from the elegant bar with a wrap-around wall mural to the plush, high-ceilinged dining room. Spacious and comfortable.

Service: Well informed and professional.

Price range: Moderately expensive.

Credit cards: All major cards.

Hours: Lunch, Monday through Friday, 11:45 A.M. to 2:30 P.M.; dinner, Monday through Saturday, 5:30 to 11 P.M. Closed Sunday.

Reservations: Necessary.

Palio is the second knockout theme restaurant in the Equitable Assurance Tower on West 51st Street (after the all-seafood Le Bernardin), and in terms of its awe-inspiring decor and sumptuous creature comforts, this stylish Italian setting is more than a worthy rival. As for the food, the wide-ranging regional menu can bedazzle at times, making for a truly memorable experience. On some occasions, though, it fails to shine as brightly as the regal surroundings.

The restaurant is run by Tony May, the owner of two other Italian restaurants in the city, La Camelia and Sandro's; he imported as chef Andrea da Merano, who has a considerable following in his native Italy. The restaurant is named after the Palio of Siena, a centuries-old festival that culminates in a reckless horse race around the city's piazza. This leitmotif is most stunningly evoked in the ground-level bar, which you pass through en route to the second-story restaurant. The bar is dominated by a bold and bawdy 124-foot-high wraparound mural of the Palio by one of the country's hottest contemporary artists, Sandro Chia.

A reverential gentleman in a dark suit escorts you on an elevator to the main dining room with its soaring coffered ceiling, colorful Palio theme banners on the walls, trellised woodwork and plush, well-spaced tables. No expense has been spared; the shimmering brass service plates have pretty hand-painted tile insets, the cutlery and glasses are exquisite, and baby roses sprout from handsome silver boxes. The lengthy, leather-bound menu looks like a diploma.

As you consider the options, a changing medley of tidbits is set out, including morsels of fresh lobster nestled in clouds of whipped cream tinged with horseradish, marinated scallops, assorted vegetables and the most supple and fresh mozzarella I have tasted in ages. Diners at my table could not stop eating the dense whole-wheat bread made with olive oil.

The Italian waiters are efficient and well informed about the menu; service is sharper at lunch than at dinner.

Appetizers are divided into cold and hot preparations, soups and pastas (the pastas can be had in half portions). In the first category, one of the best was fresh baby octopus, remarkably tender and faintly sweet, bathed in a blend of strong olive oil, tomatoes, capers and celery. Two other heady starters were marinated salmon swathed with a woody truffle paste, and a sparkling patty of chopped, seasoned raw beef with fresh artichoke disks for garnish (the beef is served at lunch).

You would be hard pressed to find a more buttery carpaccio anywhere. The sheets of florid red beef were so good I didn't even mind that the advertised balsamic vinegar was missing and that the smattering of fresh foie gras over it added little. Bypass the delicatessen-quality turkey in a light tuna sauce.

The best hot starter is beautiful fresh mussels in an aromatic saffron broth. Baby squid in a vivid olive-oil-and-parsley-based sauce would have excelled had it not been for undercooking, which left the squid crunchy. A good strategy is to have as a warm appetizer risotto, which is among the best I have had in some time, or one of the pastas. The rice is barely resilient, as it should be, and the cooking broth is deep and richly seasoned. One risotto is made with rare-roasted pieces of quail, another with tiny sweet peas. Two pastas can be highly recommended: fettuccine in a lustily seasoned Bolognese sauce and fusilli carbonara, with postage stamps of pancetta in a mildly tart pecorino sauce.

Gnocchi also is a winner, tossed with morsels of tender frogs' legs and infused with garlic. Spaghetti with artichokes and olives, though, was undercooked and over-saffroned. Ravioli filled with zucchini flowers could have been stuffed with mashed potatoes for all the flavor they had.

Seafood fanciers can't go wrong with the lustrous steamed bass fillets festooned with asparagus and zucchini in a vernal herb-flecked broth; another spirited creation is rolled salmon fillets, rare pink in the center, brushed with a blend of black olives, spinach and pink peppercorns—a nice contrast of flavors. Shrimp coated with dill and parsley arrived dry and overpowered by herbs.

Finally, among meat entrees the best bets were sage-perfumed roast squab, and poached breast of capon stuffed with prosciutto and set over a vernal green sauce. A veal chop was tasteless and medallions of lamb were dry.

It is rare these days to find a first-class assortment of cheeses, and at Palio not only is the selection diverse but also in peak condition. If you crave something sweet, try the fabulous homemade fruit sorbetti or the intriguing black polenta pudding, light and bittersweet, in a velvety white chocolate sauce. In fact, most of the desserts are smashing, with the possible exception of a flossy "nueva cucina" rice pudding.

Like the original Palio, this majestic new restaurant is ablaze with color and pageantry. With a bit more discipline behind the scenes, it could well become an enduring tradition too.

✦ PALM ✦

★

837 Second Avenue, near 45th Street, 687-2953.

Atmosphere: Sawdust-covered floors, wooden chairs, caricature-covered walls. Loud and bustling.

Service: No-nonsense veteran waiters are affable and generally efficient.

Price range: Moderately expensive.

Credit cards: All major cards.

Hours: Lunch, Monday through Friday, noon to 5 P.M.; dinner, Monday through Saturday, 5 to 11:30 P.M. Closed Sunday.

Reservations: Necessary for lunch; accepted at dinner only for four or more.

It is impossible to be dispassionate about Palm, the archetypal New York steakhouse that opened as a restaurant and speakeasy in 1926. Judging from the clamorous, standing-room-only crowds at the bar nightly, one might think these fervid Palmists somehow missed news of the 21st Amendment, which made it possible to have cocktails before dinner elsewhere.

To love Palm one has to be the type who revels in a Pamplona-like atmosphere with sawdust-strewn floors, smoke-smudged walls festooned with celebrity caricatures, wham-bam service and lumberjack-size portions. I get a kick out of steakhouses like this—that is, assuming the food is equally engaging. At Palm, unfortunately, that is no longer the case. You can still get a first-rate sirloin here and, if luck is on your side, good brittle cottage fries. The rest, however, is as unpredictable as the stock market.

One vexing affectation at Palm is the lack of a menu. A waiter comes to your table and runs off several varieties of steaks, chops, lobster, broiled fish and two or three appetizers. If pressed, he will concede a veal dish or two. To get more out of him (and there is more) requires the persistence of a district attorney. In fairness, though, the waiters, mostly affable, wisecracking veterans who do their job well, are simply trying to steer customers toward the best dishes.

The seventeen-ounce sirloin steak that made Palm famous is

still a winner—seared under a superhot broiler to impart a blackened crust while remaining juicy and succulent within. The thin disks of cottage fries and tangle of deep-fried onion can be fresh and crunchy one night, tepid and leathery on another from sitting in the kitchen too long. Other vegetables range from acceptable to cafeteria-style. The wine list is thin and undistinguished.

Another of Palm's erstwhile favorites is called steak à la stone, featuring sliced strips of sirloin steak over a mound of sautéed onions and pimientos. Once again, the meat can languish in the kitchen too long and begin to turn steam-table gray from the heat and moisture of the onions. Veal chops and double-cut lamb chops are generally reliable and tasty. Filet mignon, on the other hand, would be hard to identify if eaten blindfolded, so lacking is it in flavor.

The four-pound lobsters that come to the table split, broiled and with melted butter are less succulent than steamed lobsters but delicious in their own right with a nice smoky tinge. In my experience broiled fish is usually overcooked and underseasoned. Except for a garlicky plate of sautéed shrimp with herbs, other appetizers are forgettable: bready and chewy baked clams, tasteless crab salad and papery shrimp with cocktail sauce.

If there is room for dessert, try either the top-notch creamy cheesecake or the awesomely rich chocolate mousse cake.

The similar if more subdued Palm Too across the street serves more or less the same fare. Although the original Palm has lost its edge as an all-around restaurant, I can still recommend it for a stiff drink and a slab of sirloin, which, after all, is what the place is really all about.

✦ PETALUMA ✦

★

1356 First Avenue, at 73rd Street, 772-8800.

Atmosphere: Expansive, open cafe with convivial bar and exposed kitchen.

Service: Composed and pleasant young staff, although amateur.

Price range: Moderate.

Credit cards: None; will accept personal checks with proper identification.

Hours: Lunch, daily, 11:30 A.M. to 5 P.M.; dinner, daily, 5:30 P.M. to 2 A.M.

Reservations: Accepted only for parties of five or more.

Petaluma is an expansive, peach-colored playroom with post-modern touches, a long, crowded bar and an exposed kitchen turning out grilled victuals, pastas and brick-oven pizzas at moderate prices.

The restaurant was standing room only when it opened several years ago, but things have calmed down since. Don't worry, though, if you have to cool your heels at the bar on a busy night, for that is considered part of the game by the mostly young, single and sociable clientele. Ambitious young executives in dark pin-striped suits and loosened ties take in a parade of leonine blondes, conservatively punked brunettes and other well-preened women, who often arrive in pairs. The food, it seems, is a pleasant sideshow—a bonus if it happens to be palatable, no great loss if it isn't. There is a good deal of food to consider, however, and its quality is variable.

Petaluma's menu carries about a dozen regular appetizers, an equal number of entrees, and as many daily specials. A good way for two or more people to start is to nibble on a pizza, then get an appetizer and an entree. Thin-crusted pizzas have the burnished edges and smokiness expected from wood-burning ovens, and the toppings are fresh and tasty, but skimpy. They come garnished with ricotta, mozzarella and asparagus; ham, mushrooms and artichokes; three peppers (red, yellow and green) with fontina cheese; and goat cheese, oil-cured olives, red onions and mozzarella, to name a few.

Another good appetizer is the moist and mild slices of smoked trout and smoked bluefish served with a dipping sauce of vinegar, parsley, capers and garlic. It also comes with a cloud of fresh whipped cream blended with horseradish. The polenta, which is deliciously cheese-encrusted and firm, is blanketed with an earthy mushroom sauce. An equally savory choice is a woodsy salad composed of sliced mushrooms, fresh fennel and Parmesan cheese. Mozzarella in carozza, little battered and deep-fried triangular sandwiches with a zesty caper sauce, could easily become habit forming. The same goes for the light and crunchy fried clams, an occasional special.

There are several clunkers to avoid on the appetizer menu. The duck terrine is fatty and underseasoned; seafood sausage that is supposed to have saffron butter is insipid; and barbecued ribs are ordinary at best.

The young waiters and waitresses belong to the "Who gets the chicken?" school, however they are remarkably composed and pleasant under sometimes highly pressured conditions. You won't get any help choosing wine from this team, so I would suggest that you stick with simple Beaujolais, familiar California labels and such.

Pasta specials are the strong suit of the kitchen. Typical of the repertoire is fettuccine swathed in a sauce combining chunks of thick, smoky bacon and swiss chard. Others might include fusilli with peas and spicy sausage in a tomato-cream sauce, and penne in a tomato base tinted with orange zest, garlic and white wine.

In contrast to the pasta crew, which toils out of sight of the public, the grill chefs could benefit from a few cooking lessons. While simple preparations such as butterflied baby chicken, duck breast and steak are competently prepared, more delicate items, such as fish, are often overcooked.

Among the desserts, the puckery lemon tart with a thin, buttery crust is a standout. Authentic strawberry shortcake, with baking-powder biscuits, fresh whipped cream and ripe berries, is a runner-up, while chocolate mousse cake is merely sugary icing on chocolate cake.

There is a side-door exit to Petaluma, but no one seems to use it. A long, slow promenade past the bar, with a pause at the open kitchen to comment on the wonderful pizza oven and check for celebrities in the front dining room, is all part of the show. This is food as theater, dining vérité, and Petaluma is a successful prototype that many have followed.

✦ PETER LUGER ✦

★

178 Broadway, Brooklyn, 718-387-7400.

Atmosphere: Old New York charm in a century-old landmark. A neighborly old barroom fills up nightly with a gregarious crowd, and the wood-trimmed dining rooms are austere and Germanic, appropriate for a no-frills steakhouse.

Service: Lighthearted and chatty veteran waiters who perform their duties in a casually efficient manner. Don't expect them to lay a napkin on your lap.

Price range: Moderately expensive.

Credit cards: Peter Luger charge cards.

Hours: Lunch, Monday through Saturday, 11:30 A.M. to 3 P.M.; dinner, Sunday through Thursday, 3 to 9:45 P.M., Friday and Saturday, 3 to 10:45 P.M., Sunday, 1 to 9:45 P.M.

Reservations: Required.

Anyone who contends that America is no longer a nation of steak eaters should journey across the East River some evening to Peter Luger, which is to carnivores what Brooks Brothers is to the plaid Bermuda shorts set. For nearly a century this landmark in the Williamsburg section of Brooklyn, in the shadow of the Williamsburg Bridge, has been a crowded, no-frills, elbows-on-the-table steakhouse. The river has isolated it from the ebb and flow of food fads in Manhattan that have compelled similar establishments to water down their menus with such "fancy food" as escargots, veal piccata and shrimp scampi.

Menus are strictly for the tourist trade, offered to those who insist upon seeing one. The first time I requested a menu, the waiter replied with the same quip that has been drawing chuckles there since the McKinley administration. "Sure you can see a menu, but first I'll ask you how you want your steak done."

Your choices are juicy slabs of broiled porterhouse steaks in portions serving one to four, and fist-thick double lamb chops. Both are nicely encrusted from high-fire broiling and succulent (roast prime rib is an occasional special, but I never had the opportunity to sample it).

Leaning on the long, elbow-worn oak bar with a man-size drink while waiting for a table, you feel as if you are a thousand miles from Manhattan. At one corner of the room, four white-haired neighborhood cronies chew on thick stogies and debate politics in Brooklyn accents as thick as Luger's lamb chops. Local couples in sports clothes banter with the bartender and sip

Bloody Marys while businessmen in pinstripes from "the city" belt down martinis and swap jokes.

The main dining room is vaguely Teutonic with its exposed-wood beams, burnished-oak wainscotting, brass chandeliers and scrubbed beer-hall tables. The veteran waiters are a jocular bunch if you get them going and are casually efficient. On our first visit we ordered a porterhouse for three and lamb chops for one. The formidable cut of singed steak had been sliced in the kitchen and placed on a hot platter. Our waiter set a small dish under one end of the platter to let juice run into a corner while commenting, probably for the hundredth time that week, "If you don't like this steak you don't like steak!" He then portioned out enough beef to sate a tugboat crew. The beef was cooked rare as ordered and had a good meaty flavor and plenty of juice for bread dipping.

The lamb chops are equally flavorful and profit from the same skilled broiling. The perennial salad of sliced onions and tomatoes is worth ordering only during peak tomato season; the dreary horseradish-tomato sauce slathered over it could be done without. Shrimp cocktail is available, but chances are the waiter won't tell you about it unless you are a regular.

Among the side dishes, German fried potatoes are usually burned around the edges and underseasoned. They also show telltale signs of having been prepared in advance and reheated before serving. The bland creamed spinach would prompt a groan in a prep school dining hall, though the steak fries are better than average.

If you finish all this and still want dessert, there is sweet pecan pie that is brought to the table with a bowl filled with enough fresh whipped cream to paint a stripe across the Williamsburg Bridge, as well as a lightweight chocolate mousse and good dense creamy cheesecake.

✦ PETROSSIAN ✦

★

182 West 58th Street, 245-2214.

Atmosphere: Plush Art Deco theme.

Service: Uneven, from friendly to pretentious.

Price range: Expensive.

Credit cards: All major cards.

Hours: Lunch, Monday through Saturday, noon to 3 P.M.; dinner, Monday through Saturday, 6 P.M. to midnight; caviar bar, 3 to 6 P.M. Closed Sunday, Christmas Day and New Year's Day.

Reservations: Necessary.

This pleasure palace in the Alwyn Court on West 58th Street strives to feed the soul as well as the body with regal silver platters of foie gras, caviar, smoked salmon and champagne. For Armen and Christian Petrossian, who own the famous Parisian caviar shop, believe there are enough New Yorkers in need of periodic pampering, as well as visitors who want to put on the dog, to keep this fantasy alive.

The dining room is a splendiferous work of art or an ostentatious conceit, depending on whom you consult. The theme is Art Deco, with magnificent rose-colored Italian granite floors and bar, snappy designer stools, etched glass mirrors, crystal chandeliers and a banquette upholstered in gray kid leather with mink trim.

The cynosure of the menu is caviar—$55 for 50 grams of beluga, $37 for osetra, $31 for sevruga, and $26 for pressed— and it can be had alone or as part of the prix fixe menus, one for $98 a person, and the others for $59 and $46. The more expensive the dinner, the more caviar or foie gras you get. You can't fault the quality of the caviar or its stunning presentation on silver-lined black-lacquer plates complete with a golden spoon. The foie gras, too, is rich and smooth. Try it with an aromatic hot truffle in its juice accompanied by a glass of Sauternes. Also memorable is the extravagant foie-gras-and-fresh-vegetable salad studded with truffle slivers.

Foie gras cognoscenti will note that the version sold here is mi-cuis, that is, partly cooked before exportation from France. It is firmer and drier but similar in flavor to the fresh domestic product now available in New York. Truffle fans must try the truffle consommé, which is so earthy and luscious you will want to lick the bowl. Petrossian's smoked salmon at best is firm, lean and buttery, although once it was too salty.

Petrossian serves only a handful of entrees at lunch and dinner. The service can at times be forgetful, awkward and imperious. The two fish dishes I enjoyed were poached salmon fillet blanketed with a custard-light scallop mousse in a butter sauce highlighted with cubes of tomato, and fillet of red snapper in a mustard-cream sauce with wild mushrooms, tomato and parsley.

The beef fillet with black pepper sauce and shiitake mushrooms was satisfying; however, veal chop stuffed with a puree of foie gras seemed a bit of overkill after the rich appetizers.

If you're still in the mood for dessert after all this, mocha layer cake with a buttery mocha cream filling is suggested. Most desserts are mundane. For some reason, the restaurant has a tendency to tell potential customers that it is fully booked when that is not the case. One evening we were told the only available tables were at 6 P.M. and 10. We arrived at 6 to find the place one-fourth empty. At 8:30, there were still plenty of tables free. That kind of treatment makes a diner feel like he's been had, and at these prices it is inexcusable.

✦ PIG HEAVEN ✦

★ ★

1540 Second Avenue, corner 80th Street, PIG-4333.

Atmosphere: Barnyard motif. Usually clamorous and crowded.

Service: Competent, amiable and well informed.

Price range: Moderate.

Credit cards: American Express and Diners Club.

Hours: Lunch and dinner, Sunday through Thursday, noon to midnight, Friday and Saturday until 1 A.M.

Reservations: Necessary.

As you enter the restaurant, past the giant wooden piglet holding a menu card at the front door, into the pink barnboard-lined dining room with a frieze of illuminated pigs all around, past tables of voracious customers chowing down like farmhands at sunset and sipping tea from mugs sculptured like pigs' snouts, oinking and giggling, you begin to question the wisdom of coming to a place called Pig Heaven for a serious Chinese meal.

The silliness at Pig Heaven, part of the David Keh restaurant empire, belies some of the most serious and authentically delicious Chinese food around. (Those who do not eat pork have a choice of many other dishes.)

Start with the excellent dumplings—fried, boiled or steamed. The tubular fried version, brashly seasoned with ginger and black pepper, is crisp and golden brown on the bottom, soft on top. Equally tasty are the hand-crimped steamed and boiled dumplings that spurt juice when bitten into—often all over your tie.

Other appetizers worth trying are the cold hacked chicken,

shards of white meat swathed in a zesty combination of sesame paste and hot oil, and the sesame-flavored scallion pancakes. Impeccably fresh kidneys, blanched and sliced in florets, are served with a Hunanese black peppercorn sauce that has a slightly bitter and numbing edge—appealing in a painful sort of way.

Appetizers that do not hold up as well are the thin crusty vegetable pie served with pancakes, which is a leaden and redundant concoction, dried out white-cooked pork, and undistinguished spring rolls.

There are nineteen pork specials. The Cantonese-style suckling pig at Pig Heaven is truly heavenly. The skin is potato chip–brittle, and underneath are a layer of fat and a strip of juicy meat. It will never make the American Heart Association's menu suggestions, but you are certain to leave the restaurant with a smile. Another good selection is minced pork sautéed with corn, bell peppers and pine nuts.

Fish is prepared with equal skill, especially the whole braised carp with Sichuan hot bean sauce and the braised red snapper with whole garlic cloves.

Three-glass chicken, a house specialty, is worth trying. The cut-up chicken is placed in a crock, mixed with ginger and assorted vegetables, and doused with a glass each of Chinese rice wine, soy sauce and water. It is covered and cooked until the sauce reduces to intensely flavorful brown drippings.

The largely non-Oriental waiters are amiable and well informed about the menu. They manage to keep their cool when nights are hectic, which is often.

Desserts are a far cry from the usual litchi nuts and fortune cookies. The crusty and custardy bread pudding with orange sauce is irresistible. Frozen praline mousse, studded with pecans, is far better than the grainy apple caramel sundae. A whimsical way to end the meal is with a Peking snowball, an igloo of whipped cream encasing a deadly rich chocolate core. Garnished with some silly cookies, it looks like something that would be served at an eight-year-old's birthday, which seems fitting here. Pig Heaven brings out the kid in all of us.

✦ THE POLO ✦

★ ★

Westbury Hotel, Madison Avenue and 69th Street, 535-9141 and 535-9142.

Atmosphere: Clubby, masculine and comfortable.

Service: Professional and Old-World European.

Price range: Expensive.

Credit cards: All major cards.

Hours: Lunch, daily, noon to 2:30 P.M.; dinner, daily, 6:30 to 10:30 P.M.

Reservations: Necessary.

Many New Yorkers remember the old Polo Lounge in the Westbury Hotel as a genteel East Side watering hole where dispirited businessmen—the kind of characters who inhabit John Cheever stories—would stop for a few martinis and an encouraging word before catching the 7:06 to Darien. The building was completely redone several years ago and with it The Polo (its new name) was transformed into one of the better hotel dining rooms in the city.

The chef, Patrice Boëly, who honed his skills with Roger Vergé at Moulin de Mougins in France, has a winsome, light touch and solid mastery of seasonings and sauces. His style is hard to pin down, except to say he blends classical and nouvelle techniques with a Provençale accent.

The Polo is like a fine old mink coat: opulent, dignified and warm. The dining room has been spruced up without sacrificing its clubby character. Horse prints on burnished mahogany walls, brass sconces, cozy banquettes, plush leather chairs, tuxedoed waiters—all add a timeless charm.

A splendid if extravagant way to begin dinner is with foie gras, and few places do it with such class. My favorite is the sautéed fresh foie gras with artichoke bottoms and a cider vinegar sauce. The fruity and slightly tart sauce cuts through the duck liver like a razor. Another civilized version is the room-temperature fresh foie gras with toasted brioche and a glass of Sauternes.

Those in the mood for a lighter starter can opt for dishes like the sparkling salad of haricots verts with warm sea scallops flavored with gin vinegar and fresh mint. A marinated red snapper infused with fresh anise is a welcome change from gravlax. The last time I had it, though, it suffered from too much anise.

A sole and salmon mousse gets an A for texture, but it fails for flavor. At lunch, a better selection is the chicken breast and goose liver terrine. It is moist, boldly seasoned and studded with macadamia nuts, with a rich core of foie gras speckled with truffles.

The service, like the room itself, is Old World and professional—no aspiring thespians or would-be sculptors here. These unflappable veterans have that rare quality of making a diner feel in command, no matter how insecure he might be.

Mr. Boëly's Provençale influence shines most brightly with seafood, starting with creations such as the fillet of salmon braised in fish stock with a touch of cognac and orange zest. It is perfumed with the flavor of fresh herbs and garnished with a rainbow of turned vegetables.

Two other preparations are memorable for their simplicity: fillet of pompano roasted with white pepper, tomatoes, pimientos, olives and anchovies, and striped bass steamed with seaweed and draped in a watercress-butter sauce. Top quality meats and game are prepared with the same light-handedness. A pair of butterflied roast quails with a black currant sauce is a good example. The brittle-skinned birds are moist and succulent, and the sauce has just the right combination of sweetness and tartness.

A longshoreman's portion of plump calf's sweetbreads with fresh coriander and port wine sauce is bracing and flavorful, served with a spinach mousse. Another rousing combination is medallions of veal with poached pears and a zinfandel sauce— the veal is milky and tender and the sauce redolent of good stock.

The dessert wagon, whose passengers change often, is appealing if not overly imaginative. Chocolate mousse layer cake with a crown of bittersweet chocolate curls is worth the guilt. Linzer torte, with its spicy, cookie-like lattice crust and raspberry jam center, is as good as you'll find outside Austria. Raspberry fans should try the airy raspberry mousse cake.

For the nostalgic commuter, there is still a small welcoming bar at The Polo. But with food like this, it will be even harder to catch the 7:06.

✦ POSITANO ✦

★ ★

250 Park Avenue South, at 20th Street, 777-6211.

Atmosphere: Airy and bustling, chic and informal.

Service: Young staff, friendly but sometimes slow.

Price range: Moderate.

Credit cards: All major cards.

Hours: Lunch, Monday through Friday, noon to 3 P.M.; dinner, Monday through Saturday, 5:30 to 11:30 P.M. Closed Sunday.

Reservations: Necessary.

Positano reflects a certain style of hip, theatrical restaurants that began sprouting in downtown Manhattan several years back. The typical scenario goes like this: Someone buys a cavernous former industrial space or bank lobby with ceilings high enough to shag fly balls. It sports neo-classical columns and acoustics like the trading floor of the New York Stock Exchange. The room gets a fresh coat of pastel paint, a long bar with a Cruvinet wine machine and an aggressive public relations agent. Oh yes, the place also serves food, but that is usually an afterthought.

While typical in many ways, Positano rises above the pack in one crucial respect—the food can be very good. The restaurant is co-owned by Bob Giraldi, the music video and television commercial director. Housed in a pre–World War II building with neo-Gothic accents on Park Avenue South, Positano has dining areas on three tiers—a large dining platform on top, a bar in the middle and tables around the perimeter of the ground floor. The room is painted pink and white, including the massive columns and overhead heating pipes. Everything from the green marble tables to the pink-rimmed wineglasses and sleek oil-and-vinegar cruets says high-toned Italian design.

Since Positano opened in late 1984, it has been filled with a mixed group, ranging from the neighborhood after-work business crowd to the artsy aviator-jacket types who stroll in after 9 P.M. The food is based on the Campania region of Italy's Amalfi coast, but there is really a bit of everything on the menu. One of the most alluring appetizers is batter-fried artichoke hearts with mozzarella—fresh artichokes are covered with a light egg batter and cheese, then fried until golden and served in a zesty tomato sauce.

Crostini is simple and good: slabs of Italian bread layered with tomatoes and slices of fresh mozzarella, all drizzled with olive oil. If your mussels steamed in wine, garlic and herbs are overcooked, as mine were, all is not lost: the broth makes for great bread dipping. Sundry salad plates are colorful and refreshing with well-balanced vinaigrettes.

In restaurants like this, I like to order a half portion of pasta before the entree; that is not possible here, unless you order a whole portion and split it with someone, at a $1 surcharge. This annoying policy notwithstanding, most of the pastas are superior. If they have it, try the rigatoni with a tomato-cream sauce spiked with pimiento and hot red pepper flakes, or farfalle, bow-tie shaped noodles, tossed with broccoli and zucchini in a satiny and herbaceous cream sauce. The list goes on: penne with a tomato, parsley and tuna sauce (a special one day), paglia e fieno with bits of ham and firm peas in a tomato-cream sauce, and penne with sautéed eggplant.

The young and casual service staff, donning oversize bowling shirts and pastel ties, do a reasonably good job until the place fills up late at night, at which time waiters and waitresses start doing confused pirouettes as requests assault them from all sides. Pay attention to such daily specials as the superb osso buco. The veal shank, nearly the size of a man's fist, is so tender that buttery seems the only word that can describe it.

Freshness and simplicity are the hallmarks of fish cookery here. Sautéed baby squid with garlic, olive oil and parsley is the kind of dish you rarely find prepared well in New York. Here the five tiny squid, served with the tentacles, are charred on the outside, resilient but not chewy. Garlic oil is all they need. Another dish that is delicious in its simplicity is broiled red snapper with a shower of vinegar and mint garnish.

The kitchen turns out an intoxicating custard cream cake soaked with cherry liqueur, a crunchy chocolate-almond torte and excellent gelati. Positano proves that a swanky scene and fine cuisine are not mutually exclusive.

⋆ PRIMAVERA ⋆

★

1578 First Avenue, corner 82nd Street, 861-8608.

Atmosphere: Formal and urbane.

Service: Uneven, depending on whether you are known.

Price range: Moderately expensive.

Credit cards: All major cards.

Hours: Dinner, Monday through Saturday, 5:30 P.M. to midnight, Sunday, 5 P.M. to midnight.

Reservations: Necessary.

Primavera, a polished, expensive Italian restaurant on First Avenue, has always been patronized loyally by its Upper East Side customers. With its burnished mahogany walls, soothing paintings, tulip-shaped lamps, women in subdued silk dresses and men in somber suits, it has the feeling of an Ivy League club. Indeed, sometimes it can be harder to get into than Yale because regulars book tables well in advance. As for the food, it offers a fairly predictable curriculum.

If you start with the seafood appetizer, you get a generous amount of baby squid along with tiny chunks of octopus in an oregano-scented vinaigrette. In my experience the seafood was a bit overcooked but otherwise flavorful and fresh; baked clams are rubbery, and stuffed mushrooms are a stodgy concoction of bread crumbs and a tasteless brown sauce.

Better choices are the hearty minestrone soup, blushing fresh carpaccio with a basil-lemon mayonnaise, and any appetizer featuring the creamy-textured and slightly nutty buffalo mozzarella from Italy. Spiedino, a deep-fried rectangle of regular mozzarella resembling a gold bar from Fort Knox, is satisfactory but not worth the $9 price tag.

Half portions of pasta can be obtained as a second course. Here again, chances of success are fifty-fifty. The best pasta I have sampled at Primavera is the tortellini with peas and prosciutto. The tortellini were resilient and tasty, while the cream sauce had a delightful smoky tinge. The penne in a fresh and lively tomato sauce with bits of bacon can be good too.

Service can be as crisp and attentive as you'll find anywhere—that is, if you are a regular. Otherwise, it is a roll of the dice.

There are no unexpected twists or turns along the entree course except for the roast baby goat, a house specialty. To those unfamiliar with this meat, one could say it tastes vaguely like lamb. The goat meat is served deliciously charred and seasoned with rosemary.

Sautéed veal with prosciutto and spinach was flaccid when I tried it, and paillard of beef was thick and without flavor. Simple grilled meats, such as veal or lamb chops, are the best options.

Primavera's wine list is a pretentious document unsuited to the cuisine. There are many expensive and prestigious Bordeaux and Burgundies running into the hundreds of dollars but scant choice for those looking for a pleasant drinking wine under $20.

One nice touch is the huge and varied assortment of fresh fruit that is presented at the end of the meal. That and the winy tirami sù, made with ladyfingers, mascarpone cheese and heavy cream, are the best desserts.

✦ PRUNELLE ✦

★ ★

18 East 54th Street, 759-6410.

Atmosphere: Handsome, understated room with burled-maple walls, gentle lighting and lavish flower displays.

Service: Staff is professional and pleasant although sometimes there are long lags between courses.

Price range: Expensive.

Credit cards: American Express, Carte Blanche, and Diners Club.

Hours: Lunch, Monday through Friday, noon to 3 P.M.; dinner, Monday through Saturday, 5:30 P.M. to midnight. Closed Sunday.

Reservations: Necessary.

Prunelle, owned by Jacky Ruette and Pascal Dirringer, is still among the most opulent spots in town. The entire dining room is done in gleaming burled maple, with Art Deco etched-glass partitions, luxurious flower arrangements and gentle indirect lighting adding to its low-key allure.

When the restaurant first appeared in 1983, the food was as ambitious and as pretty as the setting, but uneven. Based on recent visits, however, that is no longer the case; the food is consistently satisfying, and sometimes extraordinary, at both lunch and dinner. Mr. Dirringer, the chef, has forged a taut menu that straddles the fence between classic French cuisine and nouvelle-style touches. Without exception his sauces are intensely flavorful while light, and presentations are appealing without being contrived. He has a penchant for baby vegetables —carrots, turnips, squash. After eating here several times, you may begin to crave foods bigger than your thumb.

Good starters abound. One of my favorites was a special one

evening of steamed shrimp wrapped in spinach and set in a lustrous velouté sauce; another winner is the sweet smoked shrimp alongside slices of translucent smoked sable paired with a tart watercress sauce. Fanciers of fresh foie gras should try the version here, seared outside, silky within and garnished with orange sections, wild rice and a rich Madeira sauce.

Lighter options at lunch include a bright tarragon-flavored crab salad nestled in an artichoke heart surrounded by spokes of firm-steamed asparagus, and a golden puff pastry atop white and green asparagus in a thyme-accented champagne-vinegar sauce. Mussel soup, faintly briny and heady with saffron, is always a good option. A cold seafood assortment mounted over ice features succulent bay scallops in a coriander vinaigrette and sparkling littleneck clams, but the selection of oysters taste as if the brine has been rinsed off.

The service team at Prunelle are highly professional and congenial; unaccountably, though, there can be undue lags between courses. I suspect this is the fault of the kitchen, not the waiters.

Among the entrees, seafood is executed especially well. Salmon, in particular, is terrific, sautéed to just the other side of sushi in the center and glossed with a red-wine butter sauce. Lobster comes in a tasty and unusual guise—shelled, steamed with shredded romaine lettuce, and served over the lettuce with fennel and baby vegetables. If you go while soft-shell crabs are in season, try the crackly browned ones here surrounded by a fresh and pulpy tomato-basil sauce. Another special, coho salmon, is delicious in its sweet-edged sauce of wild leeks.

One of the special meat dishes sounded as if it might be cloying but turned out to be among the better entrees I sampled. It combined medallions of first-rate veal paired with a seductive lobster sauce and a disk of beef tenderloin in a refined stock sauce. Confit of duck is the real thing, crisp and buttery, escorted by florid slices of duck breast speckled with ginger. Crunchy disks of roast potatoes are the perfect accompaniment.

Finally, there are firm and well-browned sweetbreads over a sward of wild mushrooms and flanked by all those baby vegetables.

Portions are copious at Prunelle, so when the well-maintained assortment of cheeses and fruits rolls your way on its marble-topped trolley, it may be necessary to choose between that or dessert. If you opt for the sweets, recommended choices are the changing varieties of splendid fruit tarts topped with everything from blackberries to kiwi, strawberries and mango. Praline layer cake is moist but undistinguished. Mimosa sherbet made with champagne and orange is so good I wouldn't mind letting it thaw and sipping it with a straw.

⋆ THE QUILTED GIRAFFE ⋆

★ ★ ★ ★

955 Second Avenue, between 50th and 51st streets, 753-5355.

Atmosphere: The long, narrow downstairs dining room has a classy glow, a convivial feeling and good sound level; upstairs is quieter and romantic.

Service: Highly professional.

Price range: Expensive.

Credit cards: All major credit cards accepted.

Hours: Dinner, Monday through Friday, 5:45 to 10 P.M.

Reservations: Necessary, usually two weeks or more in advance.

The Quilted Giraffe, Manhattan's celebrated monument to self-indulgence, has undergone several changes since it garnered four stars in 1984. The young chef, Noel Comess, left to pursue private goals. The owners, Barry and Susan Wine, have taken on the burden of a second, more casual, restaurant in midtown. Fortunately, though, what has not changed at The Quilted Giraffe is the entire staff's dedication, energy and passion for quality that placed this restaurant at the top of a crowded and competitive class.

What struck me over the course of several recent visits was how even the most straightforward preparations—grilled salmon with mustard, roast chicken with aïoli, calf's liver and endives —receive the same attention lavished on more intricate creations. Even a sliced tomato with basil can be absolutely symphonic when the ingredients in question have been picked earlier that day in the Wines' country garden and raced to town before the mist dries.

The restaurant's two dining rooms are filled nightly with a soignée crowd that believes—or in many cases whose corporations believe—that prix fixe meals of $75 and $100, not including wine, mandatory 18 percent tip and tax, are reasonable fees for an evening's gastronomic entertainment. The $75 prix fixe dinner includes appetizer, entree, cheese course and dessert; the $100 menu allows one to choose from two six-course meals.

The downstairs dining room, which seats about forty-five, exudes a glow of civility and class. It has soft cream-colored walls, handsome wooden wainscotting, flattering lighting and a sound level that usually allows a convivial backdrop of conversation but rarely at distracting levels. Two intimate upstairs dining rooms are quieter and more romantic.

Mr. Wine's cooks have a knack for extracting every last drop of flavor from ingredients. Consider, for example, his cool celery soup with lobster. Never have I tasted the essence of celery so clear and bright, and it marries beautifully with the tender morsels of lobster.

First-rate sautéed sweetbreads take on an arresting texture in a coating of ground pecans, flanked by firm fresh kernels of corn speckled with minced red pepper, while thin slices of pink-red duck breast rouse the palate with a left-right combination of tart lime and hot peppers. Only the coriander-cured salmon seems lifeless by comparison, the herb failing to assert itself in the marinade. Mr. Wine's much imitated beggar's purses—gossamer crepes filled with beluga caviar and a touch of crème fraîche secured with scallion strips—are the type of treat one should consume while prone on a couch with a bottle of champagne. A portion of five carries a $30 supplement.

The service team is exemplary in every respect. Waiters stand at a distance and study every table, ready to swoop down at the sight of an empty glass or bread basket. Unsolicited chitchat by waiters is eschewed. The computerized wine list, which is printed daily, is deep if a bit pricey. The sommelier is good about pointing out some superior wines at the lower end of the scale.

Simple preparations such as grilled Norwegian salmon make most others I have had pale by comparison. The fillet is exquisitely fresh, and the mild mustard glaze combined with olive oil lends a mildly sweet, almost orange-like sensation. Another recommended seafood option is the succulent lobster sections set in a light cream sauce made with a concentrated lobster stock aromatic of basil, fennel and radish.

More substantial entrees include a superb confit of duck, cooked to the point of buttery tenderness with thin blistered skin. It comes with lovely homemade creamed corn and ripe tomatoes. Two other earthy winners are tender calf's liver with braised endives, and rare-roasted rack of lamb swabbed with Chinese mustard along with brittle homemade potato chips and sugar snap peas.

You don't see many interesting cheese platters in this abstemious age—dieters usually forgo those calories and zero in on dessert—but this one should not be dismissed. About a dozen varieties of American and imported cheeses are offered, all in peak condition.

The all-American desserts are an adolescent's dream—and not bad for older kids either. Hazelnut waffles under an igloo of unstintingly rich vanilla ice cream and maple sauce may be a bit excessive after a full meal, but it is suitable for sharing. In the same category is phyllo crumple, a pleated disk of fragile dough combined with apples, strawberries and vanilla ice cream. Raspberry mousse puffs suffer from tough, stale puff pastry, and white chocolate mousse is grainy and nearly curdled; go instead with the luxurious pecan squares—they are fresh and not overly sweet —or the embarrassingly good chocolate soufflé whose crater oozes espresso ice cream that is so intense it could be served alone in demitasse cups. For a $10 supplement, you can have your table loaded down with a bit of everything. I do have one gripe, though. I wish Mr. Wine would stop giving out cigars to customers while others are still trying to dine.

The Quilted Giraffe is entering its eighth year in New York, still uncompromising, still unconventional. For that, its four stars continue to shine brightly.

◆ THE RITZ CAFE ◆

★

2 Park Avenue, at 32nd Street, 684-2122.

Atmosphere: Sprawling Art Deco cafe with two long mahogany bars and an informal open dining room.

Service: Hovering and eager when empty, but generally enthusiastic and efficient.

Price range: Moderate.

Credit cards: American Express, MasterCard and Visa.

Hours: Lunch, Monday through Friday, noon to 4 P.M.; dinner, Monday through Friday, 4 P.M. to midnight, Saturday, 5 P.M. to midnight. Closed Sunday.

Reservations: Recommended.

The Ritz Cafe on Park Avenue, sister of a glittery establishment in Los Angeles, is a handsome Art Deco Cajun-Creole restaurant. The dining room is a wide-open arena with a high ceiling, period chandeliers, etched-glass room dividers, period wall moldings and full-length glass panels facing 32nd Street (unfortunately, in winter they retain heat about as well as rattan). Two long mahogany bars flank the front of the room, and along the back are semiprivate booths—perfect for discreet business meetings or impassioned trysts.

A variety of shellfish samplers are offered for starters; you can have them at the bar with one of the house cocktails or in the dining room. The oysters sometimes taste overly rinsed and bland; Gulf shrimp with a piquant version of remoulade sauce made with peppers, tomatoes and mustard are firm and tasty; the best appetizer is crab cakes, which are loaded with sweet meat, flavored with crunchy scallions and lightly fried.

The touchstone of a Cajun restaurant is its gumbo, and this version—viscous and inky, filled with spicy sausage, oysters and rice—is the real thing. It is appealing in small doses. Bright red crayfish that come as part of a combination shellfish platter look more savory than they are—the meat, which one excavates by hand, has little flavor.

Waiters tend to hover at night, but who can blame them? The restaurant is much busier at lunch, when the local business trade streams in, and the waiters manage to keep things going at a brisk pace. One of the best entrees is called Cajun cassoulet, an earthy red-bean stew with hot red sausage and tender portions of duck breast and thigh. Three moist and flavorful quails, smothered in a thick browned chicken-stock sauce with mushrooms, carrots, celery, ham and rosemary, is another winner. It comes with dirty rice, which is sullied with bits of duck liver and confit of chicken and duck gizzards.

Lunch specials represent some of the best bargains, particularly the delicious hot chicken salad. It features strips of moist chicken breast dusted with mildly hot ground peppers and spices, perched on a thick nest of fresh watercress and enhanced with roasted pecans, julienne strips of ham and a balsamic vinaigrette.

Unfortunately, the pan-blackened entrees—blackfish fillet, steak and lamb chops—share the same basic fault that mars many other Paul Prudhomme imitations. Instead of merely searing the mixed ground spices that coat the food, the chef carbonizes them. The result looks like something that has fallen into an open campfire, and tastes that way too.

All the liquor-laced desserts are superior—heady Jack Daniels chocolate ice cream, cognac ice cream set in a blueberry compote, a semisweet pecan-chocolate pie cut with rum, and lovely bread pudding with raisins that is doused with bourbon.

✦ RIVER CAFE ✦

★ ★ ★

1 Water Street, Brooklyn, 718-522-5200.

Atmosphere: Romantic dining room on a barge with stunning views of Manhattan and the East River.

Service: Professional and well informed; waiters tend to disappear later in the evening.

Price range: Expensive.

Credit cards: All major cards.

Hours: Lunch, Monday through Friday, noon to 3 P.M.; dinner, daily, 7
P.M. to midnight; brunch, Saturday and Sunday, noon to 3 P.M.

Reservations: Necessary.

Even the most jaded I've-seen-everything New Yorker cannot help feeling a slight rush of the pulse upon entering the dining room at the River Cafe, situated in a barge on the Brooklyn shore of the East River. The Oz-like vista of lower Manhattan at night serves to confirm what so many citizens of the metropolis have always maintained: This, indeed, is the center of the universe.

Civic pride aside, there is another compelling reason to cross the majestic Brooklyn Bridge: some of the most provocative food to be found anywhere in the city. The chef, Charles Palmer, who replaced Larry Forgione several years ago, has an authoritative style, a fusion of American and French that is clean and bold yet never contrived.

This can be seen in some of his stellar appetizers, such as the seared, pepper-encrusted yellowfin tuna, just this side of sushi in the center, set in a pool of faintly tart cultured cream speckled with golden and black caviars. The three flavor sensations—piquant, tart and saline—constitute the most uplifting trio since the Marx Brothers. Lightly battered and fried Wellfleet oysters served in their shells over shallot mayonnaise are another felicitous marriage. Even a simple cold lobster salad is made memorable by presenting, in the shell, the perfectly cooked morsels of meat between alternating leaves of different-colored lettuces. The dish comes with two mayonnaise sauces, one zippy with cayenne pepper, the other soothing with ripe tomatoes.

Two specials are worth noting. One combines delicately smoked sea scallops and slices of grouper fillet in a clear and oceanic fish stock garnished with pearl onions and lima beans;

the other is a remarkably vibrant eight-layer vegetable terrine made without cream and bound with yellow pepper puree.

The service captains get so fired up when describing the food that I half expected one to sit down and join us for the main course. The dining room operates at full throttle from early evening until after midnight. Service is generally attentive and well paced until about 11 P.M., when the staff starts to run out of wind. Customers tend to linger after dinner in this romantic setting, with its soft lighting and buoyant pianist, so be prepared to spend some time at the bar or outdoor cafe waiting for your table. There are worse places to kill time.

The entree list is a virtual Chinese water torture for the congenitally indecisive—everything appears so seductive that a firm decision is nearly impossible. You wouldn't go wrong with the fruitwood-grilled pheasant, which is extraordinarily succulent, slightly charred and infused with woody flavors. A heady wild mushroom risotto is a wonderful accompaniment.

Roast lamb chops, cooked a notch more than requested, came in a sweet-edged honey sauce with a terrific charlotte made with eggplant puree. Fruitwood grilling contributes to the best Black Angus steak I have ever tasted: smoky, tender and enhanced with a bourbon-laced stock sauce. Other spirited offerings are the pan-fried red snapper with moist corn cakes and circled by a colorful corn relish; sea bass fillet baked with basil oil, lemon confit and sun-dried tomatoes with an airy asparagus sauce, and first-rate sautéed calf's liver with morels and onion-laced corn pudding.

Among such a glamorous cast, the veal steak seems somewhat of an introvert. The meat is not terribly distinctive, nor does the pepper and lemon thyme seasoning add much. Another also-ran is the slightly dry salmon flanked with delicious crab and zucchini fritters.

The River Cafe has one of the better wine lists in town, particularly strong in American selections.

There are more than a few outstanding desserts to fortify you for the voyage back to home port: frozen praline soufflé ringed by crunchy praline clusters and a shimmering caramel sauce, a bursting ripe raspberry tart, excellent sorbets (chocolate and raspberry) and double-chocolate mousse with a pecan base.

Crème brûlée is a pale rendition of the real thing, and lemon mousse has too many egg whites whipped in. I rarely order cheesecake after a multicourse meal, but the one here is the best I have had in ages—smooth yet light, lemony and encircled with fresh raspberries and strawberries. It takes real audacity to serve whipped cream with cheesecake. I ate it all.

Charles Palmer and his crew not only have kept the River Cafe afloat, but they have also released the spinnaker and sailed it to dramatic new destinations. It is a voyage not to be missed.

✦ ROSA MEXICANO ✦

★ ★

1063 First Avenue, at 58th Street, 753-7407.

Atmosphere: Elegant grill restaurant with restrained Mexican decor and lively ambiance.

Service: Knowledgeable about the food and accommodating. The back room moves at a better pace than the front.

Price range: Moderate.

Credit cards: All major cards.

Hours: Lunch, Monday through Saturday, noon to 3:30 P.M.; dinner, daily, 5 P.M. to midnight; Sunday buffet, noon to 3:30 P.M.

Reservations: Necessary

I'm not sure where young upwardly mobile professionals in Mexico City dine these days, but I suspect their haunts have a few things in common with Rosa Mexicano on 58th Street and First Avenue in Manhattan: a stylish ambiance, gregarious clientele, a good-time bar and a diverse range of bracing foods. Rosa Mexicano eschews the leaden and starchy clichés of most Mexican restaurants in New York and attempts to serve what Mexicans really eat. It's also one of the few such places where you will not wish for a stretcher to carry you home after dinner.

The menu, orchestrated by Josephina Howard, who helped open Cinco de Mayo in SoHo several years ago, is notable for its clean and bright seasonings and relatively light touch. Moreover, the fare is well balanced, offering moderate portions of stimulating appetizers followed by a host of grilled meats and fish, stews and soups.

The front room has a long, often crowded bar where exceptionally good margaritas flow like the Colorado River in March. The more elegant back room is done in rose-colored stucco with pink banquettes and a magnificent cluster of flowers in the center. The house special margarita, made with pomegranate, is more accessible to the novice than the slightly more aggressive traditional rendition made with tequila, Triple Sec, lime juice, salt and crushed ice. A few of these on an empty stomach will put you in such a mañana mood that anything the waiter suggests will seem just dandy. It's worthwhile to go over the menu carefully, though, because some arresting selections are available for all tastes.

Rosa Mexicano does not belong to the fire-thrower school of Mexican restaurants. Hot peppers and spices are added for seasoning, not scorching—although some dishes come with condiments on the side that you can add to taste. Two authentic and zesty appetizers are taquitos de tinga poblana and taquitos de moronga. The first combines tasty shreds of roast pork, chili chipotle (actually smoked jalapeño chilies), diced onions and tomato rolled in soft flour tortillas like thick cigars; the other taquitos hold morsels of earthy blood pudding, sliced onions and fresh coriander.

The guacamole is justly famous. A waiter brings a ripe avocado to the table and prepares it to the preferred degree of hotness. The avocado is cubed, not mashed, and blended with tomato, coriander, assorted minced peppers and fresh lime juice. Another engaging starter is briefly sautéed oysters served chilled and in the shell with the natural brine and lemon juice—a rousing summer dish.

Starters that don't make the grade are fishy-tasting steamed clams in a chili-laced broth and bland jalapeño peppers studded with dry sardines.

Service in the back room is better than in the front, where understaffing can lead to delays. Waiters are well versed in the menu and are usually happy to accommodate special requests.

Grilled entrees are particularly well executed, whether it is the crusty seared shell steak under strips of sautéed chilies poblanos and onions, mildly piquant chicken, or fist-thick beef ribs basted with lemon juice and beer and accompanied by four garnishes (tomatillo, spicy tomato, coriander-onion salsa and beans). Grilled marinated red snapper is fresh and well cooked but oddly lacks flavor at times. Try the coriander-flecked baked snapper instead.

Unfortunately the roast duck breast and leg consistently suffer from overcooking, for the sauce of pureed green tomatoes, green chiles and pumpkin seeds is terrific. Fanciers of chili rellenos will find the version here more refined than most: a single large poblano chili is stuffed with mild white cheese, lightly battered and fried, then presented in a sparkling tomato broth.

The consistently best entree to my taste is carnitas, a simple but delicious combination of succulent cubed pork paired with soft flour tortillas and four sauces that you add to taste, at your own risk: fiery mole sauce, coriander-onion vinaigrette, red tomato and green tomatillo.

A few tropical desserts are worth considering. Flan with coffee sauce is a good combination, and mango fruitcake—sort of a bread pudding with frothy mango sauce—is a nice twist on the north-of-the-border version. While I found the crepes smothered with caramelized sauce of goat's milk and sherry too sweet, several diners at my table liked it. Mango ice cream is a ripe and refreshing alternative, although papaya is pale and icy—maybe dropping it into a margarita would help.

◆ ROXANNE'S ◆

Satisfactory

158 Eighth Avenue, at 18th Street, 741-2455.

Atmosphere: Engaging little restaurant with two narrow dining rooms and an outdoor garden.

Service: Friendly but distracted and inattentive.

Price range: Moderately expensive.

Credit cards: MasterCard and Visa.

Hours: Lunch, Monday through Friday, noon to 2:30 P.M.; dinner, Monday through Saturday, 6 to 11:30 P.M. Closed Sunday.

Reservations: Necessary.

Rarely have I seen such a meteoric fall in a restaurant as at Roxanne's, which received two stars shortly after opening in 1984. If there are any herbs or seasonings in the kitchen—or even a salt shaker—they rarely got near my food. What's more, the kitchen specializes in overcooking and undercooking. Unaccountably, the restaurant is packed to overflowing nightly, testimony perhaps to the sorry state of gastronomic affairs in Chelsea.

Roxanne's is an attractive spot with a lively bar in the front and dining areas on two descending tiers that lead to an enchanting garden in the back. The service staff is good-natured but often distracted and inattentive. The owner, Roxanne Betesh, is an accommodating hostess who darts around the place trying to fill in the gaps. The biggest gap, however, is in the kitchen.

Among the sorry appetizers is a ballottine of salmon—a ring of salmon stuffed with a tasteless mousse of scallops, sole and Alaskan king crab—in a tomato-basil sauce. Poached mussels with squid rings look tempting with their colorful garnish of diced onions, coriander, tomato and herbs but are utterly bland. And undercooked sweetbreads in a grossly sweet framboise-and-port sauce were inedible. Only one starter, a special, was satisfactory: bay scallops glossed with a Pernod-tinged sauce.

Roast red snapper surrounded by snow peas, carrots and potatoes was the only good seafood dish sampled; tournedos in a sweet zinfandel-stock reduction received a split vote at my table.

The remaining entrees are dreary: flabby and oily soft-shell crabs, chilled galantine of chicken overloaded with thyme and served with a cloying cranberry mayonnaise, insipid chilled lobster with capellini in tomato vinaigrette, and a sprightly gazpacho that suffers from the addition of oddly watery and flavorless shellfish.

Several desserts rescued our flagging spirits. Lime cheesecake is exceptionally vibrant and light, and pot de crème under a layer of chocolate shavings is wonderfully rich.

✦ THE RUSSIAN TEA ROOM ✦

★

150 West 57th Street, 265-0947.

Atmosphere: Exuberant holiday feeling with Christmas colors and the sense that important things are happening around you.

Service: Routine and at times slapdash, especially for unrecognized customers.

Price range: Moderately expensive.

Credit cards: All major cards.

Hours: Lunch and dinner, daily, 11:30 A.M. to midnight.

Reservations: Requested.

The "RTR" is theater, business and tourism in equal parts. The theater is in the decor. The dining room has pine-green walls, Santa Claus–red banquettes, mismatched paintings, gleaming brass samovars and tinsel-lined chandeliers supporting shiny red Christmas-tree balls. The upstairs sports a less prodigal version of the same color scheme. There is really nothing wrong with the second floor unless you can't bear to eat without the possibility of seeing Dustin Hoffman.

The business side of the Tea Room is evident at lunchtime, when theater gents and notables from the entertainment world cut deals over caviar and blini. Some days it seems to take an Actors Equity card to get a downstairs table. The crackling ambiance is repeated in after-theater hours. As for the food, it has become less consistent in recent years, although many of the house specialties still hold their own. The highly pressured waiters tend to be a mirthless lot, at least to strangers, and fine points of service have all but vanished.

Stay with the well-known specialties. Cliché though it may be, côtelette à la Kiev is worth trying. The moist breast of chicken, rolled and lightly breaded, spurts butter like an unplugged garden hose. Don't confuse it with côtelette de volaille, which is dried out.

The karsky shashlik, a delicious lamb fillet with kidneys, is superior to the shashlik caucasian ($2 supplement) with its sinewy cubes of dry lamb on skewers with onions and tomatoes. The only fish on the menu is salmon, and it is fresh and nicely broiled, blanketed with a thick lemon-butter sauce. Lightness is not the hallmark of RTR cooking. The cherry-and-mushroom sauce on the roast duckling Vereniki is syrupy and overly sweet; beef à la Stroganoff, which also has a sweet undertone, was so viscous and rich I could eat only a third of it; leathery strips of beef throughout didn't help.

The borscht, both hot and cold, is still a winner. Zakuska, a Russian appetizer plate ($2.75 supplement), is the best way to start a meal because you get to sample miniportions of many dishes. One of my favorite selections is the eggplant Orientale, a puree blending eggplant, onion, green peppers, tomatoes and spices. The lunch menu is similar to the dinner menu with the addition of several sandwiches and salads—salmon salad and chef's salad are lunchroom quality.

The most regal dish at the Tea Room is caviar and blini. You feel like an old-world Russian aristocrat as a waiter fusses at tableside swathing the earthy buckwheat blini with snowy sour cream and sparkling caviar. All kinds of firm and briny caviar are available with blini: beluga costs $44, osetra $41 and sevruga $39. A fitting accompaniment is champagne (available by the glass or carafe) or one of the bar's twenty types of imported vodka ($4.25 a shot).

The wine list is small for an establishment this size. If you start the meal with one or more of the house-vodka cocktails, which pack the strength of a Soviet wrestler, chances are you won't notice.

The best dessert is cranberry kissel, which is essentially a puree of cranberry sauce, cream and sugar. It is refreshing and both tart and sweet. Dense clouds of Russian cream flavored with vanilla are hard to resist, as is the kasha à la Gourieff, a sweetened farina garnished with kiwi, strawberries and almond slivers.

✦ SABOR ✦

★ ★

20 Cornelia Street, between West Fourth and Bleecker streets, 243-9579.

Atmosphere: Small, informal and rustic dining room with Latin music piped in.

Service: Friendly, enthusiastic and casual.

Price range: Moderate.

Credit cards: American Express, MasterCard, Visa.

Hours: Dinner, Sunday through Thursday, 6 to 11 P.M., Friday and Saturday, 6 P.M. to midnight. Closed Christmas Day and New Year's Day.

Reservations: Recommended.

Sabor is one of those quietly competent restaurants that could remain anonymous only in New York City. Anywhere else it would be widely hailed as one of the best little spots in town. Working out of a kitchen the size of a bus shelter, the cooks turn out a lineup of Cuban and Spanish food that is authentic-tasting, boldly seasoned and utterly delicious. At Sabor, hot means hot, sweet means sweet, spicy means spicy. Every dish might not be to your taste, but it is guaranteed that all of them will make your taste buds stand at attention.

Sip one of the fresh-fruit daiquiris or lime margaritas while scanning the appetizers, which include marinated fresh squid rings in a spicy tomato sauce, pickled kingfish mackerel and a zarzuela of mussels. The squid is bright, resilient and flavorful. Mackerel fillets are delicious in the pickling of carrots, onions, fresh bay leaf, olives and capers.

Frituras de malanga, bite-size nuggets of a tropical potato-like vegetable pureed with garlic and parsley, are reason enough to consider warming relations with Fidel Castro. They come with two hot sauces. Empanadas filled with chorizo and tamales are better than most available in Mexican restaurants around town. The entrees may take some explanation, and the two waitresses, who are friendly and efficient in a languid sort of way, are more than willing to walk you through the gastronomic thicket. Highly recommended are any seafood dishes with salsa verde (green sauce). A whole baked snapper comes out deftly roasted and blanketed with a slightly pungent and citric sauce of pureed fresh parsley, white wine, garlic, capers and lime juice. The same sauce brings life to a plate of sautéed shrimp.

The zarzuela de mariscos is identical to the mussels appetizer with the addition of clams, shrimp, scallops and squid. Bacalao à la Vizcaina, a Spanish specialty that to some is an acquired taste, is faithfully reproduced here. Dry salted codfish that has been soaked in water to moisten and desalinate it is served in a warm salad tossed with potatoes, olives and assorted vegetables in a tomato sauce. Don't miss the side dish of sautéed plátanos. Two kinds are offered: the ripe, which are dark orange and wonderfully sweet, and the green, which have little appeal without some hot sauce.

Cuban food is not restricted to seafood and vegetables. Two tasty beef dishes were the carne estofada (stuffed meat) and ropa vieja (it translates as "old clothes," but it's really shredded meat). The former is a well-braised pot roast with an exotic brown gravy made by pureeing vegetables with sherry and fresh orange. The other dish is a sinewy but tender flank steak in a piquant red sauce perfumed with cloves and cinnamon. Of the two chicken dishes on the menu, pollo con comino is the better—boneless chicken breasts marinated in lime juice, garlic and cumin served in a light sauce with red peppers and onions.

Sabor turns out a knockout Key lime pie. It is served in a fragile tartlet crust, and the semisweet, lime-loaded filling is more like custard than a pie. Another winner is the coco quemado, a hot coconut custard with a blistered coconut crust. It's flavored with sherry and cinnamon and is served with a dollop of fresh whipped cream.

Sabor will prepare a feast around a roast suckling pig for groups of eight or more. It is well worth trying. The succulent pig is presented to diners before carving resting on a bed of lettuce with grapes for eyes and a red apple in the mouth. The meat was moist and smoky while the skin was brittle and grease-less. The pig comes with many of the appetizers and side dishes mentioned, plus saffron-chorizo rice, for about $40 a person, including dessert and coffee.

✦ SIAM INN ✦

★

916 Eighth Avenue, at 54th Street, 489-5237.

Atmosphere: Informal, dimly lit dining room with Tai artwork on the walls.

Service: Friendly and competent.

Price range: Inexpensive.

Credit cards: American Express and Diners Club.

Hours: Lunch, Monday through Friday, noon to 3 P.M.; dinner, Monday through Saturday, 5 to 11:30 P.M., Sunday, 5 to 11 P.M.

Reservations: Suggested.

Siam Inn, a dimly lit, pleasantly appointed restaurant, is fairly typical of the genre of Thai restaurants in town, perhaps a notch better than average. It turns out several bright dishes that reflect the exotic allure of this cuisine.

Start with an appetizer called curry puffs, inflated crescents of light pastry stuffed with a sweetish combination of curried ground chicken, potatoes and onions. It comes with a vinegar-based cucumber sauce that foils the sweetness nicely. Another good preliminary is spicy fish cakes made with ground kingfish, which are crusty and browned outside yet moist within.

The best entree is the steamed seafood combination. It comes to the table enclosed in aluminum foil that is molded into the shape of a swan. Inside are mussels, shrimp, squid, cubes of salmon, fermented black beans and ginger in a pool of aromatic fish broth enlivened with fresh lemon. You could round out this meal with a platter of Bangkok duck—the meat is rich and succulent, the skin crisp, and the mildly sweet sauce tinged with tamarind and curry. So much for the menu's A-team; now for a tour of the dugout.

If the kitchen has one overriding flaw that debases some otherwise good preparations, it is a relentless sweet tooth. The cold spring-roll appetizer, for instance, is a cool combination of bean sprouts, Thai sausage, bean curd and minced vegetables wrapped in rice paper, but a lollipop-sweet sauce overwhelms it. Thai salads—lettuce, cucumber, bean sprouts and bean cake—suffer the same fate under a shower of sweet coconut-milk-and-peanut dressing.

Even the most famous Thai dish of all, pla lad prig, is marred

246

by a sucrose attack. The deep-fried red snapper set over a bed of spinach is mired in a thick sauce that is both aggressively sweet and aggressively hot at the same time—the ensuing battle on the palate leaves the fish all but lost. Another familiar preparation, beef saté, was disappointing. The strips of meat had been overmarinated before grilling, leaving them unpleasantly mealy. You would be better off with the shrimp in mild curry sauce cut with coconut milk and red peppers.

Two satisfying entrees are the broiled salmon with a garlic-and-scallion sauce and frogs' legs in a straightforward garlic sauce. At lunch the sautéed shrimp in garlic sauce was drenched in oil. The best side dish is pad Thai, a tasty mélange of minced shrimp, egg, dried bean cake and bean sprouts.

Probably the most suitable beverage with this assertive cuisine is beer; wine fanciers will find a tiny but relatively decent selection. The staff at Siam Inn is accommodating and efficient in a laconic sort of way, and the setting is usually tranquil enough for easy conversation. Don't bother with the commercial-tasting desserts—carrot cake, assorted pies and the like. Siam Inn, which earned two stars in 1981, has slipped a notch to one-star status.

◆ SISTINA ◆

★ ★

1555 Second Avenue, between 80th and 81st streets, 861-7660.

Atmosphere: Spare, bright, cheerful.

Service: Patient and attentive when waiters aren't overburdened by crowds.

Price range: Moderately expensive.

Credit cards: American Express.

Hours: Lunch, Monday through Friday, noon to 2:30 P.M.; dinner, Monday through Saturday, 5 P.M. to midnight, Sunday, 5 to 11 P.M.

Reservations: Necessary.

Run by a group of young, first-generation Italians, Sistina serves dishes with an inventive spark, a cut above the pack, even when reinterpreting some of the old standards.

The rectangular dining room is trim and cheerful—unstained oak walls, bent-cane chairs, rows of tables with starched white napery. Trim Italian waiters make everything sound irresistible as they describe the food with finger-kissing gesticulations.

Among the better starters are the two types of crostini. The crostini supremi features two thick slices of Italian bread coated with intense olive oil and layered with roast peppers, mozzarella cheese and anchovies; the polenta crostini is made by topping crisp slabs of cornmeal toast with white beans in tomato sauce, fresh parsley and Parmesan cheese.

Delizia di mare, or seafood salad, is sparkling: a briny assortment of squid, octopus, shrimp, black olives and tomato in a mild oregano-scented vinaigrette. One exasperating feature of this restaurant is the untranslated Italian menu. Some of the dishes' esoteric names leave even Italians scratching their heads: pollo Vesuviano (exploding chicken?), filetti di sogliola gran successo and so on. As a result, waiters spend all evening lunging from one perplexed table to the next.

One item that doesn't need translation is fresh white truffles, served in the fall, which a waiter waved under our noses, making his easiest sale of the night. They are shaved over tonnarelli (thin spaghetti) with a light cream sauce ($20 for a generous appetizer portion; $35 as an entree). Nearly all the pastas are superior, including the penne ai sette re, tubular noodles swathed in fresh tomato, basil, arugula and garlic; the same noodles all'amatriciana, a lusty sauce made with tomato, garlic, basil and chunks of smoky pancetta bacon; and lustrous, fresh linguine ai frutti di mare, overflowing with shrimp, squid, scallops, mussels and clams.

When they have fresh giant Spanish shrimp, ask for them grilled and with lemon wedges. The grilled bay scallops, on the other hand, tasted poached and were mired in a watery, tasteless sauce. Better are the crisp and golden fried calamari and the striped bass cooked in parchment paper. By far the best side dish is deep-fried zucchini sliced into threads so thin they crackle and break when you touch them.

Top quality veal is served here, and among the better preparations are costoletta Val d'Aosta, a thick, tender chop stuffed with prosciutto, mozzarella and mushrooms that is roasted and served with a white-wine sauce, and veal scaloppine sorpresa, breaded medallions sautéed with artichoke hearts and fresh peas, lemon and wine. The sauce has a stimulating citric edge.

Desserts are satisfying if unexciting—crème caramel, ice cream, chocolate mousse cake. Strawberries with winy zabaglione are better. The most intriguing dessert, however, is fresh raspberries with a dousing of balsamic vinegar. The unlikely combination, both sweet and tart, is absolutely ethereal.

✦ SPARKS STEAKHOUSE ✦

★ ★

210 East 46th Street, 687-4855.

Atmosphere: Bustling and masculine steakhouse ambiance in large, wood-lined dining rooms.

Service: Efficient in a brisk manner.

Price range: Moderately expensive.

Credit cards: All major cards.

Hours: Lunch, Monday through Friday, noon to 3 P.M.; dinner, Monday through Thursday, 5 to 11 P.M., Friday and Saturday, 5 to 11:30 P.M. Closed Sunday.

Reservations: Required.

Everything at Sparks Steakhouse is oversize—the dining rooms, the steaks, the chops, the lobsters, the wine list, even the customers. This bustling, masculine outpost is, in my view, everything a good steakhouse should be.

It sports dark burnished woodwork that glows under amber lighting, starched white tables that are well separated and a bonhomous bar where whiskey still appears to edge out white wine and Perrier. Moreover, the rosy, dry-aged steaks with charred, salt-edged crusts are among the best in town.

Sparks is not the kind of place where you go for a romantic evening or for people-watching. A sizable percentage of the nightly crowd consists of ex-college-linebackers-turned-pin-striped-businessmen who congregate at large tables to tackle thick steaks and swap tall tales. Service is efficient in a brisk sort of way. The place spins at 78 rpm in order to keep up with the huge volume, and consequently dishes sometimes appear a bit too quickly for comfort. If you are in a leisurely mood, make it known.

Typical steakhouse appetizers are offered, and on the whole they are superior to those in similar establishments. The lump crab meat and scallop starter is fresh tasting, buttery and not overcooked (the scallops, however, look and taste like ocean calicos, not bay scallops as described on the menu). The combination of sautéed shrimp and breaded baked clams is also well prepared. Icy bluepoint oysters on the half shell and oceanic little cherrystones are first rate.

The menu carries an adequate selection of fish. However, going to Sparks for grilled tuna is like spending a winter weekend in Aspen playing tennis. My favorite steak is the unadorned prime sirloin—broiled exactly to order, incredibly tender and intensely beefy. Close runners-up are the thick and buttery rib lamb chops and the juicy charred veal chop. Filet mignon, which so often is textureless and bland, is anything but that here—juicy, firm yet tender. Side dishes include hash brown potatoes —golden and moist once, a bit dry another time—baked potatoes (same inconsistency) and nicely cooked spinach and broccoli.

Only when the kitchen tries to get a little fancy with beef does it get into trouble, so in general avoid sauces.

Of the seafood entrees sampled, swordfish steak, tuna steak and rainbow trout usually cannot be faulted. Enormous lobsters, split and broiled, are available in three sizes: small, medium and something resembling a Japanese subcompact. Our nearly 3½-pounder was fresh and well cooked, with lots of briny roe. I just wish waiters would reveal prices as they describe the selections —in this case $45.

The Sparks wine list is legendary. I find it curious, though, for a restaurant that takes such pride in the depth of its cellar to lack a sommelier who could help guide customers through it. For dessert the highlights are a good creamy cheesecake and a base-ball-size chocolate-covered tartufo with whipped cream.

Sparks is a well-focused restaurant that knows exactly what its clientele wants and how to provide it with impressive consistency. For first-rate steak, it is my prime choice.

◆ SUKHOTHAI ◆

★

149 Second Avenue, between 9th and 10th streets, 460-5557.

Atmosphere: Pub atmosphere with brick walls, brass rails, long bar and high ceiling. Noise level moderate.

Service: Slow and confused when the restaurant is more than half full.

Price range: Inexpensive.

Credit cards: American Express, MasterCard and Visa.

Hours: Dinner, Sunday through Thursday, 5 to 11 P.M., Friday and Saturday until midnight.

Reservations: Suggested for weekdays; required for weekends.

Sukhothai, a relative newcomer to this raffish block of cafes and bars, is in the forefront of a creeping renaissance in this neighborhood. The restaurant is on the second story of an aging building in a former English-style bar and grill. The Thai family that took over did not try to Orientalize it. Instead, they left intact its long wooden bar, brick walls, brass railings and garish multicolored-glass ceiling panel. The air-conditioning system leaves much to be desired at times, so dress lightly on warm days.

Most of the wooden tables are a bit wobbly—and so is the service. The small staff, besides having difficulties with English, becomes easily overtaxed.

These inconveniences aside, there are several good reasons to visit Sukhothai. It offers some zesty hot and spicy dishes as well as a few nicely fried tidbits at budget prices. Foremost among them is the appetizer of deep-fried minced shrimp with Thai spices wrapped in bean curd. The cooks are deft at frying, and these flavorful little dough pockets are light, mildly seasoned and strong with the flavor of shrimp. They come with an invigorating sweet-and-sour sauce. Exotic and equally tasty starters are the kingfish dumplings perfumed with curry. They are served with sliced cucumbers soaked in a tart fermented fish sauce that has just a hint of sweetness. The kingfish has a chewy texture and a flavor not unlike pork.

Both of the satés—char-broiled morsels of marinated chicken or beef swabbed with peanut sauce—are moist and delicious.

Another pleasing offering is a deep bowl of plump mussels steamed in peppery broth flavored with scallions, green peppers, bay leaf, lemon and lime. The fried bean cakes are greaseless and crisp but devoid of flavor, and Thai salad is a lackluster mound of pale greens and sprouts.

Thai food embraces diverse taste sensations—hot, spicy, citric, sweet, herbaceous—so when you order, remember to choose dishes that span the flavor range to get the full effect. This is easier said than done at Sukhothai because some of the asterisks printed on the menu, which supposedly indicate dishes that are hot and spicy, seem to be tossed around at random.

Soups are accurately labeled, and some are exceptional. The hot-and-sour shrimp soup, redolent of fragrant lemon grass, combines fish sauce with Oriental mushrooms, chili and lime to achieve just the right balance between hot and sour, pushing you right to the threshold of peppery pain, then backing off and soothing the palate with fresh lime. Another multidimensional taste sensation is set off by the exotic chicken soup that combines coconut milk, lime juice, chili paste and loads of fresh coriander. The coriander imparted a dry edge that foiled the sweet coconut.

The entree list looks impressive large at first, but upon closer inspection one realizes that many of the preparations are the same, only the main ingredient is different. Seafood seems to be the best bet. Aside from the aforementioned grilled shrimp, deep-fried whole sea bass under a blizzard of garlic is a good rendition of this standard Thai dish. Another good selection is the seafood combination with Thai spices. The food came out in an inflated foil bag the size of a football. When pierced, it releases a cloud of saline steam. When the air clears, it reveals the familiar Thai cast of characters—shrimp, squid, mussels and scallions tossed with rice noodles and stoked with whole red chili pods. The combination is fresh, evenly cooked and resting in a pool of broth that is dotted with explosive mines of hot chili pods. Navigate around them at all cost. While Sukhothai has limited ambitions, it does enough things well to give you a taste of Thailand's intriguing cuisine at budget prices.

✦ TANDOOR ✦

★

40 East 49th Street, 752-3334.

Atmosphere: Roomy and comfortable with dim lighting and low noise level.

Service: Indifferent and slow.

Price range: Moderate.

Credit cards: All major cards.

Hours: Lunch, daily, noon to 3 P.M.; dinner, daily, 5:30 to 11:30 P.M.

Reservations: Required.

The fare in most of New York's Indian restaurants is fairly predictable: scarlet curtains in the dining room, dim lighting, a hushed ambiance and soft-spoken managers wearing tinted, black-framed glasses. The best you can hope for is well-made breads, tandoor-roasted specialties, authentically hot and spicy stews and fresh vegetable-rice preparations. That, in short, is what you get at Tandoor, the spacious, low-key midtown restaurant.

The main dining room is accommodating with its tufted red banquettes, ornate wall moldings and Indian paintings. Unfortunately, the phlegmatic waiters do not contribute to a welcoming atmosphere—they tend to be distant and slow—but if you are willing to endure that inconvenience, there is some pleasing food to be had.

As the restaurant's name implies, the ancient art of baking foods in the clay tandoor oven is a specialty. Tandoori chicken, in which the meat is marinated in yogurt and spices and tinted bright orange with a natural dye, is right on target—succulent, complexly seasoned and faintly smoky. A similar dish in which the chicken is deboned before baking, called tikka, is the best of all, buttery tender and suffused with complex spices.

I rarely like fish cooked in the super-hot tandoor oven because it tends to dry out quickly, but the chefs here could teach their counterparts at other restaurants a thing or two. Both the tandoori fish tikka, made with tilefish, and the tandoori shrimp are delicious, spiced just enough to give them a sharp edge without masking their delicate flavors.

To serious Indian food enthusiasts, vindaloo, the smoldering dish from Goa on the southwestern Indian coast, is the real test of a chef's mettle. Both the lamb and the fish vindaloos at Tandoor are among the better ones in town. The slow-burning tomato-based sauce, kindled with hot peppers, ginger and garlic, is as warming as a potbellied stove in January.

In the vegetarian category, the best dish is alu bengan, grilled eggplant and potatoes in an engaging blend of herbs. Navrattan curry sounded tempting—nine vegetables cooked with nuts, mild spices and cream—but it turns out to resemble something you might find in a suburban Cantonese restaurant.

I suggest you bypass most of the appetizers and go right to the entrees. Traditional starters such as chicken chaat, for example—cold slices of tender white meat in a mint sauce—had an old and acrid flavor; on another occasion the alu chaat, a coriander-spiced potato salad with the same sauce, was much fresher. Samosas, the deep-fried pastries stuffed with spicy potatoes and peas, were satisfactory, while the bite-size fritters called pakoras, filled with individual vegetables, were thick-skinned and greasy.

A safer bet is the mulligatawny soup, a soothing and subtle blend of chicken stock, lentils, complex spices and cream. It is especially good with any of the wonderful homemade breads: puffed and charred tandoor-baked nan; exquisite onion kulcha, a nan stuffed with sweet spiced onions and coriander; earthy whole-wheat chapati and the buttery multilayered paratha.

In addition to the handful of dessert items on the menu, there is a small pastry cart carrying lovely sweet honey buns soaked in syrup called gulab jamun, as well as rasmalai, the sweetened cheese dumplings flavored with rose water and nuts (which was dry), and a bland coconut cake. The standouts, however, are the two fresh and intensely flavored ice creams—mango and fig.

A good lunch bargain is the daily buffet for $9.95, which features a wide range of the menu selections. Tandoor is a restaurant I will return to whenever I need a dose of spice in my life. And if the sullen staff cheers up and tightens its act, it may well merit two stars again.

✦ TAVERN ON THE GREEN ✦

Satisfactory

Central Park West at 67th Street, 873-3200.

Atmosphere: Enormous assortment of public and private dining rooms. Tongue-in-cheek garish and loud decor with abundance of fresh flowers inside and illuminated trees outside.

Service: Personable but overextended and slow.

Price range: Moderately expensive.

Credit cards: All major cards.

Hours: Lunch, Monday through Friday, noon to 3 P.M., Saturday and Sunday, 10 A.M. to 3 P.M.; dinner, Monday through Friday, 5:30 P.M. to 12:15 A.M., Saturday and Sunday, 5 P.M. to 12:15 A.M.

Reservations: Suggested.

Tavern on the Green is a balloon-popping, birthday-partying, boisterous and brassy institution that dazzles out-of-towners and locals alike with its outlandish rococo decor and stunning Central Park backdrop—dining by Disney. Almost all the thrills and spills, however, are visual.

This enormous restaurant, with its glittery glass-enclosed main dining room abloom with azaleas and every sort of wacky tongue-in-cheek design hyperbole, is unlikely ever to be in the front ranks of New York cuisine. It is simply too big to get out of its own way. It could, however, do much better. The unworkably large menu flirts with many types of popular cuisine—a little California, some Italian, French, and even a Chinese accent here and there—but embraces none with passion.

Take a fatuous creation such as grilled scallops in lime-butter sauce with sesame seed–coated grapes—even if the seeds had not been slightly burned in the deep fryer, the combination would have been jarring. And who wants perfectly decent smoked chicken upstaged by a chorus line of chichi fruits (kiwis, strawberries, plums and raspberries) in a cloying blackberry coulis? The two best starters sampled were lobster salad with green beans and artichokes, and boneless quail stuffed with apples and raisins wrapped in a crepe.

Considering the throngs that pass through the restaurant every night, the service staff is remarkably composed and good-natured, but not very efficient. Waiters and waitresses get lost in the crowd when you need them.

The best entrees were the simplest. A grilled veal chop one evening was excellent, thick and tender, served with little pancakes of Gorgonzola cheese. Grilled salmon steak was first-rate too, but please, hold the sweet lemon and lime chutneys. You expect to find prime rib of beef here, and you surely get it—the enormous hulk is the size of a catcher's mitt, beefy and cooked to order, escorted by a papery-dry Yorkshire pudding. Desserts present the same rocky road.

257

Tavern on the Green cannot be dismissed entirely, however. It is still an enchanting place to have outdoor drinks and snacks under the illuminated trees. And children always get a kick out of the place, especially during the holidays, what with the balloons, festive lights and all. If the kitchen eventually shapes up, it could be fun for grown-ups too.

✦ TERRACE ✦

★ ★

400 West 119th Street, 666-9490.

Atmosphere: Romantic, low-lit dining rooms with panoramic views of Manhattan.

Service: Straightforward and professional.

Price range: Expensive.

Credit cards: All major cards.

Hours: Lunch, Tuesday through Friday, noon to 2:30 P.M.; dinner, Tuesday through Thursday, 6 to 10 P.M., Friday and Saturday, 6 to 10:30 P.M. Closed Sunday and Monday.

Reservations: Suggested.

The Terrace's rise in recent years could be attributed to the gifted chef Dušan Bernic, but his death in 1984 raised doubts about its future. Mr. Bernic's widow, Nada, took over the reins and with the help of the former sous-chef, Dominic Payraudeau, attempted to carry on in her husband's fashion. I am happy to report that on the whole they are succeeding.

The Terrace has many enticements, foremost among them the sensational view from its glass-enclosed perch on the fourteenth floor. Off to the northwest, one sees the illuminated bracelet of the George Washington Bridge, and to the south, the brilliant spires of midtown Manhattan. The two spacious dining rooms are romantic in an old-world manner, with low lighting, tall candles, harp or piano music and a solitary rose on each table.

As for the food under the new regime, it continues to lean heavily on classic French preparations that are carried out with a light touch. Superior appetizers include the fresh and vivid poached oysters served on the half shell—the shells are lined with minced mushrooms and shallots and the oysters are glazed with a champagne sauce. The house pork terrine is well seasoned and bolstered with just a touch of liver, while the sautéed foie gras with raspberry vinegar and truffles—somewhat of a cliché these days—gets high marks for flavor and texture. Near misses are a crayfish terrine that, while bright and fresh, failed to convey the flavor or texture of those delicate little critters, and rather dull marinated raw salmon.

The tuxedoed captains know their jobs and perform them congenially and efficiently. The wine selection runs deep, especially through Bordeaux, and prices are more or less in line.

The entrees may not dazzle with bold juxtapositions of exotic ingredients, but that's not the intention here. The Terrace offers reliability over rakishness: a Mercedes versus a Ferrari. Florid and tender rack of lamb with fresh mint puree, sweetbreads in a port-and-truffle sauce, lobster cloaked in a Pernod beurre blanc, duck à l'orange the way it should be (not too sweet), beef tenderloin in a tarragon-and-green-peppercorn sauce—all are straightforwardly pleasing.

Other winners are two specials: a deftly grilled red snapper accented with garlic and herbs, and blush-pink poached salmon ringed with scallop mousse and spinach. Two dishes that fail to deliver on their promises are flaccid veal with morels and sweet onion mousse, and bland quail with shallots, ginger and herbs.

It is only fitting that such a traditional restaurant will roll out the old multitiered, silver dessert chariot. In this case, though, showmanship superseded logic, for several nicely made cream-based desserts—rum-spiked chocolate cake with mocha filling, and hazelnut meringue cake with strawberries and butter cream —got too warm sitting out all evening. The kitchen excels at puff pastries and tart crusts. Try the exceptional raspberry napoleon, orange-chantilly pie and a bulbous caramelized apple tart (mislabeled tarte Tatin). And the crème brûlée here is one of the best in town—with a burnished glassy sugar lid over a silky custard.

Overall it is reassuring to see that, despite its recent trials, the Terrace has upheld its classy and conscientious reputation—an Ivy Leaguer all the way.

✦ TRASTEVERE ✦

★ ★

309 East 83rd Street, 734-6343

Atmosphere: Tiny rectangular room, dark, candlelit and romantic in a confined sort of way. Tables are frustratingly small and chairs spindly and stiff.

Service: Adequate. Pacing of the meal is leisurely but not laggard.

Price range: Moderately expensive.

Credit cards: American Express and personal checks accepted.

Hours: Dinner, daily, 5 to 11 P.M.

Reservations: Necessary.

Trastevere is a Roman-style sliver of a restaurant on the Upper East Side owned by the energetic Lattanzi family, which has since expanded its domain to include another restaurant a block away, Trastevere 84, as well as Erminia's on East 83rd Street and Lattanzi on West 46th Street. Dining at the original Trastevere is like watching the late show on television—there is nothing new or surprising on the schedule, but some of the oldies are as enjoyable as ever.

The menu carries pasta with such traditional sauces as amatriciana, white sauce with clams, and primavera, in addition to such familiar dishes as chicken with Marsala wine and mushrooms, veal scaloppine, and shrimp with garlic and wine.

The tiny candle-lit dining room adorned with old prints is romantic—that is, if you don't mind the undersized tables and stiff chairs. Waiters are usually within arm's reach, literally, so it is easy to get their attention.

You would do well to start with one of the better appetizers, such as the lightly fried and tasty spiedino alla romana made with prosciutto, mozzarella and anchovy sauce, or the bright vegetable salad for two combining green beans, artichoke, zucchini, roast potatoes, broiled tomato wedges and red peppers.

Many patrons split a portion of pasta as a first course—at about $16 a bowl you don't order profligately. Linguine with white clam sauce is a model of how the dish should be done. It is made with aromatic basil leaves, lots of garlic and good olive oil. The sparkling little clams are cooked to tender perfection and arranged, still in the shells, over the pasta. Trastevere's version of capellini primavera is a welcome change from the run-of-the-mill preparation, which is so often filled with woody hunks of underseasoned vegetables; this one blends al dente capellini with firm, steamed morsels of broccoli florets, zucchini and fresh peas in a vibrant tomato-and-basil sauce. The fettuccine Trastevere, featuring a sauce made with peas, prosciutto, mushrooms and cream, slowed a famished diner at my table from a gallop to a saunter in just a few bites. The sauce also suffered from an overpowering mushroom flavor.

One expects a much better wine list in a restaurant of this caliber and price range. Some of the commonplace Italian whites and reds are significantly overpriced.

Among meat entrees a nod goes to the vitello Trastevere, a pummeled piece of top-quality veal that is breaded and nicely fried, then served under a knoll of tomatoes and lettuce in a subtle vinaigrette—it makes a fine warm-weather dish. That old Italian workhorse veal piccante benefited from the same tender breaded veal in a lemony wine-and-butter sauce. Of the chicken dishes sampled, pollo alla romana—moist chicken nuggets in a tomato-wine sauce bolstered with green peppers, onions and rosemary—packs plenty of flavor; not so the pollo alla Gaetano, which features the same chicken, this time dried out, in a nondescript garlic and mushroom sauce.

Shrimp are exceptionally well prepared, whether in the scampi Angela (sautéed with garlic and wine) or as part of the excellent zuppa di pesce replete with whitefish, clams, mussels, lobster and squid in a lively tomato-based broth.

And for dessert? Just what you might expect—a baseball-size tartufo with a dark chocolate "hide" enclosing chocolate ice cream. The surprisingly light and flaky napoleon is a winner, while the leaden, fudgelike chocolate mousse is guaranteed to energize you for the evening.

In this era of anything-goes Italian food, Trastevere holds to the old verities and demonstrates their enduring appeal.

◆ 20 MOTT STREET ◆ RESTAURANT

★

20 Mott Street, 964-0380.

Atmosphere: Bright, bustling, three-tiered restaurant.

Service: Waiters can be helpful when you get their attention, however they are easily distracted.

Price range: Inexpensive.

Credit cards: All major cards.

Hours: Lunch and dinner, Sunday through Thursday, 8 A.M. to 1 A.M., Friday and Saturday until 2 A.M.

Reservations: Suggested.

If you are a fan of Chinese-style roast duck, hop in a cab and scoot down to 20 Mott Street Restaurant, a Cantonese restaurant in Chinatown. The duck is one of the best in town—remarkably succulent and flavorful meat, lustrous burnished skin and a base of earthy black bean sauce.

Not everything is so memorable; nevertheless, there are other reasons for trying this bright, airy, three-story restaurant. Start with the unusual spring rolls, dark golden thick cylinders stuffed with Chinese mushrooms, pork and tofu, or the fried dumplings made with rice-flour dough around an aromatic blend of tender spiced pork. Pass over the salty spare ribs; instead, get the plump golden-fried crab claws.

The menu at 20 Mott Street is typically encyclopedic. But if you can get the undivided attention of one of the waiters, who seem to enjoy hobnobbing with Oriental customers to the exclusion of befuddled Caucasians, ask about off-menu specials. With a little luck, you'll discover the delicious deep-fried squid and buttery scallops served on lettuce leaves with a sweetish sauce.

One evening, we spotted a waiter darting out of the kitchen with an overflowing platter of steaming hard crabs in a glistening sauce. We quickly ordered the dish by pointing furiously, only to discover it is called crabs with black bean sauce on the menu. Excavating crab with chopsticks is no picnic, but the effort was worth it, especially with that spicy bean sauce. The restaurant serves beer and plum wine to quell the fires, but nothing else. Among the soups tried, a tart and fresh watercress and sliced pork in tasty broth was better than the pallid sliced-fish soup (the latter was an off-menu special).

The entree list is so large one can offer only a cross section based on more than two dozen dishes sampled. While the plain roast duck is superb, the more elaborate Peking duck is disappointing. It comes out in two courses: the first featuring small overly thick pancakes sandwiching fatty duck skin, scallions and hoisin sauce; the second is a platter of the duck meat mixed with julienne vegetables, which was better.

The salt-cooking technique, an ancient one in which foods are submerged in salt and either baked in a very hot oven or deep fried, works exceptionally well with delicious little shrimp in the shell as well as lightly battered fried oysters. One of the more exotic dishes is a Malayan specialty called Singapore mai fun, a platter of al dente rice noodles laced with scallions, shrimp and pieces of ham in a light and zesty curry sauce.

Some of the Chinese mixed vegetables are flat-tasting; pan-fried noodles with seafood and vegetables also are humdrum. If you want greenery, get Chinese broccoli with oyster sauce, or watercress with a tart bean-cake sauce.

Chinese desserts are always a dubious proposition to the uninitiated. Nonetheless, curiosity compelled me to inquire about the Chinese red-bean drink.

"It is a warm soup," our waiter explained, adding with a sheepish grin, "It is a little, uh, strange." "All the better, bring it on," I replied in a silly show of gastronomic bravado. In a word, the sweet, milky dessert is, uh, strange.

◆ UNION SQUARE CAFE ◆

★ ★

21 East 16th Street, 243-4020.

Atmosphere: Low-key, comfortable dining rooms with a neighborhood feeling; good oyster bar.

Service: Young, enthusiastic and well informed about the food; sudden rushes of customers can lead to a slow pace.

Price range: Moderate.

Credit cards: American Express, MasterCard and Visa.

Hours: Lunch, Monday through Friday, noon to 3 P.M., Saturday, noon to 4 P.M.; dinner, Monday through Thursday, 6 to 11 P.M., Friday and Saturday, 6 P.M. to midnight; oyster bar, Monday through Friday, noon to midnight, Saturday, 6 P.M. to midnight. Closed Sunday.

Reservations: Suggested.

The recently spruced up Union Square area has become fertile ground for a new crop of restaurants. Union Square Cafe, an inviting, low-key newcomer on the site of the former Brownies, a health food restaurant, is one of the most appealing of the lot.

Unlike so many of the new stadium-size establishments with decibel levels rivaling those at Madison Square Garden, the Union Square Cafe is designed on a human scale, which allows for that rarest of commodities nowadays—civilized conversation. On entering, you pass a long, handsome bar where a changing roster of sparkling fresh oysters is served atop iced seaweed with black bread and butter. In the back is a cozy room with a double-height ceiling and winsome murals painted on the wall; the main dining room is characterized by simple rustic touches, kind lighting and well-spaced tables.

Union Square Cafe is a lunch haunt for the downtown publishing crowd. Both the locally commissioned artwork and the sensitive design give the dining rooms a nice feeling of being part of the neighborhood, not something imposed on it.

The food, like the decor, is genuine and eclectic. The menu of the boyish-looking chef, Ali Barker, formerly of La Côte Basque, straddles the border between France and Italy. This leads to some unlikely juxtapositions. It's possible to begin with a boldly seasoned spaghettini alla puttanesca generous with coarse chunks of olives and garlic paired with anchovies, capers and tomatoes, then move on to a French classic such as crusty confit of duck, flanked by garlic potatoes and chicory salad (a Monday dinner special).

A lighter way to begin is with pappardelle of zucchini, thin flat strips of zucchini in a fresh tomato sauce flecked with garlic and shallots. The kitchen is not timid in the seasonings department. When a dish advertises garlic, brace yourself. This is wholesome rustic cooking, not dainty big-city fare. The best new pasta on the menu is spaghetti all'amatriciana, a lusty creation melding chunky pancetta bacon, tomatoes, onions and spices.

Lobster ravioli in a Pernod crème fraîche sauce, while tasty, was marred by thick, chewy dough. One of the side dishes, bruschetta with roasted peppers, is so good it should be considered as an appetizer. Simple and delicious, it combines garlic-rubbed toasted Italian bread with roast sweet peppers.

Danny Meyer, the young owner, is passionate about his wines, and his highly personalized list offers many good selections in the $12-to-$20 range. Union Square Cafe is one of the few restaurants in town that offer a good selection of dessert wines by the glass. The young service staff is earnest and well informed, although unexpected waves of customers can occasionally throw the place off stride.

The most unusual dish on the menu is the marinated "fillet mignon of tuna." Recommended for fish lovers only, this whale-size slab of florid tuna is seared on the outside and progressively rare toward the center; the core is virtually warm sushi. A confetti of ginger shavings adds a vibrant dimension. A deliciously whimsical club sandwich is made with this tuna on sourdough bread with niçoise olives.

Among meat and fowl dishes, worthy options are the nicely grilled lamb steak, rare-grilled duck breast with green olives and garlic confit, and a beefy rosemary-scented Black Angus club steak. Venison, a Wednesday special, was overmarinated and mushy recently; so was the mushroom polenta that came with it. Although vegetables accompany all dinners, try the homey side dish of mashed turnips with a snowfall of shallot crisps.

Union Square Cafe is a delightful place for lunch. You can get anything from a freshly ground hamburger and good french fries along with zippy black-bean soup—made with duck and veal stock—to a rosy salmon steak in a red-wine sauce colored with saffron potatoes and carrots.

For dessert, go with the thin-crusted apple tart, Italian pear torte in a cornmeal crust or the fudgelike ganache cake with hazelnuts. My favorite finale to a meal there, though, is a glass of sweet vin santo with almond biscuits. Dunking is not only allowed, but expected.

✦ WATER CLUB ✦

★

On the East River at 30th Street, 683-3333.

Atmosphere: Glass-enclosed barge on the East River with a panoramic view of Queens and parts of Manhattan. On deck is an alfresco bar.

Service: Amiable and efficient.

Price range: Moderately expensive.

Credit cards: American Express, Carte Blanche, Diners Club and Visa.

Hours: Lunch, Monday through Friday, 11:30 A.M. to 2:45 P.M.; brunch, Saturday and Sunday, 11:30 A.M. to 3 P.M.; dinner, daily 6 to 11:45 P.M.

Reservations: Suggested.

Credit should be given to Michael O'Keeffe, creator of the River Cafe in Brooklyn and its sibling, the Water Club, just upstream on the Manhattan side, for holding to the near radical notion that good food and panoramic waterside views are not mutually exclusive. In fact, before Mr. O'Keeffe came along with the River Cafe in 1977, this major seaport city had no notable restaurants on the harbor at all.

The Water Club was designed in 1982 as a middle-class alternative to the splashy River Cafe. The Water Club's ambiance is a bit less starchy, the food more familiar and prices closer to sea level. Even the view—oil tanks and factories of Queens as opposed to the glass-and-steel redwoods of Wall Street—reflects this distinction. Nonetheless, if you order wisely at the Water Club, you can have an enjoyable meal in one of the more inspiring settings the city has to offer.

The entrance to the restaurant resembles a pricey yacht club, with a long, burnished bar along one side and, along the other, an iced display of various fish and shellfish. Before entering the main dining room, which is in a barge tied to the pier, you might want to walk up deck to the open-air bar. It is a delightful spot in which to enjoy an aperitif while watching barges and pleasure boats ply the river.

The three-tier main dining room is wrapped in glass, offering views from every table. Little nautical flags hanging from the ceiling add to the clubby feeling.

The menu is expansive, and there are always a half-dozen or

more specials. They are worth considering because some of the better dishes sampled were among them. For example, it could be creamy fresh salmon rillettes accompanied by a slice of light scallop mousse garnished with two buttery whole sea scallops (the delicate roe was attached). The combination comes in an aromatic tarragon sauce. Another delicacy is the foie gras terrine, two slices of silky foie gras veined with truffle-laced gelatin. Fresh oysters of different varieties—Belons from Maine, Malpeques from Cape Cod among the best—are icy and glistening fresh. The chef knows how to fry shellfish without destroying it. His oysters and clams are lightly breaded and minimally fried in good oil, letting their flavors shine through.

The Water Club's setting naturally puts one in the mood for seafood entrees, however one must exercise caution. Poached halibut, a special one evening, had been submerged a little too long and then dressed up in a bland champagne-hollandaise sauce. Grilled swordfish may be well cooked but in my experience lacks flavor.

The Water Club turns out some of the best crab cakes in town—plump little golden-brown disks loaded with well-seasoned crabmeat. A hillock of crunchy deep-fried parsley in the center of the plate is a pleasing mate. Tuna steak, a heavyweight delicacy of the deep that is often roughed up more than a Saturday night wrestler by careless cooks, is remarkably good here. It was crosshatched on the surface and blush-pink in the middle, set in a soy-based sauce and garnished with julienne of leek and carrot.

On the other side of the menu, slices of duck breast with a semisweet fresh cherry sauce and wild rice suffer from overcooking. Another dry combination is pork chops stuffed with corn bread and bacon. Better selections are the prime ribs of beef and broiled lamb chops with a fresh mint sauce.

Some inventive side dishes enliven the meals. Try potatoes

colcannon, which are good old-fashioned buttery mashed potatoes topped with chopped scallions and lots of fresh pepper; potatoes O'Brien don't look anything like those you'd find on the
old sod, but they are engaging nonetheless—crunchy little cubes
of fried potatoes tossed with bits of sweet bell peppers. Lumpy
corn fritters are as down-home as a Kentucky farm breakfast.

The blue ribbon for dessert goes to the warm apple tart with
its thin and buttery puff pastry crust, followed by the towering
frozen Amaretto soufflé. Cheesecake tastes as though it had a
surfeit of gelatin, and a cloying concoction called chocolate
raspberry barquette is more suitable at a Little League banquet.
Both fresh berries with sabayon and coupe aux marrons (ice
cream sundae with glazed chestnuts) could prompt a smile at the
end of the meal. If the Water Club would trim its sails and
concentrate on seafood with a few good light sauces, and retain
its best meat dishes, it would easily merit two stars. Even with
its shortcomings, though, this stunning spot on the water can be
one of the more diverting places to impress out-of-town visitors
or, if the mood strikes, to treat yourself to a dose of nautical
tourism.

✦ WILKINSON'S SEAFOOD ✦ CAFE

★ ★

1573 York Avenue, between 83rd and 84th streets, 535-5454.

Atmosphere: Brick and aged wood, soft lighting and handsome bar
make for a relaxing cafe setting.

Service: Congenial and well informed.

Price range: Moderately expensive.

Credit cards: All major cards.

Hours: Dinner, Monday through Saturday, 5:30 to 11 P.M., Sunday, 5:30 to 9:30 P.M.

Reservations: Recommended.

A mostly young, well-turned-out Yorkville crowd frequents this informal, inviting dining room with its exposed-brick and aged-wood walls, friendly bar, overhead blade fans, soft frosted lights and etched glass. Cool piped-in jazz strikes a laid-back tempo. The seafood is invariably fresh and treated with respect, service is congenial, and the setting is soothing and cheerful.

Start off with one of the house signature appetizers, either brittle, light, fried calamari rings in a pulpy tarragon-tomato sauce or the lustrous warm oysters glossed with orange butter —the success of this preparation is the invigorating blend of briny oyster juices with the tart-sweet butter. Shimmering gravlax paired with a mild horseradish-and-caper sauce is another winner. Less appealing is the underseasoned seafood sausage.

Carnivores would enjoy the scarlet sheets of first-rate carpaccio brushed with a zippy combination of capers, onions and mustard.

Even when entrees fall short, it is not for lack of freshness but rather misjudgment with herbs and seasonings. Poached gray sole in a sloppy coriander-and-red-onion vinaigrette that separated at the table was one example; watery and bland mako shark was another. Aside from these, however, every other fish selection I sampled was a winner. One of my favorites was broiled marinated swordfish, something I rarely order because so often it is cooked to the consistency of newspaper. This succulent steak had been broiled to barely pink inside and coated with its pungent soy-based marinade. The leathery string beans, woody carrots and unseasoned broccoli added little. Two other recommended fish that shared an Oriental touch are the grilled salmon steak in a bright lime-teriyaki butter, and flaky red snapper set over a terrific sauce made with sake and fermented Chinese black beans.

Closer to home you can enjoy the big pearly sea scallops nestled in spinach leaves with a lovely lemon-saffron sauce or a golden strudel filled with dill-accented crabmeat and surrounded by a sweet leek puree and sugar-snap peas. Passable steak and chicken are available if you lose your sea legs.

Portions are generous but not overwhelming, so chances are you will have room for the deceptively light and semisweet white chocolate mousse, the cleansing lemon tart or the caramelized baked apple tart.

If Wilkinson's were closer to midtown, it would probably be mobbed every night. I'm glad it's not, for it's always nice to know there is a welcoming port of call over the horizon.

✦ WINDOWS ON THE WORLD ✦

★

1 World Trade Center, 107th floor, 938-1111.

Atmosphere: Wide, glass-enclosed wraparound restaurant with panoramic views of New York City.

Service: Professional and reasonably prompt.

Price range: Moderately expensive.

Credit cards: All major cards.

Hours: At lunch the restaurant is a private club. Dinner, daily, 5 to 10 P.M.

Reservations: Required.

272

Windows on the World, perched a quarter mile above the earth atop the World Trade Center, poses a troublesome challenge to one of my long-held maxims concerning restaurants: that food quality varies in inverse proportion to a dining room's altitude (airplanes being the extreme example). Now more than a decade old, Windows on the World, the highest and grandest dining room of them all, has proved that being a serious restaurant and a sky-high tourist attraction are not mutually exclusive. The restaurant's performance is even more impressive considering that its expansive glass-enclosed dining rooms, seating three hundred, would probably be packed even if the kitchen served sautéed Spam and frozen pot pies.

The Continental-style menu is nicely balanced and contemporary without lapsing into trendiness. Stock is obviously homemade, the quality of provender is top-notch, and seasonings are generally employed with skill. When the kitchen stumbles, it is usually a consequence of trying to feed the estimated four thousand customers who pass through weekly—similar sauces show up in a variety of dishes, and a few items must be prepared in enormous quantities a bit too long in advance.

Windows offers good value for the dollar, with a $29.95 four-course dinner as well as à la carte options. The prix fixe menu has considerable appeal, beginning with a platter of sparkling Cotuit oysters on the half shell paired with a tart mignonette sauce, or the lovely chilled pea soup suffused with fresh mint. A double beef consommé is clear and intense, garnished at the last minute with strips of scallion-laced pancakes, an unlikely but winning combination. Only the salmon-and-leek terrine fell short because of dryness.

The expanded à la carte offerings include sheets of bright mint-marinated fresh salmon with an Indian-style yogurt-and-cucumber sauce. A smooth duck-liver terrine is lusty and fresh.

Once again, the fish terrine—this one made with puree of salmon encasing a core of crayfish—was arid.

Two pleasing entrees on the prix fixe menu are succulent roast baby chicken with an intensely reduced veal-stock sauce garnished with miniature vegetables, and pale slices of buttery veal in the same stock sauce bolstered with white mushrooms—this veal stock, albeit good, is the fuel that propels most of the kitchen's meat dishes.

Standouts on the regular menu include most steaks and chops, such as the pink-roasted rack of lamb for two, the double-thick lamb chops with savory gratiné potatoes, and a crusty and beefy sirloin steak for two in a heady red-wine-and-stock sauce sweetened with shallots and beef marrow.

Soft-shell crabs did not fare so well; the dizzying ascent to the 107th floor left them pale and lifeless. A fricassee of lobster and crayfish was better. The lobster, cooked to a turn, was arranged in a pretty pattern on the plate over a lustrous shellfish-flavored cream stock garnished with delicate lacy pleurote mushrooms. Another recommendation is the roast breast of duck, rare and lean, in a mild plum sauce paired with addictive sweet-potato chips.

The army of service personnel somehow manages to keep this multiring circus moving right along, and with relatively good humor. The complexion of the multitiered dining rooms changes dramatically on weekends, when it is inundated by tourists who are forever jumping out of their seats to press their faces against the windows while trying to illuminate the entire island of Manhattan with flash cameras. At such times the noise level can be jarring.

The wine list at Windows is justly famous, not only for its wide selection of French and American labels but also for its prices, which are among the lowest I have encountered anywhere in town, in some cases only 25% above retail.

The best desserts are the luxurious frozen raspberry soufflé, a rich and creamy hazelnut dacquoise, and a classic New York–style cheesecake that is so weighty you may not need the elevator to sink to ground level. Floating islands must react badly to heights, for they are more like flaccid islands, and the white chocolate mousse is gelatinous and pallid.

But all in all, Windows on the World, while not a dazzler, is a solid and conscientious restaurant that would have appeal even if it were on ground level in midtown. In fact, I would be happy to go there even on the foggiest day with absolutely no view. Well, maybe a light cloud cover.

◆ WOODS ON MADISON ◆

Satisfactory

718 Madison Avenue, at 63rd Street, 688-1126.

Atmosphere: Bright, trim and pleasant.

Service: Amiable if haphazard.

Price range: Moderately expensive.

Credit cards: All major cards.

Hours: Lunch, Monday through Saturday, noon to 3 P.M.; dinner, Monday through Saturday, 6 to 11 P.M. Closed Sunday.

Reservations: Suggested.

Woods on Madison has been going through a difficult adolescence. A menu that seemed so bright and invigorating back then has become riddled with clichés and silly affectations—do you really want raspberry-and-shallot compote with your duck liver mousse? What's more, sauces and vegetables that should be warm arrive cold, and seasonings are often way off target. The smart dining room is done in shades of beige and blond wood with soft lighting that highlights safari photographs taken by the owner, Zeus Goldberg. It is still a popular spot among Madison Avenue shoppers, especially at lunch, where you can spot more furs in one hour than during a daylong trek in deepest Kenya. The mostly young service staff is long on personality and short on skill.

As for the food, the only consistently good appetizers were soups, pizza rustica, and a fresh and well-seasoned salmon and brook trout terrine with a tomato-sorrel sauce. Among the soups were soothing and light cream of carrot, bracing onion and beef stock and, at lunch recently, a pulpy puree of zucchini and tomatoes. The pizza was topped with a basil-scented combination of tomatoes and buffalo mozzarella.

Vegetable fritters—deep fried pieces of broccoli, cauliflower and onions—were delicious the first time we tried them. The hot curry-laced batter, fried to brittleness, was an eye-opener. The dish came with a zippy yogurt sauce flavored with both curry and mint. At lunch a week later, the fritters were flaccid and tasteless.

Other disappointments included over-refrigerated duck liver mousse with the sweet raspberry compote, the chewy and under-marinated Oriental beef salad, and a fussy mélange of lettuce, roast peppers, smoked whiting and mascarpone cheese in a sweet vinaigrette.

An exotic-sounding champagne-poached lobster with coriander corn cakes and garlic mayonnaise was a flop. The boiled split lobster was fine, but where was any evidence of champagne? The corn cakes tasted as if they had a bad case of freezer burn. So did an inedible portion of pheasant.

One of the few high points was the individual portions of cassoulet, made with firm-cooked navy beans, assertive garlic sausage, tender lamb, duck, tomato and herbs.

Desserts are some of the best dishes at Woods: dense and moist chocolate–macadamia nut cake with chocolate sauce, crusty apple bread pudding flavored with cinnamon, and apricot praline tart. One dessert is more notable for its size than quality, an adolescent dream called waffles with three ice creams—chocolate malted, strawberry (icy and tasteless) and vanilla—all slathered in whipped cream and strawberry sauce.

If Woods is not turned around soon, it will soon become merely a glorified watering hole for Madison Avenue shoppers.

Diner's
Journal

The Diner's Journal column in *The New York Times* is a vehicle for ferreting out special dishes, offbeat restaurants, great bars, breakfast nooks, little-known bargains and scores of other colorful dining spots that might otherwise be overshadowed by the gastronomic sequoias that get the star treatment in the weekly dining column. It is a casual, chatty and highly personal forum. I have more fun scouring the city for these little gems than with anything else. We have attempted to make some order out of the chaos by organizing the material thematically; a listing of the categories can be found in the table of contents on page ix. Prices mentioned in this section are subject to change.

✦ AMERICAN ✦

Irving Place has sprouted a rustic little breakfast and sandwich shop that looks as if it belongs in an upstate hamlet rather than in the belly of Manhattan. In fact, the young couple who created **Friend of a Farmer**, 77 Irving Place (between Park Avenue South and Third Avenue at 19th Street), hail from upstate—and so do most of their provisions. Terry and Carrie Morabito have been an instant hit since they opened their restaurant and carry-out in the summer of 1986 in this tranquil neighborhood and started selling their earthy homemade whole-wheat bread, moist zucchini bread, lacy apple pie, brown-egg omelets, buckwheat pancakes, wholesome sandwiches, homemade preserves and more. Beverages include cappuccino, sparkling cider, iced tea and the like. Sandwiches and breakfast entrees are in the $5-to-$6 range.

The Morabitos operate out of a sliver of a storefront that is redone in an authentic-looking barn motif. Several wooden tables tumble onto the street. Friend of a Farmer is open from 11 A.M. to 5:30 P.M. Monday through Friday and for brunch on Saturday and Sunday from 10:30 A.M. to 3:30 P.M. with regular service until 6 P.M. Telephone: 477-2188.

The handsomely renovated Loeb Boathouse on the lake in Central Park, with its spiffy new glass-enclosed cafe and outdoor tables overlooking the water, is a delightful spot to pause for a drink or a light meal in the warmer months. The brick Colonial-style boathouse, built in 1954, previously had only a snack bar; it has now been ambitiously redone to include a new wraparound blond-wood counter serving sandwiches, soups, salads and daily specials (in the $3-to-$5 range) that can be eaten at tables in the glass-enclosed terrace or outside patio. On another side is the bright new **Boathouse Cafe**, a full-service restaurant that also offers the choice of dining inside or out.

The cafe serves soups, pastas, omelets and the like for lunch (a three-course meal runs about $15) and more ambitious fare for dinner: crayfish seviche, barbecued short ribs of beef, roast duck with champagne sauce and grapes. An adequate wine list is offered at reasonable prices.

The food complex is operated by a company called TAM (Time and Management). Catering and party facilities are available. For those who would rather not walk in the park at night, the company runs a free shuttle bus that resembles an old-fashioned trolley. It makes the rounds every fifteen minutes to and from Fifth Avenue and 72nd Street, and Central Park West and 72nd Street. The service begins at 6 P.M. and runs until all patrons have left. The Loeb Boathouse is on the east side of the lake near 75th Street. The Boathouse Cafe is open daily from late spring to early fall from noon to 4:30 P.M. for lunch and 6 to 11 P.M. for dinner. The snack bar is open 9 A.M. to 6 P.M. Telephone: 517-2233.

Tenth Avenue and 46th Street is not the sort of neighborhood frequented by window-shoppers pondering a cute spot for lunch. If David Ludtke has his way, however, his eccentric little restaurant, called **Mike's American Bar & Grill**, might be reason enough to venture into Manhattan's western frontier. How about grilled game hen with moist and crumbly corn-bread dressing and vegetable salad? Or nicely charred fresh vegetables on a skewer with a red pepper—cream sauce? Or grilled bluefish with red tomato salsa? Entree prices are generally under $15.

The restaurant is the reincarnation of a former shots-and-beer bar by the same name. From the outside, with its smudged aluminum facade and a grimy sign that looks as if firemen used it for hatchet practice, it is hardly the kind of place you would be attracted to. Inside, however, is all spruced up in a funky kind of way, and the vintage rock 'n' roll is dynamite.

An enormous wooden bar takes up most of one side of the room. The yellow checked tile floor has been scrubbed down, the walls painted brash yellow, and wooden tables are covered with last year's Christmas wrapping paper. An assortment of soups and salads sampled were homey and flavorful; the dinner menu offers a wider selection, with items such as grilled smoked duck and marinated leg of lamb. Telephone: 246-4115.

. . .

Broadway theatergoers looking for a snack or light meal before the show have a new option at a sleek little restaurant called **Square Meals** on 45th Street just west of Eighth Avenue. Square Meals offers a wide variety of appetizer-size dishes in the $3-to-$5 range.

Square Meals is a comfortable little spot done in black-and-white tiles and with a long bar along the dining area that features piano music nightly. A sampling of a dozen dishes suggests that one should order carefully; however, enough satisfying dishes exist to constitute a good light meal. Some of the better selections include the sesame chicken squares ($3), rosemary lamb kebabs ($5), hot chicken salad ($3.50), smoked duck ($5.25) and baby grilled lamb chops ($4.50).

Square Meals is closed all day Sunday, and Monday for lunch. Telephone: 489-6357.

One of the more delightful lunch spots in Fifth Avenue's shopping district is a little-known restaurant perched on the fifth floor of the Trump Tower at 56th Street. Called **Terrace Five,** this charming bistro offers engaging salads and entrees as well as a superior little wine list with many selections available by the glass. On clement days, you can sit on a tiny outdoor terrace that affords a striking view down the avenue; even from the indoor seats, the view through the wraparound windows is inspiring.

Among the bright and tasty salads you might find are a copious seafood combination featuring large, pearly white sea scallops, squid rings, shrimp, tomatoes and mixed greens in a pleasantly tart lemon vinaigrette, and chicken salad with sliced poached chicken breast, lettuce and sections of oranges and grapefruit. Sautéed shrimp in mustard sauce is fresh and piquant, while good starters include the salmon carpaccio marinated in lime and fresh mint, and slices of mozzarella and tomatoes marinated in fresh herbs. Waiters and waitresses wear white shirts, black bow ties and welcoming smiles, conveying a real enthusiasm for their jobs—maybe it has something to do with the altitude.

A small wine bar is open from noon until closing. The reservations number is 371-5030.

If you have a nostalgic longing for the ingenuous hash-house grub of simpler days, you might stop by the **Broadway Diner,** at Broadway and 55th Street, for a cup of java and a wedge of pie, or maybe a hot open-face sandwich flanked by volcanos of mashed potatoes and lava-like gravy.

Broadway Diner is a faithfully re-created specimen of that gastronomic icon of the 1940s and '50s: gleaming white tile walls, a long slate-colored Formica counter holding plastic-topped cake stands, steaming coffee urns, lots of chrome and stainless steel.

The food is for the most part unfussy and solid luncheonette fare. A breakfast might include homemade corned-beef hash with poached eggs. At lunch, a grilled chicken sandwich with avocado mayonnaise is satisfying, as is the deluxe hamburger platter. The waitresses are pleasant, but they lack one quality that could impart absolute verisimilitude: bubble gum. The Broadway Diner (765-0909) is open daily from 7 A.M. to 11 P.M.

✦ BEER ✦

New York City is often touted today as one of the wine capitals of the world. Long before the wine boom came to this country, however, it was a mecca for beer drinkers—more than seventy breweries existed in the five boroughs at the turn of the century.

That era is long gone, but there are still a good number of taverns and restaurants that stock a wide range of domestic and imported beers. Among them are:

American Festival Cafe, Rockefeller Plaza, 20 W. 50th Street (246-6699)

Empire Diner, 210 10th Avenue (22nd Street, 243-2736)

First Avenue Restaurant, 361 First Avenue (21st Street, 475-9068)

Fleming's Bar and Restaurant, 232 East 86th Street (988-1540)

Gage & Tollner, 372 Fulton Street, Brooklyn (718-875-5181)

Joe Allen, 326 West 46th Street (581-6464)

Landmark Tavern, 626 11th Avenue (46th Street, 757-8595)

North Star Pub, 93 South Street, in the South Street Seaport (509-6757)

P. J. Clarke's, 915 Third Avenue (55th Street, 759-1650)

Rathbones, 1702 Second Avenue (80th Street, 369-7361)

Ryan McFadden, 800 Second Avenue (42nd Street, 599-2226)

Shelter Restaurant, 2180 Broadway (77th Street, 362-4360)

Tastings, 144 West 55th Street (757-1160)

SPECIAL PLACES

Beer, unlike fine red wine, does not improve with age. The fresher it is, the better the flavor. The only way to find fresher beer than that served in the new **Tap Room** at the New Amsterdam Amber Brewery would be to put your mouth over a barrel spigot. In this cavernous industrial setting on 26th Street and 11th Avenue, you can have drinks and a light meal while watching beer being made in huge copper brew-kettles.

New Amsterdam Beer, an all-malt, heavily hopped brew with a flowery aroma, is sold on tap at the large two-tier bar. Patrons can also sit at tables facing the vats and order from a menu that offers hot and cold appetizers, sandwiches and snacks. Sandwiches are in the $5 range and a draft is $2.25. The Tap Room is open daily from 11:30 A.M. to 1 A.M. It is in a rather isolated location, so be prepared to walk several blocks to a busier street to hail a cab. Telephone: 255-4100.

The **Tap Room** at the Manhattan Brewing Company, 40-42 Thompson Street in SoHo, is one of the first beer-making facilities to open in New York City after the last one, F&M Shaefer Brewing, closed its Brooklyn plant in 1976. It attracts a good-time yuppie crowd nightly in its cavernous tavern room dominated by massive copper brewing vats. These vats are not for show; they each hold about 7,000 liters of the beer, including a refreshing light ale, a slightly bitter amber ale and a dark, heavy-bodied special porter.

The Tap Room, which has long, communal copper-topped tables, sawdust on the floor, a fifty-foot-high ceiling and a long open kitchen, serves a variety of pub food. It is open from 11:30 A.M. to 1 A.M. Tuesday through Saturday, and Sunday for a buffet brunch at 11:30 A.M. to 4 P.M., $9.75. Telephone: 219-9250.

Have a craving for a frosty beer on a hot summer day? How about a bottle of Kulmbacher Schweizerhofbräu from Bavaria, or Tooths Sheaf Stout from Australia, Tiger from Singapore, Chihuahua from Mexico or EKU 28 from West Germany, billed as "the strongest beer in the world."

These and about two hundred other domestic and imported brews can be found at a remarkable bar in the West Village called the **Peculier Pub** (the unorthodox spelling comes from Old Peculier Ale from England, the manager's favorite brew).

The pub, at 182 West Fourth Street, is small, with eight chairs at the bar and about a dozen tables along walls lined with bottles and cans of beer from around the world. All beers are kept in five packed refrigerators. Customers order from a two-page beer list; daily specials are listed on a chalk board. Telephone: 691-8667.

The pub's manager, a former chemist who identifies himself only as Tommy, is a walking encyclopedia of brewing lore. Prices range from $1.75 for domestic beers (fifteen of them) to about $5 and more for special imports such as St. Sixtus Trappist Ale, a wonderfully creamy and flowery dark brew from Belgium. The Peculier Pub is strictly a burgers-and-sandwiches spot, presumably to keep the spotlight on the beers.

✦ BRAZILIAN ✦

For those who want to sample earthy Brazilian cuisine, there are two choices on West 45th Street: **Cabana Carioca** and its newer sister establishment, four doors down, **Cabana Carioca II**. Both serve wholesome soups, stews and broiled meats in portions large enough to sate a couple of soccer goalies.

The original Cabana Carioca, a floor above street level, offers a more tropical atmosphere. It has colorful folk murals and a crowded little bar where excitable Brazilian men, some with mustaches so thick and bristly they could be sold as shoe brushes, watch soccer games from Rio and drink beer.

The rows of tables in the small dining room are so close you can't help but sniff the aroma of your neighbors' food—and given the friendliness of most Brazilians, don't be surprised if you are offered a taste of their feijoada (pronounced fezh-*wa*-da), which is served on Wednesdays and Saturdays. This is the Brazilian national dish, an immense and savory mixture that gets its name from the shiny black beans called feijoes. There is nothing subtle or spare about the food here, whether it is the spicy Portuguese sausage, the seafood stew or the grilled pork chops with black beans and rice. Cabana Carioca, 123 West 45th Street (581-8088) and Cabana Carioca II, 133 West 45th Street (730-8375).

✦ BREAKFAST ✦

Finding a tranquil and elegant spot for breakfast in New York City is not always easy. Dining rooms in luxury hotels such as the Carlyle, the Mayfair Regent and The Polo restaurant in the Westbury come to mind. Another luxurious choice is the renovated **Cafe Pierre** in the Pierre Hotel at Fifth Avenue and 61st Street.

This fabled room, which for decades has been a favorite hangout for celebrities and America's industrial barons, has retained its aristocratic French charm. The room is done in light gray with painted cloud panels in the ceiling, comfortable chairs, soft-fabric banquettes, starched white tablecloths, fresh flowers and colorful china.

The old-world waiters make you feel like one of the privileged

289

few—even if they discover that you are not staying in one of the hotel's $250-a-night double rooms.

The extensive breakfast menu carries all the usual egg preparations as well as kippered herring, corned beef hash with a poached egg, and smoked salmon with cream cheese. A refreshing starter is the fresh papaya with lime. A low-calorie breakfast of sugarless cereal with fresh strawberries and skim milk, a bran-carrot muffin with apple butter, and coffee or tea costs $10.50.

The Cafe Pierre serves breakfast from 7 to 11 A.M. daily. A Continental breakfast is offered from 11 A.M. to noon in the regal-looking rotunda just outside the restaurant. Brunch is served in the cafe on Sunday from noon until 3:30 P.M. The number for brunch reservations is 838-8000. No reservation is necessary for breakfast.

A spacious and tranquil morning alternative to clattering coffee shops is **Cafe Un Deux Trois** at 123 West 44th Street. This airy, columned dining room, which is crowded and clamorous at lunch, is remarkably serene in the morning. For about $5 one can have fresh juice, coffee and entree (eggs, cereal, pancakes and so on). The brioche French toast with a side of applesauce is particularly satisfying. Breakfast is served from 7:30 to 11 A.M. Telephone: 354-4148.

When the thermometer plummets and steam rises from the manholes, mother's age-old plea to put "something warm in your stomach" before heading out the door seems to carry a belated aroma of logic. But even the most enthusiastic home cooks may find preparing anything more than strong coffee too much of a challenge before noon.

Residents of the Upper West Side have a pleasant solution in a cozy little cafe called **Good Enough to Eat,** on Amsterdam

Avenue between 80th and 81st streets (496-0163). It has a narrow dining room with exposed-brick walls sporting copper molds and other Americana as well as baskets of dried flowers and knickknacks. The regulars who drift in when the door opens at 8 A.M. sit at small wooden tables and read their morning papers to the background of mollified pop music—the most one could handle at this hour.

The menu offers such homey fare as eggs and omelets with buttermilk biscuits, old-fashioned oatmeal with cream, brown sugar and cinnamon toast, as well as banana-walnut pancakes with strawberry butter, pecan waffles, apple pancakes and a combination platter called "the lumberjack," two pancakes, three strips of bacon and two scrambled eggs. Prices are in the $4-to-$8 range.

The pancakes and waffles are made with thick, eggy home-made batter. The banana-walnut pancakes, three huge disks, are sprinkled with chopped walnuts, sliced bananas and an orange slice. They should fortify you for any challenges in the day ahead.

If you want to butter up your co-workers, take out some of the grainy bran muffins, bulbous scones or banana-walnut muffins. Breakfast is served from 8 A.M. until 4 P.M. daily, except week-ends when service begins at 9 A.M.

Good Enough to Eat also has a larger downtown location, 162 Duane Street, that serves a more extensive menu of homey roasts, potpies and the like for lunch and dinner. Telephone: 693-0559.

Those seeking a cross-cultural experience may want to try the special Shanghai-style breakfast at **Pig Heaven,** the winsome Chinese restaurant with a barnyard decor at 1540 Second Avenue (corner 80th Street). Served from noon to 3 P.M. on Saturday and Sunday—which makes it more of a brunch, really—it consists of two kinds of soybean-milk soup, one slightly sweet, the other on the sour side. The soups are eaten with two kinds of traditional Shanghai bread. One, called yu tiao, is a long piece of fried dough that is sometimes referred to by Westerners as a Chinese cruller. The other, shao bing, resembles pita bread covered with sesame seeds. The Chinese usually insert the cruller into the pocket bread, then dip both into the soups. It may not be the most elegant way to start the day, but it is assuredly authentic. All other items on the regular menu are available as well. Telephone: 744-4887.

If you like your eggs sunnyside-way-up, try the breakfast at **Windows on the World.** From 7:30 to 10:30 A.M. on weekdays, an à la carte breakfast is served in the glass-fronted Hors d'Oeuvrerie high above New York harbor. Prices range from about $4 for Irish oatmeal with honey and cream to about $10 for smoked salmon and cream cheese. Windows on the World is at 1 World Trade Center. Telephone: 938-1111.

✦ CARIBBEAN ✦

Two sizzling nightspots in town—Sugar Reef and Bayamo—are among the restaurants that serve that tropical smorgasbord collectively known as Caribbean food. Both offer island specialties such as barbecued shrimp wrapped in banana leaves, conch fritters and peppery jerk chicken. A third restaurant, the palmy West Village spot called Caribe, offers everything from Jamaican-style curried goat to Barbados codfish stew with tomatoes and onions.

Rounding out the island fare are Victor's Cafe 52, a Cuban restaurant in midtown, and Sabor in the West Village.

Aside from variety, the homespun fare in these restaurants offers some of the better bargains in town—three-course meals can be had for $25 or less at many places. Here is an informal culinary cruise to the city's major Caribbean ports.

Sugar Reef (93 Second Avenue, near Fifth Street, 477-8427): This clamorous, funky restaurant is hotter than a Havana afternoon. Be prepared to cool your heels with a tropical drink at the elbow-to-elbow bar, which is rimmed with plastic ferns and fake bananas. The bartender wears baggy shorts and a billowing Hawaiian shirt sporting an ornithological theme.

The dining room, with its Day-Glo green wall, corrugated plastic ceiling, pulsing music and T-shirted waitresses, is hardly the sort of place that inspires faith in the kitchen's output. I was surprised, however, to encounter several authentic and tasty regional dishes. Among them were a lusty rendition of callaloo soup, the peppery mélange of kale, pork and crabmeat. Another good starter is mango pepper pot, half-moons of ripe mango tossed with red onions and Jamaican hot peppers —it is sweet and mildly hot at the same time. The Jamaican meat pattie is leaden, so go instead for an entree called Bajan kingfish. This meaty deep-sea fish, not unlike swordfish in texture, is mildly spiced and nicely fried and is accompanied by sweet cabbage and pumpkin-flavored rice. No reservations, cash only.

Bayamo (704 Broadway, near Fourth Street, 475-5151): This soaring two-level restaurant, with massive green Ionic columns, paper-covered tables, a rakish bar and a noise level approximating Yankee Stadium's, describes itself as the home of Chino-Latino cuisine. This curious combination, the result of Chinese immigration to the United States via Cuba, yields a menu of disparate specialties such as ropa vieja and pan-fried lo mein noodles.

I was more curious about the Caribbean fare and found some satisfying renditions in the cavernous crock of ropa vieja, which combines flavorful braised meat with rice, peppers and cinnamon-tinged beef stock; picadillo de camarones, which includes zippy stir-fried minced shrimp that you wrap in soft tortillas with cheese and hot sauce, and lime-marinated conch-and-vegetable salad.

Not everything works well on this encyclopedic menu; the best advice is to keep an eye on the daily specials and stick to simpler dishes. Reservations recommended, major credit cards accepted.

Caribe (117 Perry Street, at Greenwich Street, 255-9191): It doesn't compare to Sugar Reef and Bayamo for glitz and high-wattage energy, but this West Village spot does offer a similar range of tropical dishes. I like the savory oxtail stew, with sweet fried plantains on the side, and the heady black bean stew.

Other offerings include a version of the French beef stew called daube, Martinique-style, cooked with red wine, garlic, onions and orange peel; spicy chicken Caribe, and deviled turkey leg (the recipe used here is said to come from the South Bronx).

Caribe has a mellow bar surrounded by a jungle of palms and tropical plants. Reservations not necessary, cash only.

⋆ CHICKEN ⋆

GRILLED

If you don't have a charcoal grill on which to barbecue chicken, ribs and the like, the next best thing is going to one of the better grill carryout restaurants that have become so popular around town.

The phenomenal success of **Chirping Chicken,** a chain of carryout shops that serve charcoal-grilled, marinated half chickens with pita bread and hot sauce for about $3 (Amsterdam Avenue and 77th Street, Lexington Avenue and 85th Street, among other locations), has spawned many imitators. One such is **Chicken Kitchen** (Second Avenue and 62nd Street, among others) which takes grilled chicken one step further. This cheerful, tiny spot has four tables in an elevated dining area.

The menu is larger than at Chirping Chicken, although the meat is not quite so flavorful. It could have to do with Chirping Chicken's marinade. A half chicken with any of five sauces—cranberry, peanut butter, barbecue, hot salsa and mustard curry —along with pita bread costs $3.50. The pulpy, fresh salsa, with just enough zip to keep you coming back, is the best; mustard curry is the runner-up.

A cup of hot, homemade applesauce, fragrant with cinnamon, is a fine winter dessert ($1.40).

Another bargain grill is called **Checkers,** three restaurants that apply the same formula of well-prepared grilled ribs and chickens in a simple, cheerful setting at reasonable prices. The original Checkers is at 201 East 34th Street. It has a black-and-white tile floor and a colorful modern mural depicting street scenes. The newer one is in a landmark building at 36 Water

Street. The other two are at 1047 Second Avenue, between 55th and 56th streets, and at 867 Ninth Avenue, between 56th and 57th streets.

The most popular dish appears to be the chicken and rib combination plate ($7.95), which offers a quarter chicken and a small portion of baby back ribs. The chicken, dusted with paprika, is moist and flavorful, while the ribs, coated with a vaguely sweet sauce, are crisp and agreeably smoky. Homemade potato salad with dill and coleslaw are above average for such places. Beer, soft drinks and tea are served.

Take-out orders are bargains: a whole barbecued chicken is $5.95 and a whole portion of baby back ribs costs $8.45.

A gleaming restaurant and carryout off Park Avenue South is doing its share to keep a lid on the 1986 Consumer Price Index. **Les Poulets,** 27 East 21st Street, offers a tasty grilled half chicken with a variety of sauces, cottage fries and homemade coleslaw for $4.50 to $4.95, depending on the sauce.

Les Poulets has a long carry-out counter in the front facing an expanse of sizzling gas grills as well as a clean and brightly lit dining area for fifty in the back. My only gripe concerns the flimsy plastic tableware—cutting chicken with a plastic knife is like trying to eat Jell-O with chopsticks.

Aside from the grilled chicken with various sauces—New Orleans barbecue, salsa, Dijon and teriyaki—there is a garlic-seasoned version as well as a wide array of salads. The curried chicken salad studded with apple chunks is a zippy alternative; chicken potpie is a near miss, a bit soggy-crusted and dry inside. Homemade coleslaw is a delicious alternative to the sour version sold in delicatessens around town.

Moussy, the nonalcoholic beer, is the headiest beverage in the house.

Les Poulets is open Monday through Friday from 8 until 11 A.M. for breakfast; 11:30 A.M. to 9 P.M. for lunch and dinner; Saturday noon to 8 P.M.; closed Sunday. Les Poulets delivers orders of $5 or more without charge within a ten-block radius. Telephone: 254-5330.

SANDWICHES

One of the best chicken sandwiches in town is rustled up at **Cafe Montana,** one of the grand grilleries on the Upper West Side. Situated in the Montana, a new apartment building at Broadway and 88th Street, the cafe is a cheerful, two-level restaurant with a tiled open kitchen, plum-colored walls, Art Deco sconces and, in the upstairs dining room, tall windows affording a sweeping view of renascent upper Broadway.

As for the chicken sandwich on the lunch menu, you get a huge, skillfully grilled chicken breast that is nicely seared outside yet moist within, served on a thick onion roll. It comes with sweet pineapple chutney on the side, black olives and sliced tomatoes—all for $5.50. In the evening, the cafe withholds the roll, adds vegetables and doubles the price. Telephone: 874-7400.

✦ CHILI ✦

In the hyperbolic world of chili, almost every cook seems to have a recipe that is "the world's best." The owners of the **Manhattan Chili Co.,** a hot spot in more ways than one at 302 Bleecker Street in Greenwich Village, are no slouches when it comes to self-promotion. On the menu, they unabashedly describe their basic chili as the best "in the universe."

And that's just one of six versions offered in this hip Tex-Mex jalapeño parlor with its sleek coral-and-sea-green walls, track lighting and piped-in vintage rock and roll. Some of the chilis are indeed tasty—though perhaps not intergalactically so—such as the basic version, called numero uno, which features ground beef, pork and beans, and ground chilies with a haunting after-taste of toasted cumin. Other chili dishes are called the real McCoy (with beef, onions and chilies), seafood chili (scrod, scallops, shrimp, clams and mussels in a hot tomato-and-wine sauce), vegetable (a variety of peppers and vegetables), Abilene Choral Society and Music Guild chili (ground beef, tomatoes, red wine, beans and basil—for "tenderfeet") and green chili with pork, carrots and roasted green chilies. Prices range from $5 to $10, with extra charges for condiments.

A good inexpensive wine list is available—and, of course, margaritas. Telephone: 206-7163.

Looking for an amusing place to have a good cheap lunch or sate the post-movie munchies? Try **Exterminator Chili,** a wacky diner-like eatery at 305 Church Street, at Walker (219-3070) in the lower Broadway section of Manhattan. The name of this seven-month-old establishment is quite apt. Chili comes in three gradations on the gastronomic Richter scale: residential (mild), commercial (medium) and industrial (Is there a gardening hose in the house?). For $5.95 at lunch, you get a hefty bowl of chili served with slaw or potato salad and, if desired, a topping of sour cream, onions and cheddar cheese. A mild vegetarian chili is also available for the same price. (At dinner, portions are larger and chili is in the $7.50 range.) The types of chili sampled—I drew the line at commercial grade—were fresh and tasty.

Exterminator Chili, which is run by a team of pot-wielding

Marx Brothers characters, is a wonderfully campy throwback to the 1950s. You sit in worn vintage booths surrounded by pop icons from the Howdy Doody era—color-by-numbers art adorns pink stucco walls with fake hewed timber cross beams, a wagon-wheel chandelier hangs from the turquoise ceiling, and all sorts of memorabilia clutter every horizontal space.

The menu also carries burgers, sandwiches, salad plates and a dense sweet potato pie right out of the Crisco Homemaker's Cookbook. If you are nice, the counterman may let you pet one of his rubber monkey heads, the ones advertised in comic books that "AMAZINGLY GROW HAIR!" when you set them in water.

Exterminator Chili is open Monday through Friday for breakfast and lunch from 8 A.M to 4 P.M.; dinner Monday through Thursday, 6 to 11 P.M.; Friday 6 P.M. to midnight; Saturday 11 A.M. to midnight; Sunday 11 A.M. to 11 P.M.

◆ CHINESE ◆

Great Shanghai, at 27 Division Street, at Market Street, in the heart of Chinatown, has an ambiance something like Grand Central Terminal on the Friday night of a holiday weekend. It specializes in the maritime cuisine of Shanghai, and one of its best dishes is Oriental fondue, which features impeccably fresh seafood, as well as a host of other ingredients.

It is best to try the dish with a group of four or more so that many of the tidbits available can be sampled. Diners sit around a circular table with a gas burner in the center. After a large pot of chicken broth is placed on it and brought to a simmer, a waiter drops in rectangles of bean curd, stalks of Chinese cabbage and thin bean-thread noodles.

While these are cooking, you should sample one or two stimulating appetizers on the menu: shredded pork with spicy bean curd, which is redolent of star anise, or egg-skin dumplings, tiny rolled omelets with diced pork in the center.

Any number of ingredients can be ordered with the fondue. When the waiter brings the first round of food, he also brings a tray of twelve condiments—fish sauce, fresh coriander, diced scallions and chili oil among them—and offers to make "a special mixture." He then proceeds to mix a little of all twelve in a small bowl. The result is, well, complex.

A good way to start is with plates of sea scallops, shrimp and oysters. They are placed in little wire poaching baskets and, if you don't overcook them, are briny and tender. Another dish worth ordering is squid, either fresh or dried—the dried, less chewy than some fresh squid, has a darker color.

This might be followed with thin slices of lamb and beef, which are best if cooked only a few minutes and eaten rare. When the poaching is finished, the broth and vegetables are served in a soup bowl. The best beverage for this steaming feast is Chinese beer. Telephone: 966-7663.

The house special at **Tang's Chariot**, a smart and comfortable Chinese restaurant at 236 East 53rd Street, is called beggar's chicken. The legend of this dish notwithstanding—something about a beggar who steals a chicken and tries to hide the evidence by concealing it in mud and burying it under some campfire embers, where, of course, it becomes a marvelous creation—beggar's chicken is fun, an exotic item worth trying.

A whole chicken is first marinated in a mixture of soy sauce, sesame oil, ground ginger and garlic. It is then stuffed with pickled Chinese cabbage, diced dried shrimp, black mushrooms, ham and herbs, then wrapped in bamboo leaves and aluminum foil. In the final step, it is coated with a thick mixture of flour and water. When the chicken is placed in a hot oven, the flour mixture hardens like cement, trapping the moisture and flavors inside.

The chicken is ceremoniously carried to the table, so diners can see the Chinese inscriptions painted on the crust (you can have "Happy Birthday" or other messages in Chinese by asking ahead of time). After the oohs and aahs have subsided, a waiter hacks open the crust and serves the moist and aromatic meat, which is infused with the flavor of bamboo leaves and nicely set off by the slightly salty stuffing. It's a fine show at about $30 for four people. You must order beggar's chicken a day in advance. Telephone: 355-5096.

✦ COLOMBIAN ✦

Along busy Roosevelt Avenue in Queens, the sights and aromas of South America belie the street's very North American name. Deep-green plantains, strings of garlic, clumps of fresh coriander and odd-shaped tropical melons are bargained for in machine-gun Spanish. Storefront restaurants, most of them owned by Colombians, display their menus, handwritten in Spanish, with come-ons such as "Plato del dia—$4.95!!!"

One of the tastiest introductions to Colombian food can be found at **Cali Viejo,** a cheerful little nook in the shadow of the elevated train tracks, and at the new, even smaller Cali Viejo II a few blocks away. The owner, Jose Bastidas, seems to know everybody in the neighborhood. The eat-and-run patrons, virtually all of whom are South American, stop by to gobble up the earthy envueltos de maíz (crispy, honey sweetened fritters) and tamales filled with spicy chunks of pork and peas. You can sit at one of the rickety Formica-topped tables and order the works, which is Cali Viejo's version of a degustation menu. It is guaranteed to have you speaking Spanish in no time.

Cali Viejo is at 84-24 Roosevelt Avenue, between 84th and 85th streets, Jackson Heights, Queens (718-424-2755); Cali Viejo II is at 73-10 Roosevelt Avenue, between 73rd and 74th streets (same phone number as the original Cali Viejo).

✦ CZECHOSLOVAKIAN ✦

Ruc, a homey little garden restaurant, is one of the few vestiges of the Slavic and Hungarian community that once thrived on Manhattan's Upper East Side.

One of the more traditional dishes on Ruc's menu is boiled beef tenderloin with dill sauce and bread dumplings. My favorite part of the meal is the dumplings. Unlike the dumplings served in Chinese and many Eastern European restaurants, these are thick, disk-shaped slabs made from flour, eggs and cubes of bread; the mixture is boiled and becomes firm and resilient. Ruc's kitchen also turns out a respectable roast duck with the same dumplings and sauerkraut as well as some earthy soups.

An appetizer worth trying is the headcheese, made with beef tongue, heart, liver and other parts most people would rather not hear about. The best drink to accompany a Czechoslovak meal is a golden Pilsner Urquell.

Ruc is at 312 East 72nd Street (650-1611).

✦ DELI ✦

New York City is synonymous with the clattering and chattering institution known as the delicatessen. To devotees of corned beef, pastrami, chicken dumpling soup and "a bagel with a schmear!" there is no place like the **Carnegie Delicatessen,** at 55th Street and Seventh Avenue (757-2245).

The atmosphere is something right out of a Woody Allen parody of New York Jewish culture—in fact, the Carnegie played a large role in *Broadway Danny Rose.* The reason Carnegie's corned beef is so superior—remarkably tender and lean yet intensely flavorful—is that big slabs of brisket are cured in-house and hand-trimmed. The Carnegie also prepares its own peppery pastrami in a slow smoker that was specially made for it in Canada. A sandwich of either is served on the the best-quality rye bread, weighing in at a pound and three-quarters and standing five inches high on the plate, fairly daring you to finish it. Perpetual lines outside the door at lunchtime attest to the Carnegie's reputation as New York's best.

✦ DESSERTS ✦

One of the most civilized ways to lift the spirits on a dreary winter afternoon is to slip into a pastry shop and thaw out with a cup of steaming cappuccino and something sweet. If you find yourself trudging around the Upper East Side, one welcoming spot is **Les Délices Guy Pascal,** 1231 Madison Avenue, at 89th Street (289-5300). Mr. Pascal, former pastry chef at La Côte Basque, opened this shop, one of three in Manhattan (the others are at Zabar's, Broadway and 80th Street, and on First Avenue, between 51st and 52nd streets).

This cheerful little shop, with a dozen tables, serves Mr. Pascal's pastries, as well as a small menu for light lunches or dinners. Of the entrees sampled, pâté de campagne and ratatouille quiche were among the best choices; ham-and-aspic pâté had a stale off-flavor, while a ham and cheese torte was overwhelmed by nutmeg. Most of Mr. Pascal's cakes, tarts, mousses and breads, however, are superior. The shop is open 8 A.M. to 10 P.M., Monday through Saturday, and 9 A.M. to 8 P.M. on Sunday.

An addition to the late-night scene on the Upper East Side is **Caffe Biffi,** a rakish Italian bar and restaurant at 251 East 84th Street. It is worth knowing about if you are looking for a lively spot for an after-dinner drink or liqueur-spiked espresso.

The cafe section in the front, enclosed by wraparound glass affording a view of the avenue, sports a semicircular marble bar, high-tech lighting and chrome accents. A rear dining area serves a variety of pastas.

Coffees are uncompromisingly Italian—espresso ($2.50), cappuccino ($3.25), espresso with liqueur ($3.75)—and a good assortment of teas is available, including chamomile ($2.50). A few of the pastries sampled are noteworthy, such as the espresso layer cake and the fudgelike chocolate mousse cake (both $4.75), which is so rich it can be split among four.

Caffe Biffi is open Sunday through Thursday 10 A.M. to 2 A.M.; Friday and Saturday 10 A.M. to 4 A.M. (288-6894).

✦ DINING ALONE ✦

Eating out is usually a social occasion as much as a gastronomic one; however, most of us at one time or another find ourselves looking for a place to dine alone in peace, perhaps to read a magazine or just get away from it all. Here are some suggestions.

Aurora, 60 East 49th Street; 692-9292. Eating and drinking bar.

The Ballroom, 253 West 28th Street; 244-3005. Colorful tapas bar (Spanish snacks).

Brasserie, 100 East 53rd Street; 751-4840. Large rectangular eating counter; many tables suitable for one.

Cabana Carioca, 123 West 45th Street; 581-8088. Communal table arrangement.

Cafe de Bruxelles, 118 Greenwich Avenue (13th Street); 206-1830. Banquettes.

Cafe des Sports, 329 West 51st Street; 581-1283. Inconspicuous small tables suitable for singles.

Cafe 212, 212 East 52nd Street; 486-0212. Wide, comfortable sushi bar.

Chez Napoleon, 365 West 50th Street; 265-6980. Inconspicuous small tables suitable for singles.

Hamburger Harry's, 157 Chambers Street (between West Broadway and Greenwich Street), 267-4446; 145 West 45th Street, 840-2756. Eating counter surrounding grill.

Inagiku, 111 East 49th Street; 355-0440. Large circular tempura bar.

La Bonne Soupe, 48 West 55th Street; 586-7650. Banquettes in front room suitable for singles.

Oyster Bar and Restaurant in Grand Central Station (lower level, 42nd Street and Vanderbilt Avenue); 490-6650. Expansive eating counters, animated atmosphere.

Prima Donna, 50 East 58th Street; 753-5400. Pizza bar and banquettes.

Restaurant Florent, 69 Gansevoort Street (between Washington and Greenwich streets); 989-5779. Long counter in converted diner.

The Ritz Cafe, 2 Park Avenue (32nd Street); 684-2122. Two large wooden eating and drinking bars.

◆ ETHIOPIAN ◆

Sitting on squat wooden stools and picking from a communal plate with your hands may not be everyone's idea of an elegant evening on the town, but it certainly makes for interesting dinner conversation. **Abyssinia,** a spare but pleasant Ethiopian restaurant at 35 Grand Street, at Thompson Street (226-5959), might be just the place to take jaded New Yorkers who think they've tried everything.

Diners sit around a colorful wicker table with a recessed center, which holds a large circular platter. Ethiopian food, at least as represented here, is serious hot stuff. Doro wot, chicken and hard-boiled eggs in a smoldering red sauce, tops the list, followed by azefa wot, which combines lentils, red onions, garlic, ginger and hot peppers in a lemon-tinted hot sauce. These can be tempered with yekik wot, a refreshing dish of split peas in a relatively light lemon sauce.

One of the best dishes is kitfo, Ethiopia's version of steak tartare; the beef is pulverized to a paste and mixed with spiced butter and chili powder, giving it a rich, elegant flavor. Diners scoop up food by hand, using flat, spongy sheets of Ethiopian bread, called injera. Entrees are in the $7-to-$10 range. Service tends to be lackadaisical, so go when you have plenty of time.

✦ FRENCH BISTRO ✦

Upper Broadway in the Columbia University neighborhood abounds with little ethnic storefront restaurants catering to student tastes and budgets. One that is worth investigating even if your diploma is getting yellow around the edges is **Au Grenier Cafe,** a sunny walk-up French bistro where lunch fare includes some tasty soups, salads and pâtés—and at bargain prices.

The clean and simply appointed dining area with its brick walls, lacquered wooden tables and tall windows overlooking the avenue attracts a casual crowd of students and area businesspeople. A chalkboard lists a dozen wine specials by the glass. Lunch might begin with a beefy and sweet-edged onion soup gratinée and chewy rye bread. Various pâtés, which come from the reputable Les Trois Petits Cochons, are reliably fresh and well seasoned—a country blend flecked with green peppercorns, rabbit with Armagnac, duck with port wine, and more are about $5 for a generous slab.

The changing selection of salads makes for an engaging light lunch (prices range from $3 for a mixed green salad to about $5). The hands-down best is firm and sprightly lentil salad in a vinaigrette blended with red pepper, scallions, red onions and parsley. The others are invariably fresh, although a few needed an extra shot of seasonings. The dinner menu offers the same salad selection as well as steaks, chops, fowl and other straightforward fare in the $10-to-$20 range.

Au Grenier Cafe, one flight up at 2867 Broadway, between 111th and 112th streets, is open for lunch Monday through Friday, 11 A.M. to 4 P.M.; dinner, every day, 6 to 10:30 P.M. Telephone: 666-3052.

• • • • •

Cafe Destinn, on West 68th Street, is a snug little bistro with lead-paned windows, a cozy bar facing a glowing fireplace and a small back dining room with high-backed wooden booths. The menu offers a range of earthy dishes at reasonable prices: appetizers about $6.50, entrees $12 to $20. Not everything on the menu shines, but there are ample good choices if you order carefully. Two of the better entrees are sausages of chicken, veal and pork with grilled polenta and cabbage, and ricotta-filled ravioli with lobster, shrimp and crabmeat.

Overall, this is a good place to keep in mind when you are in the Lincoln Center area. Cafe Destinn is at 70 West 68th Street (496-2144). Dinner is served Tuesday through Sunday, 5 P.M. to midnight; Saturday and Sunday brunch, 11 A.M. to 3 P.M.

Chez Jacqueline, run by Jacqueline Zini and her Italian-born husband, Giovanni, is a trim little bistro that formerly was on King Street and Avenue of the Americas. It offers a solid range of country fare such as the garlicky codfish and potato puree called brandade de morue, escargots in a pastis-perfumed tomato sauce and meaty fresh mussels in a zestily seasoned tomato-and-white-wine broth. A special entree is tender tripe in a soothing tomato sauce. Herb-encrusted rack of lamb is delicious, as are stuffed quails in potato baskets. With a good bottle of wine and lovely homemade desserts, dinner for two runs between $50 and $60 before tip. Chez Jacqueline is at 72 Macdougal Street (505-0727).

La Bohème, a striking and congenial French bistro at 24 Minetta Lane at Avenue of the Americas in Greenwich Village, is a good, moderately priced option for dinner in this animated neighborhood. It is a comfortable spot that melds country French and high-tech—barn-board wainscotting, pink banquettes, bare test-tube-shaped lights dangling overhead and an open kitchen.

The menu features such items as rustic pork pâté, soups, oysters (prices vary), as well as French-style pizzas and pastas. Ravioli niçoise, with meat and spinach in a tasty tomato sauce, is also pleasing. Entrees I can recommend include a nicely grilled Cornish hen with tarragon sauce, monkfish with saffron, and roast duck. Entree prices range from about $11 to $17.

The young staff is affable and eager to please, which adds to La Bohème's appeal as a place to keep in mind on Village visits. Dinner Tuesday through Saturday 5:30 P.M. to 12:30 A.M., Sunday 5 P.M. to midnight; Sunday brunch noon to 4 P.M.. Telephone: 473-6447.

Le Madeleine, an engaging little French bistro on West 43rd Street near Ninth Avenue, is often overlooked as a moderately priced dining option in the theater district, although it shouldn't be. It is a lively spot at night, where theater people gather at the long bar to leaf through issues of *Variety* and talk shop. The dining room is low-key and charming, with brick walls, wooden banquettes and butcher paper–covered tables. During the warm months, a backyard garden is open for dining.

The menu is straightforward bistro fare with more than a few appealing dishes. Mussels marinière are plump and well cooked in their flavorful white-wine-and-herb sauce—they make a good light lunch along with a salad and some French bread for dipping in the broth. Soupe au pistou, while thicker than the traditional version, is tasty and well seasoned. Simple grilled fish are usually nicely done as well.

Not everything is so successful, but you should do well by sticking to homey soups, stews and salads. Dinner entrees range from about $7 to $16. Le Madeleine, 405 West 43rd Street, is open daily from noon to midnight. Reservations: 246-2993.

I am often asked for restaurant recommendations within walking distance of Fifth Avenue's museum row, from the low 70s to about 92nd Street. One worth seeking out is **Le Refuge,** an enchanting French bistro on 82nd Street near Lexington Avenue, where you can have a tasty light lunch in a tranquil setting. Le Refuge is reminiscent of a family-run restaurant in rural France—exposed woodwork, pale yellow walls, fresh flowers and open shelves where you can pick up a jar of mustard or preserves on the way out.

The lunch menu carries several omelets, salads and light fish and meat entrees. A typical lunch might be a light and deftly seasoned vichyssoise as well as a delightful salad composed of extra-thin julienne of zucchini, yellow squash, red and yellow peppers in a mint-perfumed vinaigrette. For entrees, try either the chicken salad made with Bibb lettuce and strips of real chicken breast or the exceptional frisée aux lardons, the traditional French salad that combines crunchy escarole with smoky bacon cubes in a warm vinaigrette. This version of the salad comes with two soft poached eggs on top. Le Refuge is at 166 East 82nd Street (861-4505).

The sunny and bucolic Provence region of France seems to strike a nostalgic chord in nearly all who pass through. For those who do not get there enough, some consolation may be found at a handsome bistro in Greenwich Village that specializes in that area's fresh and herbaceous cuisine. Called **Provence,** it is owned by Michel Jean, former maître d'hôtel at Régine's and captain at Le Cirque, and his wife, Patricia. They took over a dark, wood-trimmed Italian restaurant with a backyard garden called Gordon's and brightened it with pale yellow walls, scallop-shaped sconces and dried flowers.

Brightest of all is the food. The Provence-born Mr. Jean offers a host of lovingly prepared dishes that will moisten the eyes of Francophiles: soothing brandade de morue (a cod puree), pissaladière (sort of a French pizza with onions, tomatoes and anchovies), cod and vegetable stew, tian d'agneau ratatouille (pan-roasted lamb with ratatouille), roasted eggplant tartines, paillard of rabbit with cabbage and mustard, and more. Prices are reasonable—dinner for two with a bottle of wine about $40. A bottle of ripe easy-drinking Bandol from southern Provence is a perfect mate for under $20. Provence is at 38 Macdougal Street between Houston and Prince streets. Telephone: 475-7500.

It's an Edward Hopper painting come to life, this World War II coffee shop turned French bistro in the heart of the gritty West Side meat-market area. Formerly the R & L Restaurant, a stainless-steel-and-Formica hash house that catered to butchers and truck drivers in the market's heyday, it was taken over by a genial young Frenchmen, Florent Morellet. The new owner changed the name to **Restaurant Florent** while leaving the period decor largely intact.

The menu has abandoned "Adam and Eve on a raft" (poached eggs on toast) for French onion soup gratinée, duck mousse, couscous, sweetbreads, grilled calf's liver and other homey Gallic fare. Not only is much of the food surprisingly well prepared, it's also a bargain—a three-course meal runs about $25, or a bit more with wine.

The duck liver mousse is freshly made, creamy and well seasoned; and rillettes of pork are appropriately rough textured and peppery. Although I had heard good reports about the tripe, my waitress steered me instead to the fresh, golden sautéed sweetbreads with thin, crunchy french fries. Two dining companions enjoyed the inky and oniony boudin noir and a nicely poached monkfish swathed with onions and leeks. The restaurant is awaiting a liquor license.

Restaurant Florent is at 69 Gansevoort Street, a half block west of Greenwich Street (989-5779). Lunch is served Monday through Friday from 10:30 A.M. to 3 P.M.; dinner Monday through Friday from 6:00 P.M. to midnight (a small supper menu is available until 2 A.M.); Saturday and Sunday from 6 to 11:30 P.M. No credit cards are accepted.

West 14th Street, where the aroma of sizzling garlic mingles with rapid Spanish, is hardly the place where an authentic French bistro might be expected. However, one has taken root there, a convivial new restaurant called **Quatorze**, near Eighth Avenue, which has brought a dash of Gallic flair to New York's unofficial Latin Quarter.

Quatorze (French for fourteen) is a long, rectangular restaurant with a clean, minimalist decor that suits its unpretentious food. There can be found some of the simple French dishes that are staples in bistros all over Paris: jambon persillé, country-style terrine, chicory salad with a warm bacon vinaigrette, choucroute garnie and oysters on the half shell. There are also lively table wines at low prices.

The earthy terrine is unlike most encountered in this country, and it is exceptionally good—alternating layers of well-seasoned beef brisket, spinach and carrots.

Quatorze is one of the few places in New York to offer frisée aux lardons, the chicory salad with a warm bacon vinaigrette that is a ubiquitous dish in France. It is nicely done here, swathed in a well-balanced vinaigrette. The seven or eight menu entrees are supplemented by a daily special.

Desserts are huge and up to the standards of the entrees, from a cereal-bowl full of fresh fruits with crème Anglaise to apple tart, which comes out the size of an individual pizza. Prices are moderate.

Quatorze is at 240 West 14th Street, just east of Eighth Avenue (206-7006).

Sel & Poivre is a tidy little French bistro on Lexington Avenue near 65th Street that, based on a recent sampling, is capable of offering solid and satisfying fare. It is the latest venture of Barbara Mora, formerly of Bistro Bamboche on York Avenue. The dining room has a warm and congenial feeling with its white walls and dark wood wainscotting, candlelight, decorative wall beams and cozy bar. It seems to be attracting largely a genteel neighborhood crowd.

The menu is small, though there are usually a few daily specials. Among those I enjoyed were a bright vegetable terrine that holds a mosaic of carrots and broccoli, surrounded by a grainy mustard-cream sauce. A scallop and spinach terrine was fresh and well seasoned too.

Entrees are straightforward and traditional: crisply sautéed sweetbreads in a brown sauce redolent of thyme and oregano, delicious soft-shell crabs nestled in spinach and doused with sizzling brown butter at the table, and entrecôte with red-wine sauce. Service is low-key and friendly. For dessert try the bulbous fruity apricot soufflé. Dinner for two runs about $70 with wine.

Sel & Poivre, 853 Lexington Avenue (between 64th and 65th streets), is open Monday through Saturday, 5 to 11 P.M. Telephone: 517-5780.

In the Provence region of southern France a favorite Friday-night meal is brandade de morue, which is a puree of poached salted cod blended with olive oil, garlic, potatoes and milk. It is

313

a delicious combination, especially when served with toasted slices of French bread, which can be used to scoop up the snowy puree. One rarely sees brandade in New York restaurants; it is probably considered too much of a peasant dish to be bothered with.

La Bonne Soupe, a budget-priced bistro at 48 West 55th Street, between Fifth Avenue and the Avenue of the Americas, serves a superlative brandade every Friday night (in winter) for the budget price of $7.25, including salad and bread. With a glass of wine and dessert, you could have a fine meal for about $10. Telephone: 586-7650.

✦ GELATO ✦

The gelati wave that washed over New York in recent years has given New Yorkers a kaleidoscopic selection of this Italian ice cream. The best gelati I have tasted is served at an Italian delicatessen/restaurant that was serving soft Italian ice cream long before it invaded the Upper West Side.

Siracusa, 65 Fourth Avenue (near 10th Street), makes three flavors of gelati that are so heavenly they belong in the licker's hall of fame. The special of this family-run trattoria is ricotta gelato, an ineffably delicious concoction that tastes faintly nutty with hints of cinnamon and cream. If you ask for the recipe, the young woman behind the counter will just smile. "It's so secret some family members don't even know it," she says. The other two outstanding flavors are hazelnut, which is incredibly rich, smooth and intensely flavored, and espresso, a dry, pure and invigorating blend with a pleasing aftertaste.

Siracusa also serves excellent espresso coffee and cappuccino at its long wine bar. About eight Italian wines are available by the glass; in the small trim dining room, a half-dozen fresh and tasty pasta dishes are prepared daily. Pastas are in the $9-to-$18 range and gelati cost $4. Phone: 254-1940.

◆ HAMBURGERS ◆

Hamburger Harry's, the sleek grillery that brought the béarnaise burger to New York, has two locations: 157 Chambers Street, between West Broadway and Greenwich (267-4446), and near Times Square, at 145 West 45th Street (840-0566). They sport violet walls, neon highlights, blond-wood tables and an open charcoal-mesquite grill. Their thick hamburgers are made with good quality semi-lean ground beef; they are served on sesame seed buns. Prices range from $3.25 for the "naked burger" (served without a roll) to $5.95 for both the caviar and sour-cream burger and the "ha ha burger" (chili, Cheddar cheese, chopped onion, guacamole and pico de gallo hot sauce). Coleslaw is freshly made and tasty, although the cooks haven't mastered the french-fry machine yet.

◆ ICE CREAM ◆

Amid all the hoopla over fancy ice cream concoctions, such as the whimsical combination of cookies, candies and nuts mixed into ice cream cones at **Steve's** (Avenue of the Americas and 10th Street) and at **David's Cookies** (Broadway and Eighth Street, among others), the notion of an old-fashioned ice cream soda may seem quaintly anachronistic. If prepared well, however, an ice cream soda is one of the most uplifting warm-weather drinks.

One of the best is served in an unexpected place, the **Fountain** at Macy's, Seventh Avenue and 34th Street, on the fifth floor. This cheerful ice cream parlor, all green and white, with a gazebo and clumps of fresh chrysanthemums, is a pleasant place to recuperate after a tiring shopping tour. The ice cream sodas are superlative because they are made the traditional way: soda water, flavored syrup, first-rate ice cream (Sedutto) and billowy fresh whipped cream. The Fountain has a wide range of regular flavors, as well as weekly specials. Aside from ice cream sodas, it serves all kinds of sundaes, malteds and sherbets.

✦ ITALIAN ✦

MANHATTAN

The invasion of the pastel pasta makers continues. First it was **Mezzaluna** at Third Avenue near 74th Street (535-9600), the colorful Italian cafe the size of a studio apartment that serves sprightly pumpkin tortellini, green cannelloni and tortellini with pink sauce. Management defies the laws of physics nightly by cramming what appears to be four people into every seat.

A clone of Mezzaluna called **Pasta & Dreams** opened awhile after at First Avenue and 58th Street. This cheerful little spot, about the dimensions of Mezzaluna, is done in bright yellow and pink with yellow cane chairs and a clay-colored tile floor.

The lunch menu carries a number of prix fixe meals, most under $12. You will find combinations such as a sparkling salad of arugula, green leaf lettuce and radicchio; spaghetti with fresh tomato sauce and basil; a glass of wine, beer or mineral water and coffee.

À la carte choices include summery dishes such as tagliatelle with asparagus, farfalline with salmon and spinach, and penne with zucchini and mozzarella. The inexpensive wine list offers some reliable Italian labels by the glass and the bottle.

Pasta & Dreams (752-1436) is open for lunch Monday through Friday from 11 A.M. to 3 P.M. and for dinner Monday through Sunday from 6 to 11 P.M.

Fanciers of veal chops know that on the infrequent occasions when forces conspire to produce a top-grade chop expertly cooked, it is one of the most sublime meats around. Too often in restaurants, this expensive delicacy lacks the subtle beefy flavor and buttery texture it should have.

One of the consistently best veal chops in New York is served at **Girafe**, a northern Italian restaurant at 208 East 58th Street. Girafe, not to be confused with the Quilted Giraffe on Second Avenue, is a starched and formal restaurant that plays the zoological theme to the hilt. There are large and small giraffes in every nook and cranny, and on the walls is a gallery of oil paintings depicting African wildlife.

Girafe turns out some formidable pasta dishes, especially a seasonal fall special of fettuccine with a porcini mushroom sauce. Its most remarkable entree, however, is the veal chop. The double chop, thick as a man's fist, is golden brown and crusty outside, pink and juicy inside. The maître d'hôtel explained that the chop is kept moist by a special cooking method that involves broiling it for crispness, then covering it with foil and finishing it in the oven. Accompanied by a small dish of pasta, salad and a bottle of bracing red wine, it is a superb fall dinner. Telephone: 752-3054.

Little Italy may have lost its edge as the epicenter of authentic Italian food, but from time to time a new place is discovered that offers a winning dish or two. **Taormina**, at 147 Mulberry Street, a relative newcomer to the neighborhood, is one of the more promising. It is a bright and airy place with a spiffy brass-and-wood bar, cheerful greenery and a friendly informal feeling. A few pastas are worth trying. One is penne with smoked salmon and vodka, a curious-sounding combination that succeeds smashingly ($13). The al dente tubular pasta is delicious in its silky cream sauce with a lovely smoky undercurrent from the chunks of salmon. Another winner is the ziti alla melezane, in which the pasta is swathed in a toasty combination of roasted eggplant, tomato, cognac and basil ($9.50).

The menu at Taormina is giant, and the wines reasonably priced. Taormina is open daily for lunch and dinner. Telephone: 219-1007.

The cafe at **Pete's Place**, ensconced in the basement of a turn-of-the-century tenement in a jagged-edged neighborhood of the East Village, looks from the outside like little more than a watering hole for the Ninth Precinct station next door. Over the years, this spot has served that function between sporadic restaurant ventures; however, current management has turned it into one of the best buys in Italian food in town, a real find in the downtown theater district.

Pete's, at 317 East Fifth Street, between First and Second Avenues (473-9863), retains its rough and unfinished look—bohemian, if you want to be romantic about it. There is an old wooden bar along one wall, flanked by a 1950s jukebox and a pool table. The dining room, partly segmented by a painted plywood divider, has a long wooden banquette with a Naugahyde strip down the middle, rickety tables, exposed heating pipes overhead and faded cream-colored walls of a shade likely to be found in police-station waiting rooms. The decorative highlight of the restaurant is a vintage espresso machine whose design resembles the front grill of a 1957 Chevy.

Everything on the small menu is freshly made every day, from a simple preparation of spaghetti bathed in olive oil with garlic and hot red pepper flakes, to rigatoni al ragu, a lusty, boldly seasoned red sauce, with sausage, pork and veal. Another fine dish is penne in a cream sauce, with prosciutto and asparagus. There are slivers of prosciutto in the sauce, as well as small cubes of prosciutto that are fried until crunchy and added at the last minute, lending a wonderful texture. The restaurant has a small wine list.

In an era when many restaurateurs value decor and service over good cooking, it is reassuring to dine in a homey, unpretentious place like **Frank's**, at 431 West 14th Street, in the heart of Manhattan's wholesale-meat district. This seventy-year-old steakhouse, with its pressed-tin ceiling, languid overhead fan, sawdust-strewn tile floor and long, elbow-worn mahogany bar, is as comfortable as an old flannel shirt. It has been known to generations of butchers and truck drivers as a place to start the day with coffee and rolls at 2 A.M. or, after the cooks come in at 4 A.M., virile breakfasts of everything from steak and eggs to kidneys, liver pancakes and bacon.

Several years ago, Frank's began serving dinner, not only steaks but also a sizable seafood selection and pasta. The steaks are better than average quality and cooked to order, but it is a pasta appetizer that shines on this menu. Tagliarini puttanesca, thin, homemade egg noodles with a sauce blending tomatoes, capers, black olives, garlic and anchovies, is delightfully executed. Puttanesca translates as "prostitute-style," named after the prostitutes of Rome said to favor this dish. The pasta is cooked al dente, and the sauce is brassy and beautifully balanced. It is served as a daily special about three nights a week; always call ahead and ask if they have it (243-1349).

THE BRONX

Some of the most lovingly prepared Italian food in New York can be found at an unprepossessing fifty-year-old family-run restaurant in the Bronx called **Amerigo's**. Easily accessible from Interstate 95, Amerigo's is a well-guarded secret among its cult-like clientele from this safe and solidly Italian neighborhood as well as from nearby Westchester County.

Don't be put off by the exuberant Neapolitan decor—filtered cocktail-lounge lighting, classical statues scattered about and, in the back, an eerie illuminated brick wall oozing water like a leaky dam into a pool below.

Tony Cortese, the welcoming owner, will take you under his wing and offer all sorts of off-menu specialties at the slightest goading. I can't vouch for the entire menu, although I have tried the Friday night osso buco, and it was the best I've had in ages. The fist-size veal shank, meaty and packed with buttery marrow, was falling off the bone and delicious in its thick braising sauce of carrots, onions, tomatoes and lemon. For starters, fresh marinated artichokes, available on weekends only, were delightful. Other good choices were the well-made gnocchi in meaty Bolognese sauce, or equally good al dente green-and-white fettuccine in a beguiling Alfredo sauce. First-rate dishes included brassy shrimp fra diavolo ringed with fresh mussels and clams and excellent tripe in a marinara sauce. Entrees fall in the $12-to-$20 range.

Amerigo's is at 3587 East Tremont Avenue. Telephone: 792-3600 or 824-7766. Closed Tuesdays.

There are no reservations, no menus, no tablecloths and no soft music, no credit cards are accepted, and no check at the end of the meal—the waiter simply tells you how much you owe.

Dominick's, a tiny restaurant at 2335 Arthur Avenue in the Bronx, near the Bronx Zoo (733-2807), is one of the last of those unvarnished pasta houses that serve an honest bowl of spaghetti with fresh sauce, rough red wine and superb homemade bread. A complete meal is the price of a fancy appetizer at some of Manhattan's Italian grottoes.

This thirty-year-old neighborhood restaurant, with its long communal tables and simulated-wood paneled walls, is so popular you may have to wait at the small bar for a while. An Ernest Borgnine look-alike offers a glass of Villa Pinza California Burgundy as you watch a hockey game on a television perched high on the wall. If you order pasta with shrimp and calamari in red sauce, it comes in an oval platter that could feed the front line of the New York Rangers. The waiter places it on the table, pats you on the back and says half-defiantly, "Mangia!" Fettuccine with fresh mushrooms and bacon in cream sauce is also fresh and tasty. The sauces and special dishes change daily, with no apparent pattern.

BROOKLYN

If you fear that Italian food in New York is becoming a bit precious, what with all those cute Frisbee-size pizzas, pastel raviolis and vegetables in every color of the spectrum except green, then you might want to venture to the Williamsburg-Greenpoint section of Brooklyn to visit **Crisci**—"A Tradition Since 1902."

In this wonderfully anachronistic setting you will find an appropriately dim bar where stocky old-timers sip red wine and watch sports on the overhead television; walls festooned with 8-by-10 glossies of Frank Sinatra, Marilyn Monroe and other luminaries; a large, simply appointed dining room with walls that exude the aroma of a half century of marinara sauce (the restaurant moved to its present location in the 1930s); and dozens of patrons chewing happily on pasta, seafood and chops in familiar colors and shapes.

You are not likely to experience an epiphany with the cuisine here; what you get is simple, fresh and generally well-prepared fare, and most entrees are about $10. Eggplant caponata is a fine fresh starter; pasta with white clam sauce cannot be faulted, especially if you like garlic slices the size of dimes and lots of oregano. And resilient homemade tagliatelle comes in a good pulpy red sauce. The list goes on and on, and the veteran waiters can steer you in the right direction. Ask for some Sambuca with your espresso, and they will plop a bottle on the table and tell you to help yourself.

Crisci is at 593 Lorimer Street, Brooklyn, (718) 384-9204, and is closed Mondays.

✦ JAPANESE ✦

You suspect you may have had one too many shots of sake. Don't fret, the three video monitors above the sushi bar at **Cafe 212**, showing simultaneous scenes of Japanese surfers, are just part of the show. This polymorphic restaurant—part Japanese, part French—is worth considering for a quick lunch in the midtown area, especially if you are dining alone. The striking modern dining room is done in soft shades of rose and pink with a spacious sushi bar in the front and tables in the back. Another dining area is upstairs. Solitary diners will find the sushi bar particularly accommodating because it is wide enough to hold a newspaper or magazine while eating.

You could begin lunch with soothing and well-seasoned miso soup colored with scallions and seaweed, followed by à la carte tidbits of fresh and attractive sushi. The French culinary influence is really minimal; salmon stuffed with fish mousse over a bed of spinach, all in a thick basil-cream sauce, is satisfying, but overall I find the Japanese entrees to be better. Aside from good sushi and sashimi, prepared in front of you by a young chef in a pastel dress shirt and stylish thin tie, several varieties of sea-weed-wrapped sushi rolls are available. Cooked entrees include chicken teriyaki, beef teriyaki and negimayaki (thinly sliced beef rolled around grilled scallions). Sake, plum wine and Japanese beer go well with them.

Cafe 212, at 212 East 52nd Street, is open for lunch Monday through Friday from noon to 3 P.M., and dinner from 5 to 10:30 P.M. (Saturdays 6 P.M. to midnight). Telephone: 486-0212.

It is said that the food at a good Japanese restaurant evokes sensations of the sea. At **Hayato**, a sushi bar and restaurant at 571 Third Avenue (between 37th and 38th streets), the illusion is taken one step further. Patrons at the sushi bar and tables in the front dining room are treated to an audiovisual display projected on two walls that shows rolling ocean surf to the soothing background music of Kitaro, the composer of futuristic-sounding "new age" works.

I wouldn't say that food necessarily tastes better with celluloid ocean spray bathing your face, but it certainly creates a relaxing atmosphere. Fresh and attractively displayed options include the sushi combination, chirashi and an assortment of vegetables and fish in seaweed rolls. Prices are moderate.

Occasionally, the video switches to dramatic scenes of surfers gliding across monstrous waves or to wind-surfing competitions. The highlight of the show, however, is when videotape cameras aim at the sushi chefs behind the bar. This allows diners who are sitting at the other end of the room to watch their food being prepared. If you happen to be sitting at the sushi bar, the camera may catch you in the unflattering pose of trying to bite a tuna roll daintily in half, only to have the rice fall on the counter and the fillet dangle from your mouth like a piece of bait. No matter, it's all part of the show. Telephone: 883-0453.

Another Japanese-style restaurant that is not so well represented is the tempura bar, at which diners sit at a counter and order various kinds of meat, fish and vegetables that are dipped in egg batter and flash fried in oil. When prepared properly, tempura is greaseless and light, with a slightly puffed and brittle crust.

One good spot to try the whole spectrum of well-made tempura is at **Inagiku**, the Japanese restaurant in the Waldorf-Astoria Hotel (the restaurant entrance is at 111 East 49th Street between Park and Lexington avenues; 355-0440). Inagiku is a sprawling full-service restaurant with many dining areas, but the room that is the most fun—and that has the best food—is the large circular tempura bar. Chefs wearing traditional Japanese outfits work in the middle of the circle tending to giant, oil-filled woks. The bar is comfortable and congenial; chances are you will strike up a conversation with diners next to you as you examine one another's selections.

There are two tempura dinner entrees: the tempura Inagiku, featuring a variety of seafood ($20 range), and the tempura and kushiage, which includes vegetables and meats (about $25). You can also order individual items. All of the selections sampled recently were exceptional.

The seafood tempura includes large shrimp, smelts, fluke and an invigorating combination of ground white fish wrapped in a vaguely mintlike Oriental leaf. Because the tempura entrees are prepared in front of the customer and served sizzling hot from the wok, they are superbly crisp and fresh. They can be dipped in a radish-flavored soy sauce or simply in lemon juice and salt. All foods are fried in a combination of sesame, camellia and olive oils. The tempura style of cooking does wonderful things for vegetables, whether they are chunks of green pepper, whole mushrooms, slices of onion or stalks of zucchini. Meat, too, is a special treat. The best version is bite-size chunks of beef with onion slices that are served on skewers.

✦ MOROCCAN ✦

Some of the best dinner bargains in New York can be found along Brooklyn's Atlantic Avenue, home of about a dozen Middle Eastern and North African restaurants. One of these is **Moroccan Star**, 205 Atlantic Avenue (718-596-1919), a simple, tidy restaurant that serves a mélange of Arabic and European dishes for prices so low you can't help suspecting they are a mirage.

The kitchen of this family-run restaurant is presided over by Ahmed Almontazer, formerly of Luchow's, the Four Seasons and the Brasserie in Manhattan, which explains the Continental accent on the menu. However, forget the beef Stroganoff and crepes, and head right for the lamb steak ($7.95), a juicy, intensely flavorful slab of meat that makes you wonder why this dish is not generally served in Manhattan steakhouses. The best side dish is al dente baby okra.

Other good choices on the menu are pastella (sometimes spelled pastila or bastila), traditionally a semisweet pigeon pie in paper-thin pastry, and tajine. The pastella is made with chicken, raisins, garlic and spices and is served in a large wedge, like a thick slab of pizza ($6.75).

The tajine, while different from the version served in Morocco, was nonetheless satisfying. It is a savory lamb stew with carrots, prunes and dried almonds, and it is meant to be eaten in large pockets of pita bread. Moroccan Star does not serve beer or wine, so you may provide your own.

Neither smog nor heat nor threat of rain nor honking traffic will stay New Yorkers from their appointed weekend rounds of outdoor cafes in warm weather—and the choices are growing every year. Stretches of Columbus Avenue, the Upper East Side and Greenwich Village are beginning to resemble Jones Beach as umbrellas pop up on sidewalks and terraces, in gardens and plazas.

Each summer seems to spawn more sidewalk cafes, and the casual observer can easily follow their migratory patterns. Where five years ago they were considered cute attractions scattered loosely in the Village and parts of the East Side, they are now an integral part of the summer social life nearly everywhere, particularly the Upper West Side.

The familiar favorites are going strong: the **River Cafe** in Brooklyn's Fulton Ferry district, where drinks are served on an outdoor terrace overlooking the East River and all of lower Manhattan; **Tavern on the Green** in Central Park, which has a leafy and magical ambiance in summer and early fall; **The Terrace** at the American Stanhope Hotel on Fifth Avenue across from the Metropolitan Museum, and the assorted restaurants at the South Street Seaport and the new Pier 17, which has a number of American grill-style restaurants and lively bars that offer panoramic views of the harbor.

The following outdoor cafes are recommended for atmosphere, comfort and service; food quality varies widely, from average to superior. Also taken into consideration is the "fume factor." All of these selections are a safe distance from the street and from the eye-burning exhaust fumes that are the bane of many urban cafes. Those who plan to go to any of the restaurants are advised to specify the outdoor cafe when calling for reservations.

The **American Festival Cafe** at Rockefeller Center, 20 West 50th Street, occupies one of New York's most popular tourist haunts. It is also worth visiting even by those who live here. The cafe, offering an all-American menu, is part of a glittering new three-restaurant complex that opened this year. It also includes the Sea Grill, a slightly more formal restaurant, which features fish grilled over charcoal, and Savories, a combination carryout, sandwich and salad shop. The cafe has a dining area called the Bar Carvery, offering steaming slices of roast beef, turkey or cold poached fish and a wide variety of American beers. None of these restaurants is memorable for food, but the setting partially makes up for it.

All the restaurants spill out into what is in winter the home of the Rockefeller Center skating rink, under the golden statue of Prometheus. Trying to figure out which outdoor tables belong to which restaurant can be a challenge, but once you settle in, you can enjoy a comfortable, fume-free meal under the red-and-pink umbrellas flanked by palm trees and potted geraniums.

The American Festival Cafe starts up at 7:30 A.M. for breakfast, which can be lovely on a crisp summer morning. Savories closes at 6 P.M., but everything else goes until 10 P.M.. You can sample from a rainbow of frozen drinks at the outdoor bar until 1 A.M. Telephone: 246-6699.

For those with a nautical bent, the **Water Club**, on the upper deck of a barge on the East River at 30th Street, is the place to go for before- or after-dinner drinks and snacks. You sit on directors' chairs under the summer sky and watch ships and tugs ply the river, or, if you are facing landward, you monitor traffic on the F.D.R. Drive. The only break in the tranquillity is the flutter of helicopters at a nearby landing pad, briefly drowning conversation at each landing and takeoff.

Food served on the outdoor deck is limited to hamburgers, hot dogs, clams, oysters and dessert in the $3-to-$5 range.

The deck is open 4 P.M. until midnight weekdays and noon until 1 A.M. weekends. Telephone: 683-3333.

One of the old standbys near the theater district, **Tout Va Bien**, 311 West 51st Street, has opened a small, tree-shaded courtyard in back with a half-dozen large tables under green-and-white umbrellas. You will think you are going on a guided tour of the boiler room as the waitress leads you through a dim back hallway to the garden, but once you are there, it is peaceful and pleasant.

Stick with the simple entrees—steak and french fries, broiled chicken, stews. Anything fancier is consumed at your own risk. Lunch is a singular bargain, with many entrees in the $7-to-$10 range. The cafe is open noon to 2:30 P.M. for lunch and 5 to 11:30 P.M. for dinner. Closed Sunday. Telephone: 265-0190.

Le Madeleine, 405 West 43rd Street, a fine place to cool off with an iced cappuccino and a tea cake, is one of the more charming little cafes in the theater district. The restaurant, which serves simple French fare in the $6-to-$10 range at lunch, slightly more at dinner, has a small but lovely enclosed backyard garden with ivy-strewn brick walls and about a dozen tables under white umbrellas.

The cafe is open daily, noon to midnight. Telephone: 246-2993.

•   •   •

Greenwich Village outdoor cafes tend to be cramped affairs, jutting out into narrow sidewalks crowded with pedestrians. **Caffe Vivaldi**, at 32 Jones Street, has the advantage of being on a quiet side street with a neighborhood atmosphere. There are a half-dozen tables outside under an attractive canopy. You can order such tidbits as prosciutto and mozzarella or quiches. There are all sorts of exotic iced coffees, ten different teas, imported sodas, mineral waters and a wide range of desserts.

Open 10 A.M. to 2 A.M. weekdays, until 3 A.M. weekends. Telephone: 929-9384.

Ye Waverly Inn, 16 Bank Street, corner of Waverly Place, a nearly 180-year-old Greenwich Village landmark, has been known in recent years more for its nostalgic atmosphere than for its food, but its backyard garden is a charming setting for a cool drink. Among the house specials are concoctions called peach fizz, lemon mint freeze and iced Alaskan coffee. There are also piña coladas and daiquiris. Lunch, Monday through Friday, 11:45 A.M. to 2 P.M.; dinner, Monday through Thursday, 5:15 to 10 P.M., Friday and Saturday until 11 P.M., and Sunday, 4:30 to 9 P.M.; brunch, Sunday, noon to 3:30 P.M. Telephone: 929-4377.

Roxanne's, 158 Eighth Avenue, at 18th Street, is an elegant oasis amid the cacophony of construction in this part of Chelsea. There is a small, handsomely landscaped garden in the back, with five tables under romantically illuminated trees. Tables are reserved for diners, but if you want only a drink, there is a tiny bar outside with five chairs. The gregarious bartender does some nice things with rum and fresh fruit.

Open for lunch noon to 2:30 P.M., Monday through Friday;

dinner, 6 to 11 P.M., Monday through Saturday. Closed Sunday. Telephone: 741-2455.

One of the livelier and stylish outdoor cafes in a relatively tranquil neighborhood is **65 Irving Place** (at 18th Street). Tables wrap around the outside of the restaurant, some under a canopy, and if you are facing the right way as the sun goes down, you will see the giant clock light up atop the stately old Con Edison Building on 14th Street. The menu is on the expensive side, and you'll have to crunch through raw green beans in any of the nouvelle-style creations. Lunch served daily, noon to 3 P.M.; dinner, 6 to 11 P.M. daily. Telephone: 673-3939.

If you are in the mood for just a drink or simple chophouse fare, there is a landmark tavern across the street at 129 East 18th Street, called **Pete's Tavern**, once frequented by O. Henry, which also has an outdoor cafe. Hours: 11 A.M. to 11:30 P.M., Sunday through Thursday; 11 A.M. to 12:30 A.M., Friday and Saturday. Telephone: 473-7676.

There is a massive red-granite outcropping in the garden behind **Lion's Rock**, 316 East 77th Street, a French-American restaurant. The rock is so startling, like a chunk of the Appalachian range transplanted to Manhattan's East Side, that you can't help suspect it is a masterly papier-mâché prank. But it is real, a glacial remnant that was a famous picnic spot for couples a century ago. Dramatic lighting at night makes the scene even more impressive as you sit at one of the eighteen tables in the tastefully landscaped garden.

Steaks and chops are the best bet here. The outdoor tables are generally reserved for diners in peak meal hours.

Dinner served 5 P.M. until midnight daily; lunch, 11:30 A.M. to 3 P.M., Monday through Friday; brunch, Saturday, 11:30 A.M. to 3 P.M. and Sunday, 11:30 A.M. to 4 P.M. Telephone: 988-3610.

Da Silvano, 260 Avenue of the Americas, between Bleecker and Houston streets, is a popular Tuscan restaurant just outside the crowded core of Greenwich Village. The once superior food has become wobbly, but the outdoor cafe on a wide sidewalk is still a lovely place to share a bottle of wine and assorted hors d'oeuvres. Da Silvano is open for lunch Monday through Friday noon to 3 P.M.; dinner, Monday through Thursday 6 to 11:30 P.M., Friday and Saturday 6 P.M. to midnight, Sunday 5 to 11 P.M. Telephone: 982-0090.

The recently refurbished Loeb Boathouse on the lake in Central Park is one of the most serene spots in town to wind down under the open sky. Aside from two restaurants, one more a snack bar, the other more formal, there is a relaxing outdoor terrace overlooking the lake. Diners in either restaurant have the option of sitting indoors or outside. The **Boathouse Cafe** is open daily in summer months from noon to 4:30 P.M. for lunch and 6 to 11 P.M. for dinner. The patio is open continuously from 9 A.M. to 6 P.M. Telephone: 517-2233.

Victor's Cafe 52, 236 West 52nd Street, 586-7714. The granddaddy of Manhattan Cuban restaurants, Victor's moved six years ago from its original Upper West Side location (which is still called Victor's Cafe but under an independent management) to a sparkling new home in the theater district. It has a pretty skylit dining area in the back and a big cool bar up front. The oversize menu carries a full range of familiar and exotic

Cuban dishes. Once again, I find that simplicity yields the greatest rewards. For example, black bean soup, corn tamales, ropa vieja and assorted spicy chicken dishes are the best. The black beans and rice are always fresh tasting and well seasoned. Reservations not necessary, major credit cards accepted.

Victor's is open Monday through Thursday, noon to midnight; Friday through Sunday, noon to 1 A.M.

✦ PIZZA ✦

From the avenue, it looks like just another slick East Side neon-and-fern bar specializing in frozen drinks sporting little umbrellas. Inside, though, the unmistakable aroma of garlic indicates something more substantial. Pizzico, an Italian trattoria-like restaurant at First Avenue and 75th Street, turns out a host of beguiling little pizzas as well as some bright and tasty salads in a friendly, informal setting.

The chef is Evelyne Slomon, author of *The Pizza Book* (Times Books, 1984). Appetizers, breads and pizzas far outshine the grilled entrees. Among the starters, you might try the engaging sweet pepper salad with roast garlic and herbed ricotta cheese or the lively arugula salad with sweet peppers, walnuts and balsamic-vinegar dressing. Air-cured beef with arugula, capers and olive oil is first-rate. For the asbestos-tongued, there is grilled hot—and they mean hot—fennel sausage with hot peppers and focaccia. It also comes with sweet sausage.

As for the pizzas, they are made with the freshest and most aromatic ingredients and can be ordered in as many variations as you want. We enjoyed one with clams, parsley, bacon, garlic and Parmesan. Pizzas are about $10 (extra ingredients can be ordered for about $1–$2 each).

One of my favorite tidbits on the menu is homemade focaccia, puffed triangles of pizza-dough bread that come with a small crock of baked garlic cloves in olive oil. You coat the bread with olive oil, then spread the soft cloves on it like butter. Garlic fans would also moan in ecstasy over the bruschetta, toasted Italian bread that is rubbed with raw garlic cloves.

Pizzico, 1445 First Avenue, is open for lunch Monday through Saturday from noon to 4 P.M.; dinner Monday through Thursday 6 P.M. to 12:30 A.M., Friday and Saturday until 1:30 A.M. On Sunday, a pizza brunch is offered from noon to 4 P.M. and dinner is served from 5 to 11:30 P.M. Phone: 737-3328.

✦ SEAFOOD ✦

Succulent fried oysters that evoke memories of lunch at a beach canteen on a blazing summer day are the specialty of a bustling fishhouse on the Upper West Side. **Docks Oyster Bar and Seafood Grill**, at Broadway and 89th Street, is an inviting, informal spot with black tile walls, simple wooden tables and a long bar with iced shellfish on display.

The menu carries an assortment of fresh oysters and clams on the half shell as well as grilled tuna, swordfish, salmon and the like for around $14. Among the best options are the plump fried oysters encased in crisp cayenne-spiced cornmeal, served with tartar sauce. Fried clams dredged in cornmeal go fast, so arrive early if you want to taste them. Get some of the rough-textured homemade coleslaw on the side, which bears little resemblance to the sour glop served in many delicatessens.

Bluepoint and Chesapeake oysters on the half shell are fresh and well iced, although the cherrystone and littleneck clams have better flavor. The oyster selection changes daily. If the shrimp chili special is available as an appetizer, go for it—firm, fresh-tasting shrimp in a zippy rice mixture spiked with jalapeño peppers, dried chilies, coriander and tomatoes.

Lobster lovers can really indulge themselves—from a two-pounder to a hulking four-pounder to an intimidating deep-sea Gulliver that could double as a bar bouncer; call a day in advance for prices, which vary.

Docks is open for lunch Monday through Saturday from 11:30 A.M. to 3 P.M.; Sunday brunch from 9 A.M. to 4 P.M.; dinner Monday through Thursday 5 P.M. to midnight, Friday and Saturday until 1 A.M., Sunday 5 to 11 P.M. Telephone: 724-5588.

CRABS

You are hit with a blast of a familiar aroma upon entering the sprawling dining room, a blend of sea air and hot spices. All over the room, animated diners wearing plastic bibs are hammering away at mounds of steaming red crabs, sending shards in all directions. **Sidewalkers'**, at 12 West 72nd Street, is about as close as you'll get to the eastern shore of Maryland without leaving Manhattan Island.

Its specialty is steamed and liberally spiced hard-shell crabs, the kind that make a mess of your hands, napkin, bib, the table and floor. The crabs are generally fresh, the meat snowy and sweet, and the spices just piquant enough to keep you rubbing your lips against an icy beer mug in between bites. The size of the crabs depends on availability; a dozen of the medium-size cost about $24, a dozen large $34.

The dining room has a freewheeling, down-home atmosphere conducive to such inelegant consumption—wooden plank floors, rust-colored walls, paper-covered tables and a young good-time crowd. In addition to the hard-shell crabs there are nicely sautéed soft shells with tarragon butter (in season), as well as some of the best crab cakes in town. Steamed shrimp with Old Bay Seasoning also is a standout appetizer. There is a full menu of grilled fish as well—the fresh tuna sampled was smoky and moist—pastas and other shellfish. Top it off with a respectable deep-dish apple pie, and you've just saved train fare to Baltimore. Telephone: 799-6070.

LOBSTER

It is always interesting to watch true lobster aficionados in a restaurant. To them, everything else on the menu has as much appeal as oatmeal. They savor their lobster slowly, rhapsodically, sensually.

The following restaurant listings are not only for purists who prefer lobster steamed or boiled and served with lemon butter and maybe a tall beer but also for those seeking more imaginative preparations.

Some of the biggest and juiciest fresh lobsters are served in New York's better steakhouses. Some of the biggest are served at **Palm** and its sister restaurant across the street, **Palm Too**. Four-and-a-half-pound monsters come to the table split, broiled and with melted butter. These lobsters are large enough to share, and at about $44 apiece, sharing may be a necessity.

Palm, 837 Second Avenue, is open for lunch Monday through Friday, noon to 5 P.M.; dinner, Monday through Saturday, 5 to 11:30 P.M. Closed Sunday. Reservations are accepted at lunch only. Telephone: 687-2953.

Palm Too, 840 Second Avenue, is open the same hours as Palm. Reservations are accepted at lunch, and for parties of four or more at dinner. Telephone: 697-5198.

One of the more popular lobster dishes in town is at **Arcadia**, the inventive American restaurant on East 62nd Street. A house special is a 1½- to 2-pound lobster, called a chimney-smoked lobster, that is grilled over a wood-fired grate and is served with tarragon butter. The meat has a hint of smoke, a wonderful extra dimension. Also try chef Anne Rosenzweig's signature club sandwich made with brioche, lobster, lettuce, bacon, tomato and lemon mayonnaise.

Arcadia, 21 East 62nd Street, is open for lunch Monday through Friday, noon to 2:45 P.M.; dinner, Monday through Saturday, 6 to 10 P.M. Closed Sunday. Telephone: 223-2900.

For an unusual, succulent variation, try the lobster pan roast at **Meridies**, an eclectic and breezy new spot in Greenwich Village. This creation features a hacked 1½-pounder in the shell set in a creamy bisquelike broth made with intense lobster stock.

Meridies, 87 Seventh Avenue South (between Bleecker and Christopher streets), is open for lunch, weekdays, noon to 5 P.M., Saturday and Sunday, 11 A.M. to 5 P.M.; dinner, Monday through Friday, 6 P.M. to midnight; Friday and Saturday late-night supper, midnight to 2 A.M. Telephone: 243-8000.

The fricassee of lobster at **Windows on the World** is one of the prettiest—and tastiest—lobster dishes in Manhattan. It features shelled lobster arranged in a pattern on the plate over a lustrous shellfish-flavored cream stock garnished with delicate lacy pleurote mushrooms.

Windows on the World, 1 World Trade Center, 107th floor. At lunch the restaurant is a private club. Dinner reservations are accepted from 5 to 10 P.M. Monday through Saturday. Reservations are required for Sunday brunch, noon to 3 P.M., and for the grand buffet from noon to 7:30 P.M. The restaurant is closed after 7:30 P.M. on Sunday. Telephone: 938-1111.

✦ SOUL FOOD ✦

To call **Sylvia's** the most popular ribs and fried chicken restaurant in Harlem, if not in the entire city, would be a gross understatement. This congenial spot, operated by Mrs. Sylvia Woods and her family, is an institution where local politicians meet over braised short ribs, and an ever growing roster of celebrities from near and far stops by for some restorative soul food that has its origins in Mrs. Woods's hometown of Hemingway, South Carolina.

Sylvia's has a pleasantly appointed dining room for leisurely meals and a long bonhomous counter for those who want to eat and run—waddle is more like it—after one of these rib-sticking repasts. Friday night is braised ribs night, and they can be ordered with peppery collard greens and moist corn bread. The congenial waitresses tend to address customers as "honey" and to encourage them to eat more than they should. Save room for the sweet-potato pie, which is so good it could stop a Baptist preacher in mid-sermon. Sylvia's, 328 Lenox Avenue, between 126th and 127th streets (534-9414). Reservations accepted for eight or more. No credit cards.

✦ TEA ✦

In what seems a throwback to a more genteel era, the cocktail terrace at the **Waldorf-Astoria** serves a formal afternoon tea, a tradition that was popular there in the 1930s and 40s. Sinking into a soft leather chair in the hotel's splendiferous Art Deco lobby and sipping tea with scones and Devonshire cream, you will feel like a character from a British movie of the '30s. Different teas are featured monthly. It might be Waldorf Darjeeling, Amaretto, Earl Grey, English breakfast or blackberry. Decaffeinated teas are available too, including such unusual flavors as strawberry and vanilla. There is also a selection of spiked coffees topped with whipped cream. You may choose à la carte from the menu—tea sandwiches, scones, fruit tarts, bundt cake, napoleons, cream puffs and the like—or go for a little of everything ($14.75). A pot of tea or coffee alone is $2.50. Throughout the afternoon, a harpist plucks out "Scarborough Fair" and other soothing tunes. Tea is served daily from 2 to 5 P.M., after which the cocktail hour begins.

Waldorf-Astoria, at Park Avenue and 50th Street. Telephone: 872-4818.

Italians are not known as tea drinkers, preferring instead to finish their meals with coal-black, 220-volt espresso. So it is ironic that one of the better tea selections around town is offered in an Italian restaurant. **Parioli Romanissimo**, 24 East 81st Street between Fifth and Madison avenues (288-2391), offers an after-dinner tea tray that would be a Briton's delight.

In addition to the standard Earl Grey and chamomile, there are cassis, mango, clementine, mint and verveine. In warmer months, you might want to try iced raspberry or strawberry. The hot teas are presented on an attractive tray, and customers may brew their own.

◆ TEX-MEX ◆

Fajitas, a staple of the Rio Grande set that combines grilled strips of beef with flour tortillas and assorted eye-opening salsas, can be appealing even to a dandified urban palate if prepared well. At the **Cadillac Bar**, a rough-edged Tex-Mex watering hole and restaurant on West 21st Street, a credible version is being rustled up at lunch and dinner. The fajitas al mesquite are made with lean and well-tenderized sheets of skirt steak that are grilled until nicely charred outside and tender within. The flour tortillas served alongside are delicious—soft, warm and not dry, as they are at so many Mexican restaurants in town. The fajitas come with rice, beans and two sauces: a lively coriander-and-onion salsa and a combustible hot sauce ($12.95). The only other dish sampled was a cloying Kahlúa mousse topped with aerosol whipped cream.

Cadillac Bar, 15 West 21st Street, is a branch of the original in Houston. It is a spacious, rowdy place with an Alamo theme and a large bar whose canopy is covered with empty beer bottles. Open daily. Telephone: 645-7220.

New York has been under a gastronomic siege in recent years as restaurants featuring Tex-Mex food as well as south-of-the-border fare have been advancing from all sides. One of the best in the Tex-Mex genre is **El Rio Grande**, occupying much of the block between 37th and 38th streets along Third Avenue (867-0922). It has two airy dining rooms, one called Mexico, the other Texas. While the decors play off this demarcation, the food is the same on both sides of the border—and some of it is quite good.

For starters, frozen margaritas, served in copious goblets, are first-rate. As you sip those, try the two hot relishes, a guacamole-type concoction and a green-tomato scorcher. A small order of chili con queso would suffice for two as an appetizer. It is a dish of mild melted cheese served with a tray of relishes, including diced coriander, chopped jalapeño peppers, diced onions, salsa verde and hot red tomato sauce. Some or all of these can be mixed with the cheese and scooped up with fried tortilla chips.

One of the best entrees is mole poblano, a perfectly cooked half chicken with an earthy mole sauce.

Hell's Kitchen is smoldering with a whimsical new Cajun–Tex–Mex–Southern–you-name-it–style restaurant in the former McGraw-Hill Building on West 42nd Street, called **Southern Funk Cafe**. Paul Prudhomme it's not, but where else in New York can you get an eye-watering bowl of Creole jambalaya replete with sausage, chicken and crayfish for $6.25? Southern-fried chicken, thickly battered, peppery and moist, is the same price—it cries out for a Lone Star beer ($2.75, no extra charge for the glass).

Southern Funk Cafe occupies a former cafeteria in this evocative Art Deco building, and the concession to hip decor revolves around splashes of neon and tinsel, a few posters and piped-in Sam Cooke. The vinyl booths and Formica tables are well worn, and the linoleum floor gets a good workout on certain weekends when live music and dancing are featured.

I only scratched the surface of the menu, which includes a muddy beef stew that will spark pangs of nostalgia among those who hung out at diners in their youth. Other specialties range from fried okra ($2.95) and chicken potpie ($6.25) to chicken-fried steak ($6.95) and "White Castle Hamburgers imported from the South Bronx" (70 cents). For dessert, how about Oreos and a tall glass of milk ($1.50)? Southern Funk Cafe, 330 West 42nd Street, is open Monday through Friday from 7:15 A.M. to 11 P.M., Saturday from noon to 11 P.M. Telephone: 564-6560.

It seems lately that every restaurant that plunks a bottle of Tabasco sauce on the table along with some corn bread calls itself "Southwestern" or "Tex-Mex"—these are still hot cuisines, and everybody wants a piece of the tortilla while it lasts. **Yellow Rose Cafe** on Amsterdam Avenue at 81st Street is the kind of place you dream of finding by chance on Route 66 in west Texas, but never do. Co-owned by a Fort Worth native, Barbara Clifford, this is a real down-home restaurant, as honest as a country preacher and as comfortable as an old saddle.

You know this is serious southwestern food when you see chicken-fried steak on the menu, a Texas-Oklahoma oddity in which a slice of well-pounded cube steak is dipped in a flour-and-buttermilk batter, then fried like chicken. It might not be everyone's idea of an elegant steak dinner, but for aficionados of this culinary hybrid, the Yellow Rose version, which is greaseless, crispy and smothered with cream gravy, is better than most served in the Lone Star state.

Fried chicken, all puffed and brittle outside and moist within, is an archetype for all would-be Southwesterners around town. Side dishes are prepared with care as well, particularly butter beans laced with small cubes of ham, fried okra and potato salad. I never thought it possible to rhapsodize over mashed potatoes, but these heartily seasoned spuds, drizzled with cream gravy, are as uplifting as a Sousa march. For starters, try the lumpy guacamole, the hot tomato-scallion sauce with nacho chips or the beanless chili with molten Monterey Jack cheese and chopped onions. A couple can eat like ranch hands for under $30. Telephone: 595-8760.

◆ VEGETABLE PLATTERS ◆

As temperatures rise in the summer months, so does the demand for lighter meals, particularly at lunchtime. A number of New York restaurants serve refreshing vegetable platters, steamed, stir-fried or sautéed. Following are some of the more imaginative ones.

Woods (148 West 37th Street, between Seventh Avenue and Broadway, 564-7340): What may be the most elaborate and colorful vegetable plate in town packs enough chlorophyll to paint a green stripe down Fifth Avenue for St. Patrick's Day. Remarkably, each of the more than a dozen ingredients is cooked to perfection: green beans, broccoli, leeks, asparagus, zucchini, snow peas, carrots, yellow bell peppers, roast potatoes, mushrooms, sweet potatoes, beets and two purees, carrot and turnip. They are artfully presented, with two sauces, lemon-butter and soy-scallion.

Lavin's (23 W. 39th Street, between Fifth Avenue and Avenue of the Americas, 921-1288): There is an Oriental twist to the steamed vegetable platter here; the selection is brought to the table in a bamboo steamer. The variety is nearly as large as at Woods, and the vegetables come with two sauces, soy and a creamy garlic vinaigrette.

Auntie Yuan (1191 First Avenue, between 64th and 65th streets, 744-4040): One of the best parts of the meals here is the giveaway marinated vegetables. One bowl contains slivers of Chinese cabbage and scallions in a bracing sesame-oil vinaigrette with fresh coriander. The other has carrot sticks and pickled Chinese daikon in a zingy hot-oil dressing. The vegetables on the luncheon platter—snow peas, carrots, bamboo shoots, baby corn, black mushrooms and more—taste as if they had been steamed, then quickly stir-fried. They are lightly swathed in oil and go well with steamed rice.

Raga (57 West 48th Street, between Fifth Avenue and Avenue of the Americas, 757-3450): A whole vegetarian menu is offered, including subji jalfrazie, assorted vegetables—carrots, cauliflower, green peppers, green beans—sautéed with herbs and served with a hot sauce and rice, and baigan bhurta, eggplant baked over an open fire and mashed with onions and spices.

The Four Seasons (99 East 52nd Street, between Park and Lexington avenues, 754-9494): The daily vegetable platter at lunch is offered as an appetizer, but you may order a larger portion as a main course. It is beautifully done—a variety of baby vegetables, such as eggplant, scalloped pattypan squash, sugar-snap peas, yellow squash—and served with an invigorating lemon vinaigrette.

◆ WALL STREET DINING ◆

The food scene in lower Manhattan has improved markedly in recent years as former factories and warehouses have given way to apartments and lofts, creating demand for bars, restaurants and night spots. Here is a selective guide to dining in the vicinity of the financial district, from haute to hamburgers.

Windows on the World (1 World Trade Center, 106th and 107th floors, 938-1111): There is no more panoramic perch in New York than this sprawling complex of restaurants and bars atop the World Trade Center. Both food and service are on a high level (no pun here) in the wraparound, glass-enclosed Windows on the World and at the smaller and more expensive

Cellar in the Sky, which specializes in pairing wine and food. Wine lists here are among the best in town for variety and price.

At lunchtime Windows is a private club catering to business clients; Cellar is open only for dinner.

American Harvest; The Greenhouse Restaurant and Bar (Vista International Hotel, 3 World Trade Center, 938-9100): These two restaurants in the Vista International Hotel, part of the World Trade Center complex, are worth keeping in mind for lunch or dinner when you are in the area. The more ambitious American Harvest restaurant specializes in regional American cuisine, while the attractive Greenhouse, with its soaring glass ceiling and ferns galore, is a nice place for a drink and a light meal.

The regional foods at American Harvest can be diverting and tasty, although the kitchen occasionally gets too cute for its own good.

The River Cafe (1 Water Street, Brooklyn, 718-522-5200): This ambitious American restaurant on a barge in the East River, under the shadow of the Brooklyn Bridge, is about as close as you can get to being on a boat. The food has continued to rise in quality, and it now ranks among the city's top dining rooms. Of course, the view of downtown is unparalleled—this is a must for out-of-town visitors who want to see the romance of New York's skyline at night.

The River Cafe is a class operation all the way with imaginative menus and a terrific wine list (especially strong in American labels).

· · ·

Liberty Cafe; Fluties (Liberty Cafe, 406-1111; Fluties Oyster Bar and Restaurant, 693-0777, both at Pier 17 in the South Street Seaport): The new Pier 17 in the East River at the South Street Seaport, a glittery, multitiered shopping and restaurant complex, sports buoyant bars and simple grill restaurants where the young button-down Wall Street set unwinds nightly with blue margaritas. Liberty Cafe and Fluties Oyster Bar and Restaurant are among the most popular, both offering a gull's-eye view up and down the East River. Both restaurants have lively bars that resemble sailors' shore leave on summer weekends.

As for the food, they both serve oysters and clams on the half shell and a mixed bag of grilled steaks and seafood. The best advice is to order the simplest dishes and ask for everything cooked rare—then hope it comes out medium. Prices are moderate.

Gulf Coast (489 West Street, near West 12th Street, 206-8790. No reservations, no credit cards): This cacophonous Cajun/Tex-Mex spot on West Street along the Hudson River serves generally fresh and satisfying fare. The nightly crowd runs from rolled-up workshirts to tieless young executives who dig into spicy steamed shrimp, tamales, soft-shell crabs and the like, washing them down with frosty Lone Star beers. The average tab for a complete dinner with several drinks is about $20. While the downstairs dining room does not have a view of the river (the front bar has a partial view), a new second-floor room does.

Exterminator Chili (305 Church Street at Walker Street, 219-3070): This campy chili parlor with a nostalgic 1950s diner ambiance is one of the best bets for downtown bargain hunters. Only a five-block walk from the Hudson River, it offers satisfying sandwiches, soups and burgers as well as its famous chili, which comes in three ascending grades of hotness: residential, commercial and industrial (each $6.95 for a longshoreman's portion). The restaurant finally has a liquor license, so you don't need to brown bag anymore.

Bridge Cafe (279 Water Street, 227-3344): This informal, vintage restaurant in the shadow of the Brooklyn Bridge, specializing in seafood, is a favorite among the financial community at lunch, when you must show up by 12:30 P.M. if you want to get a table.

Le Zinc (139 Duane Street, 732-1226): A Parisian-style cafe with a polyglot, stylish crowd, Le Zinc is worth considering if you revel into the wee hours. It's only a five-minute walk from the Hudson River near Chambers Street, and the food is tasty and moderately priced (a fresh and well-seasoned steak tartare with french fries is $14.50). The service is harried but functional. Be sure to reserve ahead when possible.

The Odeon (145 West Broadway, at Thomas Street, 233-0507): Always fun, always busy, the Odeon is worth a special trip. This Art Deco diner-theme restaurant has a wide-ranging menu of bright and creative American-style dishes and exceptional desserts. Quality has slipped a notch in the past year, but stick with steaks, roasts and grilled fish and you will do fine. The Odeon has an engaging wine list too.

Hamburger Harry's (157 Chambers Street, 267-4446): This handsome streamlined cafe is a good bet for a charcoal-grilled burger and beer, everything from a simple cheeseburger ($4.25) to a deluxe model crowned with caviar and sour cream. Wine, beer and champagne are available.

Montrachet (239 West Broadway, between North Moore and White streets, 219-2777): A contemporary French restaurant with light and herbaceous food and first-rate wines, Montrachet is always in demand. The menu is French, and some of the best bets are inventive seafood preparations. À la carte entrees are in the $18 to $25 range.

La Tour d'Or (31st Floor, 14 Wall Street, between Broadway and Broad Street, 233-2780): Few people seem to know about this clubby rooftop restaurant housed in the former downtown hideaway apartment of J.P. Morgan, the famous financier. It has a wonderful old bar, a bright and cheerful main dining room, and some cozy semiprivate rooms tucked away up a flight of stairs. The Monday and Tuesday buffet lunches are particularly popular among Wall Streeters. The regular menu is a bit stodgy, with old-fashioned French food of unpredictable quality. But the waitresses are engaging and motherly, and the room definitely has a sense of history and drama. Dinners are irregular, depending on demand.

El Internacional (219 West Broadway, between White and Franklin streets, 226-8131): This eccentric Spanish bar and restaurant is a good spot to have a drink and some tapas, or Spanish finger foods. Don't be put off by the jarring decor or the occasional purple hairdo—some of the food, especially at the bar, is quite good.

·   ·   ·

Barocco (301 Church Street, at Walker Street, 431-1445): This relative newcomer to the neighborhood is a high-ceilinged, spare and spacious trattoria serving some delicious Tuscan fare. The pastas are fresh and rustic, the salads sparkling and well seasoned, and grilled seafood is generally reliable. Prices are reasonable.

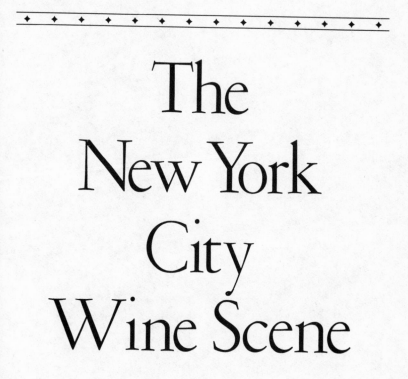

The
New York
City
Wine Scene

Just a few years ago, wine enthusiasts who wanted to make comparative tastings—say, three or more California Chardonnays from the 1981 vintage—had to go out and buy three bottles at a liquor store and try them at home. A handful of bars in town offered a range of wines by the glass, but they were mostly low-key neighborhood places. And the typical house wines at restaurants and bars were limited to an inoffensive and inconsequential white paired with an overchilled, underwhelming red.

Today, however, one does not have to look far to find wine bars that offer all kinds of tasting opportunities for the connoisseur and the novice. The SoHo Kitchen and Bar, which sells a remarkable number of wines by the glass—more than 120—has special "flight tastings" for each category on its wine list; for example, 1½-ounce glasses of eight sauvignon blancs are served on a platter for about $14. This is an excellent way to learn about different styles among producers. It can also make for a diverting evening with a group of friends.

The Wine Bistro at the Novotel Hotel, Broadway at 52nd Street, offers similar tastings on a more limited scale.

Perhaps the term "wine bar" as it applies to New York City is a misnomer; some of the bars here are traditional Scotch-and-water haunts that have yielded to changing consumer tastes and started offering a reasonable selection of fine wines by the glass. This addition has been made possible by a technological innovation called the wine-preservation machine, commonly referred to as a Cruvinet (the trade name of a major manufacturer).

These machines, which hold up to eight bottles attached to tubes and spigots, replace dispensed wine with a layer of nitrogen, thereby maintaining an airtight seal. Fragile wines, which formerly were sold by the bottle only, can now be served by the glass over a period of hours or even days without risk of deterioration. It is not an exaggeration to say that these machines have revolutionized the wine scene in New York.

Buying wine this way is no bargain. Prices range from about $3 to $7 or more a glass depending on the wine; buying by the bottle is usually cheaper, even at the high markups most restaurants impose—at least twice the retail price. But then, you taste only one or two wines by the bottle in an evening; the machines allow greater experimentation.

For purposes of this survey, a wine bar is defined as an establishment that sells ten or more wines by the glass and where the staff has at least minimal knowledge about the selection. The wine bars are listed in alphabetical order.

Cafe Chardonnay, 414 East 73rd Street, 772-9191. This uplifting little nook tucked away on a residential street was started by four marathon runners who prefer Chardonnay to Gatorade. About twenty-five wines are available by the glass, more in bottles, from California, New York and France. The enthusiastic owners strive to offer little-known quality wines. You can try an interesting range of California and imported wines. From time to time special festivals are held, such as for New York State or Washington State wines, which offers a good opportunity for comparison tasting—about $3 to $5 for a 2½-ounce glass, $6 for a 5-ounce serving.

Wines in bottles represent some real bargains. Soups, sandwiches and light meals in the $7-to-$10 range are served in the pleasant pastel-colored dining room. Bill Abraham, one of the partners, who is usually found behind the bar, enjoys nothing

352

more than discussing labels, vintages and so on with customers. The cafe recently began a series of special wine tastings with guest speakers.

Open Monday through Saturday from 6 P.M. to midnight (the kitchen is open until 11), Sunday for brunch noon to 3 P.M. and for dinner 6 to 10 P.M.

Cafe Europa & La Brioche, 347 East 54th Street, 755-0160. This is a most unlikely setting in which to find a high-tech wine bar, a charming old-world restaurant specializing in earthy stew-like meat, and seafood preparations that are served in carved-out brioche loaves the size of softballs. The colorful dining room, festooned with rustic artifacts, looks as if a team of Gypsies could dash in at any moment and begin dancing on the tables. It has a tile-fronted fireplace, stucco walls, rustic wooden beams overhead, ornate brass chandeliers and a loyal clientele that looks as if it was cast for the role.

In the back of the dining room is a snug little wine bar featuring a huge stainless-steel Cruvinet. Selections range from the Margaux's Château Kirwan to Frog's Leap sauvignon blanc from the Napa Valley. A nice option is the snack menu to accompany the wines, including rillettes of pork with French bread, garlic sausage brioche and rabbit-duck terrine with Armagnac.

The bar serves during restaurant hours: lunch Monday to Friday noon to 2:30 P.M.; dinner Monday through Saturday 5 to 11 P.M.

Cafe 43 Restaurant and Wine Bar, 147 West 43rd Street, 869-4200. This is a fine spot to meet friends for a glass of wine before or after a Broadway show. The bright and cheerful interior is in the grand-cafe style, with lots of mirrors, deep banquettes and a long brass-and-wood bar where twenty-six wines, including champagnes, are poured by the glass. The bottle list is impressive as well, especially the California selections. Prices are moderate.

The food at Cafe 43 has had its ups and downs recently. If time is limited before a show, you might want to order an assortment of appetizers to accompany the wines and have a full meal afterward. Open for lunch Monday through Friday 11:45 A.M. to 3 P.M.; dinner Monday through Saturday 5 to 11:30 P.M. Bar open between services. Closed Sunday.

The Drake Bar, in the Drake Hotel, 440 Park Avenue, at 56th Street, 223-3876, 421-0900. Just off the busy lobby of this swank hotel is a plush two-tier lounge surrounding a wood-and-marble bar. This is one of the more sedate and formal bars in the city, a good place for a romantic interlude or a tranquil business meeting. The only exception might be when a pianist starts tinkling away in the early evening, exposing you to the potential risk of a tipsy frog-voiced conventioneer performing a painful rendition of "New York, New York."

Because the Drake is owned by Swissotel, the regular lineup of wines by the glass, nine by last count, includes a few labels from Switzerland. The bar stools are plush and the peanuts keep coming. There is also a good selection of champagne and sparkling wine, from Henkell Extra Dry to Cuvée Dom Pérignon.

Open daily 11:30 A.M. to 10:30 P.M.

Golden Tulip Barbizon Restaurant, at the Barbizon Hotel, 140 East 63rd Street, 838-5700. The wine selection may not be the grandest in town, but the setting is one of the more genteel. This renovated 1920s hotel with its long polished bar and tables facing animated Lexington Avenue is a fine place to unwind with a glass of wine or champagne. An eight-bottle Cruvinet carries mostly California and French labels, while during the Christmas holidays three kinds of sparkling wines are available.

Open noon to 2 A.M. daily.

Grapes, 522 Columbus Avenue, at 85th Street, 362-3004. The wacky appearance of white walls sawed open to reveal brick underneath and buoyant murals depicting city scenes belies a serious approach to wine at this lively spot on the Upper West Side. More than fifteen wines, including champagnes and ports, are available by the glass—everything from 1984 Preston Gamay Beaujolais to Château Mouton-Rothschild. The restaurant is building a solid wine list that is well balanced between California and French selections. Grapes is also one of the few places in town where you can find an intriguing dessert wine from California, the 1983 Quady Orange Muscat Essencia. If wine could be made from orange blossoms, it would taste like this.

The restaurant serves a mixed bag of pastas, grilled fish and roasts. Open for dinner Monday through Thursday (and Sunday) from 6 to midnight, Friday and Saturday until 2 A.M. Sunday brunch is served from 11 A.M. to 4 P.M. The bar is open daily from noon to 4 A.M. All wines are half price from 5 to 7 P.M. daily.

Greene Street, 101 Greene Street, between Prince and Spring streets, 925-2415. Just next door to the SoHo Kitchen and Bar, and under the same ownership, is this cavernous restaurant featuring jazz nightly. The wine list has been upgraded significantly in recent years and now includes about eight wines by the glass, plus champagne. In the fall sixteen nouveaux wines from France, Italy and the United States are poured. The extensive wine list also has a fair number of half bottles.

Wines and light meals are available at the bar, full meals in the stunning multitiered dining room. The food has improved markedly in recent years.

The bar serves Monday through Saturday 5 P.M. to closing (varies from 1 to 3 A.M.), Sunday noon to midnight. The restaurant is open Monday through Thursday 6 to 11:30 P.M.; Friday and Saturday until 1 A.M.; Sunday from 11:30 A.M. to 8:30 P.M.

Il Cantone, 294 Columbus Avenue, at 74th Street, 496-9226. Stucco and brick, hanging plants and Mediterranean accents set the informal scene at this ethnic Upper West Side hangout; rugby shirts and crewneck sweaters set the fashion tone. Il Cantone is known primarily for its lilting opera singers, who perform in the rustic downstairs Wine Cellar at 9:30 on Friday and Saturday nights.

The wine selection is as diverse as the music, with more than thirty selections by the glass and even more by the bottle. Prices are on the low side, and there is a wide roster of cheese plates, terrines, empanadas and sandwiches.

Open Monday to Friday from 11:30 A.M. to 11:30 P.M., Saturday and Sunday until 1:30 A.M.

Jacqueline's, 132 East 61st Street, 838-4559. Named after the effervescent proprietor, Jacqueline Ferrero, this gregarious spot is actually a champagne bar and restaurant. The bottle list carries a well-chosen range of domestic and imported sparkling wines, four champagnes by the glass (they vary from day to day) and nine exotic champagne cocktails, which Jacqueline calls "elixirs."

If you are in an extravagant mood, there is a champagne–foie gras combination for two at $30—two glasses of champagne and a serving of imported foie gras. Even more sumptuous is the bottle of Dom Pérignon and one ounce of beluga caviar for $99.

Jacqueline's is open for lunch Monday through Friday from noon to 3 P.M., dinner through Saturday from 6 P.M. to midnight.

Lavin's, 23 West 39th Street, 921-1288. Few restaurateurs take wine more to heart than Richard Lavin. The genial bar in his handsome, wood-paneled restaurant is one of the classiest places to sample a wide range of familiar and up-and-coming wines. Close to twenty selections, including champagnes and sparkling wines (and a dozen ports), are poured.

Mr. Lavin's particular interest in California is reflected in his list, which is updated weekly, so there is always something new and interesting to try. You can sip wine and order appetizers at the bar or have a full dinner in the dining room.

The Académie du Vin holds classes in the same building and sponsors many special tastings at Lavin's all year, some of which are open to the public, others for Académie members only. Open Monday through Friday from noon to 2:30 P.M. for lunch, 6 to 10 P.M. for dinner.

Marvin Gardens, 2274 Broadway, at 82nd Street, 799-0578. This informal Upper West Side institution that features a Cruvinet has been steadily beefing up its wine selection, which now includes twenty labels by the glass and three sparkling wines. Three-ounce samples are in the $3-to-$12 range, with a few higher-priced offerings, from Burgundy and Bordeaux.

The menu is generally more modest than the wines: steaks, chops, game and fish.

The bar is open from noon to 2 A.M. Monday through Wednesday, until 3 A.M. Thursday through Saturday, and until 2 A.M. Sunday. The restaurant is open Monday through Friday

357

from 7 A.M. to 2:30 A.M. and Saturday and Sunday from 10 A.M. to 2:30 A.M.

Siracusa, 65 Fourth Avenue, near 10th Street, 254-1940. About a dozen wines, nearly all Italian, are served by the glass in this engaging family-run spot in the downtown theater district near Astor Place. Just a few years ago, it was an undiscovered little Italian delicatessen with a few Formica tables scattered in the back, where those in the know relished Sicilian and Neapolitan fare like that made by an Italian grandmother (in fact, an Italian grandmother was in the kitchen making it). Since then its menu has vastly expanded, prices have shot up, and a bar has been added. This once strictly neighborhood spot is now frequented by the likes of Jack Nicholson and Meryl Streep.

A wonderful match to the hearty Italian red wines is the cold appetizer plate, which includes mozzarella cheese with sun-dried tomatoes, little ricotta-cheese fritters, eggplant salad, fried sardines, marinated mushrooms and broccoli pie. Pastas are still lustrous and fresh, and the homemade gelati are the best in town —ricotta and hazelnut are unbelievable.

Open for lunch Monday through Saturday noon to 3 P.M.; dinner Monday through Thursday 6 to 11 P.M., Friday and Saturday until 11:30, Sunday from 5 to 11 P.M.

SoHo Kitchen and Bar, 103 Greene Street, between Spring and Prince streets, 226-9103. This is about as close to oenophile heaven as you'll ever see. More than 120 wines by the glass, eleven special "flight tastings" in which patrons can sample up to eight wines of the same type side by side, seasonal wine festivals, weekly wine festivals and much more. Aside from the first-rate list of French, Italian and American labels, there are many unusual selections such as Australian cabernets and German Eiswein. Even the setting is bigger than life, with a soaring ceiling, mile-long bar and multitiered dining areas.

The bar is open Monday through Saturday from 4 P.M. (closing varies, but is usually well after midnight); the kitchen Monday through Friday from 5 P.M. to 1 A.M., Saturday from 4 P.M. to 1 A.M. Closed Sunday.

Tastings (144 West 55th Street, 757-1160)—Home of the International Wine Center, one of the major wine schools in the city, Tastings is one of the older wine bars in town. The relaxing setting with brick walls and strategically placed wine crates, offers twenty-five by-the-glass selections. It is often populated by students and instructors from the school, which is upstairs. When a class lets out at about 9 P.M., you will encounter clusters of grinning students, full of good cheer from their vinous curriculum, stopping at the bar to get a head start on their homework. The staff is exceptionally well informed and can answer any questions.

The International Wine Club, which holds excellent tastings and seminars weekly, is worth considering. You might call the International Wine Center (757-0518) about a free introductory session; annual dues for full membership are $400, or $700 for couples. There is a $40 initiation fee.

Tastings is open for lunch Monday through Friday from noon to 2:30 P.M.; dinner Monday through Friday 5:30 to 11 P.M., Saturday from 5:30 to 11 P.M., and Sunday from 5 to 10 P.M. The bar is open between service offering cheese plates and snacks.

Tastings on 2, 953 Second Avenue, between 50th and 51st streets, 644-6740. This offshoot of the West Side Tastings restaurant regularly sponsors interesting and educational events—

comparative samplings of the same wines from different vintages, champagne festivals, Alsatian festivals, specials on ports and Madeiras, and much more.

The congenial bar offers about thirty wines by the glass (changing weekly). The wines are chosen to offer the widest possible variety. The list of bottles is one of the most varied in town, and it is priced well. Tastings on 2 is also affiliated with the International Wine Center.

Open Monday through Friday from noon to 2:30 P.M. and from 6 to 10 P.M. and Saturday evening from 5:30 to 11 P.M. Cheese plates and terrines are offered throughout the day and evening.

Terrace Five, Level Five, Trump Tower, 725 Fifth Avenue, at 56th Street, 371-5030. It may be surprising to learn that amid the hustle and bustle of this vertical shopping mall is a relaxing little oasis where you can get a good salad and simple grilled fish while sampling from about fifteen well-chosen wines. Prices are on the high side, but so, too, is the view—and the rent.

A small bar with an eight-bottle Cruvinet extends to the shopping arcade, while on the other end are little tables in a cheerful back room with a stunning view down Fifth Avenue. Desserts are most tempting.

Bar open Monday through Saturday noon to 9:30 P.M.; restaurant, lunch Monday through Saturday noon to 3 P.M.; afternoon tea from 3:30 to 5:30 P.M.; dinner Monday through Saturday from 6 to 10 P.M.

The Wine Bar, 422 West Broadway, between Prince and Spring streets, 431-4790. The granddaddy of New York wine bars, this airy, informal spot still has a vaguely bohemian SoHo feeling. You might see a bearded young artist wearing a lumberjack shirt sketching at a corner table, a couple playing chess, and lots of people trying to read books in the dim light. Moreover, the roster of wines is one of the best around: close to thirty from major producing regions in the United States and Europe. Prices are fair across the board.

The Wine Bar offers a changing-daily menu of omelets, soups, sandwiches and homey entrees. A nice accompaniment to the wines is the special snack platter: smoked salmon, smoked turkey, roast beef and a variety of cheeses, fruit and vegetables.

Open Monday through Friday from noon to 2 A.M.; Saturday and Sunday from 11:30 A.M. to 3:45 P.M. for brunch, until 2 A.M. for drinks and dinner.

The Wine Bistro, at Novotel, 226 West 52nd Street, 315-0100. This French-owned hotel has one of the better wine-by-the-glass selections in midtown, and surely one of the best settings. The Wine Bistro, a glass-enclosed bar and lounge perched on the seventh floor, offers a pigeon's-eye view down Broadway. Two dozen wines are served by the glass at competitive prices.

The Wine Bistro also offers terrines, duck liver, cheeses and tartines (open-face French-style sandwiches) to accompany the wines. A wine club organizes special tastings regularly. Open daily from 11:30 A.M. to 1 A.M.

Best Dishes

To locate the review and neighborhood map for each restaurant in this section, please consult the index beginning on page 393.

No one is immune to occasional food cravings, whether for a rosy slab of steak, Chinese spare ribs or a gravity-defying cheesecake. The following list is your road map to satisfaction. It is always advisable to call the restaurant in advance to make sure the dish you are yearning for is currently on the menu.

Angulas	Harlequin
Apple pandowdy	An American Place
Apple pie	The Coach House
Baba ghannoush	Andrée's Mediterranean Cuisine
Beef brisket	Carolina
Beef, prime ribs	The Coach House
Beef ribs, grilled	Rosa Mexicano
Beer	Joe Allen, Peculier Pub
Black bean soup	The Coach House, Union Square Cafe, Victor's Cafe 52
Boudin noir (blood sausage)	Cafe 58, Restaurant Florent
Brandade de morue	Chez Jacqueline, La Bonne Soupe, Provence
Bread	Barocco, Montrachet, Palio
Bread, Indian-style	Akbar, Bukhara, Tandoor
Bread pudding	Lavin's

Bread pudding, chocolate	Arcadia
Bruschetta	Nanni il Valletto, Union Square Cafe
Calf's liver	Brive, River Cafe
Carpaccio (beef)	Le Cirque, Palio
Carpaccio (swordfish)	Alo, Alo
Cassoulet	Cafe 58
Caviar	Petrossian
Cheesecake	Palm, River Cafe
Cheese plate	Le Régence, Palio, The Quilted Giraffe
Chicken, fried	La Louisiana, Yellow Rose Cafe
Chicken, grilled	Chirping Chicken, Jams
Chicken paillard	Cafe Luxembourg
Chicken potpie	The Coach House
Chicken salad (warm)	The Ritz Cafe
Chicken, salt-baked	The Nice Restaurant
Chicken sandwich	Cafe Montana
Chicken, tandoor-baked	Bukhara, Tandoor
Chicken wings, Buffalo-style	Morgans
Chili	Exterminator Chili
Chili, venison	Arizona 206
Chinese hot pot	Great Shanghai
Chocolate cake	Jams, Lavin's
Chocolate pudding	An American Place, Morgans
Corn bread	Sylvia's
Corned beef sandwich	Carnegie Deli
Corn fritter	Water Club

Couscous	La Metairie
Crabs, steamed	Sidewalkers'
Crab cakes	The Coach House, Jams, The Odeon, The Ritz Cafe, Water Club
Crabs with black bean sauce	20 Mott Street Restaurant
Crème brûlée	Le Cirque, Le Cygne
Crostini	Sistina
Desserts (overall)	Aurora, La Tulipe, Le Bernardin, Le Cirque, The Quilted Giraffe
Drinks (mixed)	Peter Luger, Sparks Steakhouse
Duck à l'orange	Terrace
Duck breast, grilled	The Four Seasons
Duck confit	Aurora, La Tulipe, Meridies, Prunelle, Union Square Cafe
Duck, roast, Chinese-style	The Nice Restaurant, 20 Mott Street Restaurant
Duck, roast, French-style	La Côte Basque
Duck terrine	Le Cygne
Dumplings, Chinese	Pig Heaven
Empanadas	Sabor
Fajitas	Cadillac Bar
Feijoada	Cabana Carioca, Cabana Carioca II
Fish, broiled	The Dolphin
Fish, grilled	John Clancy's Restaurant
Fish (overall)	The Dolphin, Le Bernardin, Oyster Bar and Restaurant
Foie gras, fresh sautéed	La Caravelle, The Polo, Prunelle

French fries	Jams, Lavin's
Frisée aux lardons	Le Refuge, Quatorze
Frogs' legs	Le Cygne
Gazpacho	Lavin's
Gelati	Positano, Siracusa
Gnocchi	Marcello, Meridies, Palio
Goat, roast	Dieci X, Primavera
Guacamole	Rosa Mexicano
Gumbo	The Ritz Cafe
Hamburger	Hamburger Harry's, Union Square Cafe
Hash, corned beef	Broadway Diner
Headcheese	Ruc
Hummus	Andrée's Mediterranean Cuisine
Ice cream soda	Fountain at Macy's
Key lime pie	Cafe des Artistes, Sabor
Kidneys	Le Périgord
Lamb chops	Peter Luger
Lamb, rack of	La Côte Basque, La Réserve, Le Périgord, The Quilted Giraffe, Windows on the World
Lamb steak	Moroccan Star
Lamb, vindaloo-style	Akbar, Tandoor
Lentil salad	Au Grenier Cafe
Linguine with clam sauce	Trastevere
Lobster, broiled	Palm, Palm Too
Lobster, chimney-smoked	Arcadia
Lobster club sandwich	Arcadia

Lobster fricassee	**Windows on the World**
Lobster, grilled	**Cafe Luxembourg**
Lobster pan roast	**Meridies**
Lobster roll	**Morgans**
Margaritas	**El Rio Grande, Rosa Mexicano**
Mashed potatoes	**Casual Quilted Giraffe, Yellow Rose Cafe**
Mussels, steamed	**Palio**
Mutton chops	**Keens**
Napoleon	**Cafe des Artistes, Terrace**
Noodles, cold sesame	**Auntie Yuan**
Oeufs à la neige	**La Boîte en Bois**
Orange beef	**Auntie Yuan, Fu's**
Osso buco	**Amerigo's, Nanni il Valletto, Positano**
Oxtail stew	**Caribe**
Oysters, fried	**Docks Oyster Bar and Seafood Grill**
Oysters, half shell	**Oyster Bar and Restaurant**
Paella	**Harlequin**
Pancakes	**Good Enough to Eat**
Paris-Brest	**La Petite Marmite**
Pasta (overall)	**Alo Alo, Marcello, Mezzaluna, Nanni il Valletto**
Pasta all'amatriciana	**Union Square Cafe**
Pasta, puttanesca-style	**Frank's, Il Cantinori**
Pastella	**Moroccan Star**
Pastrami	**Carnegie Deli**

369

Peking duck	Auntie Yuan, Fu's
Pheasant	River Cafe
Pig's feet	Cafe 58
Pizza	Meridies, Orso, Pizzico
Potato chips (homemade)	Morgans
Potatoes, sautéed	Maxim's
Profiterole	Lavin's, Maxim's
Quail, barbecued	Arizona 206, Auntie Yuan
Quail, grilled	Jams, Orso
Quail, roast	La Réserve
Rabbit paillard	Provence
Rabbit sausage	Huberts
Ribs, beef	Sylvia's
Rillettes of pork	Restaurant Florent
Risotto	Alo Alo, Nanni il Valletto, Palio
Salads	Gotham, Jams, Woods 37th Street
Salmon, grilled	The Quilted Giraffe
Salmon, sautéed	Prunelle
Salmon terrine	Brive, Le Cygne
Scallops	Le Bernardin
Seafood (overall)	Le Bernardin
Seafood salad	Gotham Bar and Grill
Sea urchin	Le Bernardin
Semifreddo	Felidia
Shrimp, grilled on sugar-cane	Cuisine de Saigon
Shrimp, steamed	Sidewalkers'

Sole, grilled Dover	**The Dolphin, John Clancy's Restaurant**
Sorbet	**Cafe du Parc, Palio**
Soufflés (dessert)	**La Caravelle, La Côte Basque, The Four Seasons**
Soup (shrimp)	**Indochine**
Spareribs, Chinese	**Fu's**
Spring rolls	**Indochine, 20 Mott Street Restaurant**
Squab (in a pot Chinese-style)	**The Nice Restaurant**
Squab, grilled	**Arizona 206, Aurora, River Cafe**
Squid, deep-fried	**Wilkinson's Seafood Cafe**
Squid, grilled	**Fu's, Ozeki**
Squid salad	**The Dolphin**
Squid, steamed Oriental-style	**Indochine**
Steak	**Peter Luger, River Cafe, Sparks Steakhouse**
Steak au poivre	**The Coach House**
Steak pommes frites (Steak and french fries)	**Cafe Luxembourg**
Strawberry shortcake	**An American Place, Morgans**
Suckling pig	**The Nice Restaurant, Sabor**
Sushi	**Hatsuhana, Mitsukoshi**
Sweetbreads	**Aurora, Lola, Lutèce, The Polo, The Quilted Giraffe**
Sweet potato pie	**Sylvia's**
Swordfish	**Jams, Lavin's**
Tabbouleh	**Andrée's Mediterranean Cuisine**

Tacos	Rosa Mexicano
Taramasalata	Andrée's Mediterranean Cuisine
Tartufo	Dieci X
Tea	Parioli Romanissimo, The Waldorf-Astoria
Tempura	Inagiku, Ozeki
Terrines (overall)	The Four Seasons, La Caravelle
Tirami sù	Dieci X, Marcello, Nanni il Valletto
Tortilla, Spanish-style	The Ballroom, El Internacional
Trifle (dessert)	John Clancy's Restaurant
Tripe	Amerigo's, Restaurant Florent
Truffles	Le Cirque
Tuna club sandwich	Union Square Cafe
Tuna, grilled	Jams, Union Square Cafe, Water Club
Veal chop	Aurora, Casual Quilted Giraffe, Girafe, Le Régence
Veal tonnato	Meridies
Vegetable platters, steamed	Auntie Yuan, The Four Seasons, Woods 37th Street
Vegetables, grilled	Alo Alo
Venison	Arcadia, Maxim's
Wine bar	The SoHo Kitchen and Bar
Wine list, American	Jams, Oyster Bar and Restaurant, Windows on the World
Wine list, French	La Côte Basque, Lutèce
Wine list, Italian	Il Nido, Le Cirque, Sparks Steakhouse

Wine list (overall)	Le Cirque, The Quilted Giraffe, Windows on the World
Zabaglione	Il Nido
Zuppa di pesce	Marcello, Trastevere

Maps

NEW JERSEY

THE BRONX

Harlem River

Riverside Park

Hudson River

1

Central Park

7

6

MANHATTAN

QUEENS

2

5

East River

3

Washington
Square

4

Battery Park

BROOKLYN

Every Manhattan restaurant in this guidebook appears on a map in this section. Those in the other boroughs of the city are listed on page 392. If you aren't sure which map carries the restaurant you are looking for, consult the restaurant index (see page 393). Each entry in the index is followed by a map number and the page(s) where the restaurant is described.

On the key facing each map, restaurants covered only in the Diner's Journal are followed by (DJ); those discussed only in The New York City Wine Scene are followed by (WS).

1. West 50th Street to West 119th Street (includes Lincoln Center, Central Park, and Upper West Side)

2. West 14th Street to West 49th Street (includes Chelsea and the Broadway Theater District)

3. Houston Street to West 13th Street, west of Broadway (includes West Village)

4. Below Houston Street (includes SoHo, TriBeCa, Chinatown, Little Italy, Wall Street and South Street Seaport)

5. Houston Street east of Broadway to East 49th Street east of Fifth Avenue (includes East Village, Gramercy and Murray Hill)

6. East 50s and 60s

7. East 70s and north (includes Upper East Side)

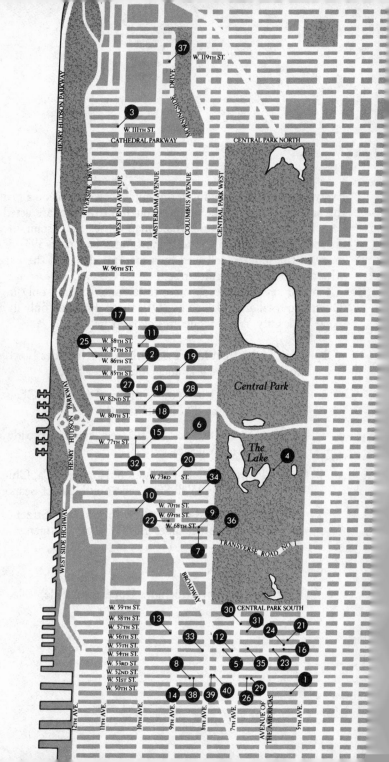

✦ MAP 1: WEST 50TH STREET ✦ TO WEST 119TH STREET

Includes Lincoln Center, Central Park and Upper West Side

① American Festival Cafe, 20 West 50th Street, in Rockefeller Center (DJ).

② Ancora, 2330 Broadway.

③ Au Grenier Cafe, 2867 Broadway (DJ).

④ Boathouse Cafe, near 72nd Street in Central Park, by the lake.

⑤ Broadway Diner, 1726 Broadway (DJ).

⑥ Bud's, 359 Columbus Avenue.

⑦ Cafe des Artistes, 1 West 67th Street.

⑧ Cafe des Sports, 329 West 51st Street (DJ).

⑨ Cafe Destinn, 70 West 68th Street (DJ).

⑩ Cafe Luxembourg, 200 West 70th Street.

⑪ Cafe Montana, 2398 Broadway (DJ).

⑫ Carnegie Deli, 854 Seventh Avenue (DJ).

⑬ Checkers, 867 Ninth Avenue (DJ).

⑭ Chez Napoleon, 365 West 50th Street (DJ).

⑮ Chirping Chicken, 350 Amsterdam Avenue (DJ).

⑯ Darbar, 44 West 55th Street.

⑰ Docks Oyster Bar and Seafood Grill, 2427 Broadway (DJ).

⑱ Good Enough to Eat, 424 Amsterdam Avenue (DJ).

⑲ Grapes, 522 Columbus Avenue (WS).

⑳ Il Cantone, 294 Columbus Avenue (WS).

㉑ Kuruma Zushi, 18 West 56th Street.

㉒ La Boîte en Bois, 75 West 68th Street.

㉓ La Bonne Soupe, 48 West 55th Street (DJ).

㉔ La Caravelle, 33 West 55th Street.

㉕ La Mirabelle, 333 West 86th Street.

㉖ Le Bernardin, 155 West 51st Street.

㉗ Marvin Gardens, 2274 Broadway (WS).

㉘ Metropolis, 444 Columbus Avenue.

㉙ Palio, 151 West 51st Street.

㉚ Petrossian, 182 West 58th Street.

㉛ The Russian Tea Room, 150 West 57th Street.

㉜ Shelter Restaurant, 2180 Broadway (DJ).

㉝ Siam Inn, 916 Eighth Avenue.

㉞ Sidewalkers', 12 West 72nd Street (DJ).

㉟ Tastings, 144 West 55th Street (WS).

㊱ Tavern on the Green, Central Park West at 67th Street.

㊲ Terrace, 400 West 119th Street.

㊳ Tout Va Bien, 311 West 51st Street (DJ).

㊴ Victor's Cafe 52, 236 West 52nd Street (DJ).

㊵ The Wine Bistro, Novotel Hotel, 226 West 52nd Street (WS).

㊶ Yellow Rose Cafe, 450 Amsterdam Avenue (DJ).

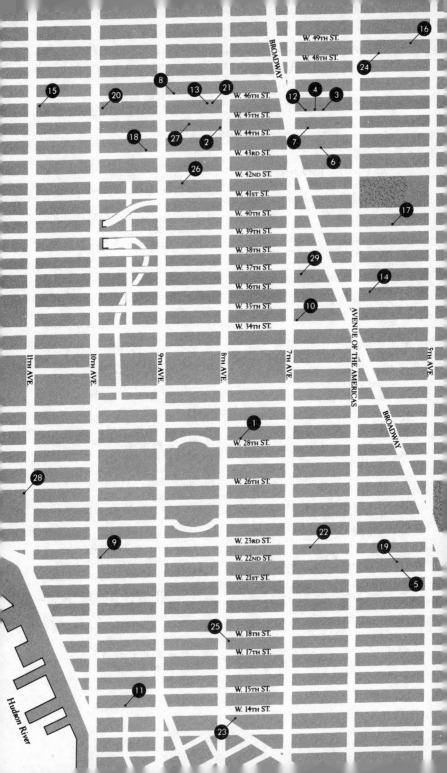

✦ MAP 2: WEST 14TH STREET ✦ TO WEST 49TH STREET

includes Chelsea and the Broadway Theater District

① The Ballroom, 253 West 28th Street.

② Barking Fish Cafe, 705 Eighth Avenue.

③ Cabana Carioca, 123 West 45th Street (DJ).

④ Cabana Carioca II, 133 West 45th Street (DJ).

⑤ Cadillac Bar, 15 West 21st Street (DJ).

⑥ Cafe 43 Restaurant and Wine Bar, 147 West 43rd Street.

⑦ Cafe Un Deux Trois, 123 West 44th Street (DJ).

⑧ Carolina, 355 West 46th Street.

⑨ Empire Diner, 210 Tenth Avenue (DJ).

⑩ Fountain at Macy's, Seventh Avenue and 34th Street (DJ).

⑪ Frank's Restaurant, 431 West 14th Street (DJ).

⑫ Hamburger Harry's, 145 West 45th Street (DJ).

⑬ Joe Allen, 326 West 46th Street (DJ).

⑭ Keen's, 72 West 36th Street.

⑮ Landmark Tavern, 626 Eleventh Avenue (DJ).

⑯ La Réserve, 4 West 49th Street.

⑰ Lavin's, 23 West 39th Street.

⑱ Le Madeleine, 403 West 43rd Street (DJ).

⑲ Lola, 30 West 22nd Street.

⑳ Mike's American Bar & Grill, 650 Tenth Avenue (DJ).

㉑ Orso, 322 West 46th Street.

㉒ Ozeki, 158 West 23rd Street.

㉓ Quatorze, 240 West 14th Street (DJ).

㉔ Raga, 57 West 48th Street (DJ).

㉕ Roxanne's, 158 Eighth Avenue.

㉖ Southern Funk Cafe, 330 West 42nd Street (DJ).

㉗ Square Meals, 318 West 45th Street (DJ).

㉘ Tap Room, New Amsterdam Amber Brewery, 610 West 26th Street (DJ).

㉙ Woods, 148 West 37th Street (DJ).

✦ MAP 3: HOUSTON STREET ✦
TO 13TH STREET,
WEST OF BROADWAY

Includes West Village

① Au Troquet, 328 West 12th Street.

② Cafe de Bruxelles, 118 Greenwich Avenue (DJ).

③ Caffe Vivaldi, 32 Jones Street (DJ).

④ Caribe, 117 Perry Street (DJ).

⑤ Cent'Anni, 50 Carmine Street.

⑥ Chez Jacqueline, 72 Macdougal Street (DJ).

⑦ The Coach House, 110 Waverly Place.

⑧ Cuisine de Saigon, 154 West 13th Street.

⑨ Da Silvano, 260 Avenue of the Americas.

⑩ David's Cookies, 749 Broadway (DJ).

⑪ Gotham Bar and Grill, 12 East 12th Street.

⑫ Gulf Coast, 489 West Street (DJ).

⑬ Harlequin, 569 Hudson Street.

⑭ Il Cantinori, 32 East 10th Street.

⑮ John Clancy's Restaurant, 181 West 10th Street.

⑯ La Boheme, 24 Minetta Lane (DJ).

⑰ La Metairie, 189 West 10th Street.

⑱ La Tulipe, 104 West 13th Street.

⑲ Manhattan Chili Co., 302 Bleecker Street (DJ).

⑳ Meridies, 87 Seventh Avenue South.

㉑ Peculier Pub, 182 West Fourth Street (DJ).

㉒ Restaurant Florent, 69 Gansevoort Street (DJ).

㉓ Sabor, 20 Cornelia Street.

㉔ Steve's, 444 Avenue of the Americas (DJ).

㉕ Ye Waverly Inn, 16 Bank Street (DJ).

✦ MAP 4: BELOW ✦
HOUSTON STREET

Includes SoHo, TriBeCa, Chinatown, Little Italy, Wall Street and South Street Seaport

① Abyssinia, 35 Grand Street (DJ).

② American Harvest (Greenhouse Restaurant and Bar), at the Vista International Hotel, 3 World Trade Center (DJ).

③ Amsterdam's, 454 Broadway.

④ Barocco, 301 Church Street (DJ).

⑤ Bridge Cafe, 279 Water Street (DJ).

⑥ Cellar in the Sky, 1 World Trade Center.

⑦ Checkers, 36 Water Street (DJ).

⑧ El Internacional, 219 West Broadway.

⑨ Exterminator Chili, 305 Church Street (DJ).

⑩ Fluties Oyster Bar and Restaurant, Pier 17 in the South Street Seaport (DJ).

⑪ Good Enough to Eat, 162 Duane Street (DJ).

⑫ Great Shanghai, 27 Division Street (DJ).

⑬ Greene Street Restaurant, 101 Greene Street.

⑭ Hamburger Harry's, 157 Chambers Street (DJ).

⑮ La Tour d'Or, 14 Wall Street (DJ).

⑯ Le Zinc, 139 Duane Street (DJ).

⑰ Liberty Cafe, Pier 17 in the South Street Seaport (DJ).

⑱ Montrachet, 239 West Broadway.

⑲ The Nice Restaurant, 35 East Broadway.

⑳ North Star Pub, 93 South Street in South Street Seaport (DJ).

㉑ The Odeon, 145 West Broadway.

㉒ Omen, 113 Thompson Street.

㉓ Provence, 38 Macdougal (DJ).

㉔ SoHo Kitchen and Bar, 103 Greene Street (WS).

㉕ Taormina of Mulberry Street, 147 Mulberry Street (DJ).

㉖ Tap Room, Manhattan Brewery, 42 Thompson Street (DJ).

㉗ 20 Mott Street Restaurant, 20 Mott Street.

㉘ Windows on the World, 1 World Trade Center.

㉙ The Wine Bar, 422 West Broadway (WS).

✦ MAP 5: HOUSTON STREET ✦ TO EAST 49TH STREET, EAST OF BROADWAY

Includes East Village, Gramercy and Murray Hill

① America, 9 East 18th Street.

② Aurora, 60 East 49th Street.

③ Bayamo, 704 Broadway (DJ).

④ Bukhara, 148 East 48th Street.

⑤ Cafe du Parc, 106 East 19th Street.

⑥ Checkers, 201 East 34th Street (DJ).

⑦ Chikubu, 12 East 44th Street.

⑧ Christ Cella, 160 East 46th Street.

⑨ The Dolphin, 227 Lexington Avenue.

⑩ El Rio Grande, 160 East 38th Street (DJ).

⑪ First Avenue Restaurant, 361 First Avenue (DJ).

⑫ Friend of a Farmer, 77 Irving Place (DJ).

⑬ Hatsuhana, 17 East 48th Street.

⑭ Hayato, 571 Third Avenue (DJ).

⑮ Huberts, 102 East 22nd Street.

⑯ Inagiku, 111 East 49th Street (DJ).

⑰ Indochine, 430 Lafayette Street.

⑱ La Petite Marmite, 5 Mitchell Place.

⑲ Les Poulets, 27 East 21st Street (DJ).

⑳ Morgans Bar, 237 Madison Avenue.

㉑ Oyster Bar and Restaurant in Grand Central Station.

㉒ Palm, 837 Second Avenue.

㉓ Palm Too, 840 Second Avenue (DJ).

㉔ Pete's Place, 317 East Fifth Street (DJ).

㉕ Pete's Tavern, 129 East 18th Street (DJ).

㉖ Positano, 250 Park Avenue South.

㉗ The Ritz Cafe, 2 Park Avenue.

㉘ Ryan McFadden, 800 Second Avenue (DJ).

㉙ Siracusa, 65 Fourth Avenue (DJ).

㉚ 65 Irving Place (DJ).

㉛ Sparks Steakhouse, 210 East 46th Street.

㉜ Sugar Reef, 93 Second Avenue (DJ).

㉝ Sukhothai, 149 Second Avenue.

㉞ Tandoor, 40 East 49th Street.

㉟ Union Square Cafe, 21 East 16th Street.

㊱ Waldorf-Astoria Hotel, 301 Park Avenue (DJ).

㊲ Water Club, on the East River at 30th Street.

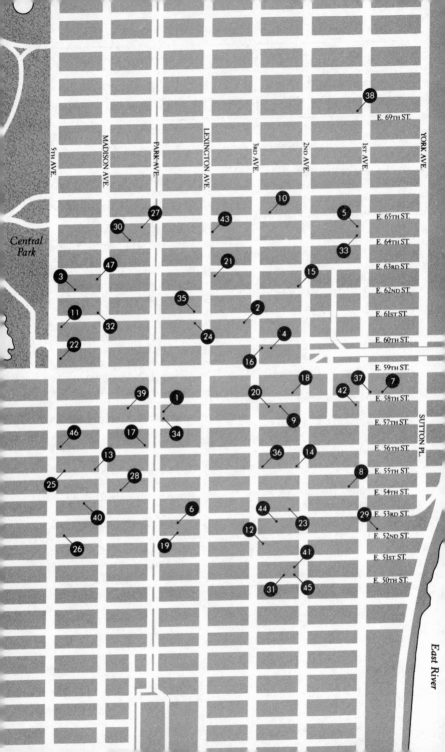

① Akbar, 475 Park Avenue.

② Alo Alo, 1030 Third Avenue.

③ Arcadia, 21 East 62nd Street.

④ Arizona 206, 206 East 60th Street.

⑤ Auntie Yuan, 1191A First Avenue.

⑥ Brasserie, 100 East 53rd Street (DJ).

⑦ Brive, 405 East 58th Street.

⑧ Cafe Europa & La Brioche, 347 East 54th Street (WS).

⑨ Cafe 58, 232 East 58th Street.

⑩ Cafe Marimba, 1115 Third Avenue.

⑪ Cafe Pierre, Pierre Hotel, Fifth Avenue and 61st Street (DJ).

⑫ Cafe 212, 212 East 52nd Street (DJ).

⑬ Casual Quilted Giraffe, 15 East 55th Street.

⑭ Checkers, 1047 Second Avenue (DJ).

⑮ Chicken Kitchen, 1177 Second Avenue (DJ).

⑯ Contrapunto, 200 East 60th Street.

⑰ The Drake Bar, Drake Hotel, 440 Park Avenue (WS).

⑱ Felidia, 243 East 58th Street.

⑲ The Four Seasons, 99 East 52nd Street.

⑳ Girafe, 208 East 58th Street (DJ).

㉑ Golden Tulip Restaurant, Barbizon Hotel, 140 East 63rd Street (WS).

㉒ Harry Cipriani, 783 Fifth Avenue.

㉓ Il Nido, 251 East 53rd Street.

㉔ Jacqueline's, 132 East 61st Street (WS).

㉕ La Côte Basque, 5 East 55th Street.

㉖ La Grenouille, 3 East 52nd Street.

㉗ Le Cirque, 58 East 65th Street.

㉘ Le Cygne, 55 East 54th Street.

㉙ Le Périgord, 405 East 52nd Street.

㉚ Le Régence, Hotel Plaza Athenee, 37 East 64th Street.

㉛ Lutèce, 249 East 50th Street.

㉜ Maxim's, 680 Madison Avenue.

㉝ Maxwell's Plum, 1181 First Avenue.

㉞ Mitsukoshi, 461 Park Avenue.

㉟ Nanni il Valletto, 133 East 61st Street.

㊱ P. J. Clarke's, 915 Third Avenue (DJ).

㊲ Pasta & Dreams, 1068 First Avenue.

㊳ The Polo, the Westbury Hotel, 15 East 69th Street.

㊴ Prima Donna, 50 East 58th Street (DJ).

㊵ Prunelle, 18 East 54th Street.

㊶ The Quilted Giraffe, 955 Second Avenue.

㊷ Rosa Mexicano, 1063 First Avenue.

㊸ Sel & Poivre, 853 Lexington Avenue (DJ).

㊹ Tang's Chariot, 236 East 53rd Street (DJ).

㊺ Tastings on 2, 953 Second Avenue (WS).

㊻ Terrace Five, Trump Tower, 725 Fifth Avenue (DJ).

㊼ Woods on Madison, 718 Madison Avenue.

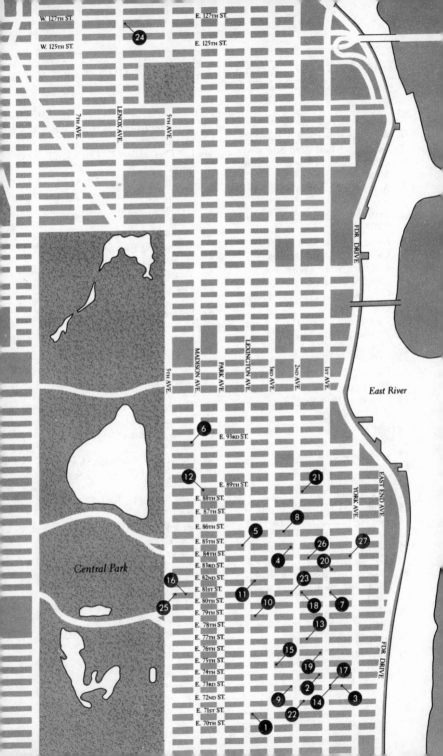

◆ MAP 7: EAST 70S AND NORTH ◆

Includes Upper East Side

① An American Place, 969 Lexington Avenue.

② Andrée's Mediterranean Cuisine, 354 East 74th Street.

③ Cafe Chardonnay, 414 East 73rd Street (WS).

④ Caffe Biffi, 251 East 84th Street (DJ).

⑤ Chirping Chicken, 1260 Lexington Avenue (DJ).

⑥ Devon House Ltd., 1316 Madison Avenue.

⑦ Dieci X, 1568 First Avenue.

⑧ Fleming's Bar & Restaurant, 232 East 86th Street (DJ).

⑨ Fu's, 1395 Second Avenue.

⑩ Jams, 154 East 79th Street.

⑪ Le Refuge, 166 East 82nd Street (DJ).

⑫ Les Délices Guy Pascal, 1231 Madison Avenue (DJ).

⑬ Lion's Rock, 316 East 77th Street (DJ).

⑭ Marcello, 1354 First Avenue.

⑮ Mezzaluna, 1295 Third Avenue (DJ).

⑯ Parioli Romanissimo, 24 East 81st Street (DJ).

⑰ Petaluma, 1356 First Avenue.

⑱ Pig Heaven, 1540 Second Avenue.

⑲ Pizzico, 1445 First Avenue (DJ).

⑳ Primavera, 1578 First Avenue.

㉑ Rathbone's, 1702 Second Avenue (DJ).

㉒ Ruc, 213 East 72nd Street (DJ).

㉓ Sistina, 1555 Second Avenue.

㉔ Sylvia's Restaurant, 328 Lenox Avenue (DJ).

㉕ The Terrace, American Stanhope Hotel, Fifth Avenue and 81st Street.

㉖ Trastevere, 309 East 83rd Street.

㉗ Wilkinson's Seafood Cafe, 1573 York Avenue.

✦ RESTAURANTS IN THE ✦
BOROUGHS

THE BRONX

Amerigo's, 3587 East Tremont Avenue (DJ).
Dominick's, 2335 Arthur Avenue (DJ).

BROOKLYN

Crisci, 593 Lorimer Street (DJ).
Gage & Tollner, 372 Fulton Street (DJ).
Moroccan Star, 205 Atlantic Avenue (DJ).
Peter Luger, 178 Broadway.
River Cafe, 1 Water Street.

QUEENS

Cali Viejo, 84-24 Roosevelt Avenue (DJ).
Cali Viejo II, 73-10 Roosevelt Avenue (DJ).

Restaurant Index

Map numbers appear in parentheses. The map section begins on page 375.